Co

TWICE BLESSED

From Hungary to America

MIKLOS MAGYAR

 www.trafford.com

North America & international
toll-free: 1 888 232 4444 (USA & Canada)
phone: 250 383 6864 ♦ fax: 250 383 6804 ♦ email: info@trafford.com

The United Kingdom & Europe
phone: +44 (0)1865 722 113 ♦ local rate: 0845 230 9601
facsimile: +44 (0)1865 722 868 ♦ email: info.uk@trafford.com

10 9 8 7 6 5 4

Preface
Two Journeys

Talking with friends about old times, a few times I told parts of my life's story. One evening, after recounting some interesting events, the consensus of the group was that it is worth writing down. I thought of doing it before in the past, but this once I said that I will give it a go, in large part to have a record to my family for those who follow. It was a half-hearted promise. The task seemed too daunting, not so much for its potential size, but the difficulty, discipline and especially my qualification -- i.e. the lack of it -- as greatest obstacles. During the ensuing months I thought more about it and focused increasingly on the subject. I thought that at least a trying was worth it. My aim all along was to document the years of my childhood and illustrate the way I saw things, the events I observed, with a sprinkling of pertinent background material. This is a personal history and a personal view, with perspective on things that happened to me, the people I knew and what I learned along the way. I made a serious effort to be accurate and left out things that I could not document to my satisfaction. This is my story and that of my two families -- my life from birth, into the first year of retirement.

The heading above refers to the two seminal events that had

great and deeply formative influence on me. -- The *first*, an extended and deeply marking sojourn, is about my family, my childhood and my experiences as a youth, ending in an *actual journey* that took nine days. A sudden departure and the ensuing long-distance travel, suddenly plucked me from a secure family environment and took me to a new and very different world and a different society that instantly accepted and embraced me, giving me opportunities to start a new life. -- The *second* was a spiritual and intellectual journey, taking place gradually and still on-going. It is about getting to know America, understanding the spirit of American exceptionalism. This to me, means *not,* that Americans are exceptional people. Rather, that the American spirit and form of government of ordinary people, as it was originally conceived, make the country the beacon that when followed and emulated, brings freedom and prosperity to people. America is a magnet, a place where people want to come, more than to any other land on earth. They are motivated by fundamental human desires, a yearning for freedom and abundance. People of all persuasions live in this country. It baffles me that there are some who *prefer* to see and dwell on the negative, and are willing to tear it down for political reasons, instead of seeing the ample good in it. They could always improve on it with honest effort, for the opportunity is there. -- In this process, I learned the history and gained an understanding of the essence of the American psyche, seeing it with the advantage of a detached perspective of being brought up in a different world. During this long journey I enhanced my knowledge of history that I learned in Hungary and in American universities. They gave me a deeper understanding of American life and the concept of liberty. I gained insight on how people live and how politics and government work in America. Life experience and incorporation of other perspectives and analyses, gave me a deeper appreciation of the work of our founding fathers and allowed me to see their *genius* as they created our two fundamental documents, the Declaration of Independence and the Constitution. Those, and the The Federalist Papers, explaining their reasoning, make fascinating reading. In them, they reflect on foibles of human nature and the fallibility, inherent in human beings, who in their view should be representing the people for a limited time in Washington, before returning to be ordinary citizens again. Alas, the founders could not forsee a curse in our time, the career politician, serving his own self interest. This belief, the gift of unusual wisdom, and their faith in God afforded them the means to found a nation. -- Principles reflecting the exceptional qualities and the generosity of the nation they created, is written on a tablet, held by a *Lady*, who is welcoming immigrants in New York harbor for over a hundred years.

* * *

Choosing my title, I wanted to convey my sense that I consider myself rewarded beyond my deserving. It was my luck to be born into a family, which gave me a secure, abundant and happy childhood. God blessed me again many years later with a wonderful wife and a lovely family of my own.

I wanted to pay homage to a *family* that gave me the foundation on which to build a good life, and to the happiness I found in *my family* as an adult. It also honors the new land that allowed me to continue after a serious disruption, by giving me opportunities, just as it offers it to its citizens and all honest people, who want to come here or reside within her borders, with generosity, to be example to the world.

Coming to America was an opportunity for me, unusual in many respects. I did not realize it at the time, for I knew little about my new homeland, her history and the principles upon which she was founded. My leaving Hungary was unexpected, unplanned and sudden. It took me almost a decade, before in my conscious and subconscious mind, I would consider my being here, permanent. In the beginning years I had manifestations of homesickness, regrets and longing. As years went by, my perspective changed by events and evolving circumstances. When I left my homeland, the Cold War dominated international politics, and the interests and politics of the Soviet Union dominated life and government policy in Hungary. At the time of my leaving, I was sure that I would never be able to return. There were times when my longing to visit home was overwhelming. When talking to friends and family, I still refer to Hungary, as home. I lived there 20 years, and here, almost 50. Those first 20 years though, were formative in the extreme. They gave me identity, forged my consciousness, sense of family and gave me my memories of parents, siblings, friends and a beautiful childhood. When measured, their weight is more than anything that followed them -- as one would expect. For me, the memories of a close, loving family, along with exemplary upbringing by my parents, made me a stable person, capable of passing on long-ago received gifts to my own loved ones. If I am a loving husband and a good parent, the germs were planted in me and nourished long time ago.

I am a lucky man. I have a home in two countries. I could live comfortably in either. The question or problem of loyalty never occurs to me. Love and good wishes for both are always in my heart. The strong bond connecting them, and connecting each with me, is Western history and culture. They are the building blocks that tie them together. As I see it, it is the best and most fitting for humans. It produced astonishingly beautiful and most human art. I am not saying, that it's perfect, but believe, that only when we stray from its fundamental principles of goodness, liberty and the rule of law, can it become evil or destructive. -- So far, we have kept the faith. I hope we have the will and wisdom to continue in the future.

* * *

1

At The Beginning

I was born, third of four boys in a row (József, Ottó, Miklós, Tamás) on a Thursday afternoon, the 27th of August, 1936.

The event took place in my mother's bed with only a midwife and servants in attendance, as it was normal practice at the time. Doctor Kovács, a family friend next door, was always on call -- so to speak. I first saw daylight in Jánosháza, a rural town in Hungary. Looking back, I see a life beginning that was a happy one and more satisfying than most people can say. I was lucky, having been blessed by loving parents, a close family, and circumstances that I consider fortunate and conducive to a happy disposition. Many years later I was again blessed, finding love and happiness after marrying my wife Ildikó, a loving, extraordinary woman. We were blessed by our children and, after more than three decades passing, their children.

Jánosháza, a *young* community in Hungary, first settled in 1254, had a population of about 5,000. This number was stable, then reduced in recent years, reflecting the traditionally low birthrate in Hungary. The boundaries of the town gradually expanded as new houses were built, showing modest affluence. Personal mobility was minimal. Land was central to the life of many, and tied people to localities. This changed dramatically after World War II, mostly for political reasons. The communist government that was imposed on us, destroyed individual ownership, as it forced farmers into cooperatives, patterned after the Soviet system.

The town has a storied past, that I occasionally heard tales about. Those were told by old-timers, who liked to recount episodes of rivalry between Jánosháza and Celldömölk, a larger community 10 miles away. Our town came out on the short end, the other being the district seat, also helped by a railroad intersection that was put there sometime early in the century. The laying down of new tracks made the decisive difference in growth of business, population and opportunity. (Jánosháza was made seat of a newly created district in 1948. It was a communist creation and had administrative problems from day one. The order was rescinded within a year and things were restored to the status quo ante. Most people agreed.)

In my town, most folks were *smallholders*, farmers who owned and tilled small plots, many living in thatched roof houses, whose stucco or adobe walls they painted with quicklime. (We had a lot of white houses.) Land was precious, fertile and productive, one of God's gift to those who made their living by working the soil. Weather was an ongoing concern and subject of daily conversation. Winters allowed time for rest, taking care of animals and repairing equipment. Farmers cultivated their land to grow staple crops: wheat, rye, barley, oat and corn. Our town was in the western part of the country, which is traditionally called Transdanubia (Latin for "over the Danube"). Romans gave it the name *Pannonia* -- from which, names of many places in the region were derived; a name that found its way even to America. A few years ago, Hungarian immigrants started a telephone company in Los Angeles: *Pannon Telecom*. (The reader will encounter the word *Pannon* in various uses, several times in this writing.)

Jánosháza was surrounded by smaller villages, where in those days almost all residents were employed in agriculture. Ours was the *big* town. It was a commercial center. Tradesmen had their stores, craftsmen their shops, where people from the surrounding smaller villages did their shopping for everyday items and used the services of tailors, cobblers, etc. To see a physician, they had to come to Jánosháza. We had two doctors, a lawyer and a bank. And yes, a veterinarian. That is how my family came to live there.

Until the mid-1940s, the town had a single Catholic elementary school, one that kids from the nearest villages also attended. A few Protestant kids also came there. They were excused from religion classes and went to their own on Saturday afternoons. When I was about 7 years old, a *civic school*, something like a junior high, was built. People were proud of it. It was a nice, modern, two-story building, similar looking to our own house (built in 1936) with a fashionable, glistening stucco finish. After the Second World War, the old elementary school became girls only and boys went to the civic school, which ceased to exist as such and became boys elementary, a public school. "Civic" was deemed a politically incorrect word, and many references and uses of it were ostracized from the official vernacular. Anything civic -- or God forbid, bourgeois -- were tabu, except in describing something from the old regime, with coloring of undesirability and connotations of *class enemy*. *Comrade* was the new, preferred -- no, mandatory -- word, to be used instead. (Official communist language reeks of political correctness, just like the language, deemed proper today, and being diligently promoted by their socialist descendants in the West.) In 1948 an academy was opened, supplanting the old civic school, but providing higher level of education, and attended mostly by adults.

Neighboring smaller towns, most of them with only a few hundred residents, were mostly populated by farmers who owned or leased just a few acres. Large manor farms, employing up to a dozen families each, were well run and profitable. They had advantage of economy of scale, expert professional help and usually, large, contiguous, good quality acres.

In many cases, the land a family owned or worked, was broken up into several plots in diverging areas around town. This developed through many years of descendants inheriting smaller plots of land upon the death of parents as the family farm was divided for the next generation. A farmer had to be clever or lucky to consolidate the acres he owned.

I whose family was not farmers, still acquired some related skills. To build our house, my father bought two adjacent lots in the middle of town and the considerable track attached to them. We had a sizable orchard in the back of the house. Also, we grew corn and potatoes, that needed care. Father was proud of his background. As a child of farmers, he liked to work the soil in a limited way, as a gentleman farmer. He also expected of his sons to do some work tending to corn and potatoes. He puttered around with a hoe, even in older age, but left major work to hired hands.

I blessed my fate and luck, that I did not have too much of farm chores. I did enough of it to appreciate, what demanding work it was. My classmates prided themselves having calluses on their hands and liked to show them off as badge of honor. It was proof that they helped out at home, knew the value of hard work and acquired a measure of expertise about land and animals. I rarely had a callus to show and was teased for it, as being soft and not really knowing the hardship of working with one's hands. It bothered me at first, but in time I summoned enough self confidence and once said to them:

"How could I have calluses, guys? My parents are not farmers. I don't work with animals, or harvest crops like you. Just cool it and get over it." That ended the matter. The subject never came up again.

Jánosháza was a pleasant town in which to grow up. Everyone knew everybody and knew, or thought he knew, many things about many people. Gossip flourished, which kept life buzzing. Most people were Catholic and mostly church-going. For older folks it was customary on Sunday afternoons, to sit on a wood bench at the edge of the sidewalk in front of the house and spend time talking into the evening.

The town looked better on Sundays and holidays. People took pride in their houses and neighborhood. Each Saturday evening, except in winter, in front of most houses the dirt sidewalk was swept, using a coarse *birchtwig-broom*. It was mostly home made, fashioned from the finer ends of tree branches. They sprinklered a little water to dampen the dust. Each stroke left a mark on the sidewalk, that I can liken to marks a vacuum cleaner leaves on a freshly cleaned carpet. It was not a big thing, but showed care, a sense of pride and neatness, wanting to have the street look clean for Sunday. When the walkways down the whole length of the street were swept, the entire village looked spruced up, ready for the day of the Lord and spending Sunday at leisure.

Each Sunday, I with my brothers attended the 8 o'clock mass. Mother also preferred this service. We liked the balcony next to the organ, with a good view of the whole church. I often volunteered to pump the bellows for the organ, the first time at about age 10. At the beginning I could not do it alone, only with a partner. Even the two of us had to push hard, putting our whole weight on the big pedal, that protruded out, through a slot, cut in the side of the huge box with the fancy pipes, that was the organ's housing. It was a kind of youthful rite of passage, to be able to pump alone. I tried as soon as I could and felt important, and on par with older guys, for whom I had various degrees of admiration. Sunday masses also gave us the opportunity to see girls in their Sunday best and usually on their best, modest behavior.

I loved to ring the big bells of the church. (We were lucky that they were not taken during the wars to be melted down for cannons, as happened to a lot of churches, especially during the First World War.) We had three of them up in the tower, but I seldom heard all three ringing together. Each individually, or in combination were assigned to different masses or other church functions. They could be rung at the back of the church, with long ropes that were dropped all the way down through holes cut in several floors. The best was when we went up in the steeple and did it there, just 20 ft. under the noisy clappers. There we could swing on the ropes and with appropriate leaps, go 6-8 feet up in the air and come down as the tolling bell let us descend. To do this, a kid had to be of the proper weight. Often it took two to do it. By the time my parents let me go up, I was big enough for the big bell, enjoying the swings and lifts by myself. It was incredible fun. For a short time I imagined I was *Quasimodo*, ringing the bells of *Notre Dame*, while scheming to rescue sweet *Esmeralda*.

Father preferred the *big* mass, at 10 A.M. He liked to sit in the single pew by the altar, within the sanctuary. Only a few people, sat there. (Mother felt better sitting with folks and was happy when we were with her. It was before we started going up to the *chorus*, as the balcony was commonly called.) I sat up front only a few times, when I went with Father to his mass. He liked the later service, that allowed him to sleep in and to visit his good friend, Monsignor Pártli after the service. (Sitting right by the altar, he once witnessed mistakes I made, on my first time as altar boy. He was more a proud parent, than a critic, and praised my efforts, encouraging me to do better.)

* * *

One of the many pleasant memories I recall, were the May Litanies and our village fair on St. Vendel day in late summer. Also, our many visits to the beautiful lake Balaton and nearby Héviz, the warm mineral spa, that has world-wide reputation as a place to cure rheumatic ailments. For family entertainment, they were our most favorite weekend destinations. Some other places also come to mind. I will describe them, as I let my mind wonder through pleasant recollections of the past, just a few turns of the page hence.

There were examples of personal commerce that I remember fondly. A Jewish woman often brought to the house, home-baked matzo, (*laska*) that she knew we liked to buy. In season, various fruits were also peddled by peasant women. These were things that were not available every day. Mushrooms had to be picked in the forest. It took time, a lot of walking, patience and familiarity to avoid the poisonous kind. (In his retirement, my father took a lesson from a priest friend in *mushrooming,* in the forest. The next day he went alone and picked a big basket-full of *good* mushrooms, based on what he learned. To be on the safe side, he showed it to his friend, who threw out almost half. -- Father was surprised, but wiser. It was a good lesson about humility and respect for learning about things, that we tend to take for granted.)

Our most favorite was wild strawberries. We had some around the yard. They grew wild, mostly under our large hazelnut bushes, in the partially shaded spots, yielding conditions, similar to those

in the woods. Picking them was tedious work. That is why the
tiny fruit was at a premium. The taste and aroma was different and
more fragrant than that of ordinary strawberry, one of my most
favorite fruits. Nothing could approach the unique taste of these
delicate berries. In season, a woman brought it in a large glass jar-
full, the kind that is mainly used in pickling cucumbers, for winter.
A 5 liter-size jar, filled with wild strawberries lasted us about two
days. We always made sure that it would not spoil on us. Mother
occasionally made preserve, but mostly we just feasted on it while
it lasted.

To publicize official town news in Jánosháza, a clerk/errand
boy, (popularly called *Little Judge*) dressed in uniform, walked
through town and read the items to be made public. This was our
version of the town crier. To ensure that many people hear the
announcements, he made noise that we heard even behind closed
doors. He carried a snare drum, hanging at his waste on a shoulder
harness and, as he was approaching the accustomed place, where
he was to read his message, he kept drumming away. Then he
stopped at the usual spot. Pounding more on his drum, he gave
time for people to gather. At the end he was drumming with a fancy
flourish, and with a crescendo, finished his noise-making. The first
words he uttered, always were: *Közhirré tétetik mindenkinek...*, an
official flowery phrase, that translates something like this: *May
the following items be known by all...* -- This official act was one
of the few mildly exciting events that people wanted to attend, or
send out a member of the family to hear. Whenever we kids heard
the rolling of the drum, we ran to the reading spot and listened
to the messages, though most of them were of no interest to us.
It was just exciting to hear the drum and gather with adults for a
few minutes. These announcements were made once or twice a
week, weather permitting. I recall very few such *drum-sessions* in
winter months. (As kids, we were not much help to our parents on
what news we heard. Later I paid attention and was able to convey
some useful information.)

Our town had a gasoline pumping station. (So what -- you say?
The next closest was 10 miles away, equivalent to 50 miles -- as
it seemed back then.) It had one pump, with twin 15 liter glass

containers at the top of the pump. We used a built-on hand pump
to fill one of the containers, before switching to the other. Then
we opened a valve and let the gasoline pour by gravity, into the
gas tank. While this was going on, the other container could be
pumped full. This way, by switching between the containers, the
process could be operated continuously. I went with my father as
often as I could. I loved to operate the pump and was intrigued
by the whole process. I also liked the smell of gasoline. It is
not possible to tell now, if my taste changed, or whether today's
gasoline is *fragranced* differently, with something that I now find
unpleasant. I only know that I avoid smelling gasoline today as much
as possible. Another reason is the adverse health consequences of
inhaling, that we were not aware of back then. The old pump
could now be in a museum, or perhaps in somebody's collection
of antiques. (I saw a similar, still operational pump on the trail
through Kings Canyon National Park. It was 1999. The old pump
in Jánosháza was long since replaced. But at this quaint, remote
rest-stop, high in the mountains of California, one may still pump
gasoline -- really pump it, using muscle power.)

* * *

We baked our own bread. Bread-day started before dawn.
Leaven was prepared the night before. One of the housekeepers
put the ingredients together very early and started kneading. Most
mornings, she was still at it when I got up. She usually made four
large, round loaves and put each in a sturdy, tightly woven wicker
basket to rise. About 10 o'clock we took the breads to the baker,
who baked bread twice a week. His huge, shallow oven was hot,
having been fired up the day before, by burning charcoal all night.
Each bread had an identifying slip of paper on top, so the about
50 breads would find their owner after baking. I loved to watch
Mr. Pernecki, one of two bakers in town, moving the breads in
the process of baking. From time-to-time, he had to shift them
from hotter to cooler parts of the oven. He was working from a
pit, in front of the oven door, so that the oven floor was near eye
level. His instrument was a large, flat wooden spoon at the end of

a handle that was at least 25 ft. long. He had a lamp to illuminate the oven. His skill in moving the breads with great speed, was remarkable. He would shove his ladle under a bread, push or pull it, thus moving it to a new spot. Then he jerked back the handle and the bread would stay put. He knew what it took to bake the breads evenly. They always came out just right.

Later in the afternoon we went to pick up the baskets and the breads. They were about 18 inch diameter, 7 inch high, still warm. They lasted two-three weeks for us, but amazingly, hardly aged during that time. On the last day, they were still enjoyable to eat. Occasionally we found small embedded charcoal pieces in the bottom crust, left over from the big oven.

Washing clothes was one of the big jobs. We had a wash kitchen, a 10x30 ft. room, part of the auxiliary building left standing, from one of the two old houses that were razed, when ours was built. We used it for a fortnightly washing, and the cooking of fat, when we had our pig-kill in winter. Mother had a strong preference for Aunt Irén, a very popular lady in town. She had expertise and capacity for work, like few others. I spent a lot of time with her talking while she busied herself in a long day's drudgery. She was always cheerful and could tell stories that a boy of 6 or 7 found entertaining. The clothes were dried on line, outdoors, summer or winter as much as it was possible. When temperatures were much below freezing, she carried things up to the attic. Even there, wet clothes stiffened by frost, but eventually dried. In late autumn, stiff sheets were waiving in the wind, until they lost most of their moisture. Then we collected them and let them fully dry indoors.

For washing clothes, we collected rainwater in a large concrete drum and used it when possible. My parents bought their first washing machine in the early 1960s. Refrigerators also became available about that time. The first machines were primitive and of small capacity. They had a simple stirrer wheel, as agitator, at the bottom. Later models were larger, more sophisticated and of better quality.

* * *

Stories -- call them gossip -- occupied the mind of adults, but I paid them little mind. I tended not to be interested in the life and stories about people that circulated in town. I was a *phlegmatic* youth, who rather saw no problems where there were none, or where others in my opinion saw problems needlessly. I mention phlegmatic, or easy-going, because I was cited as an example for that psychological group, by students in a psychology class at the local academy. ("...Stoic self-possession, imperturbability" -- as stated in my Webster -- giving me perhaps more credit than I am due.)

The word and the concept were new to me, for I just learned of the four main personality types myself from my piano teacher, Mr. Bella. He told me what happened the day before in the class, he was taking at the academy. It intrigued me how a group of local people saw me. When they searched for someone typical, they thought, Miklós Magyar would best exemplify this psychological group. I was about 13 years old. Mr. Bella agreed with the choice of his class and enjoyed telling me the story when he came to my piano class the following day.

I was certainly not a *sanguine*, or explosive type person. I believe, those are now called Type A, or extroverted. Nor was I *choleric,* which indicates irascibility. Perhaps a little *melancholic* at times, but on the whole, I thought they pegged me just right. I was then, and am now, in most things an easy-going guy. Not to say that worry-thoughts never possess me, but generally I am an optimist, looking at the bright side even when it is illusive. -- It surprised and fascinated me that in that whole town I was so clearly the example of a type.

If this brand of psychology is too arcane in the 21st century, I apologize. Back then, this is how they taught it in school. This classification made sense to me. I liked myself. It seemed, I had the best of the four available types, though I didn't ponder much on the subject through the years since then.

In the two psychology classes I took in college, these terms or definitions were never mentioned, though my professor confirmed that they were prominently taught at one time. They are listed as the four governing *humours*, that determine the human state of mind, mood and inclinations. This psychological theory also occupied the mind of Danish composer Carl Nielsen (1865-1931). His *Second Symphony* is subtitled, *The Four Temperaments* (Allegro *collerico,* Allegro *comodo e flemmatico,* Andante *melancolico* Allegro *sanguineo).* In four movements he attempts a musical illustration of the known types, as he and experts of his day saw it at the time.

This instinctive behavioral make-up and optimist outlook served me well, but also got me into trouble a few times. Those were the occasions when unfounded optimism, lack of diligence in the examination of facts and indications resulted in painful lessons.

* * *

Our town was thriving in the 1930s, helped along by the lively commerce, for which it was known in the region, despite its size. We had a relatively high Jewish population. There was even a popular little song about it -- one might say, a *rap* of its day. I heard it from locals and others I met, sometimes people from far away. Occasionally, when I mentioned that I was from Jánosháza, hearing the name of the town was the trigger. Some asked me reflexively: " What whistles the Jew?" -- referring to a popular jingle about the Jewish shopkeepers of Jánosháza.

Of course, I felt obliged to answer: "He whistles about things he has for sale." (Here, in the original: *Jánosházán fütyöl a zsidó. Azt fütyöli, mi van eladó.)*

Jews were known, among other things, for enlivening commerce. Wednesday was market day, a kind of shopping holiday and favorite day for most people and for us kids. Folks from near and far came to do business. I often went with my mother to the farmers' market, where she scrutinized everything, that she considered buying. Sometimes I was embarrassed when she bargained with market-women. After all, we were one of the well to do families in town. She was able to afford things better than most. But no, she wanted value for her money. I now think she did it just right. Besides, my father was a little tight with the money. Mother had to resort to a ruse or two, to obtain her necessary funds to run the household.

-- One method of judging the value of a chicken (always live) was when she held it by the leg upside down and lifted it up and let it down in a horizontally swinging motion, to more closely feel the weight. That was her trusted manual scale. She used it to decide if the fowl was big enough, or the price fair. We did not formally weigh poultry.

To weigh commodities, crude scales were used, but we did all right with them. They were of the type, that blindfolded bronze ladies hold atop of courthouses, as a symbol to measure men, their thruthfulness, character and adherence to the law -- a powerful symbol in the service of justice and fair dealing. It is recognized as the instrument of fair measurement. I suppose, handled well and with care, satisfactory commerce can be conducted using these old reliable measuring instruments. It was customary by the sellers to top the pan with a little extra product, after the scale has already tipped. Most sellers did that. It was commerce with a touch of magnanimity and a gesture that promoted good will. I never heard argument between buyer and seller questioning fairness.

The more serious business, with intense bargaining was done on the commodity and animal markets. I knew a few Jewish men, who were very active on Wednesdays, buying and selling (often the same day) pigs and cattle, to make a quick profit.

This was also my father's resort. He was the veterinarian who certified animals to be shipped, as free of disease. He too, looked for an occasional good buy there -- two or three pigs each year, to be fattened for a winter kill.

In the old days he had them shipped out to the manor, where they were fattened for us to about 250-300 kilos and brought in early on a January morning. By the time we had to leave for school, the hog, sometimes two together, were already dismembered and were ready for processing. Once Mother let us stay home for the entire day. Also, for a while after the war, our school was run in two shifts, and I went in the afternoon. On those days we could see all the interesting early activities of this annual event. Usually we killed one hog in late fall and two together, in January.

The day began in pitch dark. When the wagon arrived, we kids were roused by the noise and happily jumped out of bed. By the time they set up, we were there to watch. A couple hands held the hog, and took it off its feet. A quick move with the knife and someone had to jump in with a pale to collect the blood. It was important ingredient for sausages. The poor creature, an unwitting servant of mankind expired soon, to become sustaining nourishment to a whole family for an entire year. The next major step was when the men pulled up the carcass, by its hind legs on a tall, sawhorse-like wooden contraption. The whole animal was hanging on this rack, without touching ground. The two hogs were thus processed in quick succession. Parts were carried on shoulders to our big kitchen, that was set up with extra tables, sharpened knives and meat grinders, ready for this specialized culinary process. In later years Father bought beef for the occasion, to be mixed in with the pork. The blend produced a better, leaner sausage.

There were two ways to remove hair. Most people burned it off, using ordinary fire, sometimes aided by a kerosene-powered flame machine. My parents liked a cleaner job, scalding the skin with boiling water. It was done in a large tub. Turning the huge body was hard work and men took care not to be burned by the hot water. After a good dousing, and skillful effort, most of the hair was removed. This method produced an almost perfect, clean and smooth skin. The butcher used a kerosene burner to burn off hair in wrinkles and hard-to-get places, especially feet. Then he carved it up on the rack to large pieces that were carried into the house for further processing.

The nicest firm slabs of bacon were sent to the smokehouse. The rest we cooked to save the fat and make delicious crackling. By the time the fat was cooking in the big kettle in the wash kitchen, we saw all that we were interested in seeing, tasted all the fresh goodies and were encouraged to leave the kitchen.

Uncle Lala Bolla the butcher, was hired for the day and presided as master of ceremonies until mid-afternoon, when all hams were lined up, properly trimmed and salted, sausages filled and were ready for smoking or some other method of storage. Of course, calling Uncle Lala's work ceremonial, would be disparaging. He was a strong man, as butchers should be and he was the hardest worker. He directed all the important activities, while doing the most demanding tasks himself. His crew included one of his regular helpers, a strong hand who helped him in the kill. After the animals were quartered, he let his apprentice go. His crew for the rest of the day was our family staff, sometimes an extra woman hired for the day and our *house man*, who on other days was Father's helper. Mother also pitched in, as she saw need for it. -- A rare man among butchers, Uncle Lala was a kind person, with a sense of humor, deferential to my parents and polite to all his customers. I'm not surprised we always called him to do the big job.

Father knew all the 13 butchers in town. He, as district veterinarian, worked with them professionally. He examined all animals to be shipped or slaughtered. Without his approval nothing moved out in or out of town, or to the slaughterhouse. I often saw him there, examining meat, bantering with the butchers and farmers, and do the minimal paperwork required. A family lived at the slaughterhouse. They too, were farmers, but took on the additional job of keeping the facility clean. When I was there, Father often entrusted me with the job of taking home some choice piece of meat. It was still warm. One might say, he bought it straight off the rack. Other times he brought it with him or had the butcher bring it to the house.

Sometimes I watched the processing of animals. I didn't think of it so much as a gruesome procedure, rather as a normal part of life that, even if I wouldn't want to do, was an important thing that had to be done. The barber cut hair, the cobbler made shoes, the tailor clothes and the butcher provided the meat for our table.

After WWII, such things changed drastically, as did most things about our life. The 13 butchers lived well, kept busy and were prosperous by the demand for their products until the communists showed us *their* way, after coming to power in 1948. The butchers, along with other tradesmen, were forced into government controlled cooperatives and had to close their shops. When the collectivization regime was done, there was only one butcher shop in town, that of the butcher co-op, for which all the local butchers now worked. It was so chronically short of meat, that it was open only two days a week for half a day, or until it ran out of stuff to sell. On those days, to buy the best of the meager selection, a line formed long before opening. The state needed the merchandise for export. People had to sacrifice to *build* socialism in some undetermined day in the future. In the meantime we had to get used to a no-meat diet. The greatest shortage was in processed meat products. To compensate, people raised fowl, geese, ducks, etc. A previously rare custom of raising rabbits also became widespread. Fattening pigs was always a custom. It provided ham and bacon, as energy-food for the hard work in the fields.

Our family also became the victim of this Soviet style life. By 1950, Father also was *nationalized*. His *co-op* was the county veterinarian group. From one day to the next he was not allowed to practice freely. Instead, he became a salaried state employee. At each visit to treat an animal, he wrote out a bill that the client farmer had to pay to the state. His lucky loopholes were two previously innocuous aspects of his practice: medication and travel expenses. These became a sort of life-line that allowed him to make some extra money in addition to the meager fix, that was his salary. Another part of the change was a punishing load of paperwork imposed by the system, that he often worked late in the night to prepare.

In the old days his practice was a veritable gold mine, though he was not a greedy man. He worked hard to establish a very high reputation among the people. At the time he moved to Jánosháza, he found, that a certain practice prevailed in town, devised by the old vet and the local pharmacist. Back then, medication for veterinary practice, came mostly in powder form to be mixed with feed. Pills became common, later. The old vet prescribed drugs mostly in bulk powder. The druggist divided it and packed it in small portions. For this extra service he doubled the price. My father found large amount of drugs in many houses, that were the result of over-subscription that were often not needed in the amount prescribed. I heard him often instructing the farmer to divide the bulk medicine into even portions himself.

As he overtook the practice, he was able to reduce the expenses farmers had to spend for medicines. He told us that he earned the enmity of the two protagonists in this matter. But the big event early in his career was not this. It was the downfall of his predecessor, because of careless treatment of a few animals. The doctor was found to carry foot-and-mouth disease from a sick animal to a healthy one. It became a scandal and he was forced to resign. He was quite old and chose to retire.

2

A Little History --
Historical And Personal

In the 1920s Hungary, practice was that veterinarians were elected, just like politicians. My father was eyeing a very attractive district of Csorna, where he campaigned for a position, right after he received his diploma. This was an officially assigned district, that became open upon retirement. He failed in his attempt in Csorna and settled in Jánosháza, freelancing, testing out the territory, hoping that people will call on him. He worked thus for 3 years and became respected and popular. After the scandal of the old doc, the Jánosháza district officially opened up in 1932. He entered the contest and was unanimously elected throughout the towns of the district. I still have the newspaper clipping, giving him high praise.

Körállatorvos választás Jánosházán. Már hónapok óta elkeseredett harc folyt a jánosházai állatorvosi állásért. Most tartották meg a választást. A 8 pályázó közül a 15 község egyhangulag Magyar József nagycenki születésü állatorvost választotta meg. A megválasztott már öt éve működik Jánosházán mint magánorvos. Hogy mennyire értékelték működését, azt leginkább mutatja a 15 község egyhangu választása.

DISTRICT VETERINARIAN ELECTION IN JÁNOSHÁZA
Fierce battle has been going on for the position of District Veterinarian of Jánosháza. The election was concluded. Selecting from the 8 candidates, residents of the 15 towns, unanimously elected József Magyar, born in Nagycenk. The elected has been working in Jánosháza for the past five years as private veterinarian. The value, the electorate placed on his practice, is indicated by unanimous votes in all 15 communities.

By the time of the scandal, Father was in good position to take over the district. His practice later included 23 villages and manor farms, each with a sizable and vital large-animal population, many smallholders and well-to-do farmers. It was time of peace and prosperity.

He was very good in dealing with people. He spoke their language, cared for their animals and cared about their problems. In a mostly farmer community, animals were important and land was at a premium.

Ironically, for that same reason Jánosháza cut off its own development. The state-owned railroad was expanding and chose the town as a future hub, where it was planning a large expansion. In the 1920s it proposed to build a double junction with trains going in four directions, changing the sleepy little station with four tracks, into one where many trains would be coming, changing and going all day. It would've had a substantial effect on the town and would have made it a center of large commerce, with all sort of associated businesses. But it was not to be -- because of the value that was placed on land. The farmer population voted not to allow its land taken by *eminent domain*, or some other rule, for new tacks or enlarged railroad yard. Private property was sacred. The 4-way expansion was split into two, 3-way junctions and forced on nearby tiny villages, that did not have the political clout to oppose the plan. They, Boba and Ukk, remained as small as they were before. The change had no impact on them. So, Jánosháza remained as it was, with the old, already established businesses and small regional commerce. What the proposed change would have brought, I can only speculate. Without it we remained more of a quiet town, one perhaps in which it was better to raise children. I think my dear mother would agree.

* * *

I learned this story years after it happened, at about age 15. I thought of it often because to me, it had a wealth of lessons about economics, politics, free choice and human nature.

My father was exceptional in his profession. He initiated surgical procedures that were revolutionary. He was a bold and original thinker. This began, of course, in the free Hungary, in the good years, between the two World Wars. He was daring using his knowledge, common sense and an uncanny feel for his profession. With his singular ability he could save animals that otherwise would have been slaughtered.

It started with his doctorate thesis, which also had another, very important consequence -- detailed later. His thesis was about curing cattle or hogs with stomach infection. He proposed to induce vomiting as the initial step. This way the doctor had a reduced amount of infected internal material to deal with. After that, antibiotics were more effective and the cure swift. He tried it out in his first years of practice and detailed it in his doctoral dissertation. He made a convincing case, backed up by examples from personal experience. The Board of the Academy accepted it and began teaching it.

Father believed that weak or short people had a disadvantage in veterinary medicine and should take that into consideration before choosing it as a profession. Later I understood why he held this opinion. Once he was training a young intern just out of veterinary school. I saw myself, how the young man, who was quite short, struggled with the examination of a cow. After trying to reach inside deep enough, and not succeeding, he asked for a footstool, so he can complete his examination. This made his work perilous with animals, that were in pain and could get jumpy. It is important to know, that veterinary practice in those days meant almost exclusively treating large animals.

I never saw Father treat any small animal -- not that he refused. People would've been embarrassed to bring to him small pets. Dogs were a little different. They were man's best friend, but more importantly, man's helper and the guard of the house. Also, dogs were biting occasionally (even back then) so rabies shots were a regular preventive treatment. Once every two years on a summer morning, as advertised by our "Little Judge", all the town's dogs were brought to the square and in a very noisy couple hours, they got their rabies shots. It was a ruckus spectacle, but entertainment for us, as I watched, usually with friends. -- One more thing on the subject. We had no such thing, as walking the dog. They took care of their own exercise, just by being outside. Thinking of it, Snoopy, that most famous beagle, never set a paw inside Charlie Brown's house -- or go to the vet, or get a root canal. Ours were tougher than Snoopy, but indispensable not only to children, but adults too. One other thing -- ours did not try to write a book, beginning, "It was a dark and stormy night".

I can think of one more exception to the large-animal rule: chickens. Raising chickens is, of course, very important part of farm life. Occasionally, to fight some pox or other disease, region- or country-wide programs were initiated to vaccinate all chickens. I, with my three brothers took part in the big effort and went house-to-house helping out. These were the only occasions when we made some money alongside Father. In fact, he did very little of this work. We kids, some friends and volunteers did it all.

There was resistance on the part of some farmers. A few thought that the shot will ruin the meat, which was nonsense. But it was an effort, backed by the force of law, and no chicken escaped treatment, if we could help it. There was even a way to tell weather a chicken got its shot. The liquid vaccine had very fine graphite in it. Every time we loaded up our syringe, we had to shake up the bottle containing the vaccine and make sure that we suck up a cloudy, and not only clear liquid. This way each bird had in its wing web a permanent little black spot. Important, because penalty could follow each infraction. -- For us, these occasional crash projects were a diversion, a source for a little cash, but quite hard work for a few weeks. Still, it came as natural that we take part and help out. -- It seems water birds are more hardy. I never recall Father treating a goose or duck. They were not as numerous as chickens, but most people raised them. I've never seen a single duck or goose, that looked sick.

Occasionally, Father took us with him on short trips to work. A few kids, up to four, could go with him in the back seat and watch him at work. These were magical times: no work, only fun and a ride in the *car* -- for some kids the only such ride in childhood. The clients often offered some treats such as cookies, fruits, candy. We were supposed to be circumspect accepting anything, not because of any politically correct rule, but just plane politeness and decorum. It was nice to see the generosity of people. It was best in the early days. We were small kids and people were prosperous. Sweets and other goodies were always around in the farmer's kitchen. It was especially rewarding for me, when my neighborhood friends could come along. They got the same treatment I received. It felt good that in a manner of speaking, the neat experience was a gift to them through me.

Father was in total charge of us kids during these trips. It was an accepted practice by the families in town, and indeed the culture in which I grew up, that adults were responsible people, automatically trusted in controlling children and having tacit permission from the kid's parents to take corrective action when needed. I saw my Father spank a neighbor boy and later receive kudos from the boy's father, to whom he had to report his punishment. (Mother just wasn't up to take charge of others' kids this way.) There was trust in people that they all, collectively helping each other, were responsible for our upbringing. I never saw any exception

to this unwritten rule or knew of a complaint of unfair treatment
by anyone. We all knew that parents were more severe with their
own kids, than that of a neighbor. After all, setting good example
was important. Good behavior, politeness and respect were valued
virtues. One of the most effective regulating factor was a self-
imposed control to avoid shame. I see this as one of the great
advantages people in a small town have over residents of cities.

This reminds me of Dr. Laura Schlesinger's comment on her
radio show a few years ago. A caller was talking about disciplining
children, how children are behaving away from home and how
they may be treated there. Referring to today's litigant society,
when parents sue willy-nilly, if anybody as much as touch their
child and perhaps covering up their embarrassment over implied
failure in raising them, she recalled times of her own childhood
and said this:

"Back then we didn't care who the parents were. We trusted
adults to do the right thing in disciplining other peoples children,
along with their own." -- As if I heard my parents talking. In
her comment she was reinforcing universal values, generations and
continents apart.

I liked the traditional way of raising children, proven the best,
since ancient times and based on respect, decency and common
sense. It recognizes that people are good and play a role that is good
for society, by correcting any child's behavior. It is not possible
today. I would be hesitant to pat on the head, a child I don't know in
approval for just because she is cute or sweet. I would be thinking
that somebody might see in the kind gesture, contrived behavior
of a potential child molester. When there are no adults around, I
do not approach a child. This kind of government mandated child
protection, is what took the place of the effective neighborhood
watch, based on trust in the fundamental goodness of people and
respect for the judgment of adults, that protected children much
better and helped their neighbors in raising their own children.
This kind of confidence in one's conduct disappeared, along
with unlocked doors and life's other simple virtues. Freedom,
combined with responsibility, is the most potent combination for
good living and prosperous society. I hope, this will be recognized

and valued again some day. We live in a different world and it is not all good.

Once Father applied his rule to me, while we were playing *bige*, a game we played in the street a lot. All we needed were a 2-foot stick, usually fashioned from a broom handle and the bige, a 6-inch piece, cut from the remaining part of the broomstick, sharpened to a dull point at each end. The game was: using the stick, to hit one end of the bige, resting on the ground and as it jumps up in the air, hit it with the stick and see how far it flies. We kept score by measuring the distance, walking it foot-to-foot. This was great fun and we spent many hours chasing the little wooden piece. Once in an argument while playing, I wanted to punish a kid on the other team by denying him the privilege of playing with my set. This stopped the game and ruined it for everybody. Father, walking by, observing our argument, soon sided with the neighbor boy - - and really all the others, against me. Instead ordering me to let the game go on, he grabbed an ax, a crude, but suitable stick, and in about two minutes, fashioned a new bige for common use. I was left there, embarrassed with my polished set, but suddenly an outcast. The kids resumed play and I realized that I overplayed my hand and left the scene a bit wiser.

3

Veterinary Medicine

By tradition, most steers were castrated and used as beasts of burden and slaughtered for beef at old age. Steak, as it is consumed in America, was almost unknown. Beef was old steer or cow meat that made the most delicious soup or stew, one of my father's favorite meals. The cow was valued mostly for her milk and to produce young. In the lean years of communist-dictated farming, people were using cows for field work, because steers were exported, to bring in scarce hard currency.

A grotesque and desperate act by many a farmer became widespread. He broke the leg of a newborn ox, which then had to be slaughtered. His two advantages from this cruel act were that he could gain a lot more milk from his mother cow and a little additional money for the calf's meat. (His share for the mandatory surrender to the state of a milk-fed calf a year later, were to be meager.) The difference between selling the meat of his days-old calf, *and* having more milk left to sell, against raising the calf for a year, then giving it up and have less milk, was clear to him. He chose the first, the option that broke to his favor. The larger part of his advantage in raising cattle at all, was the milk. This was his attempt to remedy an unfair deal.

After the communists with their planned economy and infamous *5-Year Plans* passed from the scene, things returned to normal, at least in this respect. Other effects of the old forced economy, mainly the confiscation and capricious and grossly unjust redistribution of land, still haunt farmers and the whole of Hungarian economy decades later. Thank God, the inefficient co-operatives, that produced gross economic distortions and misery throughout the society, are only a painful memory. Complete recovery from the sorry legacy of the that despotic regime is not yet on the horizon. To forgive is not easy. The road to repair is slow and it may take a generation. The old guard still has a grip on power and is holding on to stolen loot.

* * *

I witnessed many minor operations by Father in farm yards and knew his routine. I enjoyed explaining them to friends. Neutering a pig, to facilitate fattening, took two men, a bowl of warm water, 4-5 minutes of his time and a lot of screaming by the poor beast. Father started by cutting a 2½ inch gash, just enough for two fingers to go inside, and within seconds he dug out the two ovaries. He cut them off and sewed up the pig right then. He used a 5 in. needle, which had a sharp edge, serving as his knife, to cut the string, that was sterilized in advance in boiling water. To keep the wound from getting infected, he spread on petroleum jelly or even virgin axle grease. It worked every time. His instructions to the owner were:

"Liquid, or very thin diet, rest and walking the animal twice daily for three days".

By the way, once I saw another vet do the same operation, that took about 15 minutes. The cut he made was 5 in. and he went into the poor pig with his whole hand up to his wrist.

My cousin Gerti told of an experience that taught her a lesson for life. She was staying with us at the time. She went with Father on one of his visits to a farmhouse, where he performed one of his operations. During that, she saw blood spill and recoiled, with expressed fear of the sight. Father gently reprimanded her. He told her that she should not fear blood, but rejoice over what it really is.

"It represents and gives life" -- he said. "Next time think of that and look at it in a new, positive way. That's why we respect it and are so careful treating it." Gerti remembered this admonition and told me the story years later, when we were talking about memories of Father. She said that it changed her attitude forever. Instead being a source of fear, she began seeing it as a precious commodity that deserves respect and is one of God's miraculous gifts. Not the indiscriminate spilling of it, but when it is spent in the service of health and honest advantage.

These type operations were a dime-a-dozen, but there were others that were truly remarkable. I was present at two of them. Father never spared effort to save an animal. He respected the farmer's high regard for this principal means of livelihood. In fact, he thought about animals the same way, the farmer did. They were also *his* livelihood. The goodwill he generated by respecting others, earned him respect and a lot of credit. He was too, son of a farmer and grew up with the understanding and concerns of farmers.

One of the potentially troublesome procedures was calving. Usually he received an urgent message that a difficult calving was in progress. That was, when the owner couldn't handle it himself and the cow's, or calf's life was in peril. I heard of his most heroic operation, when he got a dead calf out of its mother, in pieces. After he was unable to deliver it, trying various ways, he went in with a knife and took out the calf in parts and by that, saved the mother.

I was with Father once and present at an unsuccessful calving. The womb was twisted, turned perhaps a full circle, constricting the birth canal. He tried for a long time to turn the womb by one large, sweeping, circular move, using one arm that was inside the cow up to his shoulder. When this failed, he lay down on straw behind the heifer and tried the same move, just by holding his arm, while four men turned the animal from one side to the other with a slow, controlled move. After an hour, he gave up. The butcher had to finish the job. He told me that this was one of only two such cases. This validated for me his belief that a veterinarian had to be strong and preferably tall person, which he was. Even he had his challenges, despite his strength and experience.

My most memorable such event was -- and I remember, I couldn't believe my luck -- when I was with him at one of his signature operations. He removed nails. *Nail* in most of these cases was wire, that accidentally ended up in silage and chopped to nail-size pieces. Often there were several, that in time could pierce the stomach or intestines and actually endanger vital organs. Definitive diagnosis could only be made quite late in the process, because of misleading signs that could indicate other conditions. They did not teach about this at the university in his days. He conceived and devised this entire process.

When he performed these operations he told the proprietor that he had to pay only if the animal lived, so he had nothing to lose. Father did about a dozen of these procedures in his career. Most were successful. -- The one I saw, took place in the yard of the slaughterhouse. The location had no special significance. It was just a convenient place at this occasion. The farmer lived nearby. (My attempt at joking with the men who gathered to help Father, was that perhaps we should consult the patient, whether she thought that the environs of the slaughterhouse were a bit ominous for comfort on this serious occasion.) Oxen are the most calm and stoic patients. Despite the crucial pain, we heard not a peep -- or moo -- out of her.

Father had about 7 men in assistance. They pressed the cow standing, tightly to a wall, using a long ladder and did not let up until the operation was over. She couldn't move throughout the procedure. Father shaved and disinfected the area of incision, just in front of the left hip bone. He scrubbed his entire right arm. Then he made an 8 inch cut on the skin and cut two more layers inside: the peritoneum -- the lining membrane of the abdomen -- than the stomach itself. He reached in, eventually up to his shoulder and repeatedly *swept* the animal clean. In about 15 minutes, he removed 11 pieces of wire, some of which he gave me as souvenirs. They looked as pieces of anodized wire, no doubt from the exposure to

strong stomach acids. He finished the operation by sewing up all
the cuts he made and disinfecting the wound on the outside. He
gave instructions to the owner and put the cow on an antibiotic
regime. This one lived, as did most of his others. As crowning
achievement the year before, a heifer calved about ten days after
this operation. My brother Józsi was taught this procedure when
he followed his father in the study and the profession of veterinary
medicine.

4

Mother -- Family Life

My mother was an exceptional woman. She was a selfless and self-sacrificing soul, who lived for her family; a great cook, an artist with many skills, gentility, good taste and exemplary decorum. I saw this every day and as a child and took it as a natural thing. She raised us, so I could observe her every day. What surprised me, especially with the perspective of long time passing, is what I recall people were saying about her. She possessed an aura of reverence that I never saw about any other person I've ever known. Hers was a gentle beauty, with noble features, evoking the sublime images, as painted by Botticelli and Fra Lippo Lippi. Hers was a soft soul with moral authority which commanded respect. She had her hands full with four boys, had to get tough often, and did too, a few times. Her wooden spoons had a secondary function. We felt their stinging pinch, if only for a minute. When she really needed help, she threatened us with the prospect of telling Father. Corrective action was used often, but my parents naturally applied the more effective method of good example, rather than that of a critic and stern disciplinarian, to influence our behavior and shape our character.

My maternal grandfather, Lajos Végh, was a well-to-do farmer, rancher and landowner. He cultivated hundreds of acres and skillfully managed sizable forests. His farm was huge and beautiful, with pristine orchards, vineyards on rolling hills and fields, tended by members of about a dozen families. We vacationed there every summer and reveled in the most pleasant aspects of farm life, where for us there was no work, only opportunities for discovery, that were endless. Our every wish came true as if by magic, through the effort of relatives, house staff and solicitous employees, as they were busying themselves tending to animals, working with crops, or doing the many chores in the yard and stables. The yard was over 100 meter long and half as wide. The house was at one end, facing the street. A row of buildings circled the yard, many for pigs and fowl, but the large ones were in a row, near the center. These were the stables for the horses, two for cattle and another for large equipment. The back gate, between two corn cribs, lead to the fields, orchard, vineyard and grazing land. There were several buildings that were not used daily and contained old or rarely used equipment. For us, they were like an old attic to rummage through and find fascinating playthings and mementos.

As evening approached, a member from each employee family, usually children, came to the open kitchen window with a milk jug and took home the family's daily allotment of fresh milk, still warm. After that we had supper and came the least popular time of the day -- early to bed. Before I fell asleep, I could only think of morning.

Csehi was a small village, about 20 miles from Jánosháza. My mother, Ilona, grew up in this world, in a protective family, that by any measure, was well off. Her mother died in childbirth when she was 3. My grandfather married again and had three more children.

The young Ilonka, as she was affectionately called by family and relatives, had the most appropriate education a girl can wish for. Girls then had no ambition to follow a career. Marrying well, motherhood, a successful family, and pride in one's children were the ultimate aim and reward for a young woman of her generation and upbringing. By those measures she was an unparalleled success. She was in demand and had many suitors. Father was a great catch, but by no means a sure winner of her hand. She was educated by nuns in an exclusive girls school in Szombathely. The nuns' mission was to provide a well rounded liberal education and skills to conduct oneself well in polite society.

After growing up in a protected cocoon as dictated by customs of the day, she was expected to be a leader in society, a leader by example to establish her good name and enhance the good name of her husband in her new circumstance. She was admired exactly for these qualities. I never heard directly, or through others anything negative, things that were commonly said about other people. I did not even know people who would be envious of her or her position. She transcended that with her goodness, and was in the good graces of those with potential malignant gossip. To the contrary, she was widely considered an exemplary and virtuous woman.

I recall once an aunt telling me:

"Nobody gossiped about your mother. There was nothing to gossip about."

We entertained a lot. Mother's parties were in great demand and talk of the town, praised as the best around. I recall among our acquaintances, a number of men who lavished their attention and praises on her. I saw this early and have in later years confirmed, that my youthful observations were correct. My conclusion as a child was, that these were all lesser men than my father. Society in Jánosháza was still small-town, but offered more than did tiny Csehi, her birthplace and childhood home. Running the house occupied her every day. She liked to read and cultivated a few select friends, all of whom I liked and got to know well. She entertained colleagues and acquaintances in Father's professional circle, as times dictated.

Mother liked to play the piano in an amateurish way. She had lessons for only a few years. I enjoyed her music, because she played the most beautiful songs, popular story- and love-songs. From her I learned a few that I played later myself. I took lessons longer than she and could play better. My style is similar to hers, more improvisational, rather than literally following notes.

She had a vice, if I could call it such: she smoked an occasional cigarette, fashionable then. Later did I learn, that this was a secret, to be tightly kept from my father. I also realized what an innocent thing it was -- a mere curiosity and the challenge of doing something that was almost exclusively a man's thing. I heard that in Budapest there were many women who smoked, but in Jánosháza, I never saw any woman engage in it. Mother did not inhale. She saw some Hollywood movies, where glamorous women smoked, as a fashionable societal pastime. So, on lazy afternoons, and I assume long before Father was expected home, she took a few puffs. I think she was confident, that Father, a smoker, would not sense the odor when he came home. Once I asked her and she gave me a puff, just to satisfy my curiosity. It was good for a few coughs. This *habit* of hers lasted a few years. I think I could count on my hands the number of times I saw her touch the stuff. I do not know why, but her occasional indulgence remains one of my sweet memories of her. Occasionally she was joined in this secret activity by her younger cousin, Mariann. She was living with us after her mother's death, but was an adult by then.

My other exposure to smoking was the occasion, when my oldest brother Józsi organized a smoking session in the back garden, as we called the field behind the garden, beyond the yard. He wanted to make sure that we will never pick up the habit, by showing us how bad it smells and tastes. We, about six of us, with a couple neighbor boys were in the middle of the corn field, well hidden from possible prying adult eyes. Józsi said that we should make cigarettes, using newspaper and dried corn silk. It was a successful project. We all coughed and spit in disgust. Józsi just watched, gleaming, knowing that his demonstration was persuasive. We had no idea if there was any difference between dry corn silk and tobacco. None of us took up smoking in a serious way, though Otti is known to sometimes engage in it, only in company. It is an irony of fate that among the four of us Józsi smoked the most, just lightly, off-and-on for several years.

Mother was an exceptional cook, well known within the extended family and in her circle. Friends often benefited from this at her famous parties on Joseph day, my father's name day in March. She used to bake cakes for charitable causes that brought in good money. She traveled to the city and took specialty cooking classes and surprised her guests with extraordinary dishes. Before large parties we were encouraged to stay clear of the kitchen. She had usually two helpers. This way she could focus on the important thing, the culinary art and the esthetic presentation of her creations.

Once, when he was our guest at a dinner party, our pastor tasted one of her delicacies, a specialty beef tongue dish. After dinner he asked her if she would make the same dish for the confirmation ceremonies, when the bishop was expected in town. She gladly offered to do it. The pastor, Father Joseph Pártli was Dad's best friend. The confirmation was in May. That year, the weather on confirmation weekend was unusually warm. We had an early summer heat wave, but the nights were still cool. Mother made the entire dish in the middle of the night, so the delicate meal would hold together. The maid took it to the rectory before dawn, in the coolest part of the day. We could get ice, but had no refrigeration back then. The best place for storing food was in the basement. Using care and optimum timing, the tongue creation was prepared and safely delivered to the priory. Mother nature complicated things a little, but ultimately the meal was a success.

She had her special way to test the consistency and quality of beaten egg white or creme. She beat it, with a whisk in the bowl in her lap for about 7 minutes. Then she visually examined it. If she judged it done, she lifted the bowl high, turned upside down to make sure it was firm. It never fell out -- except once. I was with her, saw the sweet suds tumble out and plop on the kitchen floor. She was as surprised as I was. We looked at each other in stunned amazement for a second -- then burst out in an uproarious laugh. I volunteered to clean up, giggling all the way. It was like a comedy act. -- She made another batch and perhaps just once, she took a really close look at her bowl before turning it.

5

Forest Scenes And A
Memorable Christmas

One nice summer day, Mother proposed a whole-day outing for the family, a sort of working picnic for her. The occasion was an ordinary weekday, when Father had a pre-planned program, an all day visit to one or two of his villages. He did this periodically throughout the district. That day, it was Zalaerdõd.

On such *körút*-days, advertised and organized in advance, he visited many houses, and encouraged the farmers to consult him regarding any animal or other concerns. People brought their animals to a central location for non-urgent operations and procedures that were done at a savings of expense and time. These were usually healthy animals that needed shots or minor preventive operations, such as neutering. On those days he got a lot done, treating animals and giving free advice. It worked out best for everybody.

On that day, körút was in Zalaerdõd. Mother asked him to take us all along and put us out at the edge of the village, that was surrounded by forest. The day was perfect for a picnic in the woods. Mother, with her four boys and a servant, wanted to hunt for mushrooms and berries. Though we picked only two well known kinds, we found so many mushrooms by noon, that we could no longer carry them. We sorted the lot and left more than half in a pile and took only the nicest, the boletus mushrooms (a lot like portabella). The load was a burden, even thus reduced. We were roaming the forest, yelling, singing, while picking berries in the early afternoon. Mother's often repeated her favored cry: "Haho", to see if anybody hears us.

Truth be told, we were lost. Mother's plan, to take us to a certain road, leading back to town, did not succeed. We ate our packed lunch earlier and were hungry again. Then, we found one of the main roads that cut through the forest, and settled down on the side, waiting. I remember being anxious, but Mother was sure, that someone will find us. The day was still young. We spotted a man far away on the long straight road, coming toward us. As he approached, we could see, he was a forest ranger, with a rifle on his shoulder. He told us, that Father was already looking for us and should show up soon. Indeed we heard the tooting of the horn and soon the car was coming, kicking up dust on the road. It was a happy reunion. We loaded all our mushrooms and the remaining wild strawberries into the car, along with our tired, famished bodies.

A very nice surprise was in store. Father took us to the rectory for supper. The local pastor was one of his favorite friends. It was not yet supper time. The cook was still working on something smelling mighty good. In the meantime they invited us to treat ourselves to the most desirable appetizer a kid would ever want. In the yard were two huge cherry trees. It may have been early for supper, but the season for the most delicious crunchy cherries was right on time and perfect. It was late June. The year must have been 1942 and I, six years old. Within a minute we were up on the branches, stuffing and spitting, gorging on a favorite treat. I ate the most delicious cherries of my life, high on the tree never wanting to stop. We were quite full, but still ate a good supper afterwards. It was one of my most memorable events, as a small boy. I can still recall details of that day, and in my mind, re-live the magical childhood adventure so many years ago.

Father had great respect in Jánosháza, because of his professional reputation, the way he could handle people and for the generosity with which he treated others. He helped out some with favors, at times in a foolishly naïve manner. I know of several cases when he did not get paid back on loans he made to acquaintances. Mother also did similar things. She gave to friends, gave to the poor and gave things to us, easier than Father did. -- Once however, I remember how she stuck to her guns and denied me some spending money, no matter how long I begged. I saw some trinket in a store and obsessed about having it. I remember the event for of the extreme frustration I felt, and how surprised I was about her firmness in resisting my incessant pleas.

She taught me to knit once. It happened when I came in very cold, after extended play in the snow and a snowball fight with my brothers and friends. I cozied up by the warm glazed tile stove by which she often sat on winter evenings. I got the hang of knitting quite fast and enjoyed it too. It was the first and last time I knitted. Why do I remember this so well? It was warm, toasty and so soothing, while my frozen limbs were warming up. It left me with a cherished memory for life.

Family time was most important and observed with few exceptions. We always had our meals together. The midday meal was the main meal of the day, so I hesitate calling it lunch. It took place when Father came home. He tried to be there between 1 and 2 P.M., but did not always make it. We waited for him, with rare exceptions. The meal was ready, but often had to be heated again for the delayed service. Cell phones would've come in handy.

Christmas by far, was the most important holiday. In our house, this holy day of Christ's birth had all the reverence of Christmas in the Christian world, but for us it was strictly our family day. Our parents kept us believe that the tree and gifts are given by Baby Jesus, and brought to us by angels.

We had our version of Santa Claus, that was separate from Christmas, on the 6th of December. That was the day of St. Nicholas, the bishop of in the 4th century in Myra, somewhere in Asia Minor, and the patron saint of children, sailors, merchants, etc. His day had its own elaborate ritual. The revered bishop, dressed very much like the Santa we know, with less emphasis on the elaborate beard, visited homes with children, gave admonitions and brought gifts. He had helpers, a *krampus* or two, dressed in black, who represented the other, the darker side of generous giving. For bad behavior, as testified to by parents, they meted out punishment in the form of symbolic flogging. Thus, parents wanted gently to invite better future conduct by their offspring. Still all kids received sweets and trinkets. -- Also this time (early December) the *Bethlehem Visitors* started to make their house calls. A few boys, with a home-made nativity scene, came around evenings and made a presentation, appropriate for the season. Their arrival was always a welcome event. They would knock on the door and ask for permission to do their act. In a typical evening we had three-four such visits, up to the day before Christmas. They carried their little Bethlehem, complete with the Holy Family, angels, shepherds and barn animals. Some also had the three kings, or were themselves dressed like them. They may put on an elaborate show with recitation, singing and play acting. I think it was a beautiful custom and a wonderful way to get the Christmas spirit. They never asked, but usually received some money or a token gift.

I remember a treasured early Christmas Eve, actually a late afternoon, I think in 1942. Józsi kept me company as we were roaming our neighborhood. It was on my parents' request. They judged that I still believed in Santa Claus, or *Jézuska* (Little Jesus) as I knew it. I was in a state of mind that I didn't, but were not entirely sure. For a reason I do not remember, I came home too early from the Jakab family, where we spent the afternoon of the 24th each year, throughout our childhood, while our parents decorated the tree and put out presents. (In that year, only Tomi and I went there. Otti and Józsi knew it already.) My brother's assignment was to occupy me until they finish decorating. Józsi was splendid company for a six-year old. He did not talk about Little Jesus, angels or anything Christmas. He told me stories of other kind, perhaps to distract me, and entertained me while we spent more than an hour, walking the darkening neighborhood on a starry, calm, all-white Christmas Eve. It was beautiful.

I have to say though, that by the end, I was onto his art, and

firmly decided, that the family magic of our Christmas Eves --
though angel-inspired -- were man made, created by the tender
hands of loving parents, and this time, a gently protective brother.
-- But I would not tell him this for anything in the world -- and
never did.

6

A Cold Winter And A Heartwarming Event In Csehi

One of my favorite romantic love stories is the meeting of my parents. As told by knowing relatives: my father, tall and handsome, with a budding veterinary practice, a ticket for a bright, prosperous future, heard about a young lady in Csehi, known as a real catch for one who meets high character and material standards. He had also to be otherwise deserving. Of course, Father thought of himself in those terms and expressed to friends a keen interest in meeting her, by devising an acceptable scheme to have an encounter with the young lady. He knew the tiny village of only a few hundred people where she lived, but nothing more about this supposed heavenly creature, except that she came from a prominent family.

A day before the coming chilly New Years eve in 1928, he and a friend went into the tiny village, to look around and within rules of decorum, meet the lady of his dreams and imagination. As the story goes, a lot of snow fell, with temperatures so extremely cold, that left them there without means to get out. The guys saw opportunity in this and after some inquiry, looked for the biggest house in town and claiming hardship, asked for lodging for the night. (Not that there was no room at the inn. Their lucky break was that for miles around, there was no inn to have.) So, they were fed and put up for the night. A memorable and lovely day followed. On New Years eve, my future parents went to their first ball together, both smitten for life.

The rest, as you dear reader might also think, is history. But it was not to be -- at least not yet. Love blossomed as if preordained by fate and courtship followed. But as things got gradually serious, there was still Grandfather, a wise, astute man, respected by his employees and people in his town, as he was loved and revered by his family. He had land and forest holdings near and far, managed and owned his beautiful, profitable farm.

He also knew the treasure he was beholding and drove a hard bargain. He acknowledged the suitor's accomplishments and recognized his bright prospects, as things stood, but gave a choice to the young man.

"If you ever want to marry my Ilonka, you have to earn your doctorate."

Needless to say, Father found this a potentially most rewarding challenge. He did his work and received his second sheepskin with distinction. History was really made then. They married on the 3rd of January 1932 -- coincidentally on another very cold winter day. I have the old clipping, the announcement in the county daily, publicizing the wedding.

I fondly remember in an important event in 1967. On that day Mother and my then fiancé, Ildikó connected spiritually and formed an instant warm relationship. The common traits, interests and temperament attracted them to each other. They shared a strong preference for gentleness and propriety, and admired in each other these qualities, while recognizing others that made them different. Mother was more a conciliator, while Ildi stands up firmly in defense of her principles. When times are hard, demand courage and integrity, each is eminently capable of steadfastly defending truth and high-minded values. I saw it as a good indication and promising for the future. And I was right.

7

My Home, Jánosháza

Our house was built in 1936 and I was the first to be born in it. It was built on a lot where stood two old houses before. Part of one was left standing and remained the home of a childless couple the Molnárs, who already lived in it for some time. They often told me proudly that they were living in our house longer than I was. More about the old couple, in a while.

Attached to their wing and converted to our use, were utility structures, the wash kitchen, wood shed and garage. Further back, between the front yard and the garden, was a second, a small *farm yard,* left from one of the old houses. Father had a fence built around it. There we let stand old structures, that were there originally for the housing of animals. We had little use for it and let them stand more or less idle, for years. We kids kept caged rabbits and raised silkworms a few times and sold the cocoons for pocket money. (I remember what chore it became to feed them toward the end. They were ravenous creatures and when big, ate a huge amount of mulberry leaves.) The outer buildings and cages came in handy after the communists took over in 1948. Then we began raising pigs and fowl to economize on expenses.

In my childhood days, the huge garden was only for pleasure.

Half of it was grass with trees and a play area with a swing. The other half was planted with strawberries and raspberry bushes. This changed in the new regime after the war. Part of the garden and much of the strawberry field was put to the more important use of growing vegetables.

Earlier, Father planted fruit trees throughout the grassy area. All together, we had at least 60. He was a connoisseur of fruit trees, familiar with grafting and special needs of treating them. He learned it from his father. We had a cherry tree, half of which brought the crunchiest bing cherries. When we harvested them, the other half was full of small, still hard, green fruits. They ripened in late August. Not the best kind, but in late summer, we were one of only a few in town eating cherries.

Closer to the house were other decorative trees, including two huge weeping willows, excellent, if not the most safe for climbing. Tomi and I were often racing to a perch near the top. We even timed ourselves. Sometimes we were asked by adults to show our skills. In time we learned that the branches of the willow tree were not very strong. We had to be careful not to tempt fate by climbing out too far. This became clear one day, when a daring climb ended in a loud *ckack*, and a jump by me, from higher than I really wanted to let a branch go, and get to the ground through thin air. The incident ended without damage, other than to the branch, but it was a useful lesson about daring bravado -- and willow trees.

After the war, the strawberry patch shrank to about 15% of the original tract, with the rest converted to be a vegetable garden. Other things changed too. We raised our own pigs and poultry. I spent much time and work, feeding and cleaning up after animals. It was not easy to get used to, but it grew on me and after a while I took pride in it, that made it easier, taught me discipline and down-to-earth values. The work wasn't hard enough to give calluses, but occasionally I thought of the guys in 7th grade.

There were other chores we had to do. My father grew up a as child of a smallholder, and in his youth was also expected to help with farm chores. It came as natural for him to demand the same from us. His favorite command was: "Pick up fallen fruits in the garden". For some reason, this always seemed to me an unending task. First, because we had all those trees. Then, in summer months, when playing was most fun, it often interrupted things that I deemed important, or at least more pleasurable.

One occasion sticks best in my mind. We, about a dozen kids, were busy on the square after a heavy summer rainstorm -- directing accumulated rainwater downstream, into channels we carved into the ground toward the village *storm sewer*, the ditch. The ground was gravel-topped dirt, not asphalt as it is now. We could do a lot with sticks, hands and bare feet. It was incredible fun -- until Father suddenly appeared, as he drove by our happy group, on his way to make a call.

"Miklós, Tamás, go home and pick up the apples." With that, he rolled up his window and drove on.

He thought of this as a most natural thing, but in my state of mind at the time, this was not good to hear. The afternoon was ruined. The contrast between our fun project and the chore we were assigned, was indescribable. No argument or defiance -- we had to go. We went home and picked up a lot of apples, though did not do the whole job. He finished it later himself, but asked us again to help him. Doing it with him was little easier. There was no immediate distraction and with Father doing a big part, the task was finished in reasonable time. Some of the apple was good enough to eat; the rest went to feed the pigs.

Our big backyard was divided lengthwise. Just back of the house we had a dirt yard, with flat stones to walk on in rain. This walkway was leading along the Molnár's house, by the garage, to a fence, separating it from the farm yard, with the pig pen and animal cages. On the other side we had grass with trees and further down, the orchard. Behind the farm yard, the garden the fruit/vegetable track continued further back.

I would not call our grass field a lawn. Grass was let grow there to considerable height and cut only twice a summer. Father let a neighbor farmer cut it with a scythe and take the hay, as feed. This grassy grove was our playground, surrounding a large sandbox, framed with wood beams. After lying idle for years, most of the sand we used in a building repair project. The swing too, became a victim to marching time.

Near the sandbox was another of Mother creations, a mushroom table and two chairs (small mushrooms) that she painted, as those we see in children's story books: red top with white dots. The original top for the table was a millstone. Mother had a mason build a leg and the rounded top for it. The chairs had a rock as base, again built up to a domed top to make for comfortable seating. She did the painting herself. We loved the set and a few times ate our lunch, using this lovely lawn furniture.

At the back end of the strawberry field was a jungle of raspberry bushes that we visited often through the summer. Fresh home grown raspberries were a great favorite, especially of my mother. It is also the best loved fruit for Ildikó. At the edge of the raspberry patch we had nettles growing wild. We avoided those the best we could, but later chopped part of it down. The rest we left, but cut paths through it and called it the *nettle fort*. With care, we could get to the *inner cave* without being stung. It became a sanctuary, requiring child's imagination to consider it a refuge from kids who were not privy to our curious hideout.

The old, childless tailor couple, two simple, tiny people (both, barely five feet) Uncle Imre Molnár and his wife, Aunt Mici, stayed in their apartment and became our intimate neighbors for the rest of their lives. Our relationship, with a few very minor glitches, remained amicable, until their death sometimes in the 1970s. Both died within a year. After that, their three-room-and-kitchen home was left empty until my mother sold the house in the mid-1980s.

Aunt Mici (Mitzi) worked with her husband in the tailoring of mostly men's suits. Uncle Imre was a Santa Claus type, but without beard, only a mustache. He was a little taller than his wife, but I reached his height when I was about 9. I remember him for his gentle humor and much kindness towards us. He had his stock of jokes that we heard him repeat often as new, and laughed each time we heard them. Aunt Mici was a lady who grew up in Vienna. She was pedantic, with a few pretenses, having grown up in sophisticated Vienna, but inside a gentle soul. She spoke Hungarian with that typical accent that I heard exactly reproduced by Aunt Pepi, or Pepike, as we loved to call her -- and years later -- also by my sister in law, Helma. All three ladies had German as mother tongue and learned Hungarian as adults. All three spoke with a sweet accent and a pronunciation, that gave a rising, singing ending to their sentences, wholly different than a German accent in English. They made the exact same mistakes in grammar, syntax and sentence structure. We found great delight in imitating the old ladies, even in front of them, though always with love and respect. They had a good sense of humor and laughed along with us.

We boys had a special relationship with the old couple. They were true homebodies and hardly ever left their neat, miniature house other then for shopping or for an occasional visit across the square, to see their only friends, Uncle Pista, the school custodian and his wife. I spent many hours in the shop entertaining them and being delighted by them in turn. They lived practically free in the house. I was already a teenager when I learned that they paid us the rough equivalent of two dollars a month. They were our trusted guards at the gate, when we went away. I was amazed how seriously they took this trust, the responsibility and the little work it involved. Upon our return they always gave a thorough report on the rumors and happenings in town, along with the messages that came in for Father regarding work. Their most notable and vital stint as gatekeepers was, while we were away for over a month, trying to escape the Russians, as they were invading Hungary in 1945.

When I visited my parents' grave on my last trip home, my brother Tomi lead me to the Molnár grave. There they rested, a few rows down from their friend and landlord, in the close proximity of many others whose name I recognized. I was amazed that I knew so many there. I checked myself by looking at the dates and markings on the tombstones. They all checked out. Some I barely recalled from early childhood, others I knew well and saw in the village for many years. And others, who were my age and younger. László Köves, a lanky lad, was a grade school classmate. His somewhat faded enamel image is on the headstone, just steps away from that of my parents. He is in military uniform, signifying that he died as a soldier. I was told, it was during a battle exercise, a victim of the collateral risks soldiers take, in addition to the peril of combat. Under his name and birth date a simple line: "Lived

20 years". Laci, as we called him, was one of the gentlest and most polite boys I remember from my early schooling. I usually stop by his grave when I go to that old cemetery. It is always a somber walk -- and more so as time passes.

The house that I was born in was one of the biggest and probably the nicest in town, reflecting our relative affluence and the esteem my parents enjoyed. The biggest room was the kids' room, with cribs and later beds for four boys. A huge, glazed tile stove heated this room and the living room. It was installed in a big wall-opening between the two rooms, reaching four feet into each. In winter days, we built a fire in it, that was going from early evening till about 9-o'clock. It was still plenty warm the next morning. There were three other large and several smaller rooms. We used the formal dining room for occasional Sunday dinner and when guests came. We had two wedding receptions for relatives who needed larger facilities than they had available elsewhere. Also, we lived in it for two years just after the war, during which we shared space for about nine months, with another family of refugees. Nine people in one room. This was, when various Russian authorities occupied the rest of the house. But more about that, later.

I remember large parties in our house when I was a boy. The biggest ones were always on my father's name day, March 19th. Birthdays were private. Only the family celebrated those. A name day was public, because everybody knew that March 19 was Joseph. I remember loud, smoke-filled evenings before we fell asleep, and the loud sounds of good times that stretched late into the night.

Next morning I might sneak a small sip of last night's liqueur, still out on the table. One unfortunate time I took a sip of something I was hoping were sweet. It was not what I expected. It was *pálinka*, a hard fruit distillate, not kid's stuff -- something rather like whisky. As I took my little sip and gagged, Father walked in. He devised an instant punishment: "Now, you finish it!" -- he said.

"Oh no", I thought, but did as told and thought myself properly punished. I hurried out and gulped down ample water to soothe my aching throat.

The attic of this big house, finished with a layer of cement, was a special place. It was the storehouse for useful things, a lot of junk and many treasures. Boxes of old stuff, no-longer-used items, commodities, such as corn and other grains were stored there at times. We also stored smoked meat products, hanging from rafters. In warm days, grease was dripping from them, that we caught on newspapers. They never spoiled, thanks to ample smoking. Usually we took them down to the pantry where it was cooler.

Attics are romantic places. This was clearly one. We chased sparrows and once even a mouse, who got up there through some crack. Many times we used it as a secret playground or just rummaged through forgotten heirlooms, old collections and junk, gathering dust in its many nooks.

8

A Trip To The Vineyard

I recall a pleasant afternoon with Father, a few years after war's end. He and I were at our vineyard on Little Somlyó Hill, about five miles from home. Little Somlyó the village, was at the base of the hill, it was named after. It was one of the smaller towns in Father's district. The Hill, where we bought a small plot, was one of the low, basalt-base volcanic rocky mounds, in Transdanubia. Not famous, but had a good soil for producing wine. There are others, like Big Somlyó and Badacsony, and of course Tokaj further east, whose wines are known worldwide and are recipients of many awards. In 1955 we sold Little Somlyó and bought a nice property in the Badacsony region, along the picturesque north shore of Lake Balaton. For us, that was a significant step up in vineyards and also in opportunities for vacationing.

But back to my story. The year was 1951. I was in my mid-teens. Father suggested that we go to the vineyard and do some needed work. It was early summer, perfect weather, but by all indications a pleasant, but otherwise humdrum day. We did some weed clearing with hoe and general chores around the cellar on top of Little Somlyó. A couple hours later we headed home on that sunny afternoon. Our conveyance was a 100 c.c. Csepel motorcycle. It was perfect for such short trips, although quite a load for a little scooter. It was not much different from two men riding a donkey, only a little faster. Father didn't want to use his car, saving it for work and longer, more important trips. Motoring this way, with light breeze on the face was fun. He let me drive and it meant a lot. I was careful but even more proud as we cruised along at about 30 mph.

But on that day, the little bike had the last word. It quit without a sputter, at about one third the way home. It was not because of overload. It could handle that. It was something mechanical. We looked it over and concluded that it was beyond our expertise to fix. We could have used the services of my brother Otti, who could fix anything. We chose the next best thing, started for home on foot. I was rolling the bike all the way. The weather was perfect, the walk easy, the vista of the winding road, lined with poplar trees and our ears full of bird song, beautiful. The scene appeared pristine, akin to a series of *impressions*, put to canvas so many times by Monet.

When one walks a road slowly, rather than zipping along it, numbed by the long line of trees sweeping by, one is able to appreciate and enjoy the beauty of the countryside. Details in the changing contours of plowed fields, greening grains and crops nearing harvest come to life. The graceful beauty of that vista, that was hidden by speed on other days, opened up to feast the eye. I saw beauty that I never knew was there. We looked at familiar country with new eyes, while chatting and carelessly enjoying each other's company, recalling old times, lost hopes and happy moments in our common past.

I had perhaps, my best conversation with Father on that walk, with the old bike as our only companion. He told me about a long ago plan of his that was foiled by recent politics. He pointed to the run-down park with a pool, at the edge of town, that I visited a few times in years earlier. I thought it was a great bathing place, despite its water being chilly. The pool was fed by a delicious tasting spring. (It was used as the source of water for our town, when they built the centralized community water system in the 1970s.) He told me that he wanted to buy the whole complex, renovate it and open it with heated pool. That was of course before the war, when free enterprise flourished in the country and people could freely enter into business ventures. But under Russian occupation and in the communist era it was not to be. The regime nixed it. They would not allow any business to be operated by private individuals.

Father was not a businessman by nature. Yet, he saw an opportunity in this and wanted to take a risk to revive the old park and pool. This story was all new to me and I loved hearing the details. I was proud. I understood and favored his concept. My earlier pleasant memories about the place were still vivid.

This was the only thing I clearly remember we talked about. The rest is a blur. Reminiscing about that day, evokes precious memories that stay with me to the present day. I remember the lightness and liberating ease of our conversation, a kind that we never had before.

I find it amazing, how a vague memory can stay fresh in me for so many years, and remain for so long such a pleasant event in my mind. -- This happened at a time when I started to assert my independence and friction between us began to appear. It seemed to me a natural thing then and it increased for a few years. Circumstances and the serendipity of a timely mechanical failure left me for life, with one of my most precious memories with my dad.

At the beginning of this, at times tense period, I was surprised that he was more tolerant at my limited defiance of his commands. I saw that things changed. We were closer to being on equal basis. His control loosened, his tone mellowed, the occasional tension eased. I was pleased with the outcome. I reckon, so was he, although we never touched on the subject.

9

Brothers, Birds, Cars
And A Trip To Budapest

Józsi was first born. He liked to follow his own bliss, finding his own pursuits. He studied and drew aircraft, mostly fighter planes. He scratched them in the dirt in the yard, with meticulous accuracy and in actual size. He once explained to me the many details he included, even inside the cockpit. Later he drew birds and made many nice drawings and tempera paintings. The nicest was a pair of blue chickadees.

Józsi loved to read adventure stories. His favorites heroes were the Indians and other stories of the Wild West. He used to tell me about his readings. This way, second hand, I still learned much about Indian life, famous chiefs, the Mohicans and his hero, *Winnetou*, the title character in the book by Karl May.

What kid wouldn't love birds? We all did, with the innocent mind of a child, but in a way, that was hands-on. We climbed any tree to get to the nest, to see what's in it. Of the interesting ones we kept track and followed the little ones' progress. We revered all birds, with the qualified exception for sparrows. Sparrows were by far the most plentiful. They ate grain, that people depended on for food. So, there was an ongoing open season on sparrows. As we saw it, they were legitimate target for our slingshots.

I missed out on one of the most important events involving sparrows. Tomi and I were at home. Józsi and Otti were vacationing in Csehi at grandfather's magical farm. Tomi and I missed the biggest sparrow feast, our older brothers put on. As a morning project, they once decided to have sparrow for lunch. It was all done with slingshots. By 10 o'clock they had about 25 birds, ready for the pot. Sparrows were plentiful, the weapons simple, and the skill and accuracy more than adequate for the task. My aunt, Márta, my mother's much younger sister did the cooking. She was barely a year older than Józsi and took part with pleasure in this youthful gourmet treat. By then, about age 11, she was a good cook, as girls of her age were expected to be. Prior to this day she made soup, she stewed, fried and even stuffed them. The only real bite-size portion of a sparrow is the breast. But that is the most tender breast this side of bird heaven. Tomi and I were sorry to miss this big aviary feast. That was the largest number of birds on one menu, they ever put on. Before this, we also had some sparrow meals, but were not there for the big one. -- It was this policy of my parents, that usually the older two went on vacation together. We little guys went later. Csehi was big enough, to accommodate all of us, but my parents wanted to avoid burdening their parents, by sending only two kids at a time.

Once we encountered a very special pair of birds. They nested around our house. The two were the white elephants of their species: albino sparrows. Actually not white, only light gray, but it still made all the difference. They mixed regularly with the others and we saw no difference in their behavior. We knew that they were of special value for their rarity. We observed them around the house, and admired these delightfully different freaks of nature. But we had to have them. After some efforts, we captured one and had it preserved in true likeness by a taxidermist. It is still displayed at our local school across the square from our house, as a unique specimen of a species. Who knows, should we have left it alone and let fate take its course, they surely would have disappeared by now. This way one is preserved, aiding students in their pursuit of bird knowledge. – Otti and I talked about this many years later. By then he had misgivings about our youthful meddling with mother nature.

I want to mention one more thing about our attitude toward birds and all animals, really. When I learned about the sacred reverence of the American Indian for animals, the forest and all things in God's garden, it reminded me of the way we also revered them. They were there for us to carefully husband. If nature's laws are abused, bad things follow. One does not eat one's seed corn. Growing up in a small farm town you learn this instinctively. God's gifts are all around you. You just have to appreciate them and with hard, prudent work, produce your livelihood through them. When we scouted the bird nests, we took care never to disturb their peace. With rare exceptions, we selectively and with discretion, amended our unwritten rule, as we did with the white sparrows, and the eggs, as I detail below. We enjoyed their presence around us and considered them friends who make our life interesting, pleasant and fun. I have to admit, however, that eating sparrows did not figure in our mind, as damaging the bird population. We were not quite on the level of reverence for God's creatures, as was Francis of Assisi.

Józsi had a bird egg collection. He painstakingly pierced tiny holes at top and bottom. Thus he was able to blow out the liquid content. The collection consisted of about 30 eggs, safely preserved. They were classified and lined up in a few boxes, cushioned by loose cotton. Eventually, he donated his collection to the school. Other than for personal pleasure, it was an educational tool for all who saw it, and we thought of it only as such, without today's often exaggerated, politically correct, government mandated preservation and environmentalist programs. Being nice to animals and respecting nature came naturally. It was not necessary to legislate being good and respectful of nature's largesse around us.

For our own purposes we created a system, a hierarchy of birds, by which we ranked many of them. At the top were swallows. Originally this was wholly Józsi's judgment, a view that we all adopted. Swallows were beautiful in their simple, shiny coat. Black or steely blue, with white belly, they shimmer in sunlight, as some of the hummingbirds. They excelled in what is most important for a bird, that of flight. They ate the bugs, that bugged us and spread disease. Swallows were *useful* birds. We loved to watch them cutting in and out of their flight patterns with great speed and agility, near ground or at dizzying heights.

Józsi's favorite was the martin, which is the fastest bird in the world, clocked up to 180 mph. (My favorite was its cousin, the barn swallow with its long, forked tail and some difference in coloring. Its flight was smoother and more sweeping. It could glide ever so gracefully. With their behavior, they would forecast some features of weather. When they were flying inches above calm lake water, where flies gathered, we expected rain the next day. Swallows drink in flight, leaving a V-streak, as they dip their lower beak into the calm water of a lake. Also, they mate on the wing, which puts them in a very select company, that of the American bald eagle.

I loved to watch them catch flies off the wall. They were cutting through the air, surveying the territory. I would look for a fly on a wall -- best, a sun lit wall. I didn't have to wait long. Soon one of my swallows came sweeping the spot, flying sideways, and the little black spot that was there seconds before, was gone.

My brothers and I were ecstatic when after wishing it for a long time, a family of martins nested under our eaves. After that, they came back every year. We followed the little ones' progress and delighted in their chirping as the parents tirelessly fed them all day. It was a big event for us. Farmer kids were more fortunate. Birds were around them everywhere, closer than they were to us. Swallows nested inside barns, often on low beams that were within arm's reach. Those neat, precision-built little nests, made of tiny mud pellets soon dried and hardened into a formidable shell structure.

There was another bird, the stork, that endeared itself to most people in Hungary, me first among them. It is known in the western world as a delivery vehicle for the newborn, which gives it a special place in folklore, mainly in central and southern Europe. (It is also possible that this lofty role was assigned to this large bird, that was already a favorite for other reasons.) I remember watching them soar, endlessly it seemed, without moving a wing, or even a muscle high in the bright summer sky, resting and spiraling upwards on rising air currents. To have them build a nest on the top of one's chimney was considered a sign of good luck and free entertainment for young and old. Once they started coming, twigs in beak and with painstaking mastery, put together a most disorganized and disheveled pile, we knew that they were claiming a long term lease, and we would be able to enjoy watching them for decades. They built those nests remarkably well so they can return year after year. They mate for life, often living on top of the same chimney, tower or church steeple. Never do I recall one blown off in a storm.

Storks are in the family of cranes, not related to the only similarly named American bird, the wood stork, which is stork in name only and is not in lineage from the eons-ago ancestors of these handsome soaring birds. In Hungary, ours were the white storks, different from the black storks only by the amount of white plumage, not much else. Both species had the long straight orange beak, an excellent tool for catching frogs and mice. -- About mice, the storks provided another form of entertainment to us, while also proving their utility. They liked to follow, just steps behind the reaper teams, gathering the harvest. They had to keep close, to catch field mice, before they scatter or hide under the sheaves, that the workers were tying and stacking into long rows, forming the characteristic, repeated cross pattern. Storks could have a daily feast this way throughout the harvest season, exactly when they had to satisfy their chicks' voracious appetite. They returned to the field after the sheaves dried and were being picked up. The mice, living under the sheaves, became again an easy meal for our storks. With their ability to regurgitate, they could stock up before returning to the nest with a bountiful meal for the youngsters. -- The arrival of the storks in the spring, coinciding with the first sighting of swallows was cause for jubilation, similar to the joy the swallows receive, when they are welcomed each year in San Juan Capistrano.

* * *

My brother Otto, two years older, exhibited attributes and talents of a leader. He had ideas that counted. Not that we the others in our group lacked ideas. But it was almost always his that we acted upon. Whatever he proposed turned out to be the one we followed. His skill with a stick, a knife, a tool or whatever, could produce things. Later this developed into a remarkable ability to fix things, that the rest of us just watched with wander. He had courage and straight-forward demeanor.

His name was Otto, Otti within family and with friends throughout childhood. But then, in high school in Keszthely, he acquired a new name that is still his today. Once in history class, the name of a famous Italian, Galeotto came up. He was Galeotto Marzio (c.1427-1497) of Narni, a very colorful and highly educated man, often in the company of kings, princes and high clergy (until he was jailed in Venice by the Inquisition, for a book he wrote). His release in 1478, was arranged by two of the true heavyweights of Europe. They were Lorenzo de' Medici and one of Hungary's greatest kings, Matthias Corvinus Hunyadi, of whom more, later. Matthias sent Signor Galeotto to Buda Castle, where for years he was the scribe and advisor to the king. -- But his claim to fame in our family is that he gave Otti an enduring nickname, that followed him from Keszthely, then Sümeg, to Miskolc University and on to Aachen in Germany, through many years. There was always some friend from the previous place to call him *Gale*, thus carrying it on to the next stage of his life. So he is Gale to this day. As student logic would have it back then in the 1940s, and promoted by his classmate, Bandi Csertõ, he already had the *Otto* part. Now he should also have the other half. He still does. For us today, *Gale* and *Otto/Otti* are interchangeable.

An incident at a street corner one spring evening is unforgettable for me. The year must've been 1948. A group of us boys went to church for a whole the month, evenings at 7 P.M. The half hour daily devotional services were the May Litanies, honoring the Virgin Mother. It was a pleasant, low key ending to those often balmy days we had in May. It was, of course a religious devotion, but for our small group of friends also a favorite evening stroll to and from church, where we spent time talking and watching girls.

Three of us were walking home together one evening: Gale, 13, a friend, Imre Gaál, about 14 and I, who was age 11. In a few minutes, a drama unfolded, had touched me for life. As we were nearing the street corner where we usually parted, from around the corner, a group of 8-10 boys stepped out -- an obviously planned encounter.

Farkas, a 14 years old, the leader of his little band of riffraff, stood in front.

"Otti and Miklós, you can go" -- he said. "We have some business to settle with Imre."

Of course, we knew what the intended business was. They wanted to beat him up. Their, or most likely, *his* issue with Imre, he never stated.

Then, Gale in a most calm and matter-of-fact tone said: "No you don't. -- Imre, you just go home."

Imre started, right away. After passing the first house, he picked up his pace and almost ran the rest of the way to his home at a block's distance.

We all just stood there, staring at each other for a few tense seconds. Thinking back on it, we all were searching for a face-saving out from an awkward situation. The main subject of the dispute already got away. The warring gang had no real beef with us, except that we foiled their delicious, though vastly lopsided rumble. (I've been saying "us". That is not really fair. I was there, of course. But I couldn't possibly do what Gale did, whatever the consequences were to be. In fact, I stood there petrified, hoping for some miracle to extricate us from this courageous, but foolish bravado. Then the miracle I yearned for, happened.) Stern stares were exchanged, but as it turned out, Otti's was more calm, exhibiting quiet confidence, indeed authority, with the air of a winner. Farkas, known for his pugnacity and experience in fighting, could have been an approximate match for him, for Otti was tall and muscular. The others were mostly my age and younger, there only for additional fighting power, easily surpassing our strength in the aggregate. The real difference was leadership and the projection of self-assured calm, that Otti clearly had. With one sentence, he reduced an arrogant blowhard to a toothless lion. We were on top. We already won the first round. Imre was safe at home. But there was more.

Saving of face was not incumbent on us. An attempt came soon in a pathetic form, from Farkas.

"Otti, don't forget this. We'll deal with you later."

"You just go and do that" -- he answered, as we parted.

We started for home relieved and glowing in victory.

"Otti", -- I said. "What would you have done, should a general mayhem ensue your confrontation with Farkas in defense of Imre? Suppose, we were left there, the two of us facing these punks?"

"I would've quickly picked Farkas and belted him the hardest I could and hope that it would take him out of action at least for a moment. My guess is that it would have ended it. The rest would've run."

It was a good strategy, looking back on it even now. It never had to be tested -- and that is its main strength. I thought of it many times since. (More recently, when President Reagan used the same principle to win the Cold War. His *Strategic Defense Initiative* and the *Peacekeeper* missile kept the Soviets in check, without ever needing to be fired. All was based on the knowledge of human nature, a strong belief in his idea of *Peace Through Strength* and the courageous application of principle.)

An incident involving a gun is instructive about Gale. It is also telling about the communist paranoia about guns and the knee-jerk attempt to control everything in which they saw or imagined a potential threat. They were suspicious of things and behavior that were totally innocent. Freedom scared them.

This was during the time of the most severe political repression by the Stalinist regime of Mátyás Rákosi. The Communist Party was recruiting neighborhood spies on anybody for any supposed infraction that was considered a threat to total party control. Recruiting took various forms. The most common were bribe, intimidation and blackmail. Their efforts produced a network of domestic spies that infested the entire society. One could not trust his neighbor, sometimes his own family members, if any one of them were vulnerable to blackmail. Kids were enticed to tell on their parents with the promise of gifts. Raids were common and could take insidious forms. Two raids were made on consecutive days. The first was used to plant evidence that was *found* the next day. No court order was needed. Secret orders came from local or district party headquarters, not through police or judges. Accountability was only within the party structure. Party authority superseded the law and was applied on the whim of high officials.

In this atmosphere, Otti was denounced to be in possession of an illegal gun. (All guns were illegal.) A friendly visit by police came first. Gale was not home at the time. My parents panicked because they were clueless about the matter and feared potential unpleasant consequences. -- Friendly visit, I said, because it was by local policemen, whom we knew. Father carried considerable clout with them, which he established through many years, based on long time of mutual good will. They agreed to wait for the return of the accused, to confront him directly. When Otti came home, Father asked him about the gun. Again some quick thinking and guts saved the day. Gale climbed the small ladder, to the junk storage in a tiny attic above the chicken coop. Soon he produced the incriminating *corpus delicti*, the proof of crime: a small barrel, attached to a crudely hand-carved butt of a *gun*.

" Here, you guys", he said. "Take it and shoot with it". So they took it and left, to a great relief for us all.

Gale said later that he quickly detached a rusty trigger mechanism while he was up there, out of sight. Even with that, the thing was useless without serious work and additional parts. It was just a challenge for him to take it apart, clean it and try to make it work, maybe some day.

Once he worked about a month on a large hydraulic car jack, which was left at our house by fleeing German troops and was probably not understood and ignored by the Russians. It seemed a hopeless wreck when he began and became a finely operating shiny green machine when he was done with it. I still remember the many pieces that were hanging on strings from the branches of a tree near the garage, like so many ornaments, while the paint was drying on them. The jack was working, but it also had to look good. After that we used it for many years. Good quality machine often can be repaired even when it first seems hopeless. This jack needed only loving care and a little know-how to make the hydraulic parts work again. He made two gaskets out of an old inner tube.

Self-apprenticeship for Gale came early. He had the aptitude, good hands and an insatiable curiosity about anything mechanical. This is still his whole world today. After he graduated as mechanical engineer in Aachen, he did not look for work in his profession. He was satisfied, continue freelancing auto repair and making his living by working on cars, repairing, salvaging and selling them. I watched one of his projects when I visited in 1964. It was an ordinary car, just bought by a handicapped woman. She had no use of her legs. Otti made the changes, so she could operate it by hands only. The car had to pass state inspection to be used on the road.

Finally Father prevailed on him. It was a matter of personal pride for him. My father was very proud of his son, the engineer. He felt embarrassed about his son the mechanic, especially one with a diploma from a highly prestigious university, bearing the name of a Hungarian engineer, scientist and inventor, Theodor Kármán. Otti the good son, also saw the merit in finding a real job, obliged. He went to work for the German national auto inspection company, TÜV. The work was somewhat confining, but he told me that he met many people there, who became a pool of important contacts for him in matters involving cars. His job became a source, supporting his hobby.

Otti and my younger brother Tomi went to Aachen, after leaving Hungary in 1956, for the excellent engineering school the city proudly claimed as its own. Tomi graduated as aeronautical engineer. His passion from childhood was aviation. His work and entertainment for a very long time was designing, flying and -- one might say -- living airplanes and helicopters.

As children, Tomi and I were the *littles*, or little ones, contrasted to the *big* kids, my older brothers. We were distinguished from Józsi and Otti, because there was a noticeable age and height difference during childhood. The two older ones were born closer to each other. Between Otti and me there was more than two years. More important, this age and height difference was a separator in several practical ways. We were not shortchanged in any way that made a serious difference. It is true, Otti was my Father's favorite, but not in a way that we would resent. His leadership qualities and skills were appealing to Father and occasionally he showed it. We all recognized the same thing in him, so this was not a problem. Although at times these leader-types may get impatient with us ordinary folk, when we are not as good with our hands, or as quick with our mind and do not see solutions to problems as clearly as they.

* * *

Going to Budapest was, for a long time, an unrequited dream of mine. Tomi was the luckiest among us. He was a cute 4-year old, when, in 1941, my parents took him on one of their infrequent visits during the first years of WW II, when the fighting was still far away. He came home with fabulous stories, fanning my imagination and desire, to go on one such trip myself. Photos, made by a professional, showed him at the National Zoo, smiling broadly on a small carriage pulled by a pony. Soon the war disrupted many similar plans and things had to be put off. In 1946 Józsi and Otti went together. The most intriguing thing I remember them telling me about, was escalators. I thought it was magical. An invention just to save steps going up and down. But other than the novelty of it, I thought it was an extravagance. Stairs were good enough in my world.

When my older brothers went to Budapest, Father found a child's bicycle, that was our wish to have for a long time. When they came home, he announced with joy, that they found a bike, that was not available anywhere else. Consumer products were poor quality and a low priority for a government, that was struggling to transform the country's economy in the communist mold and revive a devastated and bombed-out industrial base.

The little bike arrived a week later. It was a girl's model. Father was happy to buy it, since it was the only one available. We took turns trying it out. Tomi and I were beginners and had to learn from scratch. The older ones already knew how to ride. We took several spills in the process, that may had some detrimental effect on the flimsy thing. After about two weeks of use, the bike's frame broke in two, not in a fall, but while Józsi was riding it. We were sad, but Father had it welded each time, in the mechanic's shop. (For the record, it broke and was welded several times near the weld, until it had a big bump in the middle of the frame. At the end we gave up and retired the little bicycle for good. In time, quality of steel and products improved and approached pre-war levels. By then we could ride adult bikes.)

In a late fall day something happened that I could never forget. I was 11 years old and have not yet been to Budapest. The capital city was 100 miles away, but it was a huge distance in many ways. Trains took about 5 hours to get there, with changes, and in part because of priority given to freight transport.

In November 1947, my parents had some important business in Budapest and planned a whirlwind weekend trip, leaving very early on Friday. I asked if I could go. They sympathized, but said that the trip will be one big mad dash from one place to another and it would not be a good time for me to come. Part of their argument was that I would be a burden and could not enjoy the trip, being dragged along from place to place. Tomi was more of an advocate for me than was I, but could not prevail either. I resigned to the situation and held my desire in abeyance for yet another time in the future.

I was sleeping and not aware of what took place next to me between 3 and 4 A.M. on that Friday, as my parents were getting ready for the trip. Tomi was up and made a long, impassioned plea in my behalf. He must have touched heart, because soon they roused me and told me to dress. They were taking me along. I was more than surprised, I was overwhelmed. I could hardly believe that Tomi's scheme was successful, at the 11th hour -- but more than that, I was touched by his passion in the interest of fairness and generosity toward me.

The trip was a wonderful gift and the fleeting weekend still seems to me like a week-long, luxurious vacation. Budapest had wonders in store for me. I marveled how wide the streets were. Bright advertisements, streetcars, traffic and the luxury department stores left in me a collection of strong impressions. I even had the chance to see the wondrous escalators I heard about. My cousin Mariann took me around separately for part of the time. She knew the city, explained things and selected suitable sights for me to see. An evening ride in a streetcar through busy sections of town showed me that the big city never sleeps. Neon signs and ample lighting kept the busy streets in a glow, that I could not imagine till then. I fantasized about Budapest before, but the visit surpassed all my expectations. Tomi's gesture of magnanimity and the two days in Budapest made the experience a cherished memory of my childhood.

I had another adventure in 1947 -- the thing, that happens to the appendix of many people. An aching stomach, localized in the lower right, was diagnosed to be it, an inflamed appendix. Father put me in the rickety old Opel Kadett and just the two of us, started off for the closest hospital in Celldömölk, 10 miles away. We were just a half mile out of Jánosháza, when we heard a screeching noise from the front wheels. He looked at it and tried a few tests to diagnose it without success. During this series of trial-and-errors, he noticed that the car going backwards, was silent . Further tries did not help and he saw no change. He decided to drive back to town, in reverse. It was a good mile to the shop where he thought we can get help. The mechanic worked on it for two hours and fixed it. During that, I began to worry. My pain increased as I fantasized about things not very pleasant -- stuff, like my personal demise. It was a relief to finally hear the good news. We were on our way again.

In the hospital they told us that the surgeon, whose specialty was appendectomy, was out of town. The next best choice was a gynecologist. Dad came to a proverbial fork and took it. He gave his OK.

Thus I gave birth to my appendix -- the closest I ever came to a Cesarean. Needless to say, the operation was a success.

While confined and infirmed, I had no need even to touch hospital food. Mother was excessively solicitous, heaping on me her cooking and baking largess -- with cream on top.

* * *

My parents are no longer living. Father died of a heart attack at 69, in 1973; Mother at 79, in 1989. To his funeral I was not able to go. He was retired, but did freelance work, mostly substituting for old colleagues. He died after he collapsed during work.

(Some of the above described events are out of strict chronological order, because they were about my family members, recalling memorable episodes that happened within a span of several years. I wanted them to be grouped together, covering times till about the year, 1948. On following pages I track back and pick up events beginning in 1942, when I was six years old.)

10

Winds Of War

For writing this early part of my life, I asked some of my elders, family and friends. I had talks with my parents during our infrequent visits home, before I even thought of writing my story. Those were just talks, recounting some family happenings, that I always was curious about. I had Father tell me again some old stories, the ones I wanted to confirm to test my memory, round out my recollection of events, so I can retain the authentic versions.

Life in Hungary in the 1930s was good, until the drumbeat of the approaching Second World War became a much-discussed topic. As the war progressed, Hungary was *peacefully* occupied by the German army. After all, we were allies -- we were told. Soldiers were all over, but housed separately, with minimal mixing with locals. Germans were an elitist, often arrogant bunch, projecting an air of superiority, but on the whole they left us alone, at least for a while. Small-town people gave them no grief, and vice versa. They cared more about big things in Budapest, such as having their kind of people in government.

They took over the local house of culture (Kulturház) and put on free variety shows that kids loved to go see. In one of these musical presentations, I saw for the first time, a *chanteuse* -- a

cabaret singer -- sitting suggestively atop the piano, as Marlene
Dietrich did, playing the *Blue Angel* somewhere in a Hollywood
studio, perhaps the same year. I was six or seven, but I liked what
they put on for us and thought it was a great show. There was
an important propaganda aspect to these programs. They spread
Nazi culture and ideas. They achieved a modicum of success, at
least with us kids.

I asked my father after one of these shows (I think, after the
one with the chanteuse) when can I join the *Hitler Jugend* (Hitler
Youth) the Nazi organization for young Germans, established in
the 1930s.

"Why would you want to do that?" he asked back.

"They are so neat. They put on such good shows. They always
seem happy".

Dad smiled. I knew I said something stupid.

"You have plenty time before you are old enough for that. By
that time I don't think you want to join."

I got the message. It sounded like an opinion born of
experience.

People did not like the German occupation and even less, news
we were beginning to hear, though not yet experienced in our
small town. But things were about to change, most of them for the
worse. Our biggest fear was the coming of the Bolshevik Russian
army, but the Germans were expected to keep them away. The
Nazi regime was potentially bad. It was frightening that they were
capable of the much rumored cruelty to those who in their view
had no right to exist in the Third Reich, the regime that was to last
for a 1000 years. There were many things we did not know. One
was, how a highly cultured nation could blindly and with such
fervor follow the lead of Hitler and his brute thugs. On reflection
after time passing, we could question the existence of a regime
with such savagery to human beings, as its basic tenet. A part of
the reason was Trianon, more about which, later. Had that peace,
imposed on Germany mete out punishment with more mercy,
Hitler could have never risen to power. Germany would've been a
force for stability and peace in Europe for many decades.

But we were sure about the Russians. In the following years all that we feared came through, with a lot more, that we didn't even dear to think about.

11

The Jewish Question

Attitude in our town regarding Jews was similar to what was typical in the whole of Hungary, with some differences. It seemed, Jews were quite content living in Hungary. There was some resentment on the part of the Christian population, saying that Jews liked to drive a hard bargain, were crafty and good in business, stuck together, et cetera. I saw nothing unusual in this and did not think that it was in itself bad. Their history dictated such behavior. However, as a part of this process, some were clannish, aloof, with a visible arrogance coupled with excessive ambition, which didn't sit well with the general population. They tried to adapt to their circumstance, by supporting each other, marrying within their kind and propagate the race in an environment in which they were a minority. They were envied or resented for their material success. It could be said that, in their pursuit of material prosperity, they adapted well to western societies but tended to take unfair advantage of people in business dealings. -- I heard of the Diaspora, the dispersion of Jews, originally after the Babylonian Captivity in 586 BC. Though they were allowed to return less than 50 years later, most didn't (hence the phrase: *the wondering Jew*), though many lament the event more than two millennia ago as the reason of their woes throughout history. It seems to me, they prefer to live dispersed, despite being kept out of banking and prestigious professions for centuries. Even after the foundation of modern Israel in 1948, only a small minority chose to live there. Had they stayed in historic Israel, others would have less claim on the land, that is so much in dispute today, with consequences that are deadly for many and detrimental for all humanity.

The situation, regarding Jews in Jánosháza was unique. In communities of such size, usually no Jews, or just a few, were living. In Jánosháza, we had about 35 families. They had more influence, by dominating commerce and the important professions. Both doctors, the pharmacist, and the old vet were Jewish. Their clout over the farmer population, engendered resentment. Some said, it was exploitative. Most others were in some kind of business, involving retail sales or buying and selling various commodities.

The only exception was Mr. Bloch. He had a trade. He was a tinsmith. Mr. Bloch was a jovial man, liked practical jokes and liked kids. I remember him before the deportations and I remember him after the concentration camp. He came back without his family, the only survivor, while several other Jewish families returned intact. The trying experience did not change him. He married a Christian woman, decades younger, and resumed work in his shop, much the same man. I spent many hours watching him and talking about ordinary things, enjoying his humor and listening to his many stories. I even learned a few things about sheet metal work, soldering and forming cooking dishes from flat sheets. His work included mending pots and pans that leaked after many year's use.

Our town boasted a very nice synagogue, a testimony to the affluence and prestige of our Jewish citizens. It was an impressive, stylish structure, rivaling our own Catholic church. As a piece of architecture it was unique and different from any other building. Richly ornamented on the outside, with a fancy, domed roof and stained glass windows. It was located on a wooded, secluded lot.

I never forget the only occasion when I, with a friend, stole inside -- during a service, no less. It was a daring thing, because we were strangers and didn't know what to expect. Actually, I thought we will not get past the door, for everybody inside knew us and knew that we did not belong. It wouldn't have surprised me, if we were thrown out unceremoniously as soon as we got in. Instead they ignored us for the few minutes we spent there.

Things I often heard about synagogues were confirmed, and they were only two: every man wore a hat and everybody was talking. We had a saying -- no disrespect -- describing a crowded, noisy place: *It is a synagogue.* Indeed, it was noisy there, compared to our own, stately, almost somber church, which was quiet, but bright, with many windows. It was Western, built in my favorite style: baroque. The synagogue was dim and very Eastern, strange to my taste. The interior was nice, as was the outside, but too dark. It was made lively by worshipers. I liked our church better. Still, our adventure was interesting and I was happy we tried. As to the religious acts and ceremonies going on inside, I was clueless. The synagogue survived the war and the Nazis, but was demolished by the communists after the war, which at the time surprised me, because the most important and top ranking members of the Communist Party and the government, were Jews. Of course not orthodox, not the old fashioned, religious type. Those guys didn't care for any religion, only for party orthodoxy. They were of the Jewish race, but not the religion. Rákosi, Gerõ, Révai and their ilk in the top leadership spent the war years in Moscow and were brought back by the Red Army and put into leading party and government positions. We learned later, that during their exile they became Soviet citizens. Yet, they took on the governing of a country, whose citizenship they renounced and, for ideological reasons turned to serving the interest of another. They swore allegiance to an oppressor, who now occupied their place of birth. How contemptible! (Rákosi died in Moscow where he emigrated, after he was deposed. -- A joke to illustrate the people's contempt: *"This Rákosi stamp doesn't stick!"* -- *"Of course not. Try spitting the back. That's the side with the glue".)*

The situation for our Jews took a drastic turn in the last years of the war. By 1943-44 Jews of Germany and its western neighbors were dealt with. Next for the Nazis was the rounding up of Jews in the occupied countries of central Europe. This included those in

our town. Big cities were first, but soon we also felt the heavy hand
of occupation. We heard a rumor of an ominous order, soon acted
upon by the Germans. Two streets in Jánosháza were emptied
and designated as *ghetto*. Our Jews and some from elsewhere,
were forced to move there. Christian residents of those streets
were moved out *temporarily*, some into the houses of the displaced
Jews. This inconvenience was demanded without compensation
and no appeals were entertained. The ghetto was filled, streets
were soon closed with a guarded gate and residents inside could
leave only with written permission that were given rarely and only
for substantial reasons. A pastoral letter issued by the bishops,
vigorously protested the establishment of the ghettos throughout
Hungary.

Before the ghetto opened, I recall an incident that is engraved
in my memory. I was witness to a very disturbing event. I saw
a young man on the square degrading and humiliating a rabbi.
He repeatedly yanked at the old man's beard, while abusing him
with insults. This took place next to a bonfire, where objects,
brought out from the synagogue, some precious, perhaps sacred,
were burning. The old man tried to rescue some of the precious
objects, but was stopped and beaten for his effort. I remember that
the young man wanted to tear up printed or hand-scribed sheets.
He tried to rip them apart but he couldn't. Someone told me that
they were written on parchment (goatskin). He went on to burn it
all. I was confused and did not understand. The atmosphere was
charged and ugly. Stunned and overcome with fear, I just watched
the senseless cruelty of it, then ran away in disgust.

One day a Jewish woman we didn't know came to our house.
She was from a city, I thought from Budapest and was just brought
into town. In her arms she had a cute little lap dog, a well groomed,
plainly pampered pet, used to care and comfort. Only city people
treated dogs that way, somewhat like dogs I see here, lavished with
more comfort than people get in many lands, which sometimes
makes me feel embarrassed. The lady was about to move into
the ghetto and had to give up her dog. She wanted us to put it to
sleep.

"I do not have such potion" -- said Father. He just didn't deal with such things. The woman said that she doesn't want to leave the creature with anyone and pleaded with him to find a way to put the dog away.

Father pondered for a moment, then said, pensively: "I will give it a bullet". She looked at him, paused a second and said with resignation: "Please, doctor".

Father reached for one of his smaller rifles, checked and loaded it. For me, standing around, it was awkward and sad. The lady caressed the dog for the last time, put it on the ground in front of the garage.

I heard a sharp *poof* as the shot went off, but was clearly not ready for what I just witnessed. I saw some movement on the ground. The poor little thing collapsed, lifeless. It was so small, the change so slight, I had to look again to believe that I was just part of this humane act, which nonetheless involved the killing of a charming little creature, another unwitting victim of our age that produced its own brand of evil. The dog, our little friend for a few minutes, had a fate similar to that of countless human beings, many of whom received even less humane final treatment. Many innocents became obstacles to the ambitions of ruthless, power-hungry people, and not given the chance to see the end of this sorry aberration.

"We will bury it nicely" -- Father told the woman. She was satisfied and left relieved, expressing her gratitude to him. For us, it was a delicate moment in a tense, unusual situation. For her, an episode of grief, and profound sorrow upon the loss of a sweet companion. -- I buried the dog in the grass, just a few steps from the spot, where the poor creature took its last breath.

Ghetto residents were gradually deported. They were treated with contempt and without pretense of humanness. One morning during the course of this process, I witnessed another wrenching incident near the railroad station. I saw it while riding in a small wagon with our friendly milkman. I knew him through Father. He was an employee at the manor farm near Keléd, just a few miles out. His six-day-a- week assignment was to deliver milk to customers in town -- us included.

Milk came daily, by a small horse-drawn wagon from the farm, which I visited many times with and where people knew me. One summer day, as he has just finished a round, the coachman asked me if I wanted to ride with him and maybe hold the rein for a while. He just finished his first round. After I climbed on, we were heading back to the farm for another load, to return and make more deliveries.

As we were approaching the station, a henchman for the local German command was walking an old Jewish man in his raggedy coat, from the ghetto, to join others in railroad wagons, parked on a side track. He had a stick in his hand and hit the man once or twice to urge him to walk faster. As I watched, I wondered, why is the old man wearing a coat on a nice summer day. Soon I deduced that perhaps, he had to make long term plans, in case he might need it on colder days in the future. He must have viewed his prospects with pessimism and diminishing hope.

At one point the old man stumbled slightly. As he tried to regain his balance, from his over-stuffed pocket, a food can fell on the ground and rolled away on his right, to about five step distance. He started to go toward it to pick it up, but he got another whack on his shoulder and was pulled back by his sleeve from behind, then pushed forward again, to continue his sad journey toward the station. He was put on the train to start his trip to an unknown future, in the crammed wagon, perhaps never to return.

I saw groups of ghetto residents being taken away before. We never knew their destination. It was always a strange sight, beside the obviously sad implications. They were herded as so many cattle. Some of them I knew, and many, I did not. We were not permitted to enter the ghetto. News about conditions slowly filtered out. It was not easy to hear about the deplorable situation inside.

All ghetto residents were gradually taken away. Most went by train in freight cars, to unknown places, that were likely one of the large concentration camps in Germany or Poland. After they left, the two streets stood there empty for a while. By then, the Germans also disappeared.

I sneaked in one day, to see for myself. It was eerie. The first house near the gate was the one used by the German guards. That was the only one I dared to enter. I found just one thing of

interest: many boxes full of small paraffin lanterns in metal cups
-- essentially, candles. I took a handful and gave most of them to
Mrs. Wagner. She was my mother's faithful helper, the elderly
woman I knew since early childhood. She was very happy with
my little gift and marveled at the *technology* of this unexpected
find. She said they all had a "machine", referring to the little metal
lever at the bottom, that adjusted the wick, as the wax burned. I
felt useful and happy and went back once more, just for her. A few
days later all the boxes were gone, leaving the building empty.

Candles and lanterns were indispensable those days, for power
failures were a regular thing. They were pre-planned and even
announced to signal their beginning, and usually lasted from 8
to past 11 each evening. We soon got used to them and had the
candles ready for the black-outs. The announcement was, the
blinking of the lights twice to warn us, just before they went out
for the night.

12

Interesting Jánosháza -- Stories, Current And Historical

Jánosháza offered many great opportunities for a kid. They were my sources for learning and fun. Mr. Bloch's shop was one such place. My other favorite was the blacksmith shop. We had one across the square from our house. I often took the short walk there. I liked to watch the activity and loved the smell of the place. It fascinated me, how a man makes a horseshoe from a straight piece of iron, with only an anvil, a hammer and a footpedal-powered blower for his charcoal fire. The smell came from the burning horse hoof, as the master kept trying and fitting the hot iron shoe several times, before nailing it on. The horse felt nothing. (Perhaps it even liked the fragrant smoke.) I learned from Father, that to keep a horse from kicking, one had only to lift up and hold one of its legs. Using this method, two men, the blacksmith and the owner, needed no additional help. Not all horses were peaceful. I never witnessed any serious incident, though heard of a few. I spent many hours watching and listening the rhythmic, bell-like pings of the hammer on the heavy steel. Our blacksmiths loved to play with the anvil. They produced a virtual musical composition with their instruments, while making horseshoes. (Giuseppe Verdi, in his opera, *Il Trovatore* composed an *"Anvil Chorus"*, where the pulsating tempo of the music is produced by the rhythmic strikes of the anvil, by the gipsy blacksmith. George Frederick Handle has a composition, nicknamed *The Harmonious Blacksmith*. I like to listen to its similar, pulsating rhythm.)

This anvil-play, also had a practical purpose. So he can bear down on the hot iron, using sufficient power with his heavy hammer, he may choose to *pause* or *idle* in the midst of his heavy blows, with one, or a short series of smaller hits on the anvil. As the hammer *dances* to his chosen rhythm, at the end he is able to lift it up a little easier, to prepare for his next series of heavy blows, as he shapes the straight bar into a shoe, that would fit his horse. A red hot peace of iron when hit, produces a dull sound. As it cools, the sound becomes sharper. A good blacksmith could monitor the temperature by the changing sound. From that alone, he would know when it was ready to go back in the fire, so he can continue the shaping of his steel. It was a master's way of *playing it by ear* -- by an expert's experienced ear.

In my early childhood days, we had one or two maids, helping Mother in the house and kitchen, run errands and to watch us during the day. A man, Joe Heiner, also came in regularly to keep up the yard and garden. He also went with my father on occasion, to assist him on the job. Joe was a simple, quiet, but lazy guy. He helped in corralling and holding down animals, but often he just carried Father's bag.

In 1954 Father was assigned a capable assistant, Vilmos Dömötör, from the village, Keléd. He took a course, received training and was indeed a help. Father sponsored and encouraged him to take the course and become his right-hand man. Vilmos was a very nice guy. He took part in some of our family activities and came to Ábrahámhegy, to help in the vineyard, that he really enjoyed. He used to tell me, it was a vacation. Father liked and trusted him. He too, was a state employee, but Father gave him time off when he requested. He used the days tending his farm, that he kept up with his wife.

Domestic help was relatively inexpensive. At the same time, it was a choice job for suitable girls from poor families. The work was easier than farm help and the conditions more favorable. A simple farm girl with ambition and industry could gain employment with good families, establish a reputation, and receive recommendations, which was the ticket to domestic service. Most of them lived with us, in a room next to the kitchen. Others, who lived in town, came in daily. At times, when we had two, one of them slept in the kitchen, in the *table bed*. This big wooden box stood in the corner of the kitchen. During the day we used it as an extra table. For the night it could be pulled out to make a bed. All the bedding was stored inside it. I remember, that in my early years I saw it only as a table and was surprised one morning, when I got up early. It was still open, not yet put together for the day. I never slept in it.

Talking of sleep, I was quite avers to sleeping all my life and saw it as a version of time wasting, however necessary -- not that I didn't waste time other ways. We, Tomi and I, were sent to nap every afternoon, until age four, if my memory is correct. I thought that I was too mature for those things and saw no use for naps. Sleeping was necessary, but only so much of it. The room was darkened, but it didn't put us to sleep. These forced afternoon slumbers were one of the few unpleasant memories of my childhood.

Our comforts gradually diminished. As we grew we needed less supervision. In fact, we were expected to take part in doing chores. Mother did with less domestic help. After the War, things fundamentally changed. The new people in power frowned on any sign of affluence. We all were expected to be the same. Very simple, uneducated people were put into leadership positions. Important jobs in town were granted by the Party, given to those it considered loyal and meeting the next most important requirement of communist dogma: appropriate class background. For their purposes the best was the proletariat, that is labor, preferably factory worker. Not many of those were found in Jánosháza. The closest to it in town were the workers in the brick factory. Even now, I can't see the men and women I knew there, as good proletariat material, though I cannot say that I knew much about political leanings or tendencies for opportunism in people of our town.

There were a few though, who surprised me. One of them had nothing to do with political office. This took place on one of the first days of Russian occupation. A kid about a year younger then me, was standing on the square next to a Russian officer. He did not speak Russian, but had help from someone I didn't recognize, a man who seemed to translate and comment to the soldier.

The boy spoke no Russian, but he spoke the language of hate and class envy. One by one going down the street, he pointed to houses and said just one -- or two -- words: *"Burzsuj"* or *"Nyet* [not] *burzsuj"*.

This strange word is a Russian, bastardized version of the French *bourgeois*, later also adopted for Hungarian, and into languages of other satellite countries, a part of the new, fashionable vernacular. We had to learn them as part of our new socialist vocabulary. It was given a special meaning, different from that in French, (middle class citizen): *rich,* or rather, *filthy rich,* to be despised as member of the *exploitive* class. -- The boy, who months before flunked out of 4th grade was here, encouraged to make critical judgment about respectable, long-time local residents. I heard these words there for the first time, but could never forget them. This scene seemed ominous to me, reminiscent of the burning of the Jewish relics two years before. Its real meaning and political application became clear later. -- The Russians did not follow up on the implied *guilty* list with any raid or open robbery. That came later, in more sophisticated form, after the regime established itself and felt secure and confident of its power and position.

The other story -- more benign -- is about our town's swineherd. Every morning, except in middle of winter, a large portion of the town's pigs were herded out of town for grazing and to get their daily exercise. On summer mornings, this was my wake-up call. As the sun was shining through the shutters, I heard through the open window, the sound of a sizable herd passing by. Cracking of a whip, dogs barking, a peculiar trumpet sound, some yelling, or swearing were common and loud enough for me to know that the herd was passing and it was time to get up. I was happy to get out of bed all my life. The habit may have been reinforced by our friendly swineherds.

My window looked to the east. Waking up to sunlight shining in, was one of my early pleasures. Summer mornings were greeted by the elaborate cacophony of birds, starting their day. The calling of the mourning dove went on and on, inviting me to see, how beautiful the world was outside. After a quick breakfast, we often gathered with a few friends on the stone steps of a neighborhood shoe store. By 7 o'clock the steps were warmed by the sun. We could sit on them barefoot, with just a shirt and shorts on, soaking up its warmth and just shoot the breeze on subjects, boys talk about. I remember nothing of those conversations, but I would give much if I could somehow retrieve at least a few minutes of it for this writing.

Back to the pigs and their herder. Father, as the chief health-watcher for the town's animals was often in contact with the *"kanász"*. (This is the Hungarian word for swineherd. It is shorter and, if you know both languages, more descriptive, with associated meanings of uneducated and perhaps crude.) The kanász informally reported to Father about visible signs of illness in a hog, since he often knew them better than their owners did. This way action could be taken and potential problems nipped in the bud.

In 1952, our kanász was a man in his early thirties. He grew up in town and we all knew him. Father called him by first his name, Steve, and he did Father, as "Doctor". He was an engaging lad, a nice guy, with a sense of humor. How it happened, that he became local party secretary, I have no idea. Knowing the system, lack of education and common labor background were advantages, or even good qualifications for the position. I do not know if he received instruction in Marxism or studied the history of the Communist Party of the Soviet Union. I wondered whose idea was to appoint him to his illustrious post, but as we all knew, higher level approval for such, was always necessary. Steve was really a nice guy and suddenly becoming the *numero uno* in town did not change him one bit. His respect toward my father remained the same. He was willing to use his powers to help people. Father used his good rapport with him to interfere in behalf of people, several times. -- We thought it quaintly weird, when he began to address my father as "Comrade Doctor".

(This reminds me how I chuckled, soon after I arrived in

America and heard the words: "Mr. Brezhnev". Comrade, maybe -- but to call a communist thug *Mr.?* It was amusing, ironic really, but in time I got used to it. It was protocol. Later, hearing "Mr. Castro", was merely half as funny.)

This elevation of our friend Steve, was early in the new communist experiment. It was a benigm interregnum between the uncertainty and cruelty of the war-end chaos, and the difficult times of the coming Stalinist terror. After a while Steve was replaced and new party bosses came from out-of-town -- in fact, from remote parts of the country. These commissars became the overseers of everything that went on in town. They had unrestricted power and reported only to party higher-ups, without accountability to anyone else.

How did this insidious system became the norm? It was imported to us by the Red Army and their *aparachicks* (party activists) and was copied in its details, from the Soviet model.

* * *

Historical notes and connections, to put 1945 Hungary in perspective:

From Hungary's past we knew about a brief, but bloody communist regime in 1919, which lasted about ten months. Peeling back a few layers of history, it was patterned in part after the 1871 *Commune of Paris* in France, that was known for its *La Semaine Sanglante* or "Bloody Week". The Commune in turn, sprouted from the germs of the *Reign of Terror*, that was presided over by the Jacobin leader Robespierre, during the latter days of the French Revolution of 1789, and was known for the indiscriminate use of the guillotine. Later, Robespierre himself went to the gallows, though for the prior three years, *he* was the one who issued orders, that sent many of the French nobility and even members of the bourgeoisie to a similar, gruesome death. (Many a French claim, their bloody revolution invented modern democracy. Yet, since the day of *invention,* France had only monarchies, dictatorships and so far five republics, but seem still to lack the wherewithal of true popular rule. Periclean Athens, 2500 years ago was a rule, better to emulate. Pericles based it on strong, reserved character. That is what we are in dire need today, not only in France, but throughout the modern, highly developed world. Good example and incorruptible character would improve our credibility and should supplant pious rhetoric in fighting contemporary evil.)

In the *Tanácsköztársaság* or "Soviet Republic" of Hungary, (Soviet means "Council", in Russian) Béla Kun, an uneducated, but dedicated communist created our own *red terror* in 1919, that claimed thousands of victims who had to be *eliminated* in order that his regime succeed.

(It is again ironic that Kun, a faithful Marxist and follower of Lenin, fled not east, upon his regime's collapse, but first to Vienna, *then* to Moscow, only to be tried and condemned a few years later in one of Stalin's purges. He was sent to the Gulag and liquidated, with thousands of other long-time followers and admirers of Stalin. The offense was familiar and a Stalinist staple: he was branded a *Trotskyite*. That was in those days, the highest crime in the Soviet Union. Leon Trotsky, a fervent communist, first followed, then rivaled Stalin, until he was denounced by him, tried and exiled by his cunning onetime friend. His ultimate demise came at the blade of an ax, by of one of Stalin's assassins -- in, of all places, Mexico City. Communists always had long arms, especially in revenge. Stalin wanted to leave nothing to chance.)

In Kun's defense, he appealed to Magyar patriotism, and reorganized the remnants of the previously defeated Hungarian army, to beat back the eager forces of the Czech-Slovaks and the Rumanians, who began occupying historic Hungarian territory, after they saw Hungary defeated at the end of WW I. (The purpose of that insane war, that wasted millions of lives, was never defined even by historians, beyond alleged wounded national pride on part of the adversaries. Just look it the long time of indecision before real fighting began. I know of no design to conquer, or a real threat to anyone's national security, as the cause for that most protracted and bloody war.

Kun was well aware of the dismal reputation of those two armies. Pushing them back was not difficult, for the Hungarians. The military of the Czechs and Rumanians were in a league with those of Austria and Italy, regarding the lack of bravery and military acumen. -- And that reminds me of a joke I heard long ago from my beloved Aunt Róza -- with a requisite disclaimer: *Question:* "Why did God create the Italian army?"
Answer: "He did, so that even the Austrians can win some battles."

* * *

World War I was started by the assassination of the Austrian crown prince, Francis Ferdinand and his wife, Sophie by a Serb, Gavrilo Princip (member of the *Black Hand,* a secret organization of anarchists) in Sarajevo in 1914 and ended on 4 June 1920, by the *Treaty of Trianon,* more commonly known as the Versailles Treaty. Europeans know it well and call it just "Trianon", with connotations of tragedy and international treachery. It was named after one of the two smaller palace retreats in the gardens at Versailles, where it was signed. The peace, forced on Germany and Hungary by the victorious powers, carried in it the seed of the Second World War, Nazism and emergence of the Soviet Union, as world power. In Germany it made the rise of Hitler almost inevitable. National Socialists sprouted up in many countries. Nazism, this cousin of communism is also a state-imposed despotic rule, often portrayed, mainly by leftist ideologues, as the polar opposite of communism. In fact, the followers of both are equally socialist utopians. Each of these movements was a tyrannical instrument of state power that devastated societies in similar fashion, with almost identical, dismal results throughout the world. In their wake, they leave severely damaged or destroyed civil and legal institutions, whose rebuilding take decades, often more than a generation.

After Trianon, Hungary's land was divided and parts of it given to six different countries, reducing it in size by more than 2/3 from its original, that stood for over a 1000 years. The historic

Hungary had a population of more than 18 million Magyars. The new Hungary had 7.6 million left, to count as her own citizens. No wonder that the name "Trianon" is remembered in Hungary by its Latin original: *"Tria Non"* (Three Times No) -- "Nem, Nem, Soha". In English one would say: *"No, Not, Never"*.

To see clearly the cruel insult to Hungarians, and to understand the bitterness they feel toward the diplomats at the end of WW I, compounded by the communist victory and the dereliction of the western powers after WW II, one should look at the map they created with their Treaty of Trianon. I looked at my map of the Carpathian Basin, which, from the Eastern Carpathians to the Adriatic, was in essence, the map of Hungary for a millennium. I counted 15 large cities, that were given to, Czechoslovakia, Rumania, Yugoslavia or Austria. All are within 10 miles, just outside the Trianon imposed borders of Hungary. Hundreds of thousands of Hungarians live near, yet so far, torn from their ancient homeland, still oppressed and mistreated, often worse than gipsies. After so many years, I came across evidence, documenting a deliberate policy to "destroy" the state of Hungary within the Carpathian basin. I do not yet know the source, only that it was expressed at Trianon. The West should carry the blame and shame of this travesty. Lately I detect a faint movement toward redress. Some people are speaking up, remembering Winston Churchill's protest about this travesty, when he saw it being forged in the palaces of Versailles. It was Woodrow Wilson's source of pride -- next his other debacle, the League of Nations. The Senate of the United States was wise to reject both. There is still hope!

To complete the circle, there was a historical example to follow in 1945. A new red terror was imposed on us by the Red Army and the leftover members of the gang of 1919, triumphantly returning from Moscow. By 1948, the regime felt secure with the occupying Red Army's backing. The establishment of a dictatorial order could be more methodical and its penetration more pervasive. They even took their time about elections. After a false start (which was actually a free and fair election resulting in defeat for the communists) they held another within a year. This was done well, in true Bolshevik fashion and delivered the preordained result: a substantial communist victory. After that, in the elections of the next 40 years, we had to get used to a 99+% approval for the Communist Party, the only one listed on the ballot.

In the process of the second of the two mentioned elections, we met the people of the *blue ballots*. They were a large number of people, recruited by the Hungarian Communist Party. On election day they were traveling on trucks early morning till evening, stopping in villages, voting at each stop. Details on how they counted these votes, were not disclosed. It was handled by the interior ministry, which sanctioned the operation. -- The educated guess was that they all voted for the Communist Party.

President Roosevelt asked and received a promise from the Soviet leader at the Yalta summit of the three wartime leaders (February 1945). Stalin vowed that free elections will be held in all the Russian occupied countries. Churchill warned Roosevelt against trusting Stalin, but FDR went ahead and left seven central- and eastern-European countries to the communists. Hard to believe that he didn't know better, even in his declining state. The communist way of conducting elections were known in the West by then.

Seasoned politicians understand this and sometimes use it. To recall a closer example, Mayor Richard J. Daley of Chicago saw such a need in the 1960 presidential contest. He put Illinois in the Democratic column and Jack Kennedy in the White House (with additional help from Lyndon Johnson's Texas). On that election evening, Mike Royko, the Chicago Sun-Times columnist was chief commentator for the local NBC television affiliate, WMAQ. A large number of ballot boxes disappeared at 10 o'clock but re-appeared after midnight. In Royko's opinion this was for the purpose of "stuffing". He knew politics and knew Chicago politics intimately. -- Mayor Daley once said, that votes didn't count as much as the counting of the votes. (He was quoting, or paraphrasing Stalin.) The Kennedys and the Daley family were very close.

(To his considerable credit, Richard Nixon did not challenge the election, despite many people asked him to, saying that he would have a good chance to reverse the results. Nixon swallowed his pride. He said that a legal challenge and recount would be traumatic and divisive for the nation.)

In 2004, we saw an improved version of election fraud -- this one also a Russian invention. Ukraine's own blue balloters delivered, at Moscow's behest, votes in numbers, that were multiples of those, of eligible voters. For good measure, during the campaign they poisoned Alexander Yushchenko, the leading national candidate for president. He barely survived an overdose of toxins, and was left with ugly pockmarks, changing, his handsome face, it seems, permanently. According to credible reports, Russian president Putin's hand appears to be dirty in the deed. He openly supported the other candidate, a proponent of continued close ties to Moscow.

After war's end, our life went through many substantial changes. The soldiers that came home, many after long imprisonment, saw a very different country. Grandfather's great estate was simply, without compensation, taken by the state. We all, including kids, had to make difficult adjustments. For the adults it was a painful transition into a world, of the *Dictatorship of the Proletariat.* The new cultural and economic model was the Soviet Union. In the socialist mode, every person was made equal with everyone else, unless anointed *"...more equal than others"* -- to quote George Orwell (*Animal Farm*) -- and protected by the Party. Free market and individual enterprise was stifled, initiative, ambition and industry killed in many. That is the main reason why the communist system is so inefficient and unproductive. The dominating policy to achieve the egalitarian goal was *class envy* -- the method: *class warfare.* (The latter is a most insidious form of political manifestation. Not surprising that Envy is one of the Cardinal Sins. In most cases, it actually benefits the instigators, much more than the incited, who bare the burden of the fight and suffer the consequences of the resulting upheaval.) Communists were proud of it and taught it to us in school. Those who prospered in the old regime, were displaced, scorned and humiliated and their property confiscated. Almost everybody was reduced to a lower level. It prompted people to perform with minimum effort -- inevitably with minimum results. The only group that was favored without any accountability, were the party elite. Today's American liberals learned class envy from the communists and use it regularly in getting votes and attacking the producers of our economy. Their aim and principal means to power is big government, social control and the power to tax. The champion of class warfare is Senator Dick Durban of Illinois. His arguments are nauseating and reek of ignorance.

One day in the spring of 1947 I was in front of our house on the square. Coming in at the far end of the square, through a thin fog of dust, kicked up by tired feet, I saw a great number of people, being marched through town. All the kids and an increasing number of adults quickly lined up by the roadside to see the procession and bring food. They were all men, 6-8 abreast, prisoners of war, being herded by armed Russian soldiers, on horseback, to a prison camp not too far from town. It was the camp we heard about, as it was built, but were not allowed to go near it. (Recently published articles describe the camp near Jánosháza. It is called: *"Hungary's Gulag"*.)

As I recall, it went on for more than an hour, before I saw the last one. I saw more people together there, than ever before. They were a very sorry lot, dejected, tired and in rags. People started to come out with food and gave it to the men, as they passed by.

One incident is vivid in my mind. A Russian officer stopped near us. He was on his horse with a large loaf of bread under his arm and two more in his knapsack. They were round loaves, the local variety, just like the kind we always had in our house. He stopped and gestured, showing that he is giving it out. Prisoners mobbed him, begging for a piece. He began distributing his bounty to the great number of outreached hands around him to the last slice he had. All the pleas were in Hungarian -- except one. An officer, speaking fluent Russian, reached up and received his piece, as soon as he asked. How important speaking another language can be, I thought. They were all equally hungry, equally in need, yet one was selected out for a privilege, for being able to express himself with words that was more meaningful to the giver.

In those days Soviet soldiers were all over the country, guarding and patrolling. This situation gradually changed. They seemed increasingly out of sight, as time went by. Local control was transferred to a newly organized political police, later known as the AVO. The Russians were allowed to bring family with them. We were used to seeing Russian women on the street, on their way shopping in their special stores, carrying their oversize *necessaire*, what must have been their regulation tote bag. They looked different, with their features, their attire and uniform shopping-baskets. They seemed to be happy in Hungary, but always kept to themselves.

As a part of consolidation of power for the regime, and as a lesson to the population, the Catholic church had to be controlled by the communists. The head of the Catholic church in Hungary was Cardinal József Mindszenti. My parents knew him from earlier times. He grew up in Csehimindszent, the town, next to my mother's birthplace of Csehi. His childhood name was Pehm. He later adopted a Hungarian name which he derived from his birthplace. Gentle, yet stern, he was a highly principled man, a thorn in the side of the regime. They denounced and hounded him. One day the papers were full of the news that he was a secret arms merchant. They conducted two raids of his home. On the second, they *found* a cache of weapons, that they *knew* were there. We were sad at his brutal treatment, but not surprised.

In 1948 he was convicted of hoarding arms illegally -- in the bishop's palace, no less -- and sentenced to a long prison term.

This was the time when I first heard the term, *brainwashing*, the method to exact false confession. It was discretely discussed in closed circles. He was held incommunicado for a year. During that time they were preparing him for trial. It had to be an extremely cruel and torturous treatment, because when I saw pictures of him at the trial, I hardly recognized him. The psychological and drug-induced torture would have broken an average person in weeks, he was a man of extreme will and determination. At the trial, he had an empty stare, that replaced the his normal, warm, humane look that I knew in the past.

A few stories circulated from inside his prison, where there were some who were willing to talk. One was that after going through months of brainwashing and administration of mind-altering drugs, he was asked to sign a confession admitting guilt. First he refused. After more work on him he signed it. As he did, he put two tiny letters after his name: *"c.v."* It took weeks of additional torture to have him reveal the meaning of the letters. He did not say what their meaning was. After searching for it, prison authorities concluded that they were in Latin: *contra voluntate* -- (against [my] will). The tenure of his torture was lengthened by about three months and at the end he signed again -- this time, his name only.

At the trial, he said hardly anything, other than agreeing with the charges. I saw a ruin of a man, who just months ago was a vigorous, energetic advocate for his flock, a saintly man of Christ.

He was imprisoned until freedomfighters released him in October 1956, from the most notorious AVO prison, at the infamous address: Andrássy út 60, (later renamed: "Stalin út"). When the revolution was defeated, he took asylum at the American Embassy and after negotiations, moved to Vienna where he died in 1975. (The Cardinal was beatified by Pope John Paul II in 2004. Beatification is the intermediate step before sainthood.)

Andrássy út is perhaps the nicest street in Budapest. Today, the building: No. 60, is a museum of torture, a place to remind, educate -- and surely, horrify visitors. The building has a past, reaching back to before the communists. I remember the hasty retreat of the German army and the Hungarian cronies they put into power. Our own nazi party was the Arrow Cross Party. The Germans had their Nazis, with their spider-like cross, the swastika. Their brothers, the national socialists in Hungary, were cut from the same cloth, but boasted their own symbol, a green cross with arrowheads in all four directions. They slavishly followed the Nazi model -- even in the speed with which they disappeared at the end. Communists quickly rounded them up, tried them, hanged the big shots and organized with great speed to establish a similar regime, while proclaiming loudly that they are truly of the people, not the oppressive party they had replaced. One of the telling events in this major reorganization was, when soon after taking power, they occupied the same building as their secret police headquarters at Stalin út 60, that the Arrow Cross guys occupied just a few weeks before. They also rehired some of the same people, the interrogators, torturers and operators, who went back to work, just switching masters, to run the torture chambers. The walls were painted dark brown, so as not to show the dried stains of blood. This was one of the gruesome discoveries in 1956 by the liberators of the building.

13

War Ending (1944-45)

I want to return to a few events of the war and related stories, that bear recounting. The war was winding down, the Germans were squeezed on two sides. We were frightened and much afraid of what might come. What came, were the Russians. The Allies were too far away and still preoccupied with fighting battles against the last ditch effort put up by the Germans in the infamous *Bulge* in Belgium and other places in western Europe.

In our town there was nothing of strategic value. Still, we were bombed on two successive days. We could never figure out a rationale for bombing a town, such as Jánosháza. Both attacks were before dawn. The town had two large squares. Both were hit. We lived on one, across and about 300 ft distance, from the civic school. It was the one of the largest building in town, two stories, set apart from others in the middle of the square. Two bombs just missed it and hit its low masonry wall (fence) along the sidewalk, that had a run of wrought iron decorative fence on top. Other bombs fell on the sidewalk, leaving gaping craters, broke all the windows and tore the stucco finish off much of the wall. Shrapnel made about a dozen holes in the outside wall of our house too, knocking stucco loose. The flying shrapnel also ripped holes in our own wrought iron fence. The other square suffered similar damage. No one was killed in the attacks.

Those rips in the fence bring back related, but more recent memories. When I visited the old house, I showed the holes in the fence links to Ildi and the children in earlier visits. In 2001, when we visited again, I told the story again, this time to their husbands. A woman, who now lives in my parents' old bedroom, was leaning out the window, listening. She was taken by my story and said that she was unaware of the holes in the fence or their origin. She assured me, that she will have an interesting story to tell her husband later that day. She invited me inside and asked questions about the house and its history. They occupy three of the rooms. I told her about how the building must have been divided by the cooperative, when it was remodeled for multiple occupancy and provide a home for three families.

Later I was also invited to tour the rest of the house by the other owners. They were interested in hearing my stories of the old place. As I entered the house, I was curios about what I would find. There were a few surprises for me, awakening memories and eliciting mixed feelings. The tour was fascinating and satisfying, with occasional moments of sentimentality. I told many stories to the new occupants and was able to answer most of their questions.

I explained how we had the interior arranged, and what were the occupancy of the rooms. I revealed secrets and resolved a few mysteries for them and saw, how the much beloved place, became something quite different from what I remembered. I thought of the hundreds of personal stories, good and sad, that still connect me to the many nooks and crannies. As I reflected on my sentimental journey in the following days, it seemed to me that I wanted to forget the new look of the interior of the house of my precious childhood. I registered a few striking changes, but overall, I still retain in my mind the old look and the spirit of the many details of the original structure. It is the repository of the many, deeply personal memories that tie me to the place as long as I live, regardless how it changed and who dwells in it now. One regret I have is that I did not ask to see the attic. It was quite late in the evening and I wanted not to impose on the people further with one more request. I might see the attic at another time.

Mother's lovely rock garden, that once surrounded the veranda, was no more. The terrace was closed in and became part of one of the apartments. With that, disappeared an important symbol, part of the essence of my Jánosháza. The rock garden, full of exotic dwarf plants, on and in-between the large rocks, was unique and serene. Mother planned and in large part, built it. Her talent, imagination and soul was in those rocks, as she tended and caressed her splendid creation each spring. Nothing I've seen could compare.

* * *

During the days of frequent air raids in 1943-44, Tomi broke his leg, falling off a wood pile during play. He broke his shin bone. The X-ray showed an 8 in. hairline crack lengthwise, an unusual thing, the doctor said. Most of his leg was in a cast. He spent much time in bed. During the raids we routinely went to the basement, although adults thought that we would be a very unlikely target for bombing. We did it as a precaution -- just in case. Tomi wanted to remain upstairs. Once I asked him, why he preferred to stay in his room, exposing himself to possible danger, we all wanted to minimize. He calmly told me that he was not afraid. God will take care of him. -- His answer, showing child-like trust in divine protection pleasantly surprised me. I understood his faith and admired the innocence it betrayed.

In the war years we had to get used to several things: shortages, poor quality goods, blackouts and the sound of sirens, signaling air raids. Toward the end, the raids became an expected daily event. About 10 in the morning, we could *watch the B-17 Flying Fortresses aloft and the Liberators* (B-24s) fly high overhead, with their characteristic dull murmur. They numbered up to a dozen, sometimes more, with fighter planes escorting on two sides. I saw many dog fights between the German Messerschmitt fighters and the Americans. Watching them was entertainment, much better than the many, I've seen in movies. Those always seem flashy and fake. Actor-pilots grimace as they affect the strain and difficult effort of flying and fighting simultaneously, without fear, but with affected contempt for the enemy.

Down below we had only one, a very long range, wide-angle view. But our view was real and panoramic, where we could follow the course of the battle. I saw bravery on both side, when the fighters went at each other head on, kept shooting and circled back again. I remember a few cases when one pilot managed to maneuver his plane behind the other and pursued it at maximum speed, often out of sight. No fighter plane did I ever see shut down, but saw one of the big ones.

One day a Liberator was on fire, heavily smoking. One by one, parachutes started to drop out and began their silent descent. I counted nine. The plane soon crashed in a field about eight miles away. We piled into the car and took off to see it. Our guide was the rising plume of smoke. It led us to a field, outside a tiny village of Gógánfa.

The plane was a smoking wreck, but approachable to a distance, where we still felt safe. Occasionally gunshot-like sounds broke the silence of the farm field. They emanated from inside the plane. We figured that the heat set off some ammunition on board. The wreck burned out eventually and I, joining others, approached close enough, to take a few souvenirs. I brought home two. They were light green colored aluminum pieces that I kept for a long time.

After we arrived home, word spread that the Americans were captured and they are being marched into town. We rushed to the street which was leading into the village from the plane's direction. It was the deserted Dukai Street that used to be the ghetto with houses still mostly empty.

There they were, the Americans. They looked tall and different, even more, in their air force garb. All were chewing gum. It was a strange sight. We heard of chewing gum before, but it was the first time I ever saw someone chewing. We snickered, but were fascinated at the same time by this strange exercise of the jaw, seemingly without ever getting the job done. -- (Much changed since then. Chewing gum spread, and now the whole world buys, makes and chews gum. When I first saw Michael Jordan chew while playing basketball without swallowing it in the heat of the game, I thought of my first encounter with gum. I understood the versatility and varied uses of this universal habit.)

There was, in the midst of this charged atmosphere, an ugly incident. Thank God, despite its potential, it ended without serious trouble.

It happened right in front of me. A young man from the crowd jumped past the policemen marching the prisoners and spat on one of the airmen. I heard a firm sound of disapproval from the throng and the man was quickly hustled away. The American calmly wiped his face, without even breaking his stride. For a moment I feared that a melee may erupt between those guarding the prisoners, the crowd and perhaps even the Americans, but nothing more happened. The stoic reaction of the flyer was an important gesture that helped to keep the lid on, I'm sure. I remember the American's dignified response to his indignity and admired him for it. The unruly young man was disciplined and warned by police, but not otherwise punished. I do not remember any Hungarian or German soldiers taking part in the capture or the guarding of the prisoners. It was all handled by local and county police, at least at that stage. After they were marched in and out of town, we never heard what happened to the unfortunate aviators. Even after I saw them only high in the sky, going on bombing missions, I sympathized with this attractive group, while feared and loathed the Russians. I heard, that at the end of the war, Hungarian soldiers made great efforts to give themselves up to Americans, rather then be captured by the Soviet and end up in the Gulag.

I thought of this incident during the Iraq War of 2003, when I saw pictures of American soldiers kissed by Iraqis and they in turn, giving candy and gifts to children. *Lucky Iraq,* I thought. That country, ruled so cruelly by Saddam Hussein, was liberated and given a government by American soldiers. Troops from all services and the reserves went to Iraq -- volunteers to defend their country and countrymen. They are the Americans of whom I'm most proud and to whom I owe the deepest gratitude. They are the brave, the dedicated, men and women who represent the best America has to offer -- with character, dedication and kind of patriotism, rarely found today in countries of the West, a result of affluence, never before seen in history.

* * *

In 1956, invading Soviet tanks and army hordes indiscriminately slaughtered Hungarians. We fought them to a standstill. Our revolutionary government desperately pleaded for international recognition and intervention by the West, particularly the US. We thought that we already did the hard part, shedding blood and fighting tanks with bare hands. We expected the West to live up to its declared creed of defending freedom of the oppressed. We thought we were in the front-line and gave the West its best opportunity to end communism and rid the world of this scourge. -- But no, the West caved, as it caved many times since, for the lack of spine -- and the United Nations. With Hungarians, America would have found a more unified, effective and loyal ally, than we now have in Iraq.

Hungary's sacrifice bore fruit 33 years later, when in another bold move, she opened the Iron Curtain to Austria, that separated her from the West. By this step she gave new hope to vacationing Germans, who prior to this, could meet in Hungary, but only to separate again. East German citizens were forced to return to communist East Germany. When the Curtain opened, so many chose to go with their cousins to the West, that the Iron Curtain became a sieve, no longer useful as an instrument of confinement. -- A few years later Ronald Reagan made a great speech at the Berlin Wall and said among other things:

"Mr. Gorbachev, tear down this wall!" Before Gorbachev could give him a hand, the Hungarians gave him the nudge, that in a few years resulted in the crumbling of the Berlin Wall, that lead to the collapse of the Soviet Empire.

* * *

The War was winding down. The time was late spring, 1945.

As news spread of the westward advance of the Red Army, it coincided with an increase of the number of evacuees and refugees in our town. They came from the eastern part of the country. The problem of housing them became more and more taxing. Then one day, my parents were thinking the same way. We locked up the house, leaving the key with the Molnárs and traveled to three places in succession, smaller and more remote, as we went. We packed up for an extended stay and went first to Csehi. The thinking was that it is better to be in a remote place when the Russians arrive. The secret hope of completely avoiding them seemed ever more remote.

We spent a few days on the Csehi farm. The adults were busy weighing the options and planning our next move. We missed Grandfather's wisdom and guidance. He died the previous year, 1944. Three days later, we loaded up wagons and went to Fenékpuszta, a little grange in his forest, quite remote from any village. One of his trusted men lived there with his family, watching the forest and farming the cleared land that surrounded his house. I never heard about this bucolic ranch before. It was a small place that became important for us only because of the war. I liked the place, our home for the next few weeks, one with the charm of a secluded forest retreat in idyllic setting, with woods and hills around.

We took care not to disturb the farmer, or intrude on his life. Thank God, we had good weather throughout our stay. He loaned us tools we needed to set up our temporary dwelling in the forest.

With us were two other families from Jánosháza. About 16 of us went to live like forest people, camping in the woods. We slept in the forest. Using a small cave-like opening in a ravine, we stretched, tied and nailed a tarp for shelter. There, for the first time, at age 9, I was introduced to eating raw eggs. All the adults told me how great it was, so I gave in. It was OK, but only for one time. For the rest of my life I returned to the regular methods of preparing eggs. During the day we spent time in the farmhouse and tried to plan for our coming encounter with the Reds. Their reputation preceded them. We knew them as primitive crudes, ready to grab women and take anything that shines or ticks -- that is, watches. The fear in all of us, including kids, was palpable. As events unfolded most fit the profile but there were a few officers that behaved well, even nobly, as I relate below.

As a part of wise planning, we buried valuables under ground and covered the spot with hay, moving a huge stack of it to cover the dig. In days before the availability of sealable plastic containers or even sheets to protect things in moist ground, the fear of permanent damage to many items was intense. I recall the adults discussing the best method of protecting valuables. We used the little rubberized canvass sheets we had. We knew that the favorite prize for the Russkies was wrist watches. A story went around, that a dead Russian soldier was found somewhere, with 28 watches up and down on his two arms. The phrase: *Davay Chassi* was well known. In English, one would say: "Come on fast, your watch!" Still today in Hungary, a colloquial name for Russians is the *Davays*. -- My uncle Miklós had two pocket watches. He was debating with himself and asked for advice, which one to bury, the better looking one, or the one with higher value. He decided on the one with higher value. I thought, how can a better looking watch be more valuable then the other, which, I thought was ugly, with big numbers and all. At the end, I realized that he chose right. Beauty, even in watches is only skin deep.

On a bright summer morning in 1945, we heard the *rat-tat-tat* of machine-gun shots from the forest. We knew that soon they'll be there. Indeed, a few minutes later, about a dozen Russian soldiers with submachine-guns were running out of the woods, down on the hilly meadow, that surrounded the farm house. They were ready to shoot, but soon saw defenseless civilians everywhere. They started searching the house and the outer buildings. *Germanski, Germanski*, I heard a hundred times. They were looking for Germans. Those would've been potential problem for them -- and also for us, I'm sure. The next thing was, as expected, the collection of watches. Other items, even more valuable, were left untouched -- unless they glittered. Things that *ticked*, were more sought after then those with *carats*. -- I saw one soldier examine some small item. He pondered for a moment and put it back. (There were only so many pockets.) They just wanted not to miss out on the *good* stuff. I also remember, I was in the room with the lady of the house, while a Russian was going through her things. She begged the soldier, not take some family heirloom. He looked at her and gave it back. It seems that even without understanding a word said, the universal human language of desperate pleading is understood and can be powerful. In the midst of darkness and confusion, there was this glow of sympathy and kindness. On his face I saw compassion and understanding. He was clearly moved by her plea.

They looked around for a while and seemed satisfied that the place was safe. Then the commander gathered them. They huddled at the far side of the yard. A few came back, closer to us. We saw that something important is about to unfold. A man from our group spoke broken Russian and interpreted. They needed manpower and the small truck that they commandeered, along with the owner. All the men had to line up. They were selecting out the ones that looked strong and healthy. Father was one of them. My mother saw the peril of the situation and quickly made her counter move. She sent all four of us crying at his feet. We turned on the tears until the leader pulled him out of the line. While somewhat contrived, it was a success. Contrived, of course, only as far as the unleashing of crying kids. Her panic was not artificial. We all knew the potential peril and the uncertainty of the situation that wore most heavily on her. To protect her brood, she did what the hour demanded. -- All was calm for a while. Then they left. We were greatly relieved, congratulating Mother for quick thinking and achieving her goal. As it turned out, the need for manpower was just that. They needed some free labor and transportation. All the men, except one were back the same evening. The owner of the truck came back a week later without his vehicle. By then we all worried about him and his wife was inconsolable. He had a harrowing story to tell. Not of abuse, only a fast-pace and hard labor, constant demand and nonstop driving from place to place without enough sleep in other parts of the country. Then he was let go somewhere far away and hitchhiked back to camp. He recovered his truck weeks later, after we were back home. It was in deplorable condition.

14

Returning Home

Soon things quieted down. The Russians occupied the entire country. We packed up, went back to Csehi and from there, home.

There were signs of fighting on the outskirts of Jánosháza. As we approached, I saw a wide track of a tank through a vineyard. It was one straight, ten-foot surgical gash, diagonally through the field.

Neighbor kids told us about the battles nearby. There were wrecks of war equipment all around. Some of it were the new playthings for us kids. Spent shells were scattered widely in the surrounding fields. We collected them in great number. Józsi and Gale still have a 3½ ft high brass artillery shell casing that we kept for years in the dining room. My mother collected dried wild flowers and fancy grasses in them. We polished our unique brass vessels regularly. The *vases* looked good in their new incarnation.

Two kid brothers in town loudly boasted about their expertise in handling and exploding land mines. The older of them blew himself to pieces with one that went off prematurely. A neighbor friend, Jóska Schlöber, had his eyebrows and part of his hair burned off by playing with gun powder from an artillery shell. There was a lot of that around. We also experimented using much care, before getting bold. The propellant was in the form of straight tube, like a long, brown macaroni. When lit in open air, it burned steadily from end to end. When the burning end was covered with sand, it shot out and ran on the ground. There was another kind, light beige color. We could make it take off, by lighting it, sticking and holding it in a pile of dirt. It smoked and when let go, it took off and flew, landing up to 150 ft away. It was foolish, but we saw no undue hazard, only the fun part and thought that we were careful enough, playing only in the middle of the open square.

I now have misgiving about our reckless daring, but then we saw it differently. The practice was based on careful planning and a lot of trial and error, within controlled conditions -- I like to think. Anyway, nobody was ever hurt in our group.

The biggest prize and favorite toy for us was a broken-down tank in our back yard. It was there, as we arrived home. It was already gutted, but soon we were all over it, inside and out. It was amazing, how much childish treasure we discovered in it. Just climbing up and down gave us a new perspective of a pretend childhood war game. They hauled it out after a couple weeks and we went back to our more mundane pleasures.

The Molnárs stayed home while we were in Csehi. They told incredible stories and gave endless details on how they managed to keep the house relatively safe. Still, when we arrived, four families were living in our house. They were refugees from the eastern parts. I have no idea, by whose authority were they housed in our home. This was just the first of a long list of things that showed us how everything changed and that there were situations that we were no longer able to control.

With that, started one of the strangest period of our life. An elderly couple occupied the small space next to the kitchen, that used to be the room of our housekeeper. An old man died in that room soon after we came back. The house was gloomy. We mourned together with the widow. My curiosity got the better of me and I asked the lady if I could see her husband. She kindly consented. I was quiet, reserved, and respectful. He was lying there as I expected, his chin still tied up with a kerchief, so his mouth stay closed past rigor mortis. He looked pale, serene and dignified. After a few minutes of quiet vigil, I thanked the lady, left and wondered if she thought I was a little weird. Reflecting on it now, the grieving widow probably did not think anything such. I hope she thought I was paying homage.

In an other room stayed the Borse family. The lady was a teacher and became a friend of my mother. Mr. Borse was nice, but nondescript and I have only a vague impression of him. They had two girls, Marika and Erika, a few years younger than me. We played a lot together. Erika especially, was a bright and gregarious girl, who liked to joke a lot. (The name, Erika was then quite rare in Hungary. I liked it and reserved it for somebody very special, 24 years later.)

Little Erika and I once witnessed something wrenching and not easy to forget -- but that story, later. The family soon moved back home, but we kept in contact for a time. Mrs. Borse even came to visit once.

The third family stayed with us less than a week and I have no recallable memory of them. -- I never asked my parents how this strange arrangement could come about. During war, things happen that one may not even conceive under normal conditions. My parents took events calmly and just wanted to help the others, even though we were practically invaded by strangers in our absence.

Things were changing fast and brought constant challenges. For a while, as a family moved out, others came for short periods. The one to stay with us longer, was the Pesti family. They had one boy, Steve, my age. I found out later, that the father was a prior member of the Arrow Cross Party. This we didn't know at first -- or at least not me. Being member, did not necessarily mean devotion to party. Just as later in the communist era, some, without being loyal followers of the party, joined to gain advantage in job or to be treated more favorably. The communists especially were not very discriminating, only watchful. The Pestis kept a low profile and had no job, which was not unusual. I remember them, as very nice people. Their secret was kept by us to the end and no harm ever came to them as far as I know.

By that time, living space got tighter because our house was desired by too many people, mainly those with power, such as the GPU. These letters abbreviate the name of the Russian Secret Police. As the Gestapo for the Nazis in their day, the GPU had its way in everything during the Soviet occupation.

(Communists then, as they still do today, like to change the names of organizations that are tainted by their actions or bad reputation along the way -- such as too much blood on their hand. After the original Soviet secret police, nicknamed CHEKA needed a makeover, the organization was renamed GPU in 1922. [As an aside, indicating the crucial role this organization was assigned, I want to quote the original acronym of this first political police agency. Its mission was made clear in its full title. "VECHEKA" -- short for -- "All-Russian Extraordinary Commission for Combating Counterrevolution and Sabotage".] Cheka -- as it became known -- was organized and run by one of the most ruthless of the original Bolsheviks, the Polish-born Feliks Dzerzhinsky. In time, Cheka became GPU, later NKVD, and in turn, GRU, though this one maybe separate, and is an arm of the military. Since 1954, it's been the KGB. KGB was again changed or dissolved altogether, after the Soviet Union collapsed. The latest these days is the FSB. As one reviews the changes through time, one may pick his favorite acronym -- Stay tuned.)

The Pesti family lived with us for about seven months. We six, and they, three, were crammed into our dining room. The room was big, more than 600 sq. ft. It had a beautiful, glazed tile stove, a large and a smaller dresser with a big mirror, a grandfather clock, a grand piano and the dining table in the middle. I don't remember what happened to Mother's sizable ficus and other plants, that used to grace the room by the window. We had no room to keep them indoors, but it was spring and they went to the veranda. Mother took her chances and moved them out as she did in previous years, only this time a little earlier.

We occupied all available floor space with mattresses on the floor for the night, that we stored piled up during the day. We cooked, ate and slept together. We were locked out from the rest of the house, with limited access to the kitchen. We had to enter from the yard, walking down from the veranda and enter through the back door, not through the house as we used to. The ladies had to share the kitchen with the various other important tenants. The bathroom was off limits. We had to use the outhouse in the back of the yard and had to wash up, using a portable basin. Our new privy was there, next to that of the Molnárs, who did not have indoor plumbing in their house. This two-seat outhouse was part of one of the old houses. I remember using it a few times, when I was lazy and didn't want to walk, up the house from the back of the yard during play. The old wooden privy came in handy during those months. Normally our household staff used it. The Molnárs kept theirs and never had to share their facility with anyone.

A note about Russians and alcohol. They really like it. I saw many drunk soldiers in the days following the secession of fighting. All episodes were frightening. I heard of shooting and killing a few people by drunk soldiers, though I did not see any. What I remember is two episodes that were scary. In one, a very drunk sergeant was brandishing his gun, complaining about something and threatening to shoot people around him, fumbling with his pistol constantly. I feared for my life and tried to get away without drawing attention. No military police came to disarm him. At the end I managed to sneak away by ducking behind a corner.

Our first important occupier/tenant was the GPU Command. They were not bad tenants, as things stood. After we resigned to the fact that they deprived us of most of our house, they left us alone and we, them. They had important business to conduct, as we will see later. We were happy not to be bothered.

Our home was about 4,000 sq. ft., all on one floor. We had the dining room for us and moved our cooking to the wash kitchen in the old building. They took the whole rest of the house: three other rooms of the same approximate size and five smaller rooms, plus the kitchen, a big pantry and the modern bathroom -- used by most of them the first time, I'm sure. *They* were: a number of secret agents, chauffeurs, officers and orderlies. We never got an exact count -- not that it mattered. The traffic of people in and out was constant and voluminous. There was also Walter, apart from the rest. He was the only important one for us, and by far most memorable, hence I remember only him by name.

Father got to know the commander, a GPU colonel. As time went on, we all picked up a little Russian. He made it his business to learn fast and made good use of his new skill. I recall a few instances when it made a big difference for us.

Walter was a tall, engaging fellow, with good humor and a very good heart. He helped my mother a lot with things that nobody in the village was able to find. Foremost of these was sugar. Not so much that we wanted things sweetened. That was a dream but there were more important uses for it. Sugar was an indispensable ingredient for the making of yeast. We were probably the first family who could lay our hands on some. What we had stashed away was gone. It took only a teaspoon of sugar for a batch, but we were a teaspoon short -- until Walter. With his help we could bake bread.

Walter and Father became friends. He was mainly involved in providing meals for his men, but had other ancillary duties. That gave him freedom and clout, that he often used to help us. He liked best, my brother Tomi. The kid returned the sentiment. He spent hours at Walter's side, entertaining him with his broken Russian, aided by his natural charm and childish stories. He got from him several little doses of sugar for neighbors.

Walter often made pancakes for breakfast, using a ready-mix batter from sealed containers. He gave us samples a few times. We marveled at the high quality and good taste, but found it strange that it was so thick. We were used to thin crepes, that was always one of my favorite treats. As I learned later, the batter was standard US Army issue supplied by Uncle Sam, as just one of the many war-time provisions to an ally. Straight out of the can, nothing to add, except a little pig fat, probably from in a Midwestern farm, to fry the cakes. (In the same vain, for a while, we kids thought that GMC was a Russian truck, since that was what they drove. They also drove another truck, whose brand name I don't remember, but it was a primitive looking, boxy, noisy, smoking truck. That was of Soviet manufacture.)

Near the end of the war, our car, an Opel Olympia, was commandeered by the Germans and we never saw it again. Before we could buy our first post-war car in 1947, horses were our mode of transportation. The local mechanic, Mr. Benedek, who was also a resourceful businessman, found an Opel Kadett somewhere. He fixed it up, painted it by brush and presented it for sale to Father, who eagerly bought it. This knocked-together car was more reliable than expected and lasted for about five years. The top speed, we were able to coax out of it, was 50 mph. Five years later Mr. Benedek got a hold of a fabulous, two-tone green convertible Mercedes Benz. We traded: mundane for heaven. -- It was out of this world.

Until the late 1950s, there were three cars in town. The two doctors and Father were the only people allowed to own one. Several trucks and tractors were used by the cooperatives, but there was no other privately owned auto. New motorcycles were available through a cumbersome state-controlled allocation system. Hopeful buyers had to register with Merkur, the state agency in Budapest, had to pay for it in advance and had to wait many months for delivery. It had to be picked up at one of the few distribution places. High level connections were key to get on the list.

Tractors used for work in the field were assigned and delivered to state farms and cooperatives, in accordance with wishes and wisdom of the central planners. The cooperatives had to buy their own, which was a great burden when much of what they produced was requisitioned by the agricultural control agency. In this respect they were treated same as before they had to join the cooperatives. As true for all equipment, nobody owned them but everybody used them. Poor quality and careless use resulted in many of the tractors being idled and rusting in the yard. They were cannibalized for spare parts, for the working units. The system brought with it corruption and graft by those in charge.

Before he had a chance to buy his Opel Kadett, Father used two horses for work. We housed them in the garage, converted to that purpose. We kept them for about two years. They were two, but did not make a pair. Their build, work capacity and temperament were so different, we never harnessed them as a team.

Szikra (Sparks) was a shiny, jet black, strong, steadfast horse, used for long trips. He was one, that could run at a steady pace all day long. The other one was Szedres, (Mulberry) a sleek light gray filly, dappled with dark gray spots. She could take Father locally, or to closer villages in a hurry. I went a few times with him on his light, open carriage. Horses wee fun for a while, but a car was still our dream.

One day Father's assistant, Joe, was leading Szedres home, after she was fitted with new shoes. Not far from the house a Russian soldier came and took the horse, saying that his commander needed it more then we. Upon hearing the story Father sprang into action. He called on our resident GPU colonel who listened sympathetically. The commander sent one of his lieutenants, to recover the horse. In less than hour we had Szedres back. In this tug of war, who had the more influential friend, counted. Our guys, the members of the military secret police, had no equals in having and applying clout.

Szikra also had his share of adventures, the most important one on the day before the GPU moved out. On the last day for our *guests*, the entire house was loud, filled with song, laughter and partying. The GPU was moving -- perhaps somewhere near Budapest, or at least closer to home. They had many guests from distant places, invited for the occasion. The rowdy, noisy party lasted late into the night. They were singing the Russian songs we all knew by then. Vodka was flowing freely.

Late in the night Walter woke us up. Apologized and asked a favor. His commander assigned him the task of recovering the nice, large accordion, that one of their guests stole. Walter needed a horse. With Father, they saddled Szikra and Walter left on his unpleasant journey. He came back at dawn, with the prized accordion. He thanked Father for the help and was about to leave on his way to catch up with his group. His farewell was awkward. He grew attached to us, as we to him, and it showed. They shook hands and he was on his way.

From the door he turned back:

"I could not say good bye to little Tamás. Please give him a kiss for me".

Father related this tender moment next morning. Walter was quite emotional about saying good bye, especially a farewell to his little friend, without at least a hug. -- We never heard from him or heard anything about him after that. But our pleasant memories about Walter remained with us to cherish.

The business of the secret police headquartered in our house, was to provide an atmosphere of security for the occupying forces (whom, by government order, we called our "liberators"). They also played a part in setting up the new communist regime, copying the Moscow model. No effort was spared to achieve the goal to initiate a new culture, where things Hungarian were shunned, and anything Russian was praised as ultimately worthy, to be admired and emulated. We were encouraged to become the *socialist human-kind*.

But even before all that, the number one task of the GPU was to eliminate any military threat and vestiges of any other perceived threat or resistance. We were witnesses to some of the workings of the GPU. Our living room was the office and main interrogation room for captured German military personnel, who were brought in from the region. I remember once that a young captive, still in his uniform was led into the building. Later, little Erika Borse and I were in the dining room and heard a long, often angry and loud interrogation. Obscenities were flying out of the Russian's mouth as so many common phrases, at times seeming to be the only audible connection between his rants. I spoke a little Russian by then and we all picked up early on the swearing, having heard it so often. They were all around us as part of the new culture. Their most popular phrase was one, that derogated the abused subject's mother as a whore, but with direct reference to his mother, not only using the stray dog as a symbol -- a Russian version of SOB.

I heard that swearing in Russian is an art. The language is rich and colorful in insults to both, God and man -- actually, mostly women. Hungarian can also boasts such dubious claim. The language is rich and expressive. It is no wonder that it extends to all of its uses. I was told by a man once, that he can go on in a filthy way for ten minutes, never repeating himself. -- On the flip side, the language of Hungarian children's' stories, is imaginative and limitlessly rich. Just for fairy tales, specialty phrases and words are made out of ordinary words that have no bounds in their variety. The language thus created, is the exclusive province of stories about princes, princesses, fairies and all kind of magic for young ears.

(As an aside -- swearing in English sounds boring and monotonous. The language, much praised for its enormous and ever expanding vocabulary and fabulous flexibility, may only have about a dozen phrases, and even of those, only three or four, that I constantly hear. It is offensive to me to hear *ad nauseam*, the same ugly words over-and-over in movies. Hollywood would serve itself better, since it is incapable of livening up dirty conversation in movies, if it limited it, to an acceptable level. To add insult to this, they call it *realism* and *art*, which is a laugh, merely insulting our intelligence and sense of decency. Instead they should be trying to entertain us with a not so crude form of realism, especially with better and more imaginative writing. Like salt, a little makes it interesting, but one should use it sparingly. It is distressing to hear schoolgirls who, as part of ordinary conversation, talk like stevedores, even near teachers or other adults. I'm sure in time it will change, but I would like to see it before I die.)

To continue, the swearing, coming from our living room was offensive, but seemed not very effective as a tool of interrogation. Such sessions went on for hours and often days. On this occasion, Tomi came and joined us in play, and we all listened. We talked about and fantasized on the proceedings, going on in the next room. The two were separated only by a huge four-winged, folding glass French door. The Russians covered the glass with paper, so we could not see anything, but the sound was coming through clearly.

The customary next phase in the process was temporary

imprisonment in our basement and, I think without exception, execution by a single shot. They took care not to have civilian witnesses to the killing. It was military matter and no one else's business. The shot to the head was done in the back of the garden.

I remember the first of these events, because I saw the prisoner and his guards, all looking somber, going to the back of the garden. Soon the trees blocked the view. When I heard the shot, I startled, but was reluctant to connect the parts to make a whole picture and draw conclusion. Later I had to confirm my suspicion and asked Father. He told me that I was right. Executions took place in the deep end of the garden, behind dense foliage. The garden was several acres, reaching back about 200 meters.

For a while the Russians held German prisoners only. They kept them without any outside contact and brought them back to the room only for further interrogation.

Our house had a partial basement, that also went through changes during these times. We used it for storage of odds and ends. It was roughly a 200 sq. ft. room, with access from the yard only, five steps down from ground level. Its height was barely over five feet. The only permanent content was a built-in water pump, that took suction from the well and provided water for faucets in the kitchen, bathroom, and the toilet. For bathing, we heated water as we needed it, by a wood-fired potbelly stove with a water tank built on top, at the front end of the bathtub. It counted as pioneering technology in the days the house was built. Having a bathroom with indoor plumbing in a small town without a water system, was rare and considered most advanced. Houses built after 1950, usually included such amenities as a regular part of homes. Municipal water and gas was installed throughout the town in the 1970s.

Normally, the basement contained temporary or seasonal storage of just about anything, for which the sometimes damp cellar was suitable. It was not heated, so we had to be careful with food items, that were sensitive to frost. Potatoes, carrots and such were fine there, if properly covered. We stored them in sand and dug them out as needed. Eggs could also be stored long term, using an old method. They were put in slaked lime. This was a messy process, but with it we had eggs that remained fresh all winter. One might say, we bought them on sale in the fall and saved them for later, to avoid the higher cost.

After a while our little cellar also became important for the Russkies. At the time in late spring, it was lightly stocked with storage. The exception was tiles in one corner. My parents bought them a few years before, but because of the war, we had to postpone installation. About six large crates, filled with two kinds of tiles were down there. They were intended for the walls of the bathroom and toilet, but were not put up for the lack of time and opportunity, with the war going.

It happened one day in the *GPU Administration.* We thought the basement was ours, but the top command requisitioned it for its exclusive use. We emptied it, except for the heavy crates. They needed the cellar for a prison. German soldiers were kept there overnight or for short periods, but eventually their number diminished. Others, who were caught under suspicion were kept for a time, while their fate was decided. Up to six-eight people were in there at a time. We were allowed to play in the yard without much curtailment, but kept away from the basement door that opened into the yard. There was no high security to keep the prisoners inside. We knew who was boss and what would the consequences be for any infraction. Nobody escaped from that basement. I do not remember anything specific about guards for the night. I think they only padlocked the door. During the day the door was usually open. We could look in from a distance without much trouble and could spot a few people.

Conditions inside were appalling. Mess, rubbish and dirt everywhere. The men slept on straw, and for all we knew, never got out or had a chance to clean up. It was a miniature Gulag. When the GPU moved out, we restored the basement to its original usage. But before we could do that, we had to fumigate it and kill the thousands of flees in there. I remember that the tremendous number colored the wall brown. It was one of the most disgusting and incredible sights I have ever seen.

The tile crates were still there. We even saw tiles through the slats. But when we looked inside, we found only a handful. It is hard to imagine why, whoever took the content of the crates, bothered to arrange it so, that the crates should look full. We never went down there while it was a prison and could only speculate when the crates' content was stolen -- maybe on the night, when Walter's accordion also grew legs. Tiles were a prize. They may now be on a wall somewhere east, very far away. We bought new ones about a year later. Those finally made it up on the walls. They were of inferior quality, something opaque white, what we called *milk glass*, low grade as everything else then.

We were looking forward to moving back in the house, since we had no *tenant* occupying it. Little did we know, that we were just days away from new and even less pleasant people, as the first of two additional phases of successive occupations. It came after the town was invaded on a titanic scale.

In the spring of 1946, more than 250,000 Ukrainians were transported back to their homeland. The German war industry was using them as free labor in the second half of the war. After Germany was defeated, the Ukrainians were held back for some reason, most likely security. Stalin was uneasy with any person, and especially with such a large number, who were exposed to anything other than Soviet life, no matter the circumstances. He is known to have killed thousands for just such reason. He did not want the germs of freedom, affluence, capitalism, or anything western, infecting his *workers paradise.*

Jánosháza's population of about 5,000, more than tripled almost overnight. Within a few days, 13,000 Ukrainians were moved into town. It was similar to what is pictured in old Hollywood westerns: coming in horse drawn wagons by the hundreds, fully loaded with people, homesteaders, claiming land for farming. -- Our new neighbors claimed the streets and any open field. They blanketed the whole town as locusts and soon ravaged everything. We had no contact with them if we could help it. Alas, avoiding them was not possible. (Highlights in my memory of these couple months, are that they could eat sunflower seed at a phenomenal rate. I saw some that fed the seed in the mouth at one side and in one continuous flow, spit out the shells at the other.)

Another, not so innocuous habit of theirs, was a penchant for open, daylight street robberies. Young gangs stopped one or a few persons and simply went through the pockets and kept what they felt like keeping. I was a victim of one such robbery. It was scary, but they meant no harm, only took things that they liked. A much fancied pocket knife was the thing I missed most.

They regularly roamed the farm fields to take anything they could find for food. Potato was ready for harvest, but we were surprised how wasteful they were in gathering their loot. They pulled up the vine, gathered what was on it and never bothered to dig for the bigger ones that lay deeper in the ground. We were angry and frustrated, but could do nothing. The silver lining of this clumsy thievery was that they left a lot of good potato buried for us to gather later.

The Ukrainian Command, under the watchful eyes of the overall Soviet authority was our new tenant. Just days after we saw Walter the last time, the Ukrainians moved in, occupying the same main portion of the house. We in the house had absolutely no contact with the people on the other side of the walls after the first day. Because of that, my memory about this phase is limited to the above mentioned events with one exception, but one that was very scary. One day news spread, that the Ukrainians were to be moved out all at once, the same way they came in at the outset. They were to be taken to eastern Hungary, before final repatriation. But before moving out, they had a request from their command.

They asked for a three-day, officially sanctioned, *free robbery*, where they could enter houses, take anything they feel taking and were able to carry. For days we were petrified in fear. At the end, the Russians decided not to grant the favor. In the following few days the town was emptied of all Ukrainians and we breathed a sigh of relief.

There was a short hiatus, and with the long awaited leave of the Ukrainian Command, we were able to occupy the entire house -- for a while.

Soon, however we got a new occupant. This one could more truly be called a tenant. Not that he paid rent. No, but he took residence in two rooms with his entourage of one, while we moved back again, this time into the dining and living rooms. We were now allowed the use the kitchen. The Pesti family has moved out by then.

The new tenants were a Russian major and his orderly. The major was a simple, about 50 years old guy of Mongolian extraction, and very short in stature, but must have had an important position. He gave us a list of what he wanted. It was two of the big rooms, toilet and bath for the two of them. He moved in the two rooms, but soon requested a third one, that we relinquished, by moving out of the living room again. Other things he wanted, were two meals and maid service for washing his clothes and such. His servant did the cleaning of their quarters. He also asked to eat with us, so Mother included him with our breakfast and evening meal every day. He sat at the head of the table. These were the only times when my father gave up that spot. Before this, it was inconceivable for him to do that.

By that time Father was fairly fluent in Russian. The daily meals were a help in one respect. Time during meals was spent often with interesting conversation between the two men, mostly about his humble origin, soldier days and war adventures. He told us many stories, but I'm sure he also left a lot unsaid. The major was a reserved and very polite man and other than the domestic inconvenience, gave us no trouble. He was a primitive man. That is why we were puzzled by most things about him.

Once we had our family photo album out when he came for dinner. He asked to see it and seemed to enjoy just looking at the photos, without ulterior motive. He had questions about old pictures, that we explained. As Father turned a page, among the glued-in photographs, there was a portrait of the Virgin Mary, loosely between the pages. Her head was covered with a shawl on the dark, photo-like, black-and-white print. It was out of a prayer book, here among family photos by mistake. The major didn't ask about it, rather, he voiced an opinion in form of a question, about what he thought it was.

"Tzigane?", he asked.

"No, it is someone else". -- (Father was too polite to say,: *No major, she is not a gipsy, she is a saint.*)

I dared not to look up. We all tried to carry on without

snickering. Thus we witnessed the huge cultural gap between us and the major. Religion was never a subject of conversation. It was not, that his background did not include western art or Christian images. Most likely, it completely lacked anything religious. During his upbringing and later life, he saw only socialist images and the fatherly figure of Joe Stalin, the Party and other perverse ideas about building a communist nirvana.

(I recall once seeing a picture of a scene in a Russian state-run day-care center. It showed a full size, standing cardboard figure of Stalin in white uniform, with a hole, where his hand would've been. The kindergarten teacher, from behind the image of the *Maximum Leade*r, gave out the daily food rations to the kids through the opening, to illustrate where everything good in life comes from. State operated day care was a Soviet invention, aimed to liberate mothers from the drudgery of child rearing, and free them to build a communist future. Indoctrination of the young, through such institutions at the earliest possible time was a bedrock policy of the Soviet leadership. Other youth programs, such as the boy scouts were also totally revamped and became an instrument of the Communist Party. These programs were forced upon us too, as they were throughout the other satellite countries. In true Soviet fashion, social institutions became a streamlined tool, along with many other insidious policies, to control and indoctrinate the population.)

The major stayed with us for about nine months. As we were eating one day, about two months into his tenure, he looked at the huge grandfather clock in the corner, as he often did before. On this day, he made another request. He wanted the clock moved into his apartment. We were stunned, but tried not to show it. The old clock was part of the dining room set. With its bold features, beautifully hand caved, it was a deep brown colored piece, totally different in looks, from the light brown set with soft lines and curves, that was our set in the living room, that the major occupied. We were jealously protective of our treasured furniture in these two rooms. They were examples of artful furniture carving. The set in the dining room was made for us when the house was built. It was richly carved, but in renaissance style, with marvelous gray marble top for the mirror set and the two-level china cabinet. -- (Our living room wardrobes were a copy of my great grandmother's wardrobe set in Ják. Mother received it as part of her dowry. Our set also included two matching dressers, one with a high mirror and the other with two levels, to hold our china and silver, both with a marble top. The set for the room was completed with a table and six chairs. The same carpenter made both sets, several years apart. The two were otherwise identical, except that the old lady's set has darkened by age.)

The major's request was a surprise and cause for anxiety. We moved the clock over to the his room. This request was unexpected, even after he took the third room a few weeks before. There were too many sad experiences to cite as precedent, though none involving him. He seemed always to be honest and proved to be such, till the end. He left everything in the rooms intact when he left. Nothing was missing. We found only a slight damage to the clock's base. We were happy and relieved.

His most becoming charm was his unassuming, simple nature. The one thing we kids observed and had a great kick out of, was what he did early each day as he walked to his office. Every morning I, with a few boys sat on the steps in front of the shoe store to get our dose of morning sun. The first step off the sidewalk was 14 ft wide, along half the width of the building. From it, a narrower, second and third step lead to the shop door and a similar one, to the show window a few feet away. We liked to sit on the top step in front of the window. It was toasty warm on early, sunny, summer mornings.

As the major walked by, he never missed walking up onto the first long step, walking on it all the way and stepping off at the end. We, 9-10 year old kids thought that *we* grew out of such things, years ago. So it was amusing for us to see such an important man, do a childish thing like that -- twice every day, no less. We never asked him about it, of course. I just remember it and think of it -- always with a smile.

One more thing about our major. Father told him once that

Dezsõ, a young cousin of Mother was a prisoner of war. He promised trying to track him down. A few days later he told us, that Dezsõ was in a camp somewhere in Austria. His sister Mariann, who was living with us then, wrote a letter, that the major promised to send on. Almost two years past before Dezsõ was released. Then we learned that the letter reached him. He told us that he received it, the only one he ever got during his capture. He also recalled, that it had some odd writings on it that he could not decipher. This was a very unusual thing in his camp, where nobody else received mail. They spent about three years working on useless projects, idling their life away. -- The little major was a good man. In spirit we thanked him for his kindness, after he was long gone from our life.

Mariann told me of another little event that she remembers, though I do not recall this myself. One afternoon the major walked over to our room, just for a chat with us three kids in the room at the time. She was the only other adult there, but took no part in the *conversation*. The major wanted only to be in the company of kids for a while. He spent about ten minutes with us, where each of us did our best to be intelligible to one another. Then, apparently pleased, he returned to his quarters.

15

Describe Jánosháza

The square on which we lived, originally was one huge open
space. Even most cities can't boast anything that size. It was
criss-crossed by major and lesser roads, tree-lined walkways, that
divided it into four quadrants and smaller sections. Two major
parts actually bore different names. Our half, named after the 19th
century statesman, was Kossuth Lajos Square, the other, Heroes
Square, honoring the veterans of WW I. The two together made
one huge oval, with houses on the periphery and a large school
in the center. It was 1/2 mile long, and less than a ¼ mile wide.
It contained three parks, separated by roads and walkways. One
was for a chapel of St. Vendel the patron saint of town. We had
a nice baroque church on a hill, near the end of town, but on St.
Vendel Day, mass was held in the tiny chapel. That was the day of
the annual town fair, when locals and others from nearby villages
gathered to celebrate and break bread with friends. To attend,
people were crowding around it, filling the garden and spilling
onto the road in front of our house, though saw nothing of the
mass inside. All joined the singing when we heard our cantor from
inside, starting a song. We enjoyed a festive day with our guests.
In stalls and tents, vendors hawked gift-ware. Carousels and other

jolly diversions filled the area. In the evening, people went to the dance hall and taverns for a good time.

Another garden was named in the memory of Prince St. Imre, son of St. Stephen. It contained the graves of those fallen in World War I. Their names were on a granite monument at the north end, adjacent to Mária Garden, the third and nicest one on the square. Mária Garden, dedicated to the Virgin Mother, had huge acacia trees. Lovers liked its well kept walkways, comfortable, secluded benches and its peaceful quiet for undisturbed rendezvous. The Virgin Mary's statue was at the center, where all the walks met. It was on top of a high column. Two other minor religious statues were near opposite ends.

This big square was a great place for many activities in my childhood. One could see the whole length from end to end, along the main road. Two large, two-story buildings could be seen near the north end. One was the Beer House. When I was growing up, I saw nothing in that building that had anything to do with beer. I heard that it housed a brewery over a hundred years ago. The building was not used for any important purpose I knew of. Occasionally they held dances on the large second floor hall. A few small businesses were located in it on the ground floor. The other building was the Coffee House, named after the café on the first floor. I was in it only a few times, but remember well the coffee fragrance in the air, mixed with floating cigarette smoke. It was closed and the building sold, when I was still a small boy. The ground floor was converted into a carpenter shop by the new owner, Mr. Váli. He renovated the second floor and lived there. He once joked that he enjoyed the easy commute to work.

Around the square, there were stores, businesses, two hotels with taverns, operated by the Barát and the Ritter families and the Town House, but most of the buildings were individual homes. There were trees on both sides of a long walkway, stretching from near one end, passing in front of the school, a doctor's residence, and ending at a major cross road. It had beautiful wild chestnut trees and some fruit trees, that we liked to harvest as the fruit ripened. In other places, walnut trees produced nuts in abundance. We loved them early in the season, when the meat was white, slightly sweet and tender. Our hands were black for days after the premature harvesting. The green shell is firm before it dries. Then it ripens, turns black and cracks open, exposing the hardened nutshell. This green shell was rich with sap, that stained our hands for about a week. Nothing could wash it off. Parents always commented on the unsightly hands, but tolerated our childish dismissal of the importance of this temporary condition.

Most of the square was dirt, gravel and plenty of grass, our favorite playing fields. Walkways were built up and improved with basalt or gravel, to save us from having to jump across puddles and avoid the mud. Our house had concrete sidewalk, as did a few others. We looked out to a grassy meadow, where we played soccer. A little further south, the school used the other half of the field for the same thing and other gym class activities in good weather. It was a useful field, for the school had no gym for indoor sports. The grass was also popular grazing field for ducks and geese. (We had to be careful, not to slip on stuff left behind.) At the south end, the square narrowed down and continued as a street, that had an official name, but everybody called it Cigány utca -- Gipsy Street, -- because as it lead out of town, it passed by a gipsy compound.

Six communal wells were spaced along the length of the square. They were used by people, who did not have a well in their yard. Some of these wells were of the old design, that tourists see on the *Puszta,* the flat middle region of the country. It is often likened to a gigantic, one-legged mosquito, sipping water from the earth. Most of the wells were the modern, crank-type, that lowered and lifted a bucket on a chain, as we turned the crank or wheel.

Other community structures were the two weigh-houses, both near square center. They were used for the weighing of farm animals and commodities. The weigh instruments were under lock inside, but kids could play, using other parts of the small building and the weighing platform. It was one of my favorite places during hide-and-seek.

Near the north end of the square, adjacent to Mária Garden, was the memorial for the veterans of World War I, many of whom rested in St. Imre Garden. In a small, fenced plot, it contained the body of an unknown, symbolically representing all our war dead.

Honoring all the long-time dead heroes, was a handsome granite statue of a rugged soldier, standing on a pedestal. Many names, those of the fallen, long ago residents of our town, were chiseled in the large slab of stone behind him.

March 15 was our 4th of July. Ceremonies were held around the hero's plot each year. The day, the Ides of March, commemorates the 1848 freedom fight, and it has been our premier national holiday since then. It was the uprising, trying to throw off the burdensome yolk of Austrian dominance and excessive taxation. March 15th was the most important national holiday for a hundred years. The momentous national fight for freedom was brutally repressed. On this early spring day each year, the entire school went out, sang patriotic songs and listened to speeches.

A requisite part of the program was the reciting of the poem by our greatest poet, Sándor Petõfi: *Rise Magyar.* Petõfi died in that struggle in 1849, at age 26. By the time of his early death, he published a large volume of poems. He wrote eloquently, not with fancy words, but with humor, about love, heroism and patriotism. He could write about simple things and ordinary people and make it interesting, beautiful, mocking and endearing -- all in just a few lines. His way with words and flighty stanzas are most unique in literature, showcasing the infinite, florid variety, and power of expression of the Hungarian language.

In the years after the war, celebrations on March 15th were subdued. May 1st became the most important day, when enthusiastic participation, skillfully faked, was the better part of valor, if one wanted to stay in the good graces of the all-knowing party authorities and ideologues. Adults and children had to go out and march, carrying red flags and salute the workers of the world, in whose name communism claimed its legitimacy. In truth, the workers were oppressed, just as much as was the entire country. A few who were willing to tow the Party line, had security and better opportunities than the rest of the citizenry.

The little Heroes Garden, with its granite monument, was expanded in 1946. Hungarian dead of World War II were not honored there, as one would expect. Six Russian soldiers were buried there instead. At first the soldiers were hastily covered with dirt in the St. Vendel chapel garden, right in front of our window, where only a wooden marker showed their common, shallow grave near the garden fence. One day, about six months later, they were exhumed, in order to give them a formal burial and a permanent place to rest.

Looking out of my parent's bedroom window, I noticed a small group gather at the site. A few busied themselves, digging. I noticed that the diggers were gipsies. I went out to take a look. People told me that it was hard to find people who would do the work. Regular grave diggers were not willing to do the job. I soon saw why. Nobody objected to burying any war dead, but the bodies, buried only inches below grade a few months ago, were a deplorable sight. I took one look and turned back in horror. The fetid bodies were covered with maggots. They were one solid moving white mass. It was my first time ever to see live, something on that scale. It gives me the shivers even as I write this.

Gipsies were always a separate breed. Most spoke with a dialect that was uniquely gipsy. Among themselves they spoke a version of Sanskrit, the most ancient of Indian languages, going back to 1500 BC. They were nomads, spreading west through the centuries. They lived at the edge of town in dried mud shacks, a dozen to a room. None that I recall had a job, or wanted one. They stole what they could lay their hands on and begged the rest, to support their miserable, but often strangely jolly existence. (An old joke, -- the gipsy recipe for chicken soup -- begins: "First, you steal a chicken...".) Some of the women were extremely daring, impertinent and limber with their fingers. When gipsies came begging, we never allowed them into the house and after giving them some food, watched them, all the way out to the street. They also carried diseases, another reason to keep our distance from them.

There were other gipsy families who lived in town. They lived in decent houses and looked very different than those other gipsies, though came from the same or similar stock, also immigrating from the Indian subcontinent, many years ago. They were our musicians, with the gipsy violin, reputation of musicianship and aura of romance. Their behavior was always deferential and overly polite. They played at weddings, fairs and other village events of merriment. The most romantic occasions were when they were hired individually or just a few of them, to serenade somebody's beloved. If the suitor was a brave lad, and wanted to show his good voice, he sang a love song. If he couldn't, he may ask a friend or hire someone to make sure that the rendition of the song is presentable. (It is similar to what *Cyrano de Bergerac* did for his friend Christian, helping him in his effort of wooing the fair Roxane, in the famous play by Rostand.)

In the effort of digging up the dead Russians, three men from the less attractive group of gipsies, were persuaded to earn real money for a little easy, though distasteful work. They seemed to do it without flinching, one of them even with flourish. As luck would have it, he found a bottle of vodka left next to one of the bodies. After some hesitation, he opened it, smelled it and pronounced it potable. He then wiped the mouth of the bottle and took a sip. It was satisfying and good as real vodka, he said. He put the cork back, completed the digging and no doubt, looked forward to finishing his jug of lucky bonus, later.

The remains of the soldiers were taken in nice coffins to Heroes Garden, which was enlarged and fenced to accommodate its new residents. Each was given a separate grave and a nice, large, black marble headstone with a red star to decorate it. They now rest in their own little cemetery behind the Hungarian heroes. There, the two separate memorials together, comprise a poignant message and a reminder. They commemorate those who went to war, fight for their homeland and did not return. They died for the hope of a better future and a world, in which we may enjoy the fruit of their sacrifice. They did it for freedom, or at least loyalty, to the ultimate extent of their courage, abilities and noble spirit. We never begrudged those soldiers. Closest to resentment was our feeling, that our own servile communist lackey government was doing the bidding of our oppressors. They ordered that these dead, members of an occupying army, receive higher honor, than our own, who died for liberty and in the defense of their country, our Hungary.

I was back at various times in Jánosháza during the last four decades. Sometime in the late 1960s, the town decided to plant trees throughout much of the north half of the square, creating one huge park, that incorporates in it, one of the three old ones. The walkways were paved and redesigned and along with other improvements, totally changed the look of the place. My impression was that of a forest or jungle. Not that I am against trees -- quite the contrary. Only, I missed the open space that I grew up with. It was too dense, even confining. The old Mária Garden is incorporated in the new project and now looks even more spacious, with its big old trees more loosely spaced than the many new little ones. To get a better perspective, I have to give it another look, after the new generation of trees will grow to a greater height. I better not pass judgment on the new look. Perhaps it just needs time to get used to.

16

Life Returning To Normal

Normal, for the purposes of this story, means putting our life back together, as somewhat resembling conditions, prior to the beginning of the War. We had to recover from two invasions. The first was by the Germans, followed by the hoards of the Red Army. We were raped, physically displaced, trampled on, robbed and humiliated. To add insult to our injury, at the end of all that, for 45 years, an oppressive regime was forcing its foreign culture upon us, aggressively and with contempt. So, normal is relative. (What I as a young boy considered well below normal, was that for almost a year we had no ball to play with. In frustration I was kicking rocks while walking on the street. It was frustrating and a poor substitute for kicking ball, playing our favorite sport, football [soccer].)

There was a serious and for many, devastating consequence of the war. Inflation affected the country's economy and touched the life of everyone. It began slowly, then took on a gallop, turning into a rampant, uncontrolled mad dash, ruining commerce, where people abandoned money and turned to barter. The *pengõ*, entirely lost its value. First it went into the millions. Then it became *mil-pengõ*, which inflated into billions. The last stage was the *B pengõ*.

A basketful of *it* still didn't buy anything. After closing banks for a few days, the *forint* was introduced on August 1 of 1946. It is still Hungary's legal tender.

I remember the time well. New bills were issued almost weekly and they looked very good, with nice pictures on them, printed on fine paper, but all for naught. The process even affected me personally. I was 10 years old. It was the town fair, St. Vendel's Day. We had a few games, hawkers in their stands with holiday merchandise and a merry-go-round, powered by kids, walking on a circular track on an elevated platform, pushing a beam round and round. Their reward for the work was a free ride. (I asked my parents for permission to go up and push with other kids, but they refused.)

On the day of the fair, coming home from mass, I saw a toy that I coveted dearly. I implored my patents for money to by the trinket. It took me some time to collect enough. Even an uncle donated some, when he heard me begging. After lunch I had the amount and went happily to the vendor to buy my prized toy -- I think, a tiny wagon. To my amazement, the price went up in the meantime, inflating in a few hours. At the end I was still short and never got my precious little wagon.

After the fighting stopped, most people got busy repairing their fences. As the Ukrainians left, hardly a stretch of fence was left intact. Throughout our town, plank or wood slat fences separated all lots from the properties of neighbors. For a few months, before most of the fences went up, we could make any shortcut in town, trekking through people's yard or garden. I liked how much time and distance we saved while this unusual situation lasted. The accepted rule was that kids, were not bothered by owners, as we walked through their yards and gardens. Nobody raised the issue of trespassing. We were ignorant of such laws and the owners were tolerant. Of course, we were careful to respect flowers and vegetables. Trampling on those would have ended the understood rule, outright. I was sorry to see the situation end. People soon fixed their fences. We again had to use the streets as our short-lived special privilege was terminated by the flow of events.

At the beginning of the war, fearing hard times ahead, my

parents tried an old method of hiding lard in the well. This was based on experience of prior generations, but took some ingenuity to do it right. We had three large bins, or tubs of lard from last winter's pig-kill. The tubs were blue, enameled steel with a hinged lid and a looped handle on each side, like a giant, two-handled, lidded cup. The bins held about 20 gallons of lard.

We tied loose wire, connecting the two handles, fashioning a large wire loop, so that they could be found easier and lifted out by an anchor or hook. Father was a little concerned at the beginning, whether a large container of lighter-than-water lard might not sink. The container proved to be of enough weight to sink with its content. We gently sank all three to the bottom of the well, carefully avoiding the area near the pump suction. We had slightly cloudy water from our faucets for a day. The well was shallow, with only about 10 ft. of water, the top being about 8 ft. below grade. It had a hand operated pump, that we used to fill buckets for the flowers and garden. It was also the sole water supply for the Molnárs.

One nice summer afternoon in 1947, we felt safe enough to recover our stash. We moved the square concrete manhole cover, looked into the dark space, but saw nothing, even using flashlight. Father and one of my uncles were working hard, lowering and retrieving an anchor with three-way hooks, hoping to snag the wire or something on the tubs without success and were becoming frustrated. After unsuccessful tries we have lowered a long ladder to the bottom, to make the work easier. The ladder, resting on the bottom of the well, extended through the cover opening, to above ground level. At this time a man, I did not recognize, walked in. He was a lawyer, who just moved into town and came to introduce himself, as it was a customary courtesy. Father met him briefly a few days before and invited him to stop by. He was a tall, friendly man and quite slim. It came naturally for him, and perhaps he wanted to show his generous side, to volunteer and go down on the ladder trying to retrieve the tubs. Father hesitated, but let him help us on his introductory visit. He was better able to fit through the small opening than Father, who was more substantially built.

As our new acquaintance was working with the hooks, trying

to catch something solid, the ladder gave way. It is possible that it was positioned on top of one of the tubs and slipped off. The ladder went down a couple feet, and with it went down our friend, into the water, up to his knees. It was embarrassing, getting wet in a well, instead of comfortably sipping tea or wine in the shade, under a tree. Our lawyer friend took it in stride, said that it was just a small inconvenience and insisted carrying on with his project. Eventually he was successful. All three tubs saw sunlight and we were happy and relieved.

This was the first and only time we did this type of preservation. In theory, water and lard did not mix, so they should not harm one another, we thought. Still, we were anxious to see if more than a year under water had any deleterious effect on our precious lard. A thin top layer of it turned slightly brown, likely from fine silt. Only a kilo of it did we waste. Even that went into the slop, feeding a new generation of pigs -- a process that can truly be called, recycling. In all, the experiment was a success.

One summer Otti and I went to Nagycenk, to spend a few weeks with my other grandparents and the family of uncle John. Father grew up in this small town, close to the historic city of Sopron, where he attended high school. At the edge of town was the castle of the Count Széchenyi family, famous statesmen and patriots. It was a ruin when I saw it and remained so for years, but now it is restored.

My father was the second child of my grandparents. His older brother John was a ruffian in his youth, who in his old age became a thoughtful, reflective man. In his leisurely retirement he became interested in reading books and talking with us on political and intellectual subjects, though he had only grade school education.

Uncle John was 45 years old in that summer of 1947, a strong, vigorous man, used to hard work. He was still private, that is, not yet enrolled into the government enforced agricultural cooperative, that was being organized and heralded as the coming socialist paradise for farmers and the promise of highly productive, modern agriculture. Paradise? Why then, did they need coercion to organize it? (This followed a similar brutal effort in the Soviet Union, where the program had a part in the mass starvation of an estimated 30 million, mostly Ukrainians in the mid-1930s. Stalin induced the famine to brake the resistance by the Ukrainian peasants.) Uncle John was complaining about the hardship of farming, the large mandatory quota the government demanded and the *kolhoz*, (Russian, for cooperative) that he would soon be forced to join. Once he lamented that he had to do the entire wheat harvest "on pears" as his source to sustain stamina -- meaning, that he was out of the energy food of smoked bacon with bread, that was the traditional staple for those, doing hard work in the field. He had to do the harvest on bread and fruits.

Otti made a request of Uncle John. He discovered three car skeletons in a nearby grove. They were left there to rust after the war, ignored by everybody, seemingly without anything that could be salvaged from them. Otti still saw an opportunity in taking them apart further.

Uncle John obliged his request and went out with his two cows. We flipped over one of the *cars* and, on its top, they dragged it, scraping the dirt, all the way into his yard. Otti worked on that wreck for more than a week and I was amazed at the stuff he took off it. He collected a lot of screws, washers and unusable parts, hidden before. But the exercise, the experience and just working on his precious project were his reward. -- Eventually the large sheet metal piece found its way to the foundry -- perhaps to become a tractor.

After we were rid of all our guests and moved back into our house, my parents assessed domestic damage. On an interior door we had a large pane of glass still missing. About a year earlier, we had to clean up a million pieces, after an accident by a drunk Soviet security guy. The captain apologized, let us clean it up and asked if we could find a replacement piece. It was a unique, stripe-textured glass panel on the door between the old Kids' Room and the Hall, our receiving room, where Mother entertained some guests or closer acquaintances, waiting for Father on some business matter. We found nothing matching the missing glass and settled for a miniature flower pattern. The two adjacent panels looked odd together, but we put up with the mismatch-collage from then on. Even the current owners asked me about it in 2001. I had to tell them the story of the drunk Russian who stumbled through it.

The other, much bigger item was the damage to our valuable rugs. Mother, after long search found a man, an expert in repairing Persian rugs. He was Mr. Tütüngyán, a gentle old Turk, (his given name was even longer and more difficult, so we just called him Uncle Tütüngyán). He said he was a busy man traveling the country, repairing rugs such as ours. He moved in and spent almost three weeks, with his needles and collection of threads, sitting on his foot-stool in the large opening between the living and dining rooms, working all day. His wages included room and board, making things simple for everybody. I spent time with him, talking about his trade and business, that I found unusual and interesting. He spoke with a heavy accent so I had to pay close attention. By the end he went through all that we had, about 20 pieces, some really large, and returned them to good condition. The only negative I remember was that he couldn't match all the colors, especially, when he had to work adjacent to faded and worn areas, part of which he replaced with new yarn of brighter colors.

17

Memories Of School
And Childhood

I fondly remember my first teacher, an old, erudite man. Mr. Ferenc László, was the principal and teacher of first grade. He exuded dignity, politeness and decorum and enjoyed enormous respect in his school and the community. He died when I was in third grade.

In the early days of Russian occupation, (1945) our schooling was disrupted. The school was taken, to house soldiers -- entirely for a while and partially later. We lost several months of the school year.

Third grade was not at all typical for elementary students. We spent the spring months in the yard of our teacher, sitting on boxes and crates. It was little chilly, too early for outdoor schooling. I often looked for the sun, hoping for its warming rays. One day our very kind teacher, Mr. Sziráki, told us that if we behave, the sun will come out. And it soon did. As patches of clouds passed overhead, he was following them, and he was able to predict momentary sunshine. After a few tries, I caught him looking up before he said it and made the necessary connection. I was proud to have figured it out, but kept it to myself.

This limited schooling had a couple other interesting aspects. The school year was short, vacation long. We all must have been good students, judging by my report card. It was straight A. First, this was a pleasant surprise but I accepted it and proudly showed it to my mother. She said: "Fine, son." I also tried it on Father when he came home. He glanced at it, but was even less impressed than Mother. He handed it back to me without comment. Hmm, I thought, all that hard work and those chilly mornings we sat through in the yard? Well, maybe our teacher was compassionate and generous, giving extra credit to compensate us for the inconvenience.

Teachers were in absolute control disciplining us, even outside the classroom. Uncle Pali (Paul) Nagy became a family friend soon after they moved into town about four years before. His son Bandi sat next to me in 4th grade. Józsi's best friend was their older son, Imre.

Once Tomi and I went with my parents to visit our brothers in Keszthely, where they were attending boarding school. There we learned the traditional Latin greeting, with which all students, saluted their teachers: "Laudetur Jesus Cristus" (Praised be, Jesus Christ). This was the scholarly equivalent of the greeting in Hungarian, that we were taught at home and in school, as we started first grade. (At the end of each school day the class was divided to small groups and, depending on the direction to home, we lined up in pairs and like a parallel row of ducks, went home together. On the way we greeted each adult, with the traditional Catholic greeting.) And with that goes a story.

Tomi and I met Uncle Pali on the street one afternoon and this time, we used the Latin version of saluting him. After we did it, proudly using our newly acquired skill, we giggled and whispered, to each other, whether he understood our Latin greeting.

I do not know whether he understood -- most likely, he did -- or if he even heard well enough, what we were snickering about. I never bothered, or dared, to find out. But Mr. Teacher, as we always addressed him in class, turned around and stopped us. He sensed some impertinent affront and told us to visit him in his third grade class room before classes were to begin next morning.

I could think of nothing else during breakfast. We did as ordered, making his classroom our first stop. Our punishment, as expected, was three lashes on the bottom. I prepared by wearing my boy scout shorts, one woven with the thickest, felt-like material. Tomi went first. As I watched him receiving his lashes, I got an idea to lessen the effect of the rod on me. I bent down just a little, so the cloth was loose on my behind. Not being fooled by such tricks, Uncle Paul ordered me to bend down more, so the lashing would be more effective on a tighter fabric. He had experience. -- As we were walking back to our class rooms, we agreed that it was not as bad as we feared.

We never learned if our parents found out about this. If he told Father, I'm sure he had concurred with Uncle Pali's story and congratulated him on his effective method of discipline.

In 4th grade my teacher was Miss Elizabeth László, daughter of my late, beloved principal, whose family my parents knew well. Miss László was different, a bit of a black sheep. She was not liked much by her students. We thought her to be too demanding and lacking a sense of humor. Once she detained me at the end of school, because I could not find a small, obscure river on the map in southern Transylvania. As a result of this incident, I forever remember the name of that creek: *Karas*. I saw kids being kept after classes every day, but I did not ever expect to be one of them. Detention was a great indignity, not to mention inconvenience. Of course, it also meant that my parents find out, with me showing up late and all. I told them the story and they sympathized with me, saying that the reason was too frivolous for such humiliating punishment. Miss László may have taught me some obscure geographic fact, but with her severe reprimand, she certainly left a memory in me that was not very pleasant.

(Talking about geography, I remember something else, also from 4th grade. In parts of some older maps we used in class, I saw sizable white fields, clearly delineated. They were in the middle of Africa, some remote parts of Asia and Australia. I asked the teacher, what they were and she told me that those areas were yet undiscovered and no reliable map could be drawn to show the terrain and geographical features in sufficient detail. They must have been old, because they were the only such maps in school.)

According to stories I heard from relatives years before, when my father was new in town -- and single – Miss László was one of the hopeful maidens trying to snare him. Lacking her sister's Manci's beauty and engaging personality, she remained a spinster, long time after her popular sister married.

Aunt Manci was a friend of my mother for years, going back to their school days. She married a teacher, Mr. Varga. The Varga family remained close friends and we visited each other often. They became Józsi's godparents. I remember a cute story my mother also liked to tell, involving a comment by Józsi, when at one occasion, his godmother offered some tasty cookies to him once more, after the tray went around the table a few minutes before. Józsi politely declined, but when encouraged to take just one more, he sighed:

"I would take more Godmother, but Mother said we should take no more than two."

This honest admission was a winner. The adults had a good laugh and complimented Józsi for his restraint and candor. All kids joined in the merriment and were not surprised that the cookie plate went twice more around the table.

In the late 1940s, Doctor Kovács, our neighbor two doors down died and a new, very reserved type, but handsome, young physician, Dr. Marosvári moved into the doctor's house to take over the practice. This time Miss László played her cards right. After the passing of some time, filled with anticipation and no doubt anxious moments on her part, he proposed. Soon they married and she lived, likely happier than before, as Mrs. Marosvári -- our new neighbor.

One day, somebody shot a hole through the window of the Marosvári house. It was with a pellet gun, judging from the tiny hole in the glass. The lady said that I did it, perhaps because she knew that we had such a gun. She had no proof, because there was none. She was vocal, pushy and demanding. The word got to

Father and he asked me about it. I told him that I did not do it, as I already told her, to no avail. Father went over and let her know that he stands by me because he believes me. After some argument he gave her the money to fix her window, saying something to the effect that it should shut her up. It was not a good day, but I was already out of fourth grade. Also, I was happy and proud that my father stood by me, based on my word against that of Mrs. Marosvári.

Our circle of family friends were mostly from town. There were few professional people, though not all of them became close friends. Father knew everybody for miles around. He counted all the Catholic clergy in his district, as friends. The rectories were prosperous manors. On weekdays the priests were farmers and managers, working together with their employees. Other farmers also helped by donating their time to work on parish land. This was possible because farming was a prosperous profession for many families.

Father's best friend was our own pastor, Monsignor József Pártli. He was Tomi's godfather.

For our family parties the guests usually included Monsignor Pártli, professionals, teachers, intellectuals and educated people, such as owners or managers of large farms. Relatives and people from out of town were also invited.

We kept a friendship with other veterinarians and doctors. Father's closest friend was his boss, the County Supervising Vet, Dr. Ferenc Mandeville, who also had his own district at the county seat. The Galgóczy family from the largest farm, some teachers and professionals also visited. Even as a kid I saw how popular parties were at our house.

Among my teachers were two others, who once also had hopes to snare my father when he was single. Marrying their daughters well in a small town, was a priority for many families, especially prosperous ones. Young maidens, wishing to find "Mr. Right", seemed always to outnumber eligible bachelors, especially those, well to do. (It is also a common subject in literature -- *Little Women*, *Pride and Prejudice*, *Gone with the Wind*, et cetera.) One such lady was Miss Perendi, who taught me in second grade. For about a year Father rented a room from her family that was his first residence in Jánosháza. Miss Perendi was a strict disciplinarian, but a dry, humorless woman. She never married.

The other was Aunt Vili Fenyvesi, whom I never had as teacher, but who became a family friend, especially close to my mother, till the end of her life. She visited us often and we went to see her also. After Mother widowed, they spent much time together. She was a delightful friend and always fun, even for us kids. She was staying with us once in her later years, while I was also visiting home from America. Senility began to set in, but it took nothing away from her vibrant, irreverent personality that I knew, going way back. It made her more colorful and just as good company as she was for so many years .

18

High School Interrupted

After 4th grade I left my class, which went on to finish its upper four grades. I was one of only three boys to do so. The system then was, that those who wanted higher education, left grade school and instead of going to fifth grade, started first year of high school, (junior high, really) which then was for 8 years.

(When I talk about the Church on these pages, I always mean the Roman Catholic Church, unless stated otherwise. Hungary was a Catholic country. Catholics were the overwhelming majority. Through history, the Church was a force, able to shape events and exercise influence. Several saints came from the ranks of Hungarian royalty. The Church was in charge of elementary and most of middle level education. This changed after WW II, but then the change was drastic, the consequences devastating. Even after the downfall of communism, much that was lost, could not be restored. The damage was huge and manifold.)

In the fall of 1946, I went to join Józsi and Otti in Keszthely, at the Premonstratensian prep school, where they were in their fourth and third year, respectively. I was looking forward to the school, the dorm in the adjoining monastery, the lovely garden and the imposing gothic church at the center of town.

I found high school a difficult transition. After 4th grade, it was a profound shock and took me a while before I adjusted to the rigorous and demanding standards of a school run by monks. We lived in a student wing of the monastery, 6-7 kids to a bedroom in a dorm run by the order. Windows of our quarters looked down to the school yard. Study sessions -- *studium*, as it was called -- were supervised by one of the teachers. When a student had trouble with his grades, he was required to report to the studium supervisor before supper and was questioned about the day's homework. More than one unsatisfactory report and the weekend pass was in jeopardy. Alas, it took me a while before I had free pass, as a regular part of my weekend.

The first written class exercise/test in Latin was for us, to copy two paragraphs from our book. I thought it was a very easy assignment. Instructions were simple: copy as is, skip a line after the title. By stroke of luck, I thought, my Latin teacher, Ágoston Ipoly, *"Guszti Bácsi"*, as everybody called him, (Uncle Gus in English) was our studium supervisor. He came in a few minutes before the 2 P.M. start and put on his desk our Latin test booklets. He was doing his own homework of correcting tests while we were studying.

I couldn't just sit down with my books. I had to see my test. Amid idle talk, I dug into the pile and put my I booklet on top. He picked up his red pencil and he was ready to begin. I was looking forward to my first and surest A. This way I expected to see my good grade before my studium really began.

He took the booklet. Opened it. After a brief glance, he drew a firm line with his red pencil, diagonally on the whole page and wrote two F-s on it, one for content, one for neatness. He closed the booklet, put it on his right, beginning to build his *done* stack. One down, some 40 more still to go.

I was stunned. In my disbelief, I haltingly asked his reason. He looked up at me.

"You didn't skip a line" -- said he with a plain face, as he was pulling down the next booklet.

I was devastated and desperate. "But *both* grades F?"

"When it is F for a major reason, it is F for both" -- he said, without flinching.

There was no mercy and no appeal.

So, I met Uncle Gus -- was my fist, morose thought. What else can go wrong? What other indignities will I have to suffer? Little did I know, that there was a lot more to the old guy than first seemed. My brothers told me in advance that he was one of the toughest teachers. A week before, when I found out that he was to be my *class master*, I still looked forward with casual optimism to my first year in high school, thinking that he can't be all that bad. My brothers were more or less right. After I got to know all the teachers, some of them only by reputation through friends, I ranked him about third on my list for toughness. Lucky me, the two top guys on my list taught only in the upper classes. Uncle Gus demanded good work in class and assigned plenty homework. In and out of the class room, he was a jovial man of frequent practical jokes at our expense -- or should I say -- for our and his own entertainment. Later we became good friends. I visited him many times in his room. He taught us Latin and Hungarian, but he was a physics expert, an electric engineer, a wizard with radios. He taught the languages, because as class master he had to teach at least one subject. As first year students -- really, just glorified 5th graders -- physics was not yet in our curriculum.

(I made up the title "class master", because I found no English equivalent for it, or a comparative title in schools here. A teacher, who was assigned to a class and had special responsibilities for that class, was the class master. Uncle Gus was that for us. He was to take us all the way to graduation, and after the end of the 8th year, to *matura* exam -- more about which, a few pages hence. -- That was, however, not to be, because the communists redesigned the school system, disrupting higher education two years later.)

Uncle Gus took us on a few picnics and was the best of sports.

Once during a class outing, he wagered with us, saying: "I will eat my head", ... if you guys can do ... whatever. I think it was that we had to walk home without whining, from about a 10 mile distance at the end of a long day's frolic and fun. This was a challenge. We had to win the bet -- and we did. He improvised a little on his bet, by "borrowing" a hard boiled egg from one of his *non-whiner* students. He peeled it. With a pencil, he drew on it a kind of *smiley face*. Under it he wrote: "Guszti Bácsi". That done, our illustrious class master gulped it down with two big bites, and pronounced the bet settled. We actually applauded him, that must have been for distinguished achievement in acting in a comedy role. We arrived home fresh, jolly and felt entertained.

He remained a friend of my parents for a long time. After his order was dissolved and members dispersed by the regime, he became the pastor in Zalaerdõd, the same parish where years before we had our memorable feast up on the cherry tree. My parents and Józsi, who also stayed in Hungary in 1956, visited and got together with him off and on, through the years.

In 1948, after the communist regime dissolved monastic orders, it placed all religious denominational schools under state control. It dismissed an unimaginable treasure trove of knowledge, pedagogic skill and scholarly devotion of several thousands of monks and teachers of the many Christian schools, and simply threw them out. Most of the friars went to small town parishes, filling spots where priests were needed. Faculties were staffed from a new generation of lay teachers with less education, dedication and with sorely deficient expertise. It was done with the goal of total control over the education of the country's youth.

My two years in Keszthely (1946-48) were mostly enjoyable. It was a new experience with dormitory living that suited me well. Breaking in us freshmen on the first day, the upper-class members took us to the "agricultural yard", separated from the school yard by a heavy wood gate, and there to the straw stack. We all had in hand our straw-sack for a filling. I was amazed, how much straw could be stuffed into one of those sack-mattresses. When I thought I was done, the guys smiled and pointed out my inadequacy by pushing down on the middle of the sack.

"You don't want to leave it like that, do you?" -- one asked. "You don't want to sleep in a donkey-sack! Stuff it hard and stuff it even, really pack it hard in the middle."

Donkey-sack was a poorly stuffed sack, that would soon sag and resemble a hammock. It would be uncomfortable, and its owner subject to daily ridicule. (Even in a well stuffed sack, at the end of the year when we dumped our straw, most of it became spent, flattened strands.)

I was fortunate. Józsi and Otti were there to help me get my feet wet in dormitory living and the trying adventure of high school. We were about 20 boys living in this dormitory, operated by the order. Ours was much better than the other, larger, hotel-like Rákos dorm, which was privately run. Here we could be in daily contact with all the teachers who had their rooms in the adjoining hallway. I liked our facilities better. It was a thick-walled, nicely decorated, old cloister building with an easy commute to school.

Only about 5-6% of the student body was girls. We had none in my class. In his class, Otti had several, mostly cute ones. Boys and girls had separate classes for gym. For boys it was twice a week in the yard, weather permitting. Gym class for the girls, all classes together, was always during the last hour of the day. At one occasion, we were up in the dorm, in our quarters on the third floor. The last hour class was canceled, for some reason. I noticed a few upper-class guys, eagerly watching and snickering at the girls, doing calisthenics in the yard below. They were dressed in the customary black, *glott* shorts. The boys got careless and gave themselves away by an occasional giggle or comment. I also looked out for a moment, but did not join the big guys. The teacher heard something, looked up and spotted them. He made a threatening comment and later demanded disciplinary action. I was surprised by the severity of the punishment. I even heard dismissal from school mentioned. They got away with restriction of upper-class privileges for a month.

To illustrate my family's relationship with the monks in Keszthely, I will recount our summer stint as harvest workers in the previously mentioned agricultural yard. The monastery owned and had been cultivating land, that supported the order and the schools. The main crop was wheat. Otti's class master, Father Gergely Porpáczi was in charge of all the farming activities. He was a strong, attractive man, always sporting a tan, a testament to his many outdoor activities. He had regular employees, who were hired full time for year-round, tilling the soil and tending to animals. They harvested the grains earlier and left it dry a few weeks. When we arrived, it was already in the yard, ready for the thresher.

For the busy harvest season, Father Gergely needed all the helping hands he could get. In the middle of summer in 1947, Father sent us to help in the noisy, dusty work, the last phase in the harvesting process. Józsi, Otti and I went and stayed in the dorm, ate with the others and worked in the yard for two weeks. Józsi really relished it. He always liked and had a good understanding of farm chores. He did the hardest part. He collected straw as it was fed out of the thresher and carried huge stacks of it on a long, wooden skewer, over his head. His huge toothpick was up-righted for him by a helper. After that it was his job to hold his top-heavy load vertical and carry it to the corner of the yard, where with his many loads, he was building a rick of straw, ready to be used as bedding for the animals or stuffed in sacks at the start of school. It got gradually harder as the stack got taller. His shirtless body was full of red dots, the marks from the hundreds of stabs by the sharp edges of broken straw. We all got a deep tan by the end. Being useful and a measurable help, was satisfying. It was a good summer job, but it was all gratis. The feeling of work well done and our keep for a fortnight was our wage. Father wanted it that way. We had stories to tell our friends at home and classmates at the start of school in the fall.

During school year we had all our meals in the main dining room and ate the same meals as our teachers. I considered this a privilege and enjoyed the elite company. The dining room was a large, beautiful, elaborately painted and decorated chamber, with a domed ceiling, in the old monastery wing. It was quite dark. The windows, cut into its heavy walls, looked down to the school yard. The thickness of the walls and the small size if the windows indicated that it was a very old building. Our dorm supervisor ate with us, dormitory residents. Good table manners and quiet conversation were expected. We took care not to violate these rules. Only a few times were students at the top end of the table reminded to lower the level of discourse. For the first year, as one of three freshmen, I sat at the end of the table, where the supervisor also chose to sit. Father Radnóczi was the most friendly of all the teachers. I looked forward to our meals every day. We learned from him a lot about a great deal of things. We did not spend much time in idle chatter, but had, what may be called light, intellectual conversation. We questioned him on serious, sometimes scholarly toppings and tried to engage him on things we found interesting. He was for us, at the low end, a free daily source of education on subjects of mostly our choosing. It is hard to imagine a better environment to open young minds and introduce them to the world of knowledge and wisdom. I am sure, those mealtime sessions had influenced my thinking and provoked my curiosity to much, in which I found intellectual pleasure in later life.

We had all three meals in the dining room. The most formal was the main meal at 1 P.M. Everybody was there for that. It was just after the last class ended. Time for the other two meals were flexible and not attended by all the monks, though the students were always there, together. We were excused only for serious reasons.

We prayed together before each meal. After the prayer of the midday meal, one of the students, a designated lector, went to the window. He read from a book for about 10 minutes. This is a custom in monasteries, where young monks provide solemn entertainment to their elders. Conversation commenced only after the lector finished and returned to his seat. Reading material varied. Ours was secular, perhaps because we students were the readers. We were assigned the task in rotation. I did not enjoy my periodic *15 minutes of fame*, when it was my turn. I found it too stressful for a ten years old, to stand up and read unknown material in front of my friends and to those erudite men. They were all scholars of the first order, whom I just might have to meet the next day, with yesterday's embarrassment still vivid in their mind. Yet, I found the reading a challenge that I had to overcome, improve my halting reading, increase my vocabulary and gain confidence.

The only serious problem I had during my two years, was with the lone lay teacher in the faculty, Mr. György, who taught math and drawing. He was a pompous ass, full of himself, often bragging of his many talents. At first I liked him -- as I liked most of my teachers throughout my schooling -- until I realized that he didn't like me. He had his favorites but a few of us he ignored, liked to ridicule and even treated with contempt. (He was just a jerk.) Math was not my strong suit. It took me a little time to digest new concepts. I should have sought out more help from classmates, as I did later. With a little help I could have done better in that class. He gave me none of that. Instead he enjoyed humiliating me. I should have had a C, but he flunked me. It ruined my first summer, because my parents made me study several hours a day. I was required to take a make-up exam before I could register for my second year. My mother took me to Keszthely a day early and sat in on my informal session with him. Mr. György behaved much better -- I could tell.

He sat down across from me. He pointed to the ink well on the desk.

"What's the circumference of this circle?" -- he asked.

I measured the radius and in less than a minute, gave him the correct answer -- no calculator, of course.

"Oh," -- he said -- "err..., what about the area of the opening?"

Similar process followed. To finish the exam, he asked me a question about the calculation process and a few more about similar easy stuff. I was done in five minutes. I could have passed this test in class, and certainly on the regular final. Now, with the load off my mind, I could enjoy the fruits of my summer's drudgery. That was the last time I was angry at Mr. György. -- I saw him about seven years later, under different circumstances in Tihany, during an international motorcycle race. It was after I graduated from high school. He did not see me. Otti pointed him out to me, at a distance. He was sitting on the grass by the roadside, also watching the bikes whiz by. I was tempted to talk to him but, did not. I kept myself from saying something I might regret. This way, I didn't satisfy my curiosity, what our conversation would have been like, after so many years, on neutral ground and under more pleasant circumstances.

In Keszthely, we continued our piano lessons with a kind old lady, Aunt Carrie. Studying with her, was more of a chore, because we had to go to her house to practice, not only for lessons. I made less progress than I did with Uncle Lala. Aunt Carrie was sweet but she did not discipline, which I would've welcomed. Instead, I just muddled through my two years with her. She was a darling old lady, but as a teacher, not very effective. We saw her occasionally during our later visits to Keszthely.

School rule was, that we were allowed to go home for two recesses, about two weeks for Christmas and one for Easter. Our parents came to visit a few times in between.

The winter of 1946-47 was unusual. One day, during Christmas vacation, we had an ice storm, with a lot of freezing rain. The quite fitting name for it in Hungarian is *"ólmos eső"*, (lead-rain) referring to the fact that it seems to weigh as lead, on the things it covers, because it sticks to anything, as it instantly freezes. This time we got an extraordinary dose of lead-rain. Damage to trees, power lines and buildings was huge. Ice covered everything for months. Gloom depressed the psyche and spirit of people. I know it depressed me. A long period of sub-freezing weather followed.

Father came home and told us that this was a different kind of freezing rain, one that he had never seen before. He had to stop every half mile to scrape ice from the windshield. It froze so fast and hard that the wiper could not handle it. (Cars then had no heat.) -- The rain kept falling all night and part of the next day. The result was a 4 in. thick solid ice layer, that covered everything. Utility wiring suffered much damage. A long cold period followed. Within days we received news that Christmas recess was extended. Later, it was extended twice more, until early March.

Józsi and Otti received new ice skates for Christmas that year. During that long vacation they lived on their skates. Roads and sidewalks were one big ice field. By the end of winter they could glide and do figures that was the envy of their younger brothers, while we stumbled, ran and just tried sliding on the ice. (I received skates next Christmas. That winter was so mild that I was able to go out only twice. I felt the thin ice bending under my feet. Tomi did not get skates even then, because Father found only one pair, despite looking everywhere.)

When we returned to Keszthely in mid-March, the ice cover was still intact. It was depressing not to see anything else solid under our feet. Slowly, the weather eased and one happy day I first spotted real dirt, next to a sewer by the sidewalk. I never forget my joy. As if the sun has liberated me from a nearly three-month long, gloomy hiatus. I felt that my exile in the wilderness has ended. Soon we could play soccer again in the school yard. A delayed, but very nice spring followed the hard winter.

I saw my first Tarzan movie in the spring of 1947. It was one of the seminal events of my student days. We were all prepared to go home at the end of the week for Easter vacation. On the Friday before, two friends were explaining to me at breakfast, that last night they saw this American movie about a family in the forest. They said it was a different kind of movie and worth seeing . They tried to describe *jungle* to me. I knew the word, but had trouble forming an image of it and especially life in the deep forest.

That evening I went to see it, quite curious, but with only moderate expectations. The title was: *Tarzan's Secret Treasure*. It was about greedy explorers, with their tropical hats, looking for gold -- but to me much more, true magic from beginning to end. Early in the film Tarzan, Jane and Boy are swinging on jungle vines. Then they follow each other in diving into a lake from their perch near the top of trees. I couldn't get enough of Johnny Weismuller, as he yodeled his signature cry.

The jungle movie took me to a world of wonder, one that I could never imagine. Saturday after school we went home in a lovely, sunny day. That, and my memory of Tarzan made me a very happy young man. There was one other Tarzan movie imported for domestic viewing. I saw that too, before it disappeared in some communist vault. It was *Tarzan in New York*. In that, he dives from the top of Brooklyn Bridge into the East River. Margaret O'Brien is Jane in both, with, I think, Johnny Sheffield, as Boy.

There were three other pictures that I remember well. One was the first movie I ever saw: *The Magic Air Plane*, an American stunt-flying picture. It was perfect as the first movie for a six year old. Fun and wild aviation tricks all the way, including flying through a hanger, that had doors open on opposite sides. -- Another was a French film in 1953: *Fanfan La Tulipe*, with Gerard Philipe and Gina Lollobrigida. Heroics, swashbuckling, love and romance in the best tradition. She was gorgeous, he handsome and the story perfect, I thought. To me, Hollywood never matched that. -- In 1955, we went to see several times, a lovely but sad Swedish movie: *And They Danced All Summer*. The main attraction was Ulla Jacobson, a haunting, sweet beauty, a Greta Garbo type in her young days. I saw her later in two Hollywood movies, but they could not compare to a love story with tragic ending, of two innocents in rural Sweden. The film was *synchronized* (subtitles) and the whole country was talking about how perfect the voices were, to compliment the acting and how they were able to recreate the sensitive, refined language of the original. Later Miss Jacobson came to Hollywood and starred in a WW II film about German preparations to produce an atomic bomb. It is based on true events in Norway: *The Heroes of Telemark*. Good movie.

In recent years I saw three of the mentioned American films on television but I really hope to see Fanfan La Tulipe. Perhaps I shouldn't. Seeing it as an adult so many years later, might damage my youthful illusions. I know, if I catch it anywhere, I will not be able to resist. -- Recently I heard that a remake was done in Hollywood. I want to see that -- but can it live up to the original? Not likely. It disappeared too fast from the movie repertoire.

I think the second Tarzan movie was the last American film imported by Hungary, for a long time. We saw no western film for several years, a loss I tried to make up for, later. Hollywood made good films then, unlike today, when special effect people create weird, grotesque looking characters. Evil or benign, I have no patience for this type of "stories". Give me human stories, that are well written about situations I can believe in . -- Theaters only showed films made in the Soviet Union, Hungary and other satellite countries. Some of them were so called "movement" (i.e. communist movement) movies, where proletariat heroes sang passionate movement songs about tractors, factories and a myriad of other boring socialist claptrap, to glorify the Soviet Communist Party. It was a different experience, but did only temporary damage in our love for movies. For school kids, they were compulsory viewing. The whole school was commandeered out to see them. They were most boring, but mandatory, made as propaganda instruments, in the style of *socialist realism.* It was considered part of our education. We saw it as monumental waste that engendered only resentment and contempt for an alien culture. We wanted none of this multiculturist junk, especially at the expense of our own.

Stalin appeared in some of them. Not in person, only played by an actor. I remember, in one movie he was gardening, with hoe in hand and was visited by a comrade for a friendly chat. I described it to Father and asked if the scene could be authentic. He set me strait.

"Son, when they show a political leader peacefully gardening in the back yard, you can safely bet that he is a despot."

In the early 1950s, they began to import Italian and French pictures. We wouldn't miss any of those. Our thirst for long shunned western culture was great, while the one imposed on us was stifling. These movies were a solace and much sought-after entertainment. Later they also imported some Swedish and English movies. By then, our home grown film industry also recovered, acquired limited freedom and was able turn away from the propaganda industry, that they exclusively were before.

After the film industry regained its independence, several notable movies came out to the West. Twice, a picture made in Hungary, won academy award as best foreign film.

Hungarian film makers and actors have a high reputation. There were some renowned directors in Hollywood, such as Joseph Pasternak and George Czukor.

19

Family Ties To Keszthely

Keszthely was a lovely city of about 16,000 permanent residents, a good number of students and a lot of vacationers during the tourist season. After my small hometown it seemed big, but soon became my favorite city. I was excited that I could attend school there. It is located at the west end of lovely lake Balaton. For many years we often went to Keszthely on Sundays, for a one-day outing. It included first a swim and time on a well kept, pristine sandy beach, then visits with friends and frequenting one of the sweet shops for ice cream and pastry.

There lived Aunt Lujza, a gregarious, lovely lady who had a gorgeous villa, part of which she rented out in the summer. She lived on that income and the meager pension she received after her late professor husband. She widowed much too young, but remained a woman of good cheer, satisfied with her lot in life. Seeing her was always the pleasant conclusion to our visits. She had elegance and style, had a deep alto voice, that she spoke with a *Palóc* accent, a kind of Hungarian twang from the northern region. She was a kind, generous woman, but did not suffer fools gladly.

Once on a balmy afternoon we were winding up our Sunday visit in a restaurant garden. Father ordered refreshments. Aunt Lujza was served her usual beer. She took one sip and poured the rest on the garden gravel without flinching, as the most natural reaction to lukewarm beer in a warm summer day. The waiter scrambled and came up with another, this time a cool glass replacement, in minutes.

We had other friends in the city. One of our best friends from Jánosháza, the Pallér family moved back to Keszthely, where Aunt Klári, Mrs. Pallér, grew up. She was my mother's favorite friend. We were still kids when they moved to Jánosháza. They were a very attractive family. Mr. Gáspár Pallér became the first director of the academy. Aunt Klári was a lovely, gracious lady, pretty, with personality to mach. I saw her only once more in later years on my visit home, by then a widow. She died in the 1980s. Their children still live in Keszthely. Mother, after she widowed, sold our house in Jánosháza and also moved to Keszthely. She bought a neat little apartment and renewed old friendships. The more important reason for her move was, so that she be close to my sister, who was by then married and already living there.

Yes, I said *sister.* I did not mention her before, because she was not part of our life throughout my childhood. She was born on 1950 September 23, when I was 14 years old and away from home much of the year. I first saw her at age three months as I came home from high school for Christmas vacation. She was a late gift to my parents. Mother was 40 at the birth of her fifth child. I saw Marika only on my vacations until she was four. After that I spent a lot of time with her. It was an interesting relationship. A carpenter made a child seat that was fastened onto the frame of my bicycle. I took her with me everywhere I went. She was sitting in front of me on her little perch, while we were riding and talking. I had time and found joy in opening her mind and teach her about a lot of things. She was the new and interesting addition to our family after such a long gap. As I was told many times, after Józsi was born a boy, they hoped that each of us that followed would be a girl. We all were elated, that after 17 years it happened. I spent a lot of time with Marika during her fifth and sixth years, when I was living home for extended times. After 1956, our contacts were reduced to my infrequent visits to Hungary, writing letters and very rare telephone calls. For this reason I know less about her adolescent and student days. She became a cosmetologist and later a private teacher of German. She married György Nagy, a resident of Keszthely, where they lived and had two children.

It can be said that eventually we all moved to Keszthely. To round out this subject; in 1998, Otti and Helma bought a house, renovated it and are staying there a good part of each summer. Klaudia, their daughter, a master jeweler, lives in Aachen. She is a world traveler, adventurer and a precious niece. -- Her younger brother is the other Miklós Magyar in the family. He is a master chef and restaurateur and a skillful manager of his two restaurants. He learned his craft in schools and by apprenticing with master chefs -- the last time in Tihany. -- On one of his many vacations in Hungary he met Anett Kiss. Soon they were talking about marriage. He asked her to move to Germany, but she preferred to live in the country of her birth. Things worked out, when Miklós moved to Hungary and opened his own restaurant, *Pikant,* that is one of most popular eateries in Tata, Anett's hometown near Budapest. In 2002 he opened his second restaurant that is also doing well. He found his place in his father's old country. He speaks Hungarian well, but with a slight German intonation.

In 1954, after selling Little Somlyó, Father bought a vineyard in Ábrahámhegy, a quiet resort village, not far from Keszthely. Tomi and I spent most of the following summer, helping the masons and carpenters, to build a cottage and wine cellar. My older brothers were in the army during that time. The building was ready by harvest time in the fall. We had the chance to enjoy it only through the summer and autumn of 1956 -- one season only, before our family was broken up by the revolution and its aftermath.

The small villa became our vacation place, where we went often to enjoy the lake and work the vineyard. It had quality grapes, including a few rows of heavenly tasting table grapes. These species we collectively called *fragrant grapes*, for they have a faint sweet, fragrant smell on the vine.

Grape harvesting was an old, honored tradition, with deeply rooted rituals, as it is throughout the wine regions of the world. *Bread and wine* are the most cited nourishment in the Bible and all literature, even more than *milk and honey*. They connote a life of plenty, good living, affluence -- and good times.

I had a chance to take part in the harvest only twice -- our first harvest, before I left the country and once more, during a visit home. It is a great party of merriment where people work hard, but do it with spirit that is laden with expectations of a bountiful harvest. Before the day came, we had to protect the grapes from hungry birds. My old Uncle Pista had that job for several years. He, the widower of my aunt Márika, moved in for a few weeks and hissed, clapped and yelled, to chase away the birds each day, especially in the pre-dawn hours.

Harvest, or "szüret" concluded with a feast with great food, last year's wine and freshly squeezed "*must*", (pr. moosht), the sweet grape juice, made only hours before.

In 1999, Tomi retired from his aeronautical engineering job in Munich and moved back to Ábrahámhegy. He built a house near the old villa that we worked on so much together. His life's pleasure is still aviation. He does it when he can, working with, and flying sail planes, even trying to make some money doing it. All his four children, Tomi, Danny, Katalin and Janine bought houses nearby in recent years. As kids, they spent many summers in Hungary and kept their attraction to the land, to old memories and to the memory of their grandparents.

Keszthely became a city while I was going to school there in the late 1940s. As I remember, the privilege was granted, when the town's population reached, I think, 15,000. It was an occasion for celebration. Uncle Gus talked to us about it in class. To him, the city was an ideal place to live. Not too big, so he knows almost everybody. People greet him on the street in a friendly way. Still it is big enough to offer many cultural advantages. He was right. Keszthely boasted many things that other larger cities lacked.

The city had a moderate level of industry, but ample amenities and services to accommodate tourists and regularly returning vacationers. In those years we were just beginning our long-term romance with Keszthely. In addition to its many attractions, the lovely park, lake shore, it boasted an agricultural college, with a beautiful baroque building. It has expanded since then and it now is a university. The city has great cultural and architectural treasures.

The family of Count György Festetics is integral to the city's history. They are first mentioned in the 15th century as prominent, influential and wealthy nobles, who founded high schools and institutions of higher learning. Their beneficial stamp is seen everywhere. The *Helikon*, a biannual cultural event, named after the home of the muses in ancient Greece, cultivated literature, which many of Hungary's noted poets (Daniel Berzsenyi, Károly Kisfaludy, at al.) regularly attended. *Georgikon* is an Agricultural University, that the count founded. He also donated 900 acres as experimental farms, to aid instruction. (His other noted donation was 20,000 acres of farmland that he divided and gifted to 4,000 landless peasant families.)

The city's greatest treasure is the imposing castle and large estate, the home for many generations of the Festetics dynasty. The lovely stone pillars and wrought iron gate is prominent at the end of the Kossuth Street, which today is a pedestrian mall, full of shops and restaurants, with outdoor seating. (The house, where composer Karl Goldmark was born, is also on Kossuth Street.) It is closed to motorized traffic. Behind the gate is a park, the palace, arboretum, stables and other outer buildings. Part of the castle complex is now a home to a museum of hunting, with exhibits of large game and hunting weapons. Other buildings are under renovation and will be used for other exhibits with different collections. Harmony and architectural beauty throughout the estate is pleasing and a feast for the eyes.

The castle is one of the best examples of the baroque style. It has a symmetrical design, with graceful wings, extending right and left from a central tower, which dominates the landscape. The main building is a home for a medieval arms museum with extensive displays. Visitors, are required to wear slippers, so the unique parquet floor is not damaged. Large unfurnished rooms can be rented for weddings, concerts and large-scale public events.

The lack of furniture is the sorry result of the plunder that took place in the early years under communism. The estate was closed for a while, then converted into military barracks in the early

1950s. This was the period when much of the buildings' contents were pilfered. The library was walled shut at the entrance and it, with its contents were saved, intact. (A cultured and sympathetic Ukrainian Soviet officer used a ruse. He declared it "contaminated" and built a wall at the door to protect the treasured content.)

A friend of mine told me years later that as a buck private in the Hungarian Army, he was housed in the castle and was witness to the destruction. People were reduced to savagery. They had no wood to feed the fireplaces and stoves, so they cut down trees from the arboretum, without care or knowledge as to which trees were rare or valuable. The largest ones made the best firewood. Restoration work today includes the planting of new trees.

An impressive bronze statue of Count György Festetics, with minor figures and agricultural symbols, was standing on the main square, in front of our high school, when I was a student there. In 1950, it was boarded up with plywood, creating a picture of an enormous shapeless box, as if to protect something from a coming hurricane. This vulgar monstrosity ruined the view and the atmosphere of the square and looked even more out of place with the existing beds of lovely flowers around it. A year later the box was taken down but the statue was moved to the castle grounds, where it still stands. In its place, they put a Soviet military monument. The statue of the Count represented the old world and his image was considered undesirable to the regime. The fact that he was a wealthy aristocrat, regardless of his many contributions and that he was dead for over a hundred years, didn't matter. He was still a threat. He was *class enemy*. His person, history and memory had to be besmirched and eradicated. In that process, invaluable treasures were destroyed or stolen. As the official opinion makers reevaluated the past and rewrote history books, things were erased and new heroes anointed. Many Russians we never heard of, were named as inventors, explorers and other honored personalities of the humanities, sciences and the arts. Perhaps the most ridiculous cultural project was the rewriting of the dictionary. I kept a copy of my *Dictionary of Foreign Words*. The most striking feature of the book is, that many entries in it are Stalin's personal definitions of words, concepts and historical events

-- just imagine... ("Proletariat" alone, is a two-page propaganda rant, with references to the evils of capitalism and imperialism. It is ironic, that the biggest imperialist was accusing others with his own sins. He had half of Europe enslaved, six satellite countries in addition to 14 of the Soviet states.) I read some entries to my friends, just for laughs.

* * *

There was a lucky anomaly in this attack on our cultural traditions. One of our teachers, Father Klempa was allowed for a time, to remain the curator of the castle library. The castle was already closed, but he had the keys. This was before they walled it off for safe keeping. People such as he were not easy to replace, so he got a reprieve. I was fortunate to be one of a very few, who could enter the library with him. Father Klempa asked me one afternoon, if I would like to go with him to the castle.

I was elated and went eagerly. I didn't really know him that well, for I never had him as a teacher. He supervised our studium occasionally, so he knew me from there and also, just for us living so close to one another and seeing each other often in the building and at mealtime. He was reserved but a very busy man. He was the class master of the graduating class that year. I was honored to be asked, but had no inkling of what was in store for me. He was perhaps the only non-government person, who had a key to the estate. The building showed neglect, but the dominating architecture with its gilded decorations was still a pleasing sight as we approached. He opened the wrought iron gate, and walked through the large wood doors. I feasted my eyes on the gold relief decorations, carved wood and ornate plaster work.

Then he opened the tall elaborately carved door to the library. I was stunned and amazed as we entered. The place was a baroque jewel -- and intact. I admired the beautifully carved walnut panel throughout, with matching shelving and ladders. A graceful spiral staircase at the far end lead to a second level walkway. Ladders with wheels, silently rolling on rails in the floor and at the top, were used to reach the higher shelves of the lower level. I looked up. Old books, on elaborately carved, two-story high shelving and ornamental wood decorations made up the walls, leading my gaze to the ceiling fresco. The books and artwork were the collection of the family since the 16th century. The floor and the chandelier added more to my visual delight.

Father Klempa came there for a scholastic purpose. He was a Renaissance man, a serious scholar, who took ample time for his research. I wasn't bored for a minute, walking around and peeking into old books that were open on lecterns. -- We took a few books, locked up and started back. Leaving the library, we took the main stairway. It was another unforgettable sight, a suitable match for the wood paneling of the library. Family portraits of several generations of the Feststics family were on the wall, in walnut frames, carved in similar style to the library interior. The frames were set in the walnut paneling, as if the entire wall were a single, harmoniously carved piece. We went down and walked through arched hallways, under the arcades along the building, to the iron gates again, and back home to the monastery.

I thanked him on the way home for the privilege and his good company. I saw Father Klempa only once after I finished my schooling in Keszthely. He became a pastor nearby and later was consecrated as bishop of Veszprém.

My sister Marika widowed at age 50 in 2000, when her husband, Gyuri died of cancer. She had no pension and only limited income. She decided to enlarge and divide her house, fashion four apartments out of it and rent three of them. This should provide her a permanent and steady income. Planning and executing the entire job was to be done by his son, Gyuri, who was good in those things and had many friends whom he helped in similar work before. By the fall of 2001 the work progressed nicely and the house looked altogether different. Replacing the old, worn slate, it received a bright orange, ceramic shingle roof, giving the house an attractive look. Gyuri made other minor exterior refinements that made a big difference. Inside, he used good materials and fine workmanship, hiding all pipes and conduits. By spring of 2002, the house was fit for occupation.

During construction Marika moved in Otti's little apartment on

Queen Elizabeth Lane, that connects downtown Keszthely with
the beach-front park. It runs along the main city park, which holds
many precious memories for me. It was the first large park I got
to know. I discovered it on my first visit to the city when I was
in second or third grade. We walked it lengthwise, which made
it look even bigger. It was a well kept forest grove. As a child
of about seven, I marveled at its huge trees, clean walks, covered
with tiny beige pebbles. It was kept in immaculate condition. The
minor walks were leading to streets that entered the park on all
sides. There were many curves and frequent intersections of those
walks. I got lost a few times, trying to walk across it . Eventually
I made it, but found myself not exactly at the street I wanted to
get to. In the center of the park, where the main paths meet is a
clearing with flower beds, statues and a memorial to the Festetics
family. Under a domed, open structure a large marble plaque lists
their grants and other contributions to the city.

In later years the park suffered from neglect. Last summer I
saw one woman collecting rubbish. She was poorly dressed and
looked as if she were a gipsy. I saw her again in the fall, doing
the same chores, and mentioned her to my sister. Marika said she
knows her well and often helps her with alms. She is a very kind
woman, simple in more than one way, who occupies herself with
doing cleanup in the city, mostly in the parks. She depends on
people's good will and kindness. I thought she could be homeless,
with the negatives that it often implies, but she finds satisfaction in
what she does and generates goodwill doing it.

Mother's old efficiency apartment is now Otti's. It is on the
ground floor of a modern condo building. Mother bought it after
she sold our house in Jánosháza. Her view was of the park across
a street with light traffic, ideal for one, who likes nature and quiet.
She lived a simple life, satisfied with her lot. Daily walks from
her place to see Marika and the grandchildren was easy. Orsi,
the older, on her way home from school, liked to stop by, to see
Grandma, whose place was only a short distance away.

Near Keszthely there was another favorite place for us: Héviz,
a famous spa. It is a lake of about ¼ mile diameter, a near perfect
circle, with an extensive network of spired wooden structures,

open decking and wood walkways in the center, over the water. The structure is supported on concrete pillars. It took formidable engineering to build it. The lake is deep in the middle, but in other places, about ten feet down, one can feel the very loose volcanic mud, that is its soul and therapeutic value. The mud is dried, packed and sold throughout the world. One can hear many languages spoken by guests.

Somewhere in the middle, are springs of hot and cold water of volcanic origin. The lake temperature at the surface is about 90 degrees. The basin is criss-crossed by short and long runs of wood railing just above the surface as an aid to easy travel for bathers between sections under and around the labyrinth structure. There are benches under water. One doesn't have to be a good swimmer to get around or enjoy this balmy bath. Guests are advised to limit their stay in the lake to one hour at a time.

The main central structure houses all the cabins, dressing rooms, showers, massage and mud-rooms with spacious sun decks between sections. Its architecture and decoration makes it an inviting place. We visited it many times. Father found that the bath helped him with his rheumatism. He befriended the local colleague and they saw each other a lot when he vacationed there, treating his aches and pains, in his later years. Marika also worked there as a cosmetician, in a posh resort. Her clientele was almost exclusively German. She enjoyed their company and worked on improving her language skills. Years later she started teaching by giving private lessons, which is now her sole occupation.

There is a large triangle bench in Héviz Lake in a remote section, over deep water. It is known for conversation on risqué themes that is often conducted by its occupants. I was still a child, when I discovered it by chance, as I stopped there for a little rest while swimming across the lake. It was then, and I checked it out a few summers ago, still is the bench for dirty jokes. It was a shock to me then, but for a reason, I cannot recall, I stayed as long as possible. I don't remember any of those old jokes but I still know their flavor. I did not tell my parents, only mentioned to Gale. "That's nothing new", he said, "Everybody knows it." What surprised me most, was that half the jokesters were women. I was shocked when I first heard a raunchy joke out of the mouth of a respectable looking lady. -- It was one of my rites of passage.

20

From High School To Grade School -- Then Back Again

In 1947 the government reconfigured the system of elementary and middle schooling. In the new system, the lower four years of the traditionally 8 year high school were abolished and became grades 5-8. (for ages 10-14). It was also the time when the teaching orders were dissolved. With this change, there was little difference between schools. Education was downgraded to the lowest denominator. My parents saw no purpose in leaving us in a distant school in Keszthely and brought us home. I continued in Jánosháza. After completing two years high school in the old regime, the next level for me, was 7th grade. The upper four years of the old high school curriculum became years 1-4 in the new system. No more Latin or religion class and no more boy scouting. Instead, I became a *pioneer*, whether I wanted to or not. The nice green necktie was replaced by an ugly shade of blue and, if one would measure up to socialist standards, the promise of a red one, just like those worn by our *examples*, whom we were to follow and emulate -- the Soviet children. It was nauseating. Occasionally leaders were bribing us with a new soccer ball and other equipment, each time accompanied by a pioneer meeting, where the state and the party were praised. We were repeatedly prompted to remember their generosity, as long as we live. -- Our beloved Premonstratensians were nationalized, as were all other religious order-run schools, and staffed with all new faculty of party approved, inexperienced amateurs.

József and Otti also left Keszthely. They moved back home and continued high school in Sümeg, a small city 12 miles away. They took the train daily, with a group of about 20 kids, Pali Hajós among them. A lot more about Pali coming in a while. I too, was expected to attend Sümeg High, but things turned out differently.

For the 7th grade, my place for school was the old civic school, that suffered bomb damage in 1945. As the opening ceremonies for the school year in 1948 were being prepared, we lined up by class. Then I noticed that the class master for 7th grade was Mr. Zsankó -- Laci Zsankó, really -- but known to us from then on, by his formal name: László Zsankó, teacher. I knew him well, as did many of my classmates. His father was a local tailor and previously I was on first name basis with him, as I was with most men his age. His younger brother was just a year older than Józsi. I soon realized that this comfortable familiarity was about to change. He became a teacher and with that, an adult. I was then at an awkward age, self-conscious in addressing people of his age group. I was still a boy, but saw people like him as grownups. I thought that it was up to them to allow boys my age, to call them by familiar names, as it used to come naturally just a few years ago. Mr. Zsankó was now a teacher, and things have changed for good -- or at least for a few years, until I caught up -- not in years, but in other ways, to bridge the gap, so to speak.

On that, his first day as a teacher, he was marching up and down the hallway, being stern, demanding respect and quiet. Soon it was obvious that it was an act, but I understood. He wanted to establish respect, before we, old friends, only several years younger, ruin it for him, by addressing him by first name or make jokes that could make him uncomfortable or subject of ridicule. He made a clever end run, to keep us in line on the first day and lay down a marker -- just in case. It took no more than a few days and everything was back to normal. Well, not entirely, because he was never again "Laci". From then on he was "Mr. Teacher". With his self-confidence secure, he again became a friendly person and a helpful caretaker of our class. His easy, good nature returned and all was well. We were perhaps the last class that knew him before he went away and got his degree. The upcoming classes knew him more and more as an adult and member of the older generation, entitled to unquestioned respect and deference.

We watched him a lot, playing table tennis. He was the best. We also played the game many hours and enjoyed it a lot. Next to soccer, it was our favorite pastime. We were playing it throughout the winter. Ping-Pong balls were the only problem. They were scarce and of poor quality, made of caoutchouck, a vegetable gum based material, the *plastic* of its day. We repeatedly used acetone to repair cracked balls and this way got a few more games out of them.

Mr. Zsankó was popular. He courted, then married Magda Lasch, the most beautiful girl in town. (A few years later I fell in love with her little sister, who seemed suddenly growing up. I never told her. I thought, it was a little early for her but also, I was timid and felt awkward approaching a girl, so much younger. She still lives in Jánosháza. She is a friend of my sister. Marika said I should tell her about my long-ago, one-sided romance. If nothing else, we'll have a chance to muse together on sweet, old, innocent times.)

Mr. Zsankó became a favorite teacher. We were happy to have him as our class master. To honor him, one year we erected for him a maypole. It was a serious class project. We went to the forest and cut a tall, (40 ft.) slender, straight ash, cleaned it of all the bark and branches, except for a 6 foot section at the top. We decorated it with garlands, ribbons and the requisite wine bottle, dangling up there, high. Raising it was the big challenge. By tradition, maypoles were put up as a surprise, the night before May 1st. When we were done with the work, we sang for him, to commemorate the event and, I'm sure, woke him up. (This was at his parents house, where he then still lived.) Such a late-night excursion was not strictly in accordance with school rules. But we were confident that this one time regulation would be overlooked.

Father was also honored with a maypole, once. I do not recall who put it up for him. I heard that it was a group of young men in the village. We were all very proud. I wish I had a picture of it.

21

Stage Plays And Other Things

I always enjoyed stage plays and took part in many, beginning in early childhood. Mother was a sensitive and artistic person. She was active in school plays in her day, and also as an adult. I saw her on stage a few times. Father enjoyed it as well and even as a middle-aged pillar of the community, had time for the theater. I'm told, by the time the play was ready for the stage, he sometimes edited his lines more to his liking, but nobody seemed to mind.

I had the lead in most plays and for some reason, I fell in love with many of my *leading ladies.* Before I get to that, I must mention Kati Barát. She was the cutest in my kindergarten class. Somehow the word got out that I liked her -- probably I blabbered -- and I was in trouble with the boys. They teased me to no end. My solution to get out of the situation no little boy should be in, I thought up a weird plan. Once carefully beat her up for no apparent reason. The act of cruelty was done only for show and I know how careful I was not to hurt her. I was severely reprehended by Aunt Karola, our sweet old teacher, but otherwise she and also Kati considered it a closed matter. Many years later I apologized to her. We chuckled over old times. She hardly remembered, but said she understood and has forgiven me. I was relieved and thought of my old, tender sentiments toward her.

My first show business crush was Snow White, Ili Fiszter, to my role as the Prince. She had a sweet face, which then, I thought was beautiful. I'm sure it was. I never dared to tell her, because I sensed nothing on her part to encourage me. Perhaps she was just bashful. -- I talked her into a customed photo session in costumes, at our house. The picture is in front of the beautiful and notorious grandfather clock of prior fame, involving a certain Russian major. Everything went well, but even that didn't do the trick and the one sided affair eventually faded. I never found out if she cared for me at all. Looking back on it, I can now take that, as a "no", for I failed to detect evidence to the contrary. There were other musicals and plays in which I enjoyed taking part. They were on stage at the house of culture, always well attended. People flocked to such entertainment, the few small-town diversions, beside movies.

During 8th grade, teachers were instructed to encourage students to continue their education. In my class of 24 students, I was one of only three, who needed no such encouragement. I was surprised that most of the kids needed prodding to plan their future by going on to high school.

Behind this otherwise laudable effort by the state, was a self serving purpose to promote the creation of a new leader class. The leadership was desperate to hang onto power in an atmosphere, where it was an instrument of oppression. Paranoia possessed the small group in power. Fear and uncertainty took over the consciousness of the rest of us. Children of intelligentsia were mostly excluded from institutions of higher learning, unless associated with the Communist Party. During the Stalinist years in Hungary (1947-1953) everything beyond the most basic family matters became the business of the state. Family matters were also under close scrutiny if they were perceived in any way a threat, or even had a potential to be such. This was a party directive -- party and state being the same -- to conduct class warfare by putting the highest number possible, into higher education, from the offspring of the worker and peasant classes.

By the end of the school year of 1949-50, only two of the kids from those selected classes were persuaded to go to high school.

After 1948, all high schools were "nationalized" and became state schools, so I applied at the closest school in Celldömölk. Early in the summer in 1950, I received a rejection without a stated a reason. Using contacts through friends we tried to gain entry, to no avail. In late July, I received a letter from the county education department, reversing the earlier ruling, stating that I was "accepted". Again, no reason was given. All was fine, we thought. Then, on the day before schools opened, a new letter came, stating that my name was "erased" from the list of students. This again, with no explanation, or opportunity for appeal.

22

Pannonhalma

A few days after final rejection something completely unexpected happened. In the last days of August, the regime returned eight high schools to the denominations, six to Catholic orders and two that were operated by Protestant educational entities before the 1948 nationalization. (Later I found out that this was the result of long secret negotiations between the state, the bishops and the Vatican, and separately with representatives of the Protestant churches. For this seemingly benign gesture, the government ratified its right to interfere in church affairs and maintain leverage over the church's activities, through the newly created State-Church Council.)

This agreement was startling and serendipitous with its impeccable timing and a fortunate turn for me. One of the schools returned to the monks was Pannonhalma, the most prestigious high school in the country. I have never visited the place before, but I heard about it, its history and grandeur.

Father said, as he read about it in the papers:

"Son, we are lucky. It seems like divine intervention. We are going there tomorrow."

On a bright Sunday morning, September 3 to be exact, the two of us took the 2½ hour drive to the sacred hill. The monastery towered over the horizon from a distance of as far as 20 miles, similar to Mont San Michel that graces the Normandy coast of France, or the famous Monte Cassino in Italy, both monuments of Benedictine scholarship and monasticism, as was Pannonhalma. It is a massive complex on top of a steep hill, in a countryside of gently rolling hills. I was impressed beyond my expectations.

A long serpentine drive leads to the top. As one is going up, the heavy stone walls are partly visible through the tall trees on both sides of the road. The steep drive ends at a plaza, with a prominent marble crucifix at the center of a traffic circle and wrought iron gates to the right and left. An old one, with classical designs, opens to the huge garden and farm field. Across from it, part of the high school, built in 1938, is the large gate, with religious designs in contemporary style under a wide stone arch. It is the main entry to monastery grounds. Under it, a wide cobble stone drive leads into the complex, curving still up by the bronze statue of St. Asztrik on a green, flower-filled patch, between the old and the modern buildings, and on further, to the highest point at the entrance to the basilica.

Bishop Asztrik has a special significance to this place. He was the emissary to Rome, of the Hungarian king Stephen, in the year 998. (Stephen, born Vajk in 975, was christened at age 10 later became a saintly king and canonized soon after his death in 1038.) Asztrik brought back with him a gold crown, richly enameled with Byzantine designs, a gift of Pope Sylvester II. Stephen was crowned king in 1000. (Scholarly evidence suggests that it was the coronation instrument for the Frank king and Holy Roman Emperor Charlemagne in 800, sanctioned by the pope. In the intervening years the crown was held by German kings, but eventually returned to the papal reserve.) Since the year 1000, it is Hungary's Holy Crown. It left the country only once, and spent 24 exile years in of all places, Fort Knox.

A statue of St. Asztrik is in a prominent place on the left side of the drive, in the S-curve, as the road leads to the basilica. With a patina of long years, he is standing tall, erect and dignified, with the bishop's miter on his head, holding the Holy Crown on his bronze pillow, as if he were presenting it to his king.

Just past the statue, the drive divides. To the right, under an arch, it leads to maintenance and supply facilities. On the left, after another turn, one finds himself in front of the basilica. Above the main entrance, a large golden and colorful mosaic depicts the royal act of founding the Benedictine order in Hungary (1020), and the restoration of church property and reconfirming of the original mandate to the church and school (1802). -- The Habsburg king Joseph II confiscated much of Church property in 1786 and squandered it during his reign. King Francis reversed his predecessor's order and restored properties and rights to the Church, in 1802. On the left side the mosaic depicts handing of a letter by King Stephen to Benedictines. On the right, King Francis returns the same rights to the church and restores the right to educate, to all the teaching orders. The first letter says: "*Predicate*", the other, "*Docete*" (Preach, Teach).

When Father and I arrived on a bright Sunday morning, the gate was open, monastery grounds quiet -- not a soul around. We found a door open to our right and went in. A custodian greeted and ushered us to a nearby waiting room in the cloister building. I looked out the window and again was impressed by the tall, modern, six-story high school across the drive, making an architectural contrast to the many centuries old buildings of the monastery.

It was in the shape of a huge "F". Lobby, offices theater, etc., were on the ground floor. From the lobby, large glass doors lead out to the terrace, on the roof of the gymnasium. All eight classrooms were on the second floor, laboratories and other special rooms were on the third story. The top floors were occupied with the dormitory and teachers' rooms. In the two right-side prongs of the F, were hallways, with small rooms to house seniors, except on the second level, which was the dining room, for about 350 students and for the teachers. The corridor on the third floor connects the school with the monastery building complex.

While waiting, I could not overcome my sense of wonder of the place and the situation we were in. The only thing I remember saying to Father was that I hoped that there is room and I would be accepted. The atmosphere was full of expectations and tension. We were not sure that our information was correct in its details and that the school indeed was ready to open in the general climate of oppression and fear.

After a few minutes entered a tall, lean, ascetic man, in his customary Benedictine black soutane, sporting a thin white collar, the *latest* of Benedictine fashions -- going back a few centuries. He had a formal, but approachable manner. He was Father Norbert Legányi, my future math teacher, principal and later, the Abbot of Pannonhalma, named to his post by Pope Paul VI. He signed me up in two minutes, after a short chat with my dad, asking only my name and address. Father told him that I would also like a place in the dormitory. This was expected. Because of the remoteness of the school from any sizable town, most kids lived within the complex. He told us that we were among the first dozen to apply. We talked for another fifteen minutes, where he explained their situation.

The high school building was still under lock and key. They were expecting to gain first entry in a few days. The third floor corridor, which connected the two building blocks, was walled off two years before. The wall had to be taken down to reopen the corridor between the school and the monastery. Then they had to remove the communist youth movement slogans that were all over the walls, and replaced them with the old Christian symbols. Thus the institution was symbolically fumigated, the school and the dormitory restored, to allow them to function again in accordance with their original mandate.

I was ecstatic. I had trouble comprehending my incredible luck. I had two weeks to digest this fortunate turn of events before school was to start. It took me all the next four years to learn about my new home. Till the last days, there were delightful things to discover. The huge building with its many secrets, the teachers, fellow students, and employees, including a lady from the staff, whose platonic friendship I will always treasure, will be among the best memories of my youth.

Father and I compared notes on the way home. He too, was pleased and recognized the intellectual and spiritual gold mine we had just found. It was the sweetest of ironies, that the despicable machinations of some distant Party hacks, whom we never met, denied my entry to high school. Their action resulted in such a fortunate turn of events for me. I was to attend an expensive prep school with dormitory living. Dad was proud that he could afford it. I am sure he would have sent me there even if our financial situation were tighter. It was an opportunity he would not miss.

I thought back to Keszthely, my years with the Premonstratensians, the times that left me with pleasant memories. But this place was in another class. I tried not to dream too high and be disappointed later.   In hindsight though, Pannonhalma exceeded all my expectations. I was so right, feeling so extremely lucky.

The foundation-stone for Pannonhalma was laid in 996 by Grand Duke Géza, father of Prince Vajk (later Stephen) the founder of Catholic Hungary. This was one of the most important steps that turned the country away from its pagan past and transformed Hungary into a Christian nation. Early in the long, politically perilous process, King Stephen invited Benedictine monks from Rome to establish monasteries and schools. As one of his first official acts he fully endowed the Abbey of Pannonhalma, to make it a bastion of religious education. (I once heard of a work of research, that followed the lineage of king St. Stephen through the centuries. George Washington is in that line, also the founder of *his* nation.)

In the annals of history, this Sacred Hill is first mentioned in the 5th century AD. St. Martin, the later bishop of Tours in France, was born in the Transdanubian city of Sabaria (now Szombathely, the seat of Vas county, where Jánosháza is located), then an important center in the Roman province of Pannonia, later Hungaria. The Hill was a Catholic retreat for centuries. It has been operating as a Benedictine university and abbey since the days of St. Stephen. Its Abbott also holds the office of bishop.

Originally the hill was a steep climb from all directions. We came up on the heavily wooded, curvy road from the south. Another road, more slowly sloping, was built later. It leads west, to a flat landscape. On the roughly level-ground hilltop are two additional smaller structures.

The Millennium monument, erected in 1896, commemorates the 1000th anniversary of Hungary's pre-Christian founding by Chief Árpád. It is a domed structure, with one large fresco all around, painted by Vilmos Aba-Novak. It depicts historic figures and deeds of important rulers of Hungary. Two of my favorite kings of the Royal Árpád House, after Stephen, were St. Ladislaus and Kálmán. László, as we knew him, established property rights for individual citizens, among many other ideas considered revolutionary for the 12th century. Kálmán is known, as Kálmán of the Books. His reign heralded a cultural leap, ahead of most other European nations. He outlawed the burning of witches, about 600 years before it was done in the American colonies, after the burning of many women in Salem and elsewhere.

The other is a chapel, named for the Virgin Mary, the protector of Hungary, is as old as the original cloister. It has been rebuilt more than once. Today it is a baroque structure with a tomb below, where the monks have been buried through the centuries. It had about 30 crypts and a bone collection bin at the far end. When a monk is buried, the bones from the oldest crypt are placed in the bin. We made a few visits there during my student years. Teachers told us about old friends they remembered. We also went down to the crypt during our 25th class reunion in 1979. This time we too, saw several familiar names and thought back to pleasant, joyful times. -- In 2004, on my 50th reunion I saw an expanded crypt, with room for many more sarcophagi. There, with silent prayers, we paid homage to our departed teachers and recalled pleasant memories of long ago.

* * *

The main monastery complex is massive, its secrets many and intriguing. I know of more than one occasion, and heard about several others after I left the place, when renovations revealed frescos or building elements of earlier construction projects, that were covered by new stucco or mortar, revealing architectural styles going back about a thousand years. They are now permanently exposed and preserved for generations to study. These finds add to the variety of the collection and the examples of building elements, from early Roman, to 20th century modern. Each age and style is amply represented.

The basilica is gothic, with a Romanesque lower chapel under the high altar. There is a massive stone chair which was made for and used by King Stephen, when he joined the monks in prayer. The cloister was a military fortification through the middle ages and till this day is commonly called, the *Fortress*. It has been successfully defended under the leadership of abbots, three times. The Tatars assaulted it in 1250 and again 30 years later. In the 16th century, the Turks tried but did not succeed conquering it.

Deep in the oldest part of the cloister, is a series of six connected cubicles, once used as placements for cannons. The cannons are long gone, but their place is still called the *Kill Corridor,* still in use, but with a very different mission. In each of these niches is an altar, where some of the several dozen priests say mass, beginning before dawn. Facing the altar is the opening where the barrels of the large guns peered out, to face the assaulting enemy. Many thousands of holy masses were said in this corridor, since the guns fell silent. The instruments of national defense and weapons of freedom were removed and replaced by stations where monks praise God and thank him for his blessings.

I lived most of my next four years within these walls. We had free access to the monastery, even invited to serve mass for the many priests who started to say them at 5 A.M., some even earlier. The Kill Corridor was my favorite. It had an intimate setting: quiet, gray stone arches and the small window looking out. Things went at a fast clip. I compared notes with friends and agreed that the fastest mass took 16 minutes. Sometime we served two, before returning to the dormitory for breakfast. It was an invigorating start for the day. The mass was in Latin. We had to learn the responses and the longer prayers, to be credible ministrants to the priest. I had to bone up on my skills, but the most important parts I knew from Keszthely and serving mass at home.

Normal wake up time was 6:00 A.M. It was hard at first. We were awakened by Father Csaba, who walked in sharp on the hour and loudly wished everyone a good morning. Most of us found this less than a cheerful moment. Then we got into the habit, strongly encouraged by him, to wash down the whole upper body in cold water, with a towel tied at the waist. After a few months, most of us picked up on it and found it a refreshing way to start the day. I reinforced there the habit of rising early, one that I retained all my life. Getting up at 5, as some of us started doing in sophomore year, became a habit.

(Ildikó, my wife believes that one needs at least eight hours of sleep, encouraging me to follow that rule. She does need the eight hours, I'm sure. It shows when she is shortchanged by circumstances. I need about five-six at the most, and often do well on less.)

Dormitory life was well regulated, but I had no serious complaint. Our day was full. From the wake-up call to 1:05 P.M., when classes ended on most days, we were kept busy. We had a five-minute pause between classes, and a 15 minute "long recess" mid-morning, when we walked down to the fortress circle grounds. This was the flat open yard, built up and leveled for an athletic field, where we held gym classes in good weather and also, our fall and spring athletic contests. At the edge of the circle, the ground dropped and was covered with tall grass and bushes. It eventually leveled off and the footpath lead to the small village of Gyõrszentmárton. This *fortress round* circled the monastery complex. It had a 550 meter (1800 ft.) path at the outer edge, that was our running track. It was handy for setting up markers for long distance races. It was also a popular trail for an easy walk. Older abbey residents liked to use it, rather than go down to the garden with its steep, rugged, rain-washed paths.

I liked to stand at the edge looking west, and watch a train below, appear at the horizon, pull into the village station, wait, again puff some smoke in the air to start, and in another six minutes disappear far in the distance, behind a hill on the other side, having traveled about 4 miles north-east, toward Gyõr. It was a true bird's eye view, looking at a wide, distant vista. A few miles beyond, looking west over the village, low, forested hills were rising, showing off their clear green splendor. The song says: *On a clear day you can see forever.* From the high point by the basilica entrance and especially from the tower, our *forever* was the Pilis Mountains near Budapest, about 90 miles away. It was remarkable to see so far away, bridging the gap between two distant points, over the wide flat land in between. Today Hungary cannot boast of high mountains. They were all taken at Trianon, at the end of the First World War.

Soon after the sixth hour ended it was lunch time. I looked forward to it, especially in later years. It was not only the food. Our menu was basic, but fine. A lot of starch to fill youthful bellies. We were served a hot lunch that was almost enough most days, but by supper I was always hungry.

With a teacher supervising, we gathered in the dining room. Standing at our designated seat by the long tables, we started by facing the crucifix on the far wall and said our short mealtime prayer. Designated boys went to the serving tables and each brought to his group of six or seven, a large platter of food. Usually we could go back for seconds. Bread or some pastry we could take to our lockers, to bridge the long hungry gap between lunch and dinner.

I remember how hungry I was on some days, especially after intense activity, during afternoon walks or sport filled studium recesses. In fact, in the first year I was most surprised to find that I did not lose any weight. I thought that being so hungry, so often, I should ended up skin and bones, but I actually gained.

We made several outings a year that included long walks. They were tiring and hard on the feet. The hungriest I ever remember being was after our day-trip to Zirc, the Cistercian abbey in the Bakony mountains. We took our packed lunch. Early afternoon, tired from a long stretch, we sat down on the grass. Warmed by the spring sun, I ate my sandwich. When I was done, I felt I had one bite. It didn't make a dent. I was hungrier, than when I began. The longer part of the walk was still ahead.

Most of the way home I was thinking about the piece of bread I had in my locker. It was a *sercli*, an end-piece, a lucky find, because it was bigger. All kids had their eyes on those. When we finally got home, it was still an hour before supper. Few meals in my whole life were ever as satisfying as that lowly piece of yesterday's bread. No butter, no jam, yet they were some of the best few bites I ever enjoyed.

On days when we had only five classes on our schedule, the sixth hour was free. Upper-class students were assigned to kitchen duty. This meant taking all the lunch meals from the *lower arcades* (actually two floors below ground level at the main gate) to the second story dining room. We were allowed to use the elevator for this work. This had two great advantages. One was that we didn't have to climb stairs with our load. Since much of the food was in large aluminum tubs, it was enough work to carry them in the hallways. Going up four floors would have made it even harder. We had to do it only a few times when the elevator was out of service. The second, more important plus for us, was that we could safely raid the food on the way up. *Bukta* was the best. Bukta is a baked, jam-filled, yeast dough. We all loved it. They were most suitable for stashing in pockets. Sometime I worried that some authority will get suspicious because too much was missing. We did our best to camouflage our deed by taking only from disturbed rows, where one couldn't tell how much of it *took flight* on the way up to the dining room. I'm sure, this loss was calculated and included in the meal plan. Any adult who ever was a kid, had to understand, that there was a price for this unpaid work. Needless to say, I volunteered as often as possible for kitchen duty. There were a few of us who showed up every time, even pinch hitting for others.

I had another reason to volunteer. There was a girl, several years older. She was one of the ladies in the kitchen. Her name was Maria, but we called her Dundi. The word means plump, or chubby, which she slightly was. She had a very nice face and I found her most kind and interesting to talk to. There was also Terike (a nickname for Theresa) maybe better looking overall, but she did not appeal to me. The two were very good friends and housed in adjacent rooms in the lower level. There was an unwritten rule, that the area was off limits for students. To my knowledge, there was no need or even opportunity to enforce the rule. I was perhaps one of only a few, ever to take advantage of the laxness of its enforcement. The ladies, both several years older than then us, were the main caretakers of food service in the dining room. This way I saw Maria at least twice a week for a good half hour. I always looked forward to our light, sometimes teasing conversations. The more we talked the more interesting I found her company. Once I hinted, and she consented, for me to come and visit her in her room. By that time I found this very exciting and could hardly wait for 8 o'clock when I went down to our platonic, clandestine rendezvous.

It was no problem to go there in the dark, empty corridors. At the other end, behind a turn, nuns were housed but I never saw any of them. They probably were at prayer. Many evenings we spent, up to an hour talking. She also enjoyed my company and occupied herself with embroidery work while I was there. Once she told me about a serious suitor, but she was not sure about him. We both avoided intimate subjects, so just entertained mundane themes of common interest and a few personal things. It was a happy time, for a few months.

Then word got around that I was not to be found many evenings after eight. Nine o'clock was lights-out time. Sometimes I missed even that. The dormitory rector, Father Oswald, tried to find me and later catch me, but never did. I wasn't comfortable with this but still found it a challenge. One evening Father Oswald came to see me after I was already in bed. He told me that he knew where I was when he looked for me earlier. I was never to do it again. Since he had no proof no specifics, he could not really accuse me of anything. I remained equally vague and confessed nothing. It was a fascinating stalemate.

I went home for Easter vacation. When I came back, there was a new glass door in the hallway, installed during the break, blocking the way to where I used to go. That, in effect ended it for us. Maria also took some risks, but Oswald liked her and other than expressing his displeasure, did nothing to discipline her. I saw her only one more time in her room, when she lent me her key. We concluded that it is too risky, under the conditions not worth it, and could lead to problems for both of us. We said a very emotional farewell, but not a real good bye. She kissed me then, the only time she did. It was more of a motherly kiss on the cheek. I did not returned it. I knew not how. I was elated and felt great sorrow at the same time. I knew something beautiful ended for me, and for us both. This was near the end of my junior year.

I saw her only one more time close up, when we encountered one another on the monastery main drive on a Sunday morning, more than a year later. She was not working for the dorm anymore. I was happy to see her. We talked about old times. It was just before graduation. I was soon to be gone for good. She lost some weight but looked a little sad. She told me that she was soon to get married. We wished each other well and said our final good byes. Our acquaintance, despite its travails was a very pleasant time, with beautiful and innocent memories, suitable for the location, where my four years are still among the most precious in my mind.

I did not have any other serious love interest in my high school years. We had four or five girls in our classes, all through the four years. None were the type that sent any boy's heart pitter-patter. One, Margot had an interesting combination of attributes. She was a poor student -- to be kind -- had a not very attractive face, but a mischievous sense of humor, a dynamite figure and a personality most kind and charming, along with humility and a sense of self worth. She was a popular girl and we all helped her to get by in class. She didn't make it to graduation. Still, she is the one I remember best.

In the class below ours, were two, the Makk sisters, I think twins. Éva was good looking, but Vera was a real beauty and very popular with boys. They lived down in the village, at the bottom of the hill and walked up to school every morning, as all girls did in the first three years. Some took the train, as did about 10% of the boy students, those who lived in the surrounding villages. They had the longest walk, all the way from the station, much of it uphill.

I also thought that Vera was cool, but she was in another class and I hardly ever spoke with her. Knowing myself, in any intimate moment I would have choked up and made a fool of myself. I think it was better that I never tried to approach her with serious intent. The only chance for any meaningful time with a girl could only be in class or during the short recesses. Even there, boys and girls didn't mix. There were very few extracurricular activities conducive to romance.

An exception was in my sophomore year, the school sponsored a ballroom dance class. I enjoyed it a lot. Our ballroom was the gym for both, the classes and the finale on a Saturday afternoon. (They didn't want to keep the girls till late.) It was one of the few occasions where romance could blossom, without breaking some rule or being the subject of gossip by classmates. Getting together outside, lovers had to be inventive and clever. I heard stories that were interesting, but I could not tell how much of them were true. -- I signed up and was eager to learn a social grace, but other than enjoy dancing, nothing else developed. The Makk sisters did not attend.

An interesting sidelight. -- Vacationing in Colorado a few years ago, in an art gallery I saw a few great impressionist style paintings by Éva Makk. I tried to find out more on the Internet. It turned out, this Makk, about the same age, also Hungarian, is a well known artist, exhibiting world wide. She, daughter of a diplomat, was born in Ethiopia, but now living in Hawaii. (By all indications, she married the brother of our Makk sisters, because her husband, Amerigo Makk, also a renowned painter, was born in Pannonhalma. Some coincidence! -- If I ever meet him, I'll ask.)

Throughout the four years of high school, we put on two plays a year. They were all well done, under the direction of experienced teachers. The play I liked most, was a court-intrigue drama by the Spaniard, Don Pedro Calderon de la Barka: *The Lady and the Maid*. The play's translator was a great Hungarian master, Dezső Kosztolányi. Some of the intriguing and humorous lines we are still quoting to each other, when I talk to old classmates.

Our director, Father Csaba talked me into singing an opera aria. I played the part of a merchant, who is visiting the castle, presenting jewelry to the countess. To impress her, (in our version) he sings "*La Donna e Mobile*" from *Rigoletto* by Giuseppe Verdi. Father Csaba taught me both verses in Italian. I did OK, and was applauded -- for effort, I guess. Father Csaba had an ironic sense of humor. When I sang the aria, I just mouthed the words, without understanding them. Later I found out that the words are mocking women, for their fickleness, as sung by a duke, known for his lecherous ways and habit of using women.

The most memorable production, however was the Russian playwright Gogol's, *The Revizor*, or with its more familiar title, *The Inspector General.* -- That's right! Danny Kaye played the role in a Warner Brothers production of 1949. I saw it in the 1970s, and must say, it has little resemblance to the stage play. The biting and cynical humor is mostly missing and the story itself is so altered that the Hollywood treatment emasculates it and renders it a pathetic farce.

The main reason I remember our production so well, is that it was shut down by the county office of the Communist Party. They said we falsified the production by omitting parts. The subject scene, eminently qualifying for being cut, was a raunchy one, with several characters, including children that our small group had no players for. Also, sexual innuendo and subject of adultery were not things we wanted to put on stage at our school. After one production to a packed gym, we were ordered to cease and desist. This, in spite, doing a Russian play that satirizes the nobility, ridicules the old regime and exalts the poor. We were politically quite correct, but still wrong. Wrong perhaps, just for being Pannonhalma.

One of my more pleasant theater related experience was during our junior year. Our class went to Budapest for a cultural outing on a long weekend. We had a few programs in museums and sight-seeing walks. The biggest thrill was an evening at the National Theater. This was my first serious theatrical experience and to top it, my favorite by Shakespeare, his *Hamlet*. I knew the play, but wanted to learn more, especially by seeing it at the most prestigious theater, played by the best the country had to offer. I was excited to go. I considered it my signature play.

I knew that the three most prominent actors in theater were rotating in the role of Hamlet. I had my favorite, based on limited exposure to their work, what I read and a few of their film roles. The consensus was that Ferenc Bessenyei had the optimum combination of experience and temperament. The other actor was Tamás Major, a later director of the theater. He was the most experienced, but and older, bald man, whom I had trouble imagining in the role, with possible exception in the graveyard scene, with Yoric's skull in his hands. (When he was appointed director, rumors that I previously heard about him resurfaced. He was a sympathizer with the regime, or at least a fellow traveler with the cultural elite of the Party.)

For wanting to see an exciting interpretation, my preference was Miklós Gábor, a young, good looking movie star, whom I saw in a comedy, with his famous star wife, Violetta Ferrari. I am putting down these facts for full disclosure, but still say that my most important reason was to see the way I thought Hamlet would be played by an energetic young man, closest to the age of the hero. The whole issue became moot, because that evening belonged to Bessenyei. We were all pleased. The production was superb and lived up to its billing.

There was no question about Ophelia, thank God. We were lucky to see the most prominent and beautiful lady, the national legend, Éva Szörényi. Her reputation preceded her as the greatest of her generation, a dignified actress, above all the rest. I considered a special treat to see her on stage. (She retired in the mid-1950s, moved to America in 1956 and now lives in California.)

On the second day I went to see Józsi, who was at the university, studying to be a veterinarian. It was a long walk from our hotel on the longest street in the city, Üllői út. As I was looking at the house numbers on the way, it seemed too far for a walk, but I kept going. Streetcars were passing by me, but I saw no need to get on. Walking was good and I saved the price of the fare. Finally I reached 121, where, at an important crossing, Orczy út, he lived on the second floor, looking out to a busy square, Nagyvárad tér. I walked up and introduced myself to his landlady. She told me that he was not there and usually got home about 2:30. That was several hours away and I thought I have to come back to see him later that evening.

I started walking back toward midtown. After a few blocks I thought, what if he happens to come home today a little early. I decided to watch the streetcars, perhaps I can spot him. As soon as the first streetcar came by, I saw him on the platform as the last, noisy car rumbled by. I sprang after it and almost caught up, when the it started to move again. I yelled out a loud: "Józsi". He turned, saw me and jumped off, before the car gathered much speed. Good work, for a snap decision, a timely scream and quick feet.

There was one more play, though a few years later, that is worth a mention. I barely remember the story, or much else. It was in Jánosháza, after my high school graduation, while I was working and looking for the chance to continue my education. During rehearsals I got to know a girl better, a girl whom I always knew. Her brother sat next to me in class for a whole year. Her name was Magdi Vári -- Magdi, for Magdalen. Our short-lived, sweet romance made our time happy, before I left Hungary.

I knew Magdi all my life. She was one grade below me in school. After I went away to high school, we saw each other only by chance, but often enough in our small town, to carry on an informal friendship. Then there was the play, put on by her employer, the local cooperative. At the time I was working and lived at home. She was a clerk in one of the stores. The director of the play invited me to play a role, where she was a fellow player. We soon discovered an attraction between us that developed in time. It turned to gentle, tender, sweet, innocent love. We were going together for much of 1956, during which time we never quarreled. It was idyllic, or seemed so. I was a high school graduate, hoping to go on to college. She came from a good family but finished only what was equivalent to junior high.

I courted her for less then a year. Was it a good match? We did not have a chance to find out. Fate intervened and our youthful love remains only a memory. Our tender friendship was in many ways untested, platonic and I am sure naïve, though we didn't know it back then. We never talked about a possible future together. It would have been too early. We were kindred spirits and our delicate spiritual intimacy was the source of our love. I left Hungary suddenly and under highly pressured circumstances. We corresponded for about a year.

Magdi had common sense, a good and pure heart. These

qualities I did not find in any other girl before, and they appealed to me. Each summer evening we went together to take home milk, from a farmer nearby. These walks were the most pleasant times we had together.

* * *

There was one minor scandal in my four years at Pannonhalma. It involved Zsuzsa Szabó, a girl from Jánosháza. I knew her from childhood. In the old regime, her family was the richest and most prominent in town. When we were little, they visited us, and we, them. Their home exuded wealth, as seen even with my 6-7 year old child's eye. It was next to their large flour mill. Mr. Szabó was in politics at the time, a parliamentary representative. He was a nice man, as I remember him from a few brief visits. His wife, Aunt Klára was a stunning beauty, but a haughty woman. She was the first woman that I knew, who colored her hair. I was astonished and asked Mother, if it is true. -- It had to be. One day her hair was a different color, from what I remembered last time. Mother confirmed it, but answering my follow-up question, she assured me that she would not contemplate doing anything such. I didn't know any other woman who colored her hair. (It was, like ladies showing an uncovered ankle a hundred years ago. You have to live in the age to appreciate societal sentiments, conventions, tabus and all the dos and don'ts of the time.) Coloring hair in Jánosháza just wasn't done. Aunt Klára was the lone exception. Ours was maybe the only house in town that they visited. I saw Aunt Klára on the street only once. I was not surprised that Mother could never warm up to her.

The Szabós had four daughters, Zsuzsa the oldest. We were four boys. The age difference for possible matrimonial purposes were ideal for all eight of us. So, there was some idle talk between parents, just to note the fitting coincidence. The girls were raised well and were expected to fulfill their mother's high expectations. Aunt Klára liked to cite their multiple talents. On one occasion, Zsuzsa sang for us after dinner. It was a well rehearsed song, deigned to impress and solicit praise. It was nice, but did not live up to its billing. The task seemed to exceed her talent. The third of the girls was little Anna. She was no doubt the sweetest one, the best looking and a gentle creature. I was the third among the boys. I thought it fortunate -- just in case.

After the communists took power, a great misfortune visited upon the Szabó family. Their sins, in the eyes of the new regime, were numerous. They were rich, prominent and in politics. Soon they were stripped of their mill, position and fancy house. Mr. Szabó even spent time in prison -- on some trumped-up charge.

Zsuzsa was in her first year in Pannonhalma when I was a senior. By then several years have passed, during which I didn't see her. The year was 1953. The Szabós were now in very different circumstances. The family lost the big mill, their house and more. They no longer lived in Jánosháza. So I was surprised to see Zsuzsa in Pannonhalma. The parents surely made the big sacrifice to provide her the best. It was not easy. Mr. Szabó, who once owned a mill, now worked in one as an ordinary laborer and did not complain.

In that year, the school set up a small dormitory for a few girls in an existing building, along the walkway down to the village. Two nuns also moved in to supervise. This was a small favor to the nuns, who otherwise were wards of the monastery, with little of meaning to occupy them. Their order was also dissolved in 1948. Those located in Pannonhalma were lucky. They could stay, work in the abbey or in the dormitory kitchens and, for example, give private piano lessons. I took lessons from Sister Ilonka. She was severe in class, but could not inspire me. Still, I blame more myself than fault her. I did not use the practice sessions well. -- I was sorry to see all these gentle ladies in civilian clothes. Nuns always were a pleasant sight. I loved those neat habits and their flying headdresses.

Returning to my little scandal, one late Saturday evening Zsuzsa and a few other girls climbed out a window and went down to the village to have some sort of a good time. The details escape me, but they were not outrages, and really, immaterial. The offense of leaving the compound without permission was grave enough for dismissal, let alone that it was committed after dark. As a result,

Zsuzsa and two others were kicked out. I would like to think that she was not the instigator in all this and just followed others. It could be that it was an occasion for her to rebel against her strict upbringing. The episode surprised me. I did not expect anything such happening at our school.

There was only one other case, where a few of my classmates were disciplined for going down to the village and drink a few bears one Saturday afternoon. But they were boys and seniors at the time. Testing the rules by boys was tolerated better. More was expected of girls. But even without that, the girls' offense was considered more serious, and in their freshman year, to boot. -- A kicker to the story was that many years before, my class master, Father Anaklét, in their youth, was a supposed beau of Zsuzsa's mother, the beautiful Aunt Klára. I asked him about it once, just in a joking manner. He saw no humor in it. He obliquely confirmed it, but went no further. I saw that he was not comfortable discussing it. I dropped the subject and we never spoke of it again. -- He tried to interfere in Zsuzsa's behalf, but was not successful.

Another event that year touched our family. It involved my brother Tomi. He was a sophomore then. His class master was Father Efrém Sulyok, an unpleasant man. He was very short and almost as wide -- not that it had anything to do with this case. Tomi irritated him to a degree that he wanted him out of the school. To save face and find a solution, Father talked to Abbot Paul. He arranged that Tomi could transfer to the only other Benedictine high school, the one in Győr, just 20 miles from Pannonhalma. Tomi realized belatedly that it would have been a better part of valor to be more respectful and hold his tongue at critical times. The other school was fine, but it was not Pannonhalma. It was in a large city and had none of the atmosphere of the Sacred Hill. Still, we were pleased with the outcome, considering a looming unpleasant alternative.

Many parents tried from home, to look after their offspring with treats, goodies and other things to supplant our rations. Every day, after the last class, and just before lunch, many kids ran down to a receiving room by the main entrance, to check out the daily package shipments. We were allowed to take them up only after lunch, but we had to know if the highly valued package arrived. Early in my first year, I saw that some kids were getting large wooden boxes. They were made especially for this purpose. Some betrayed signs of master carpentry. They were solid, designed for many trips and rough treatment on the train. For easy handling, some had sturdy handles. They all came with a sliding top that was guided in grooves and closed easily. A latch and padlock secured the content. For some kids the box was always in transit between home and the dorm, exchanging sweet goodies for soiled clothing. I asked my parents to have one made for me and they soon did. I felt I joined the rank of the elite.

About Pannonhalma, I had so many interesting and beautiful memories that it would take many pages to recount. Most involve teachers whom we loved and respected and criticized only in our intimate circle.

Father Geláz taught biology. Beside all his Ph.D.-s, (I heard he had three) he was a true artist. He played the violin like a pro. He gave some concerts that were free and just for our pleasure - - and of course his. We all loved him, despite his stern demands for excellence. He had a heart of gold but only one good eye -- at least it seemed that way. As he looked at us with one, the other seemed to shoot away, upward and to the side. Still he seemed to catch everything in class and gently asked us to please pay attention. Maybe he could switch between the two, or even use them independently. I never found out.

Father Oros Bajtai was young but a very big man. He taught religion. One day he expressed his disappointment that we young lads are too lazy to make a decent genuflection. Then he demonstrated how to do it properly, bringing his knee and large body to the floor and rise again. Even after 50 years, when I do it in church, I often think of him. I saw him a few years after I graduated. He was very ill with bad kidneys, a condition that affected his vision. I was reminded to announce myself as I entered, because he would see only the outline of my figure. After we greeted each other, the first thing he said was: "And how is Tamás?" We had a short talk, for he tired soon. He died within a year. On my return I visited the crypt under the Chapel of Mary and stopped by his name, as I did at others I also knew.

I was especially saddened by his passing. I thought back to the good times, his humor and the seriousness with which he took his calling and the kindness he showed, directing young boys toward the right path. He emphasized the importance of a spiritual advisor in the life of young boys like us. I chose him in my heart, but did not feel comfortable asking him. I was afraid that it would affect our *good relationship*, by making it too serious. I thought I might feel, as if I am going to confession every day. After thinking long and hard I thought I'd ask him to be my *spiritual guide*. I found hard to utter those two words and fudged a little. I asked him if he was willing to take me "under his wings". I didn't have to say, "You know what I mean, Father Oros". He knew. It was in my senior year and I had only a few talks with him, but he was my gentle guide even in formal settings.

There was also Géza Karsay, our literature teacher. My father knew him a long time, going back to high school days with the Benedictines, where he was one year under Father's class in Sopron. Father Géza was not at all athletic, as I will illustrate. His exercise was a gentle stroll around the abbey, or maybe, on a good day, down in the garden. Long walks, such as one from the train station, up the hill, taxed him more than others, although he was quite trim and only 48 years old.

One day, coming home from Gyõr, we stepped off the same train and walked together all the way up to the abbey. He carried a very thin briefcase. It was either empty or had only a few sheets of paper in it. As we began the climb, I was thinking of asking him, if I should carry his briefcase. I decided against it, thinking that it might embarrass him, it being so light. As we approached the bottom of the hill, where the incline became steeper, he asked me if I minded carrying it for him. I did it gladly, but was angry at myself for not offering, regardless of what I thought earlier about his capacity or attitude toward exercise.

I could cite a few of his idiosyncrasies that, without any conscious effort, I find permanently etched in my memory. His pet peeve was underlining our textbook. He had his all prepared and just read to us the lines that we had to mark in various ways, to distinguish the several levels of importance. That was before the invention of highlighters. We used plain, or red pencil, wavy lines, broken lines and at times blocked out entire paragraphs. This was a kind of editing, whether or not we agreed with his method, ranking of hierarchy, or importance of the details. He was the teacher, and though we privately questioned it and joked about it among ourselves, we followed his instructions.

We were discussing the work of poet Endre Ady, who lived a good part of his creative life in Paris. While admiring his poetry Father Géza pointed out, that the poet consorted with a woman, Léda, while she was married to someone else. This was scandal then, but behavior with which, kings, some celebrities and famous artists could get away with, even in those days. He castigated Ady for his loose lifestyle. He said, this was most prevalent in the *City of Lights* -- or in his phrase -- "city of sin". He also had unfavorable opinion about the French, or to be more accurate, French culture. He said that it is decadent and in his phrase, *tired,* past its dynamic, influential zenith. I did not understand this then. I knew very little about the French and lacked experience to judge the nature of a culture, or make comparisons. A few years passed since then. Now I think I know what he meant and I tend to agree with him. A dominantly secular view of moral issues leads to decadence and nihilism. This is one of history's most important lessons. One more thing about the French. They seem to be inclined to live off their glorious past, and resent the world, that in many ways passed them by. (Note the apoplectic reaction to Donald Rumsfeld's 2003 comment about *Old Europe/ New Europe.* France, Germany -- *old*, small countries, that recently emerged from communism -- *new.* The French instinctively took it, that it was about them -- though Rumsfeld never said it. How telling! Being so defensive, they validated his opinion.)

* * *

Socialism has its stranglehold on much of Europe. It is robbing France and other countries of dynamism, energy and, of which they were always so proud: *élan.* Society as a whole is legislated by opportunistic politicians, to support a growing class of parasites and do-nothings. I saw examples to this in most of the countries we visited in recent years. As our Scandinavian tour guide told us in Sweden, answering a question: those who do not work *earn* (i.e. receive) close to the amount of an average salary. The results are evident and they influence cultures in a fundamental way throughout Europe. I hope and pray that the United States will not lose its compass and will avoid similar effects, or at least, they will be less.

A regrettable side-effect of this European phenomenon is a movement, based on envy and resentment of America, that swept the continent in recent years. Europeans blame America for the world's woes, which they are cowards to honestly face and confront, and hope to solve by negotiating with terrorists, and immigrants that they are unable to absorb or control. They fail again in recognizing, that evil must be defeated and not appeased, if the West is to avoid future calamities. Rome was defeated in battle, by the Alaric of the Visigoths (410 A.D.) only because it was weakened by an unchecked invasion by unwanted hoards of groups from the East, and the well documented moral decay and corruption. -- America saved Europe in two World Wars, twice from German expansionism and once from state socialist Nazism. She stood guard against threats from the cousin of fascism, the other state socialism: Soviet Communism. All these destructive movements spawned in Europe and it was for Yankee GIs to set things right. To ensure peace on the continent, she sent and sacrificed her sons and daughters, and spent billions. -- All this in the span of 75 years. Now, Europe is again allowing in foreigners who dilute their culture, do not assimilate and make demands on the state. This is eroding sovereignty and national identity, while imposing new burdens on the people. It may soon cause serious disruption and social upheaval.

* * *

Father Lukács Hajdu taught history -- to say a little more on the subject. He was an orator in class. He could make history come alive and make sense, far beyond dates and strange names. I loved his classes and looked forward to his two hours each week. I still remember a few of his vivid descriptions of little known episodes, that caused major turns in history, or were catalysts in great changes and new trends.

Father Tibor was a wizard in his chemistry lab. Once he did a fast pace experiment, where the color of liquids in his beakers kept changing, so that we had hard time following which ingredient caused what change. (It was some barium compound.) This was one of his more flamboyant experiments. It was amusing to see how a humble monk can take delight in showing off a little once or twice a year to impress his pupils.

Everybody was afraid of Father Edgar Sámson. Not that he was rude or mean. He was overly polite, but in his class it was hardest to get a good grade. He had perhaps the most feared reputation. For some reason, I don't even know what, I was not intimidated by him. Without any direct contact, I perceived him personable, gentle and having a sense of humor. This was by observation in the hallway and just my hunch. I never spoke to him before our junior year, when he took over Latin. Nothing interesting or memorable happened between us for a few weeks, but then there was something I remember well.

The teacher's first task after he walked in, was to record in the large *Class Book*, the date, subject, etc. and any short message or reminder for himself, as he saw the need, to keep track of the class' progress. The Book, held open at the proper page, was presented to the teacher by a designated student at the beginning of each class. In it, continuing on his page, on the next blank line, the teacher signed in, put down the class code and remarks if he so chose -- if nothing else.

One day I was the designated student. I gave him the Book and stood facing him waiting, as he was making his notations. He started writing in the date, (in the accustomed format) but stopped after "1952 szeptember…" -- then paused, thinking. He seemed not to remember, and was searching in his mind for what the day was.

I was watching and said reflexively: "23".

Father Edgar looked up at me, visibly pleased -- as one, who has received welcome help he did not ask for. He smiled and said with emphasis:

"Thank you". Then, he finished writing his lines.

This was early in the school year and made an impression on me that, based on later experiences, I found to be in character.

He guarded his little personal notebook, more than other teachers, in which he recorded all the grades that he gave us on his impromptu oral quizzes in class. Once, in one of my giddy, careless moments, I said about his little book, containing sinister secrets, that it has an appropriately dark green cover, similar to a color of *dragon's blood*. As soon the words left my lips I wished I could take them back. I thought it was stupid or rude, likely both. Not Father Edgar. He took a strange delight in my description. He was proud of the reputation, his little book earned in class.

Another story goes with this. Miklós Farkasfalvy was the brightest student in class, possibly in the whole school. He was the studious type, smart *and* diligent. He didn't have to study but still did. He knew everything, perhaps Latin best. He was repeatedly called on by Father Edgar, to explain to the class stuff, the sort of which we never heard before, such as: the case and application of a dependent clause, or the correct use of gerund. (Oxford Dictionary: "Gerund -- case of Latin infinitive, constructed as a noun but governing like verb".) Wierd, I'll say!

But one day, Miklós was immersed in something else than Latin and was roused only by having heard his name by his teacher. He emerged from his thoughts and rose upon being called. In true fashion, he simply said the obvious.

"I do not know the answer because I did not hear the question. Could you repeat it, please?"

In the world of Father Edgar, that was out of the question. Instead, it was an automatic F -- case closed.

Not that it made a difference. His A has long been assured. It was delightful to see the glee on Father Edgar's face, that he caught Miklós off guard for once; also, how he insisted on going

through with this application of mock discipline in class. -- About
a month later, when similarly called on, and after again displaying
stunning linguistic gymnastics, followed by praise from his
teacher, our Miklós asked him a question: could he, instead of
giving him another A, please erase that notorious F, of old. Father
Edgar wouldn't hear of it. He must have thought it better this way
and certainly more interesting. It was a delightful exchange and
entertainment for the class. I enjoyed the humor in his pretense-
negotiating, before pronouncing *sentence*. He was clearly delighted
and just sat there satisfied, smiling.

Father Csaba Pulay was our dormitory supervisor for the first
year. He also taught physics. I found out during the second year
that he was a distant relative on my mother's side. This revelation
affected our carefree relationship, as I perceived it. I wanted to
make sure that he shows no favoritism toward me. I shouldn't have
worried. He was a straight arrow and behaved as he always did.

He was an avid walker. He took us on that long one to Zirc,
where I, and several of my friends had our *christening*, or initiation
in the exercise of walking long distances. After a while I realized,
why I liked him. He reminded me of Father Radnóczi, and the
memories of those neat mealtime talks in Keszthely.

I was surprised that all the teachers were expressing their
opinion openly about the communist regime, under which we
all had to live. I thought it a little risky. In our newfangled text
books, all explorers and inventors were Russian. Father Csaba
openly ridiculed this blatant deception and wondered aloud, where
those other well known men and women of science, he had been
teaching about in the past, disappeared to. He ridiculed one guy
who, according to his vital data, died before he was born. (A slight
misprint about dates of birth and death in our textbook , became
his joke about those wondrous Russians.)

As I think of these men of God, these dedicated men of science
and intellectual curiosity, my heart is filled with joy and gratitude
for the opportunity of being able to spend my formative years in
their company. To paraphrase Isaiah (64:2-7), as he was talking to
his Master: ...*we were the clay and they, the potter. We were all the
work of their hands.*

Our parents entrusted us to them for an important time. They were confident that we receive the best liberal education in the country, along with excellent moral guidance. Even years after leaving that institution, when we gathered in smaller number for our 50th class reunion in 2004, I saw the discernible imprint they put on us, in our most formative years so long ago. It pleased me, how little change I saw in most of my classmates in this respect.

Let me mention another advantage of living on the Hill. Our friars spent their time praying and studying, but also were dedicated to imparting knowledge. Afternoons, students were free to visit teachers for help or additional instruction. My friend Miklós took advantage of this opportunity. He befriended the prelate, Father Mike and took free French lessons from him for several years.

Once, when I visited a novice friend, I found him studying at his desk by the window. The building, with its very thick walls, was one of the oldest in the complex. His desk and his chair were in a nook, a sort of horizontal *window well*. The right end of the desk was set directly against the window. The other end of the desk was still in the wall opening that was cut out for the window. The wall was so thick, that a desk and chair fit into its window nook. I was fascinated when I saw it the first time. To see these cubbyholes, used as little niches for scholarly pursuits was intriguing, and seemed so fitting for monastic life. To take a break by a fatigued monk, he had only to look out at God's green earth, receding into the distance. Refreshed, he could return to his books. His mind might wonder about a planned walk later, in the midst of that picturesque vista that spread out below.

The religious and cultural atmosphere of the sacred hill was of great value to me. As part of everyday life, living next to, indeed being part of, this thousand-years old place, I had the chance to see and experience things that were such that in any other place were not available.

Soon, after things were organized in my freshman year, a program called *Collegium Musicum* began. It was Father Kilián's project. He did not teach at the school, only in the teachers college at the monastery. He directed all things musical in the basilica. He played the organ for each Sunday mass and directed the Gregorian choir. But on a Sunday once a month, he came over to the school and at 10 o'clock conducted a master class for us amateurs, his fellow monks and anybody who was interested in coming. It was held in our chemical classroom. He found this most suitable. The room had gradually elevated seating, excellent view of the lecturer and the three huge chalkboards. The room was full most days.

I had no idea what to expect, when I responded to the announcement, advertising the first session. As I entered the room, I was delighted to see the entire Beethoven 5th Symphony on the board. Notes from each of the four movements were detailed in different color chalk. (That was the first time I ever saw colored chalk. That alone was impressive.) Father Kilián began with a few general things about Beethoven and his Fifth. Then, he went on for 1½ hours, detailing the work and its genius composer. I felt I was in heaven. Not only that I enjoyed the lecture. I was riveted to his words and the parts that he played on a phonograph. I was overwhelmed with the feeling of being part of such experience, where teachers of his caliber were donating their time and showered their intellectual and cultural largesse on kids like me. At the end of the lecture we heard the entire work uninterrupted, as a dessert treat. Month after month on Sundays I was in the chemlab at 10 o'clock, absorbing and enjoying many other famous compositions. The unique power of first impressions is why Beethoven's 5th remains seared in my memory, while details about others are less clear. (Beethoven and Shakespeare were premier in my youthful experiences. A work by each left a mark on me. Other than movies, there were few other creations of art left such lasting impressions. Important ones of those are the ballet *Giselle* and Richard Strauss' opera, *Der Rosenkavalier.*)

When I was growing up, opportunities to hear classical music was only on radio. Regular programming included a few hours of serious music, usually in the evening hours. Many were live broadcasts of concerts or productions from the National Opera. I could hear lighter works, such as operettas and waltzes any time of the day. They were often included as requests in *Heart-to-Heart* ("Szív Küldi Szívnek Szívesen") the most popular daily program. I was naturally drawn to serious music and took best advantage of my few opportunities. I had my own radio bedside and a room for myself, for about two years before I left Hungary. I often listened late into the night and was familiar with programming of Radio Vienna, which played a lot of Mozart, Schubert and Beethoven, though not as much as Johann and the other Strausses, who clearly dominated the Austrian airwaves. Of my brothers, only Józsi liked classical music at the time. Mother had her favorites and taught me a few, but my father had no such background. Józsi told me, that on Father's visits to Budapest, he took him to the opera a few times. Father resisted at first, but Józsi chose good ones to introduce him to the high art of musical drama. After he saw *La Traviata*, then *Rigoletto*, he relented and said that it was melodic, enjoyable music. He said that he wished he would've been introduced to opera before. Lately Tomi also became an avid fan of serious music. -- My wife Ildi had a good background of the classics. Her stepfather listened to them all the time and had a state-of-the-art sound system and a large collection of phonograph records. Our tastes merged in many ways and there is a great repertoire of classics that we both like to listen to.

23

An Unusual Summer Job

My activities and duties during summer vacations were evolving during high school. After my freshman year a classmate, Kálmán Gerencsér visited -- of which more, later. In time I was expected to find some useful occupation, at least for part of the summer.

In 1953, after my junior year I did some work that earned me some money. In mid-July, Father asked me if I wanted to go on a trip and earn some.

Earlier on that Wednesday he examined and approved three cows, that were sold for export. They had to be transported to Yugoslavia. The animals were put in a railroad car in Jánosháza. After that, the car was in the hands of the railroad. This kind of transport was a low priority for all concerned. It meant that the roughly 120 miles journey could take any route and any number of days. It was subject to the railroad's discretion and convenience, so as not to interfere with their other needs or schedules.

My job was to take care of the three, feeding them and keep the car (and myself) clean during the journey. Our intended destination was the border town, Barcs.

That afternoon I packed a bag, containing some food, clothing, books to read, some odds and ends that I thought I will need to sustain me and sufficiently keep me from boredom. I knew very little what the trip might hold in store for me. Father stuffed some money in my pocket but said that I can still keep my take. He didn't know either, how long my trip will be and gave some extra, to be sure. I doubt that he expected to come out better than even, on our deal with its uncertain outcome. He was willing to pay for my gaining a little life experience.

The work was not hard, but I was to spend several days in close company of my charges. It will be boring, I thought. On the other hand it was a train ride, where I would see the country, in fact maybe even a little of *old* Hungary -- now another country.

Our car was part of freight trains, I do not remember how many. We could be moved, detached, attached from-and-to any train that was in a station, or let lie idle for any length of time on a track, at the far end of the yard.

I fell asleep in Jánosháza. By next morning we traveled four miles. I was aware of some movement, and bumps, as we were unhooked and shoved out of the way, but wasn't interested looking out. My suspicion was confirmed. We were in Boba, the tiny village, still in Father's district.

I temporarily befriended a few railroad men and line workers that eased my tedium. I was looking forward to terrain that is not familiar and more interesting. The following days brought some variety. We traveled south to the county of Somogy, that was new for me. Prior to this trip, I only saw the resort towns along the south shore of the lake, when we visited relatives in Balatonfenyves. This quiet little resort town held pleasant memories from my early childhood.

We spent three weeks there with Mother in a little house we rented: *Fészek* (Nest) a neat little villa. Father visited us on weekends, otherwise we spent the time on our own, and with one of our favorite relatives Mariann, and her brothers, Dezsõ and Szilvi, Mother's cousins. They were vacationing in their own villa, where they spent time each summer. We were their guests in earlier years and learned the basics of swimming. -- While staying in the Fészek, we ate in a restaurant every day. I found that a welcome change from the old routine. -- I thought of those long-ago meals, as I consumed my sandwiches during the first two days. Later I ate in restaurants and food stands at the stations.

One morning I woke up in Balatonfenyves. The only way I was able to recognize it, was by reading the station sign -- and it took me a double take. The sleepy little station of old, became a busy freight handling center. In 1940 it had a single track, just to let vacationers on and off. Express trains didn't even stop there. By 1953 it became a large switching station with many tracks and busy traffic.

The larger towns I remember on the way south, were Kaposvár and Pécs. These places were among those that were hometowns of classmates from my days in Keszthely or Pannonhalma. Looking on the map, one can see what a circuitous route my cows and I took to reach Barcs.

My journey on rail took eight days. I settled into a routine after a few, and adjusted to the habit of my cows. At each stop I had to do some cleaning, because I did not know what I find at the next stop and how much I have to wait to reach a station with comfort facilities -- human, or one for my companions. With a little ingenuity, I always found a way to get done what was necessary. I enjoyed the trip, but was relieved to hand over the animals and be again my own boss without the extra burden. My little area in the middle, by the big sliding door, was about a quarter of the car. (Wagons in Hungary are about 2/3rd the size of railroad cars in America.) I had my fellow passenger cows on either side, tied to the wall by their neck pretty tight, but their rump was loose and I had to be always ready to move fast when one swung out toward me. I had to watch the distance between us and not let it become uncomfortably close. I was lucky. They were calm through most of the nights.

Barcs was on the river Dráva, that once upon a time was one of our four great rivers, exalted in a semi-patriotic song, that also told of the many mountains and the fruited plain of the Carpathian Basin, that was once Hungary. The mood of the song was similar to the melancholic American tunes, telling tales of the Shanedoah or the Mississippi. After Trianon, the Dráva became the boundary with Yugoslavia. When I first set my gaze across it, half of it belonged to another country -- to be technical about it.

Barcs, a medium size city, was important as a border town with a country that was considered friendly enough for trade. Marshall Tito was its leader. He was a communist, though in those days, denounced by Moscow, as a lapdog of capitalists. He was looking for friendly relationship with the West, thus to gain a modicum of economic advantage over his backward, fellow *commie* leaders in the countries surrounding him. I remember many cartoons and slogans that showed him as a bulldog, with a chain around his neck, held with contempt, by his big imperialist master, Uncle Sam. Articles railed him as a traitor to the cause of the workers of the world and the Party, then undisputedly lead from Moscow.

I finally got rid of my uddered companions and turned them over to custom agents. With a sigh, I once more looked across the Dráva and planned the road back home.

Since I was close, I decided to see Pécs, this historic, and one of the nicest cities in the country. Turkish occupancy left a visible mark on it. The minaret, though not used, became an attraction for visitors. An old mosque was rebuilt and turned into a beautiful Catholic church. From the outside one could not tell, except for the cross on the top of its Byzantine style copper dom. I was told that if one goes to the 10 o'clock mass, he will see a fashion show each Sunday. I laughed when I heard it the first time, but it was true. Pretty women in their Sunday best made for a splendid show.

Another purpose for my visit to Pécs was to see if I can look up a classmate, Géza Várady. I knew little about his family situation. I just wanted to say hello and meet his family and return home. Pécs is situated at the foot of Mecsek Mountain, a wine growing and mining region. There were several mines in the hills, including Hungary's only black coal deposit, supporting heavy industry. (The nearby uranium mine was closed for the country and operated exclusively by Russians. Nobody could get even close.)

My problem was, that I had no address to go to and no idea how to find out where Géza's family lived. As luck would have it, strolling downtown, I ran into my friend. He was on his way to the library. This was fitting, for he was one of the known bookworms in class.

He invited me right away for a visit. What came of this, was a special few days for me, where the Várady family went to great length to convince me, that they were very happy to have me and I was in no way in their way, despite my sudden appearance without notice. The short visit became a three-day stay of which I still think fondly after more than 50 years. My stay stretched into the weekend at their insistence. On Sunday the family had plan to visit Géza's grandmother in the Meszes, half way up the mountain, in wine country. The lady lived by herself in a small house, overlooking the picturesque city. We walked all the way, that alone was a treat and stayed till dusk, loosing the sense of time's passing.

Mr. Várady was a postman. A happy and optimistic man, full of humor and cheer. Mrs. Várady took care of me as if I were her son, maybe better. Géza had a six years old sister, Éva, who found me interesting company. I had some practice with little girls; my sister was three at the time.

Saturday afternoon, while the family was busy preparing for the trip up the Meszes, I asked Mrs. Várady if I can take little Éva to the sweet shop, for an ice cream. She said, yes and off we went talking all the way. I am not sure I would still remember this event, at least not as well as I do, were it not for an unexpected consequence. I like ice cream, like most people, and bought for me a medium. To make sure that I do not appear cheep, but against my better judgment, I bought little Éva, the same. A complicating factor was that the next size down was a lot smaller, so I decided to go with medium for her too. She took her time, but ate the whole thing.

We didn't make much of it, other than it was good ice cream, until evening, when the little girl started complaining of a stomach ache. General conclusion was that it was the ice scream. I apologized and professed ignorance about the capacity and limit of little stomachs. We were relieved the next morning, when the pain passed and she was her happy self again. This way, the Sunday plan with grandma did not have to be scratched. She walked with us up the hill, without any sign of yesterday's woes. A great time was had by all.

Next day I boarded a train and returned home. My complicated journey, with my one-of-a-kind traveling companions was a first for me up to that time and became a subject of conversation at home. It was unique travel, where I was alone, responsible for myself. I was in charge, to deliver live cargo and I successfully carried it off. When I told my story to family and friends, it acquired an aura of a romantic adventure.

24

Wilderness Years -- Two Jobs (1954-56)

After graduation at Pannonhalma, I applied for admission to medical school. We mobilized friends and used other connections in the cause, but my family background again was an obstacle. Having gone to a religious school added to my problems when, in a just world, it should have been an advantage. I was better prepared for college than most high school graduates.

I spent the summer, trying to gain admission. It was a lot of effort, seeing people, writing talking with friends -- all to no avail. In the fall I secured a position in a pharmacy as an apprentice technician in Zalaegerszeg. Our thinking was that a little experience will help next year when I would apply to pharmacy school.

Zalaegerszeg was a neat city, a seat of our neighbor county. My cousin Mariann lived there with her family. Her husband Uncle Paul, had a medical practice there. I stayed with them during the week and took the train home on Saturdays.

After a period of adjustment, I enjoyed the simple work and picked up a little druggist know-how. The Dobribans, the manager and his wife were friends of my parents. They were smart and shrewd in business and I tried to learn from them. They put me under the supervision of their elderly, trusted family friend, Aunt Teréz. I was under her watchful eyes, while learning the ins and outs of putting ingredients together for simple prescriptions. She was a kind, good humored elderly lady, with her hair in a bun, and whose simple looks concealed her shrewdness and wisdom. It took a few days before she felt comfortable with me. No doubt, my introduction from her bosses, for whom she had great respect, shortened the time. Yet, I saw that she wanted to make sure for herself. For decades, she alone has been doing the preparation of prescriptions in a back room. She was a long-time *technica* (female technician). The Dobribans trusted her more then any other of their employees. She was intimate to much of their personal things, of which there were many. The Dobribans were clever capitalists in a communist world.

Aunt Teréz liked me, and I her, and we had a good time in the back, hidden behind a tall divider, separating us from counter and the retail area. She made sure I followed instructions and proper procedures in the preparation of my prescriptions. I was working only on creams, ointments, etc., not on medicine prescription. For a long time she had to know all my moves, methods and materials I used to put things together. I learned techniques as innocuous as in which direction to mix ingredients in a mortar (counter clockwise), the right way to hold a pestle and what grade was fine enough for her, when I pulverized ingredients. (Pulverized coffee beans used in a cream had to be shiny on the wall of the mortar before I could scrape it off to test it. It became the finest of all the powders I worked with.) Desired fineness depended on the consistency desired for a particular prescription. Later I could help out at the counter during busy times. This was mostly at my own discretion, considering my workload, store traffic, and with the tacit approval of Aunt Teréz. -- She taught me an old method, a special way of packaging medication in powder form. We started with small pre-cut sheets of paper laid out on the counter. On a prescribed number of the little slips, I measured out even amounts of powder. Then I used her special way of folding, making a neat package of all the doses. -- Today, when I want to package small items, powder or granular for storage, I just fold up my little packet, using the old, neat method.

I bought weekly meal tickets in a public kitchen. Later I upgraded and ate my lunch in the dining room at a nearby hotel. Although more expensive, it was a much nicer place, had better quality food and old fashioned, excellent restaurant service. It was worth it.

The pharmacy was closed for what the Spanish call, siesta. It was a 2½ hour lunch break. Nobody that I knew napped in that time. In Europe, lunch is the main meal and people take their time with it, run a few errands, unless it involved a store, that is also closed for lunch. Time was too long and I was often back early, as were several of the others. I did not want to miss conversation that I always found interesting.

There was a lady pharmacist, Olga, whom I liked a lot. She was pretty, kind and excellent company. She had a reserved modesty that appealed to me. Everyone knew that I liked her and teased me gently. They teased her to, but not for anything she did, because she was always discrete. It was an infatuation on my part over an intriguing women about 10 years older than me and it showed. She liked me also, but never let it show overtly. Perhaps she was flattered by the attention paid her by a youth. We just had a pleasant time together, whenever I worked by her side at the counter. The fact that she was married was never a problem or subject of discussion by anyone because things were always low key and under control. I never as much as touched her or intimated anything improper or suggestive. I took care to be respectful and had no intention to embarrass her in any way. Aunt Teréz showed jealousy once in her own way, not in any romantic sense, but simply saying, that lately I liked to spend more time at the counter, when Olga was working there. "Do I really?" -- said I, before switching to another subject.

I visited the pharmacy a few times in later years, once on my trip home from America. On that occasion Olga was not there. She moved to the other pharmacy. Aunt Teréz retired, followed by the Dobribans, to concentrate on wines. The old place looked less interesting, but otherwise fine, just as I remembered it.

The Dobribans had a sizable vineyard on the north shore of the

Balaton, not far from ours. My parents got together with them occasionally on the lake, after they retired from the pharmacy. They were always engaged in some sort of business and did very well, even with imposed restrictions, carefully skirting regulations. They were gingerly gaming the system, using their many friends for advantage. The pharmacy was their own before the regime nationalized all businesses. They were lucky. They were able to make arrangement through friends and connections, and were allowed to stay and continue managing their beloved *patika*. They were proud that our pharmacy made three times the business of the other, nicer one, in a better location.

Early in the spring of 1956, I moved back home, to start a very different project. The state initiated an insemination program for cattle. Before that, each little village owned a few choice bulls that were used for all the village's cows for fathering calves. That was old tradition, but a lot of expense in keep and care. The more important reason for the switch, however, was the improvement in animal stock that could be achieved by this centralized, nationwide initiative. Father told me about the program and asked if I had any interest doing it. I signed up and went for a two-week course to Szombathely, the county seat, where a new facility was built the year before, to house the animals, provide the sperm and coordinate the project. It was an interesting job, that I started after short training and was doing, until I left the country on November 14th. The course was easy, leaving a lot of time for fun in the city.

I stayed with a family, the Joós, whose son Gyuszi, just finished the course and was already working on organizing his district with my father's help. He had Jánosháza and a couple other villages. Gyuszi had a younger sister, Zsuzsa, a bubbly, sweet, gregarious girl. We fast became friends and only because of my timely departure at the end of my course that more serious things did not develop.

Mrs. Joó was a wonderful, kind, friendly woman. I liked her from the moment we met. She wouldn't hear of me paying for my stay, saying that it is small repayment for the help we gave her son. All this, after Gyuszi stayed with us a mere week, before he set himself up in an apartment. Mrs. Joó naturally assumed the role of a surrogate mother, as if she knew me from childhood. She treated me as one of her own, yet with deference as to my individual wishes. I tried to be a good guest and gave her as little extra work as possible. My stay with them was an enjoyable one. I went home for the weekends.

There was a woman, Marie, a few years older than me, who worked in the lab. I heard she paid attention to younger men. It seemed, I qualified. She lived on the premises. I worked with her as a regular part of my training. One day I invited her to a movie. She told me to buy tickets for seats in the fifth row on the balcony. I did as she asked, but wondered, why there. When we went up, I saw that it was the last row. The area was sparsely occupied. I understood. I do not remember what movie we saw...

Later she invited me to her place. This was the day before the training course ended. I got home very late. On that day, or really, the night, she gently guided me through a young man's seminal rite of passage. -- I was 19 years old. I found the experience not quite what it was cracked up to be -- at least not on that day. Mrs. Joó saw me come in early that morning. She greeted me with a polite hello. I knew, that she knew, but we talked only about ordinary things. I thought it was a good day to go home. I saw Marie a few more times, in a strict business setting. I was self-conscious and wanted scrupulously to control gossip, of which there was some. I thought I'll die if my parents hear of it.

The new job was interesting and kept me busy at the beginning, while I organized my daily round. I worked three-four hours a day, visiting my villages. It was a best *full* time job I ever had, unless I count retirement. My objective in the starting up process was to persuade farmers that this new method held great, manifold promise. Change is hard, even when it is for the better. Old habits and ideas are held, against persuasive new ones, often because of laziness and accustomed comfort. The most amusing excuse for not participating was, when the owner said that he felt sorry for the cow, and the poor bull, who was now deprived of his life's main pleasure. The bulls were kept for a while, they said in case I didn't show up one day. The real reason was that many did not believe in the new way and wanted a backup.

Advantages abounded from this new program. It was a great idea and had potential promise. In the training course they told us that the method was patterned after a Soviet program, which has already proven successful. Father told me that it was really an American pioneered way to improve livestock. We did not only inseminate cattle. We also treated those with uterus infection or cyst problems. I learned how to recognize ovarian irregularities, that prevented ovulation. I treated them on the spot. Within two weeks, the cow was back, ready to conceive.

Treating infection in the uterus was also easy. I flushed it out with a disinfectant, three consecutive days. I was surprised and pleased with the results. It worked every time -- except one, but it was my fault. I aborted a 5-week old fetus. The case, soon after I started, taught me my most important lesson. I mistook a pregnant cow for an infected one, because I thought, the lump I felt, was a sign of infection. The information by the farmer, about the animal's behavior also indicated a problem and confused me. At that stage, I was clueless, at least in the practical sense, about distinguishing between benign and malignant swelling, symptoms and problems, that later became routine and easily remedied.

It was a shame. It was my first and only abortion. I apologized to the farmer who was understanding, or at least polite. I did not even hear from my superiors. Such mistakes were probably expected from beginners and happened also to others. I saw the cow again in a few weeks. It conceived on schedule.

I talked to Father about this, as we often did about other "collegial" concerns. His explanations improved my understanding and made my job more interesting. I became proficient in confirming pregnancy.

By mid-summer, for the first time, I could inform a client farmer, that a healthy calf was growing in his cow. The first successful calving occurred while I was still working. It was just days before I suddenly left my homeland forever. By then my work gained respect. The farmers calmed down and resigned to the new order. As positive results began to show, things became easy and my work, popular.

The insemination procedure was simple. In the breeding station they had about a dozen bulls, the best studs in the country. I have never seen bulls like those before. Julcsa, despite given a girl's name, was the best of that great lot. Marie in the office saw to it that my daily shipment was almost always by Julcsa.

Each weekday morning I picked up a small cooler at the rail road station, handed to me by the man in the caboose. A 50 c.c. tube in ice, containing about 10 % sperm in egg yolk. I had a 2½ ft. tube, with a rubber ball at the end for suction and injection into the uterus, just by a squeeze of my palm. I needed a mere few drops. The pregnancy rate, using such a small amount of this diluted sperm preparation (more than 1:100) was greater than the old, natural method -- never mind the other health advantages.

Some of the farmers rubbed the back of the cow. They said it helped to compensate for the old pleasures, their prized animals were forced to give up. -- And about the poor bulls? They lay idle for a few months and, one by one were gone. -- Instead of producing beef in 9 months -- they became beef.

I visited each of my six villages every morning, spending a good half hour working or waiting, depending on the cow-traffic of the day. It was satisfying to see how I began to gain the people's trust and respect. Soon news spread about pregnancies and later, healthy calves. I provided improved, free service, which otherwise would have cost them money and extra bother. Father was proud to hear the positive feedback.

A valuable perk of my position was a brand new red Pannonia motorcycle, a new model, a deluxe 250 c.c. edition from the Csepel Motorcycle Works. I was as proud riding that bike then, as I am now, driving my Cadillac DTS (Ildi's gift to me at retirement in 2001).

It had a modern, sleek design with the latest features, among them telescopic suspension, front and rear. I had to wait only a month for delivery, I'm sure, because of my *lofty*, politically correct job. My days of waiting passed slowly, full of expectations. In the meantime I used our little 100 c.c. Csepel. After the Pannonia arrived, for months it was the only one in town. It was a source of pride and brought a new freedom for me. Within the county I could use it without limits. I bought gasoline with vouchers I was given. I found it hard to stay within the territory and took a chance to go down to the Balaton one Sunday. As luck would have it, I ran into a police check. They demanded papers, which I had, but not a special pass outside the county. It cost me some anxious moments, but after some negotiation, only a small fine.

Once I managed to finagle a permit to take the bike to Budapest for service. The trip became a fun-filled, long weekend in the big city. Tomi and I went together and had a great time.

Later that summer I had, what I now see as an amusing incident, involving an AVH man; AVH being the Hungarian communist secret police, the same as the GPU was for the Soviets. It was a domestic security police, which also had a political watchdog arm, the most vile AVO.

Coming home from work one day, I passed a slower guy, riding another bike. Before I went home, I stopped for a chat at Szeci's, the shop owned by a friend, a local mechanic. Soon after I got there, a man I didn't know, pulled up for minor service. I paid absolutely no mind to him, nor did I recall, that he was the one on the road earlier. After a short time chatting with Szeci, I left. -- Next day he told me that the guy was an AVH man in civilian clothes. Szeci also said that he asked who I was, and told my friend that I turned back, and laughed, after I passed him on the road, earlier that morning. "Rubbish" -- I said, but his comment to my friend gave me concern:

"What is this? Doesn't the man know that he is dealing with a party member?"

I told Father about the *incident* on the road and what followed. I told him as I remembered it. I looked back to check the clearance between us, before I returned to my lane on the narrow road. (I had no right side mirror on my bike.) Father did not share my worry. He was bemused by the strange reaction of the man and said something to the effect that, in his view, it was not much of an "adult thing". With that, he dismissed the event, that he would not lose sleep over. I, gladly and with relief, adopted the same view.

The summer of 1956 came and passed. We decided to try again, this time to gain admittance to veterinary school for the fall. I hoped that my past year of experience will help, but I was not accepted. The reason given was again, lack of opening in the freshmen class. It looked hopeless after trying in vain three consecutive years.

We knew that in cases like mine, there was at the county or state level of the Party, a master file, superseding all other relevant documents. That file was determinant in deciding things such as entry to school, jobs or institutions, or even getting pension.. This method of control was widely used for blocking promotions or city residency permits for many. The name of this ominous file was "káder". It was one of the most ubiquitous and for many, otherwise innocent people, the most feared document. It was only for the eyes of the anointed and all powerful decision makers in the Party.

Closest to it in America is a raw FBI file, reserved for use by grand juries only. Such files were blatantly abused by the Clintons. More than 900 FBI files were illegally taken to the White House and used for intimidation and blackmail. The subject was barely mentioned by the friendly media.

I could recount a number of cases where people I knew were ruined by their káder file. It held them back, kept them from using their knowledge, skills, talents and ambition --   or even take up residence in Budapest.

I will cite the cases of two, whom I knew well. An urbane and well schooled man, Gyuri Lippai was a family friend.

He had a Ph.D. in sciences, was from a well-to-do family, the brother of Aunt Klára Szabó, of whom I wrote earlier. Being educated and coming from a privileged background was two strikes against him, especially the latter. He was branded as one from the "exploitive class". After he came home from a Russian prisoner-of-war camp about 1948, he was unemployed for a time. Finally he was able to secure a job as (overqualified) driver for the local soda bottling company. He collected empty bottles, filled them and drove the horse-drawn wagon to make deliveries in town. We looked forward to his visits. When he came to our house, he often took time out for a little chat. Whatever we talked about, he exuded optimism, industry and responsibility, proving the old maxim: there is no job, that is not worth doing well. He did his with a happy heart and good cheer.

There was another interesting aspect to Uncle Gyuri. One late afternoon I saw him coming for a dip in the lake, when I was about to leave for home. We were, I think, the only people on the beach. He dove in for a swim. Soon he was doing the butterfly stroke, which I never saw done before. The butterfly is the most difficult stroke in swimming. He did it with ease, swimming at a speed that amazed me. I stayed on and waited for him on shore. After complimenting him on his style and pace, he told about his swimming career. It was something to hear.

He was on the Hungarian Olympic swimming team and a good friend of Ferenc Csik, the 1936 gold medal winner at the Berlin games. Csik was his mentor and coach when he trained to be a competitor. Back then, Olympic sports were for amateurs.

As an aside -- the 1952 Helsinki Olympics was the first one I followed closely. (The games were canceled during the war, so there were no games in 1940 and '44.) Hungarians really shined in Helsinki, winning 10 gold medals, and 42 overall. Hungary was the third in world ranking, beating all other European countries, and many others with much higher population, e.g. Japan, Brazil, Mexico. A country of 10 million, in the true Olympic spirit, showed what amateur sports should be. Till today, Hungary is first in proportion to population, including the data from all modern Olympics. This was before East Germany started the extreme opposite practice of developing champions by the vile method of drugs, doping and a punishing training regimen. They learned from the Soviets who, in the first Olympics they attended (1952) won a series of medals in gymnastics with their obviously mature looking team. As we later learned, their gymnasts were accomplished circus performers. They were put in the Red Army as cover, dazzled and perplexed the judges and took home a lot of gold.

In other areas of sport, the aggressive drive to prove the superiority of the "Soviet Man", contests with athletes of satellite nations were often arranged using intimidation, to favor the Soviets. A blatant example was one notorious soccer match. Moscow Dinamo, a premier Soviet team came to Budapest in 1953, to show off its prowess against *Fradi* (Ferencváros) one of our top teams. The game was fixed. The much better Hungarian team was intimidated by the highest levels in the Party to *take a dive* and lose the game. A farce in the first half, it became something grotesque, yet witty and imaginative by our guys. In the *epic struggle*, as it was billed, we witnessed a clever deception by a Hungarian player. Toward the end of the lopsided contest, with the score tied 2:2, the ball was traveling on Hungarian feet, as it did through most the game. Then our star striker got down close to the goal. Only the goalie was in front of him, after he dribbled his way by the defenders. He dribbled by the goalie too, who tried to dive on the ball. Then he was facing the empty goal and lead the ball to the goal line and stepped on it, to stop it. Then, instead of kicking it in, he turned around and kicked it back, in the other direction. At the end, the Russians went home with the game won. Word got out that some players were deeply embarrassed with the win. Perhaps, they felt as much the victims of that system, as did the opposing team, thus robbed of victory.

* * *

Although qualified, Uncle Gyuri was prevented to go to the London Olympics, or to Helsinki, and quit competitive swimming. Watching him swim, I admired the powerful kicks that give the forward thrust to a swimmer, at the moment, his arms are in the air, moving forward in unison for the next stroke, as wings of a bird -- or if you prefer, butterfly.

(At the time I did not know, and neither did he, that the frog-kick he was using so effectively, was soon to be a relic of the past, that no serious butterfly swimmer will ever use again. In the early 1950s a fellow swimmer, his countryman, invented the "dolphin kick" that proved to be a better propellant for the butterfly swimmer. The man's name was János Utassi. He was an Olympic athlete, but won no gold medal. His teammate, György Tumpek, was able to apply the new kick better than its inventor and *he* became one of the most successful swimmers of his day, winning bronze in Melbourne, 1956.)

Uncle Gyuri drove the soda wagon at least until I left Hungary. My sister tells me that years later, he was "rehabilitated" from his class enemy status and had a successful business career.

The other friend, with a similar story, was one of my best in Pannonhalma, Kálmán Gerencsér. He and I spent a lot of time together in our freshmen year. For months we planned to visit each other during the coming summer. We needed parental permission. We both were successful with our requests. I had no problem with Mother. She just asked me a few questions and approved. Father was not even part of the decision, as I knew it, though they talked about it between them, I'm sure.

After I got Mother's OK, I sat down with a post card and exuberantly wrote to Kálmán: "Everything is OK. Come soon. -- Miklós". In my eager impatience I thought this was all that we needed to celebrate the success of our months-long planning. Mother saw the card and threw it out.

"You want to send *this*?" -- she asked. "What kind of invitation *is* this? Think of it Son, would you want to be invited anywhere, with a card like this? What would Mrs. Gerencsér think, should she'd see it?" -- I wrote another card.

Mother was gentle, but persuasive in her own way, but there were times when she did not suffer fools gladly. I think, to lead one to solution of a problem, questioning, the Socratic method is most effective. When done well, the unwitting subject of persuasion might think that he was the one, who discovered the truth or found the way to solve the problem. This was an example of that method.

Kálmán came that first summer and stayed three weeks with us. Father took us with him several times. I was proud to show him a slice of small-town life. We did things that came naturally, everyday stuff that came along, just to share and have fun. We biked around, went to the beach and spent time with my brothers and friends and went a few times with Father. He seemed to enjoy his time with my family. -- Later I went to his home in Kõszeg, a small border city near Austria, with a lot of history and unique medieval architecture. Things like that are more interesting to me now than they were then. As for things to do for boys, I thought it did not have the variety that my little town, my house and my family offered, though I may be biased. We went to the city pool a lot and walked around town. Kálmán had a comic side that was natural. He had a gift of gab, humor not humble, and a certain panache to make it all work. He could turn a phrase or comment on ordinary action and create a funny situation.

We were at the railroad station in Jánosháza, when a train pulled in. I put a 2 fillér piece, on the track, ahead of the huge steam engine's first wheel. We wanted to see what happens to the small copper coin, size of a penny, after the big locomotive rolls over it. We were standing by the engine, waiting. The engineer was leaning out toward the station, looking back for command to move on. Then Kálmán called up to him:

"Mr. Engineer, we put a coin on the track. Lean down hard, please. We would like it well flattened". A little corny perhaps, but illustrated his simple whimsy. -- The man, up in his cabin smiled and promised full cooperation.

A few words about our train station. It was one of the most pleasant spots in town, if one discounts the occasional noise. To me as a child, the trains, coming and going, were not noise, but sounds that had an aura of travel and romance. The station was impeccably clean, well groomed with trees, flower beds and decorations, that made it a nice place to visit. The station master, in attractive uniform, greeted and gave the signal for departure for the trains. -- On quiet Sunday afternoons, it was a stop for courting lovers, to sit for a while on a bench, painted bright red on the boards and white for the concrete support frame. I remember, as if I saw it yesterday.

Kálmán had no sibling and, by the time I met him, no father either, who died in the war. His widowed mother sent him to the best school in the country at a great sacrifice for a widow with no pension -- perhaps for similar reasons, I ended up there. But even in his death the dead soldier was an outcast that put a permanent stamp on his family. Mr. Gerencsér was an army officer in the pre-communist era. This stigma followed Kálmán through almost the whole of his remaining life. He was denied entry to the university. He worked in a mine for several years. Eventually he became an engineer through part time night school. After that, his professional progress was stymied for many years. He became ill and died much too young.

We corresponded for several years, after I came to America, but lost contact after one of his change of addresses. I talked to some of my classmates who told me Kálmán's sad story. Several tried to help him in employment, as occasions arose. After drifting through life with menial jobs, he was finally cleared by the Party, for suitable employment. Even then, through a presumed bureaucratic snafu, the letter, restoring his new status, was not passed to local authorities and the all-important paper never reached his káder file.

I prefer recounting happier stories, that fit his personality better. I could tell stories of his humor and talents. He lead in most categories. He was a star in soccer, basketball, track and theater. Near the top of the class, he didn't have to exert himself too much. All seemed to come naturally for him. In ball sports he had feet and hands whose accuracy was uncanny. He could hit the basket, nothing but net, from as far as where the 3-point line is now. He could thread the needle with a soccer ball as well. He demonstrated it often. Not one of us could match his accuracy.

One winter afternoon we were standing with several other friends at the popular gathering place, the top of monastery garden. In this tiny spot, just inside the gate, was a geographic direction table, a finely carved stone platform on a pedestal, with lines cut from the center, pointing to many directions. The distances in kilometers, to many world cities, were carved along the lines. The most distant city, I think, was Rio de Janeiro.

This part was on level with the road and the entry to monastery grounds. From there, as we entered, we would overlook the whole garden and farm fields. We were looking down, at the top of tall trees, bushes, the drained pool and serpentine walks, that lead to the lower, gentler slopes, where the monks were growing crops and fragrant lavender. As if watching a wide view from a high platform, or as from a floating hot air balloon, we saw the land drop steeply before us just beyond the railing, then leveling off in the distance, presenting a magnificent vista for miles. Two walkways, one to the left and the other to the right, were leading down inside, along the garden fence that followed the road, then after a straight run made a couple sharp turns and lead to the lower area of the garden, where the friars took their walks. We usually ran down in big steps as we hurried toward the field. Lower down, past the fragrant purple lavender rows, was the soccer field where we played in spring and fall. (Our team was the best. Even as sophomores, we beat the teams of the other seven A and B classes. In all four years, we lost only a handful of games.)

On that winter afternoon we were talking, overlooking the garden. Nobody felt like going down on the slippery steps. Kálmán, after carefully squeezing some snow into a tight ball, pointed down, toward the pool and said:

"Do you see that manhole cover?" -- We nodded. -- "I'm going to hit that."

"OK" -- we answered his boast, paying increased attention.

The cover was down, about a 45 degree angle, at a distance of 120 ft or so. Not a great distance, but I thought quite a tricky throw, because of the direction, steeply down, not often attempted.

He wound up, aimed down, and hit the spot right on. Then he made another snowball. " I'm gonna hit it again."

This time he threw the snowball *up* at a like angle. It landed on the spot, after traveling nearly twice the distance of the first one. Artillery officers would appreciate this feat. It was all in an afternoon's work for Kálmán.

Our class was unique for a high school class, though not so much for a class at Pannonhalma. All young people who wanted to join the priesthood, had a very limited choice in secondary education. Catholic schools numbered just a few in the entire country. Of those, ours had by far the best environment as preparation for the priesthood. From my class of 32, seven became priests. Five became doctors, another six engineers and one an Egyptologist. -- A sad statistic: three of my classmates died of suicide. I know little about their circumstances, but they all occurred during the communist era; two from the same, small town, each with doubtful future, because of family origin (landowner), took their own life within a year.

At Pannonhalma we received the best education in liberal arts, one would ever want. I was in the A class, that stressed the humanities. The B class emphasized the sciences and was more for engineer types. Our curriculum included more language and art, with less math and sciences. It is one of life's ironies that I became an engineer, and pursued it for 25 years, with my high school literature, Latin, history, etc. (Even in college, in my sophomore year, I changed my major from chemistry to international relations. I studied political science, diplomacy and finance and earned a BA. In the first job I held, my official title was "engineer", as it was also for my colleagues, all with a genuine engineering degrees. What helped me to get the job, was an Associate Degree in Chemistry and Metallurgy.)

Our advantage over other high schools was the atmosphere of the old monastery and the isolation and seriousness of our life there. I talked about the history of the place. The physical facilities themselves were monastic and scholarly. We occasionally grumbled against our monk-like life, although knew what a privilege it was to be there, especially in the midst of an oppressive, godless, materialistic, communist world, that was Hungary in those days. We had religion class, as part of our curriculum. Three times a year we had a retreat, to spend time in prayer, meditation and introspection.

The first few hours in these retreats were always hard. Suddenly everything stopped and we were to look inside and forget the world for a while. The two short retreats were just a weekend, 1½ days. Walks were encouraged to be solitary, or at most, in pairs. A solemn theme dominated our time and by the end, it took a while to get back to reality. I remember several speakers who inspired me. I remember Father Pius as the best. He conducted one of the long ones, Wednesday noon till Sunday evening. He left a lasting impression on all of us and we talked about him for a long time.

Throughout the year, the weekend -- Saturday after school till Sunday evening -- ended with the appropriately named "Completorium" -- completing the week, as the Latin word indicates. This was closest to a true monastic event, with settings that fit the occasion. The entire dorm walked over, through the dark, deserted corridors of the monastery to the equally dim basilica. We prayed and sang away the last waking hour of the weekend. The music and the nature of the event was new to me. I was familiar with many Catholic ceremonies, but this was a little too somber. We joked about it at the time, but even years later, when we got together we often sang its hymns. The most memorable verse was about the Virgin Mary, who as God's instrument, *saves us from asps and vipers, and keeps us away from the nest of dragons.* (A bit medieval, don't you think?) All sung to gentle music of a cloister. -- With the passing of time, our Sunday send-off seemed more amenable and I learned to like it. It was a truly unique experience and now I think of it fondly and with nostalgia.

A few times a year, the Abbot said a high mass in the basilica. Those were grand occasions. A sizable entourage of assistant priests and "ministrants" busied themselves throughout the 2½ hour mass. We heard Gregorian chants and magnificent organ music throughout. We were standing or kneeling all the way through. Our math teacher, Father Szabolcs was the "ceremonarius" -- master of ceremonies. Like in a large stage production, he had to know the next move at any moment and direct the various groups and individuals to their places and prompt them to sing, pray or bring up instruments for the next phase of the ceremony. He was as smooth there, as he was in class, where he could breeze through a long, involved mathematical process to prove some obscure theory, without ever taking a pause.

The basilica was the center of the monastery complex. It was a massive, stern, gothic structure with high granite walls, arches and columns. Seldom did I see it full, because of its size and the fact that only the hardy or the resolute of the village people were regular attendees. Instead of taking the long, steep walk up to the abbey, most went to their small village church. Each of the two side entrances lead to a different part of the cloister. Often, just on my own, I liked to roam the empty corridors that exhibited a great variety of architectural styles and contained paintings sculptures and religious items, the monks created or collected through the centuries. I got to know some of the several hundred, who lived in the complex. We greeted one another with "Laudetur Jesus Cristus". Often they were reading the breviaries, or the *Imitation of Christ* by Thomas Kempis, parts of the daily, four-hour mandatory devotion.

Benedictines are a teaching order, established by St. Benedict (b. 480, Nursia, Italy), sanctioned by Pope Gregory the Great. The order in Hungary was established by Duke Géza in 996 and deeded by his son, Hungary's first Christian king, St. Stephen, whose original stone chair is still in the lower church, or as we called it, *crypt*. He endowed the abbey magnanimously and visited it often. Since then, the order has been operating a university within monastery walls. Young monks were coming in, preparing for priesthood, monkshood and to be teachers and scholars. -- "A good priest keeps learning till death", the saying goes. Many on Pannonhalma hill lived by that creed. Theirs was a life of becoming devout Renaissance men, a life of praying, learning teaching and contemplating eternal life.

Some instead of teaching, devoted their time to physical labor. They worked in the fields, cultivating their farm acres. The order traditionally was a land owner and employed a sizable staff of field hands. The profit from the agricultural operations supported the order and its schools. They received no support from the state. (This regime, that worked well for centuries, was turned upside down in the communist era. Land, schools and most of their property was confiscated.)

During my sophomore year a young novice arrived in the monastery to begin his studies. He was Józsi's classmate in high school. One Sunday, when my parents visited me, Józsi came along. We received special permission and went to spend a short time with him. In the first year of novitiate, his class lived in silence. Verbal communication was used for the most basic communication reasons and only during designated hours. Most monks were happy in this state and considered it an important part of preparation for a life of discipline and self denial. They were living a monastic life and were studying to be teachers.

Their professors were the same fathers who taught us in our school. Most teachers held a Ph.D., some two, and Father Geláz, three. I wonder, if for that, I should know more about birds and flowers. I like nature and her creatures, but if I lack sufficient knowledge, it is surely not for any shortcoming on his part.

25

Un-anticipated Experience
In A Chapel

Among the many nooks and crannies I liked to visit, there were a few special areas in the monastery of Pannonhalma. In those days everything was open. No permission was needed and I walked over to the old buildings often, finding any excuse just to take in the atmosphere of the austere stone walls and hoping to bump into some of the monks I got to know. During my sophomore year the abbey took on additional responsibilities. The spacious buildings had extra room to accommodate more people. Part of the cloister became home for retired friars. They added some color and traffic in the hallways. Some liked to talk to us, as they were taking their slow walks through the corridors, the monastery drive and some even in the garden.

The main dining room was a baroque jewel. I eagerly looked for opportunities to show its beautiful and elaborate splendor, when I escorted visitors, friends or family through the buildings. I saw it only in afternoon hours when it was empty. It must have been a splendid sight, seeing it full with monks during dinner. It had a small lectern on a dais in the corner where, at the beginning of each meal, a novice read something sacred -- or maybe profound

-- just as I tried once in Keszthely a few years earlier.

My special and most favorite was a large chapel, the "Káptalan". Many years ago it was a meeting chamber, later made into a chapel. It was lofty, serene, decorated white and gold in the Renaissance style. I loved to visit it and found it most inspiring. Beautiful frescos decorated its walls and ceiling. There was talk among teachers and students that a miracle happened there a few years earlier. I do not recall the details, but the subject of the miracle was Father Szulpic. He was a humble, kindly man, but I never had him as teacher and talked with him only occasionally. He outlived most of my teachers and was the one who was called down and came to greet us at the gate, and escorted us through the monastery in 1996, when I visited the old abbey, with my brothers and cousin, Sabina.

I myself had a seminal experience in the Káptalan that, with some trepidation, I would like to relate. I was not going to write about this but changed my mind. Since the event more than 50 years have lapsed. For a long time I was reluctant even to recall what happened to me there, although it is one of my most precious personal experiences. I thought that it may have been an aberration and it should not be disturbed out of reverence. I never followed up on it or tried to replicate it. Maybe I should have?

As a sophomore, I was in a small group of students on an educational tour through the abbey. We stopped in the Káptalan. After a short presentation by our guide we stayed for a prayer. I took my place in a pew and was overcome by the spirit of the chapel. Inspired by the aura of the place, I was immersed in a meditative devotion. I remember going ever deeper inside me and enjoying a steadily elevating feeling. I felt in my mind that on this one occasion I was able to leave the physical world. I was traveling deeper and deeper and felt that I was on a beautiful spiritual journey, that gave me enormous pleasure. After a while -- I lost track of time -- I was, if I dare to think, in what seemed to me a state of ecstasy. The feeling effected me to the deepest essence of my being and down to the marrow of my bones.

My memory of the event is clear and precious. Perhaps, with my amateurish trying on my visit to the Káptalan, I gained an inkling of what the saintly devoted had been able to perfect for themselves, as their form of prayer and spiritual exercise. It is a state, in which one, for a time is able to free the self from the ordinary trappings of this world, that drag us down in our quotidian concerns and rise above mundane thoughts, to reach high and accept the gift of momentary grace.

May I share some of the writing of the late British scholar, Kenneth Clark, one the most cultivated persons I ever knew. In his book, and his television series, *Civilisation,* he describes a glorious, and "...one of the most deeply moving works of European art", the allegorical sculpture by Gianlorenzo Bernini: *Ecstasy of St. Teresa.* This beautiful white marble statue can be seen in the Cornaro Chapel in Santa Maria della Vittoria, in Rome.

Clark writes of Bernini:

...his gift of sympathetic imagination, of entering into the emotions of others -- a gift no doubt enhanced by his practice of St. Ignatius' Spiritual Exercises -- is used to convey the rarest and most precious of all emotional states, that of religious ecstasy. He has illustrated exactly, the passage in her [St. Teresa of Avila] *autobiography in which she describes this supreme moment of her life: how an angel with a flaming golden arrow pierced her heart repeatedly. 'The pain was so great that I screamed aloud, but simultaneously felt such infinite sweetness that I wished the pain to last eternally. It was the sweetest caressing of the soul by God'.*

Not trying to compare. I know it is too daring, but I see a vague parallel with the spirit of Bernini's work of deep meaning, and my memories of those brief, sublime moments, so long ago in the Káptalan. I did not think of this for a long time but did again, after I saw Clark's TV series and later re-read the passage in his book.

I never wanted to take this experience seriously and told only Ildikó and my friends Imre, and Father Denis, many years later. -- (I read an early draft of these paragraphs to Father Denis. He thought it moving and gave me his opinion: "Such an experience is a rare gift of God and seldom granted more than once in one's life".)

26

Audience With Abbot Paul

Near the chapel of the Káptalan, was the entrance to the magnificent library. It is the second largest in the country, after that of the House of Parliament. (Not a surprise. The parliament's is less than 200 years old. This venerable collection dates back to more than a millennium.) It is a four-story high enormous chamber, containing countless invaluable volumes of rear and old books. Architecturally pleasing with high columns and carved wood throughout. It was closed to students. With escorts we could enter and even had limited use of its treasures, but it was a rare event. The library was reserved for the pursuit of serious scholarship. Scholars and researchers were regular users. I had the good fortune to go there a few times, but only to look around and admire this cavernous temple of knowledge and architectural treasure.

The library operated its own bookbinding shop. A few of my friends had a paying job, that was granted with consideration to their material status. The money they made was an indirect, small financial aid. There was a lot of work in keeping old, valuable books in good shape. I know anecdotally from those who worked there, that in time they acquired skills in the special art of rescuing and restoring books that were handled by too many hands through the centuries and were just ravaged by time. The few kids who worked there valued this job to earn some cash, a rare opportunity on our isolated hilltop.

The separate large art gallery contained many rare paintings. They were occasionally rotated out and shown on the monastery corridors, that were an open gallery for many, mostly religious paintings and portraits of abbots, long passed on. In time I could count the abbots back to before the turn of the century. Teachers and especially old friars told stories about prior heads of the order and imparted valuable historical knowledge about them and their time.

I regret that I saw the main collection only once. Not one painting do I recall specifically. I have just a vague memory of many saints and Madonna's, darkened by age and perhaps, in need of cleaning. Once I saw an extensive list of contents and was amazed at the number of great, world-renowned artists that are represented in the collection.

My ultimate adventure in art, beauty and grandeur was when we visited the abbot's apartment. While I was a freshman, the Abbot, Krizosztom Kelemen died. Paul Sárközi was named abbot by Pope John XXIII. This new head of the order grew up in Jánosháza, but left before Father moved there. They met later through our pastor. -- On one of the spring weekends for parental visits, my parents and my little sister, Marika came to visit Tomi and me. Father asked for an audience with Abbot Paul, who obliged him. The apartment and adjacent areas were under "clausura", that is, restricted to men only. Nuns were allowed during designated hours to do assigned work. The Abbot's invitation came with the requisite exemption from clausura to my mother and sister, for the duration of the visit.

When we arrived, his secretary motioned toward the entrance then escorted us into the waiting room. After a few minutes we were asked to go on. As I turned and entered the next chamber, I saw ahead, about six rooms at a glance. The view resembled royal palaces I've seen. The rooms were in a straight line, each with a door at the center of opposing walls. All doors were open and I could look all the way, into the abbot's office at the far end. One long runner, through all door openings, led from the waiting room to his quarters. If one stood in the center of the doorway at one end, he could see all the doors in a row, gradually smaller, as they receded. As we walked through the rooms, we saw tapestry, paintings, sculptures, religious articles and a lot of rich, mostly red drapery. The rooms exuded dignified splendor and lot of history.

Through the last door we entered his office. Abbot Paul greeted us kindly. There was no planned agenda. We just came for a friendly chat, and spent about a half hour. He and Father covered the current topics of church and politics.

We said our good byes. On the way out he gently touched the head of my sister, who then was three years old. It was one of only two occasions when I talked to Abbot Paul one on one. At a later time, he was coming unescorted into the monastery from his walk. We chatted for a few minutes. I saw him a lot on holy days, during high mass. He was quite old then, seldom walked far, and not down those steps and steep walks of the garden. He preferred the *quadratura*, the monastic interior square garden, surrounded by high buildings, and columns of the arched open corridors, that were looking into the enclosed yard, with its sculptured flower beds, gravel walks and a few benches. He liked to spend solitary time there, reading his breviary and perhaps contemplating on his problems, running the order in difficult times.

I felt lucky and privileged that I had the opportunity to see this special sanctuary of the Holy Hill. I got to know the Abbot personally through Father, and for the coincidence of our common hometown. (Once I saw a picture of the papal apartments in the Vatican. There was a resemblance.)

On one of my visits to the library, I saw an old drawing, a view of the monastery from the south. In the forefront it showed a wall with towers and gun emplacements. It was the first time I saw how the abbey looked for centuries, before a big change was made. In 1938, a large modern high school, building, with a four-story and two lower levels replaced this part of the structure. It was opened as an *Italian High School* and so remained, until the state seized it in 1948. I asked a student who also attended, before the

state took the school and returned after the give-back. He told me
that Italian studies were emphasized, with lot of Dante, Galileo
and Machiavelli. Italian was part of all curricula. Students had
informal conversation hours two afternoons a week, that were
conducted entirely in Italian. When the school was returned to the
order, the Italian program was not restored. I was a little envious
of that earlier group.

In New York in 1964, I was shopping once in the famous
Hungarian grocery store, Paprikás Weiss on Second Avenue. This
store had the look of the haberdashery of our distant relative, Mr.
Sik, back in Jánosháza, down the street fom where I lived. He lost
it to the local cooperative soon after the war's end. It never looked
the same after that.

Paprikás Weiss had that old touch. As if the place were lifted
from the pre-war Hungary and dropped in the middle of Manhattan.
After I stepped in from the street and left behind the cacophony of
midtown, I felt as if I traveled back many years. I was in a small-
town general store of my childhood, except this was bigger. It
had the most nostalgic air. By the door, I saw large burlap sacks
containing grains, flour, lentil and other dried commodities. As a
sack was gradually emptied, the top rim was rolled out, forming a
ring that was getting thicker as the sack's height diminished, and its
content depleted. Uniformed clerks, behind the long counter were
serving customers. Behind them the high back wall was taken up
by a myriad of wooden drawers, with white porcelain knobs. They
came in many sizes: large, small, tiny or flat, with various widths.
Clerks had to use a ladder to reach the top rows, that contained
items less in demand.

There on a card rack, among modern, colored postcards of
Manhattan, and Hungarian scenes, pictures of Buda castle and
the Parliament, I found one curled-up, black-and-white photo, from
prior to 1938. It was, the last copy, a postcard photo showing the
scene I have once seen in the library about a dozen years earlier.
I saw Pannonhalma, as it was before they built the high school.
The old fortress walls were still there. I had to wonder how it
survived on the picture rack for so many years. By blind chance,
this special gift was waiting there for me all these years. It was the

first time I gazed on a postcard from that far back. It was a small size version of the big picture I once saw in the library at the abbey. Had I not seen it there, I would've had trouble recognizing the old fort, replicated here on a post card. Only the basilica steeple and maybe some building features of the old fortress would've been the giveaway.

The school when built, was equipped with the most modern technology and conveniences for its day. They built a huge modern kitchen in the cloister, where all the food was prepared for the monastery and for students in the dormitory. On a visit to the abbey kitchen, I saw the shiny, all stainless steel equipment. I marveled at the beautiful setup. Nearby I also saw the huge drum of the automatic washer, they also provided, to handle laundry for the dormitory. I saw similar type wash machines only during my insurance inspection visits to commercial laundries in the US, 30 years later. The washer's huge drum turned 17 revolutions, then reversed. The guide said, it was the optimum number of turns, so contents do not tangle. They were right about the number of turns -- I counted. -- The fancy kitchen and laundry served only the monastery, after the nationalization of the school.

When the abbey was closed off by the brick barrier in the joining hallway in 1948, the school and dorm had to operate independently. With the connecting corridor walled shut, they had to provide new facilities for the school. They set up a make-shift kitchen in the basement, a poor cousin of the original, to do the dorm's cooking. When I attended school, it was staffed mostly by nuns in civilian clothes, who considered themselves bound to their original vow, but had to practice their devotion discretely. We had the use of a simple, self-serve laundry, and only a few other conveniences previous student generations.

27

The Big Test

At the end of the fourth year, early June in 1954, we had our big test. It was the "matura exam" -- a reference to the student's maturity and a testament that he is ready for the real world. We received our regular senior year final grades, and thought little about them, while concentrating on the matura, that was a separate series of exams, apart from regular high school curriculum examinations. The matura tested comprehensive knowledge, and encompassed the material for all four years. It was geared to test ability to think independently, by using disparate knowledge and facts, connected by common elements, that in our minds, long receded into obscurity. This test aimed to measure deductive ability and creative prowess to analyze facts, compose solutions, recognize relationships and predict results. It was the test for college acceptance. -- One of our sage teachers, with a touch of cynicism opined: "The preparation for this test will give you skills to use the library." -- I felt I had to memorize the entire library. (If you think it was an open book exam, you are wrong. We had only our pencil and paper we were given.)

We took written exams in four subjects a week before the oral tests. These were in ordinary classroom setting, except for the cryptic seriousness befitting the occasion. For Hungarian, it was an essay on an author or a major work. In Latin, and Russian, we had to translate at least a page of fairly difficult text.

The Latin test was a letter by Virgil. I made one big mistake in the translation, that was yet ambiguous. I realized it after I turned in the paper. I hoped that the way I wrote it, the reviewer might take my error as a play on words, or poetic license by a brazen, would-be translator. I never inquired, so it remains a mystery. Combined with the score of my oral exam, I got a B and was happy.

Details about the Russian test I don't remember. It is not surprising, because, as if by will, I forgot most of my Russian since then. I never spoke it since, so it may not be so strange. However, I do not speak Latin with anybody either, but I retained a sizable part of my knowledge of Latin till today. It was an enormous help for me in learning English, which could explain it. I still find use for it every day. But Russian was forced on us, which engendered resistance. We never wanted to learn it but had to. So I forgot almost all, despite studying it for six years, while I took Latin for only four. -- The math exam closely resembled an ordinary classroom test, just bigger and covering diverging areas of the discipline.

I have a tale about Russian. Our teacher was our class master, Father Anaklét. At the beginning of our freshmen year, he arrived to school a few days late, because he was recently released from a prisoner of war camp in the Soviet Union and just resumed his normal life. His qualification was the skill in the Russian language, he supposedly picked up in camp. Poor Anaklét! He had knowledge that was not very impressive. I had a couple year's Russian behind me from my last two in grade school. I could dance rings around my teacher when we began the year. Most of my friends were the same way. I breezed through first year of Russian, did OK later, but was increasingly forced to apply myself better as time went on. Imagine the hubris of a kid, who is good enough to correct in class the mistakes of his teacher. I was that kid for a while, along with others. Father Anaklét, as a good monk, plowed on and soon was able to teach us as a teacher was expected to. By graduation he was really good.

The oral part of the matura was like nothing else, ever. The school invited a panel of examiner judges from other schools and professors from the abbey. They sat in a head table on an a dais with their papers in front, facing the tense, nervous subjects of their scrutiny. The exams took all week. We were 32, the B class 28, I think. That meant 10 kids a day, half in the morning, the others after lunch.

My time was Tuesday morning. We gathered by the door and were called, one by one. Tests were on the main subjects, eight in all, including the ones for which we did the written tests earlier. -- We received our test questions. In history or Hungarian, they were of a general type, tracing a trend or movement through time in literature or history, comparing the influence of various authors or movements, illustrated with examples. The sciences were like other tests, only more comprehensive. The candidates repeatedly rotated in and out. The process had a flow, like a well oiled machine. We finished one subject, before turning to another, but while the last guys were making their presentations, the first in the group was back, preparing his on the next subject. Solutions in math had to be shown on a black board. At times, a member of the panel asked a question or requested clarification. This was by far the most pressure-cooker atmosphere I have ever experienced. By noon it was all done and by Saturday afternoon the whole thing was over. We were done with four years of high school and the huge aftermath. It was an extremely liberating feeling.

Suddenly all of high school was behind me. I had three days with absolutely no duties or purpose, only time to unwind and enjoy life without stress or pressure. As we were freed from our burden, increasingly larger groups gathered to discuss what we just went through and walked around the circle, the garden, out to the Millennium, the Chapel and back. The weather was ideal. It was very sweet time, but also one, nostalgically sad. A few days later we received our diploma in a rather simple ceremony and said good bye to the old Hill for good.

In the monastery, there lived a famous poet who, in effect, was hiding out. His name was László Mécs. I heard about him from my parents who knew him from years before. Rumors, entertained by only a few students said that his situation was precarious, because earlier he was jailed by the regime for several years, as punishment and to stifle his voice for his religious and patriotic poetry. Mother was not sure, whether the regime allowed him to live there undisturbed, or what his actual status was. Someone said that he was there incognito. It was hard to believe, for the authorities always knew everything. It was not realistic to believe that they would overlook it, or fail to follow one of their old enemies. Maybe he was neutralized as far the communists were concerned -- neutralized by intimidation. I never spoke to him, was circumspect asking about him, but I saw him occasionally on his walks. He liked to go down in the garden. Sometime after I graduated, his apartment was raided and he was imprisoned again.

In 1979 I had my 25 year reunion. We were five, Ildikó and daughters, Erika, Andrea and my mother. The girls were 9 and 8 years old. We arrived the night before and slept in one of the smaller rooms in the old dorm. In the intervening years, the dormitory's capacity was increased by installing high, double-deck beds. The upper bunk was up, at about 10 ft. The girls soon claimed it for themselves. We were the only ones in the room that had place to sleep a dozen. They were happy at their high perch. -- It was my first opportunity to get together with old classmates. We went to mass as we did in days gone by, this time with our families. Two sisters, read from the scriptures. They were the daughters of Marci, Dr. Breier. I do not recall the text, only the clearly enunciated delivery by two adolescents, as they were reading alternate passages. The quality of the reading was pleasing, but hard to put in words. The pleasant, undulating tone of their presentation earned the admiration of the group.

With Otti, Tomi, and cousin Sabina, I visited Pannonhalma in 1996, just a week after Pope John Paul II came to see it on the 1100th anniversary of Hungary's founding. I was pleased to see that the place was renovated, with application of fresh paint in many areas, that gave it a look it deserved. The library and adjacent corridors contained an extensive exhibition of Hungarian scientific achievements. That is where I saw the model of the first electric motor, invented in by Ányos Jedlik, one of the more famous monks of Pannonhalma. He took it for a demonstration at a Vienna science conference in 1856.

In those days, and especially after high school, I kept up with the *news*, mostly by reading a society magazine. (Coverage of politics in newspapers or radio was slanted and just propaganda. This magazine was full of pictures and not-too-serious news. It was a simpler, but not so tabloid version, of today's *People Magazine*. In one issue they had a contest. On one page, were 54 pictures of people from history, politics, society and of celebrities, a lot of bad pictures in the bunch -- I thought on purpose -- to make the game difficult. (A few pictures I recall, were Galileo, Elizabeth Taylor, Goethe and Leo Tolstoy.) It was a nationwide contest, with a large number of potential entrants. I knew my important people then. Being good in trivia, in a short time I made up my list. I was certain of the answers for 51 and made a guess on two. I thought there will be many, who will have all the 54 names, I, being one short, did not send in my entry. When the results were announced, I learned the following: Nobody got 54 or 53. The winning number was 52. My two guesses were correct, so I threw away my chance to win a nationwide contest. Too bad!

28

Convulsive Changes

In the summer of 1956, I was facing a precarious future. To find a slot at the university seemed hopeless. I was repeatedly denied entrance. What I received instead, was the first notice for the draft. There was no way to get out of it unless one had a disability. I was getting ready to join the army sometime in the fall. This process was interrupted by the revolution that began on October 23rd.

I did not serve in the military in any country. Not to serve in a communist army was fine. I thought about joining the US Army, but after I learned some English and started school, I thought it better to first finish that. As it happened, I was never called, initially because my automatic F4 status, being a full time student, then because of a low draft number. The Viet Nam war was not yet an important factor. -- I feel that I missed out on something important, never being called to serve. I miss the satisfaction one gains, by serving his country. Of course, I could have volunteered, but never did. The Viet Nam war was still going on while I was in school and getting uglier on the home front, that first surprised, then disgusted me. I am not sure that I should have volunteered. Not so much for the risks and hardship of military service, but the bitter atmosphere, whose residue is still with us today. The atmosphere was scary, mostly for the lack of support by Congress and the defeatists' anti-American attitude. I am convinced that we lost the war because of the *Hanoi Jane* leftists, and their allies in the press. It was a shameful thing and a humiliating lesson.

Today, I see similar efforts by liberals in government, the media, Hollywood and a segment of the population, who would rather lose the war in Iraq, then let the credit go to George Bush for winning it. They do not recognize that we have a war on us, by Islamio-terrorists, and the fact that they all want us dead. They rather ignore the threat and deny the country proper protection. What they want more, is to regain power.

By midyear 1956, political control in Hungary seemed to be easing. Stalin was dead for three years and left a huge power vacuum. Nobody could fill his despot shoes. After a couple rounds of musical chairs, Nikita Sergeyevich Khrushchev emerged to take the party helm, but we knew that it could never be the same. (To see a repeat of that, watch Cuba after Castro -- never mind Raul -- mind only Fidel.) In February 1957, Khrushchev denounced Stalin in a secret party meeting. It was a sea change.

As a natural consequence of incremental gains in freedom, the people wanted more. Gradually, signs appeared that the heavy hand of the state and secret police was less threatening and controlling. By fall, students started demonstrating for more freedom and reinstatement of ordinary rights and privileges that were a natural part of living before the communists. Excitement was in the air, rustling beneath, as people's expectations heightened. Radio reports were rare and masked in obscure language about what was really afoot. Regular party propaganda still continued to fill most newscasts.

In the Stalinist Rákosi regime, they were promoting and selling radio sets, that had only a couple settings: the two wavelengths of the state radio stations broadcasting from Budapest. (The one country still doing this in the 21st century, is North Korea.) I had a radio by my bed that I turned on routinely, as I woke. It was an older set, with the regular scale, able to receive all channels and short-wave, that I used evenings, to listen to the Voice of America jazz programs. -- In the morning of October 24th I heard only

static. I was confused. I didn't know that during the night the
studio on Brodi Street was taken over by student revolutionaries.
The program resumed after a while, but what I heard was not the
usual music with intermittent news. It was all news and it sounded
very different from what I was used to hearing. It was clear that
something momentous happened. Since the dawn hours, the radio
station was in the hands of students. -- They were protesting in the
streets a few days before, with special permit. The regime tried to
keep the lid on, by granting permits and hoping that things remain
under control. On October 23rd they requested another permit, but
when it was denied, the students had none of it. They went out,
testing the increasingly stretched limits of freedom, as one would
expect, and human nature dictates. The regime forgot, or never
knew, that freedom cannot be doled out piecemeal. The Party
perceived a threat and called out the AVO. Gunfight ensued. Fully
armed secret police against the bare hands of students. It was a
one-sided bloodbath, with hundreds falling dead and wounded.

An ambulance pulled up. It contained no medic, no equipment,
but arm supply reinforcement for the AVO. Soon another
ambulance came. The students stormed *it* and seized the guns and
ammunition inside. Patriotic employees at the armory, also gave
out rifles to fighting revolutionaries. The level of violence shot up
and blood flowed on the streets. Students with others joining in,
went to the radio station, occupied it and eventually took control.
What I heard on my radio that early morning, was the last phase
of that tumult.

There were several Soviet divisions in Hungary, a favorite
assignment for the occupying army. Many had family along,
housed in secluded compounds. We often saw large Russian
women with their shopping bags in stores. They came to shop in
our stores too, for variety or different merchandise. Their families
lived much better in Hungary than they would have at home. This
fact was a determining factor in the Soviets' decision not to use the
occupying troops for the repression of locals.

Heavy fighting and chaos lasted for several days. The enemy
was not the Russians but the Hungarian AVO, the goons of state
security. We fought for freedom, they, for restoring and maintaining

control. Up till then they had a free hand in their terror and had no accountability, except to their superiors and the Interior Ministry. These facts defined the battle. They knew that for past atrocities they can expect no mercy. They were well armed, took and caused many casualties, but after a few days they were defeated. The papers were full of pictures, documenting the fighting and showed many ugly scenes. On one picture, a man was hanged by his feet and the money from his pocket stuffed in his mouth. I still have many of these pictures of the events from *Life, Look, Saturday Evening Post* and other magazines, that I saved in the first weeks after I arrived.

It seemed incredible, but we won. The revolutionary government declared Hungary independent. Russian divisions were moving out of the country. We were in this unbelievably happy state for three days. Truckloads of farm products and meat were delivered to feed cities by farmers, to people in the cities. My father walked the streets evenings for several days, to calm passions of town youth and keep them from exacting revenge. He urged patience and told them to let law punish the guilty.

The crowd invited Prime Minister Imre Nagy to speak. He soon appeared and began his speech:

"Dear Comrades". -- He could not continue. The crowd, with one voice shouted: "We are no comrades! We are Hungarians, fighting for our freedom". -- Nagy continued: "My dear fellow compatriots..."

I recall hearing news that stunned and depressed me. I heard on radio, about an October 27th speech in Dallas by American Secretary of State, John Foster Dulles. He stated that the United States does not consider Hungary or Poland, possible allies. President Eisenhower repeated the message in a radio and television address a few days later. Henry Cabot Lodge quoted Dulles at the United Nations. It is without doubt, that this message was meant for the Soviets. This in effect, gave a free hand to Khruschev the top Russian military and the hard-liners in the party, who were advocating all along, the strongest suppression in Hungary. It is still incomprehensible to me, why the United States took a position, that was a cruel knife in the back to those, who wanted to throw off the yoke of tyranny and carried the banner of liberty bare handed against a world power. The ultimate irony is that while these messages were sent around the globe by American and world media, Hungarian heroes were celebrating victory. There were examples, in the days of October 28-31, where the members of the ragtag, army of revolutionaries were congratulated by soldiers of the Russian army, for throwing off the yoke of their despots. The Hungarian army also sided with the rebels. I saw pictures of Russian military families packing, ready to return home.

An explanation I heard many years later, was that in Eisenhower's judgment, though sympathetic, he believed that it was useless for a country of only a few million people to take up arms against the confident, best equipped nuclear power, the flagship of an empire, determined to hold onto power for the indefinite future. What a cop-out! We saw it as a cowardly retreat, after hearing promises for years in the Voice of America and Radio Free Europe about help from the west when needed, to freedomfighters behind the Iron Curtain. Even during the fighting we were encouraged to hold on and await help that was already on the way. To learn the truth was crushing. (How much *more* did we give and do for Iraq! But of course, there was 9/11. Hungary was too far away.)

True, Hungarians could have chosen not to challenge the great power. Initially, the movement and the uprising was entirely against domestic oppression and against those who carried the water for the occupying Soviets. It started by trying to throw out those who devised and executed one of the most harsh rule, a system of terror and exploitation of a people, in behalf of an occupying army and for their own thirst for power. -- Looking back with a perspective of 50 years, one might ask, what if we had chosen the road of placid acquiescence, as did the Czechs, hoping that their *Velvet Revolution* (a pathetic oxymoran) would be the road to freedom. -- No, we took on our oppressors. We could also have chosen to give up after the tanks and artillery returned. Many patriots would have escaped death in fighting or the indiscriminate slaughter after the uprising was crushed. After *their* "revolution", the Czechs had their country stay communist. It remained so for two more years after all the other Soviet satellites gained freedom.

(For the record: About 3,200 fell in fighting. In the retaliation, and to preemptively suppress anything similar in the future, 350 people were hanged. This included youth, who were held and sent later to the gallows, on their 18th birthday -- to make it *legal*. About 35,000 were indicted, of whom 26,000 were convicted and jailed. We had 13,000, who were sent to labor camps. It was risky to inquire about their case, status or whereabouts. An estimated 200,000 escaped, while the border to Austria was open for a short time.)

Also for the record -- indeed for history to remember -- the Hungarian revolt was the only one I know of that was a *pure* rebellion of people against its oppressors. During the free 12 days, when the mass of people, including all segments of society were fighting and were in control, nothing material was touched. People were fighting or walking by open stores and broken show windows, never touching contents inside. Some at the beginning were guarding shops and department stores and warehouses, but it was not necessary. The establishments were state owned, many with broken windows, yet they were not looted. We were fighting only for freedom, not for material things, despite massive country-wide poverty. Looting and destruction are common in less vital struggles, or even in celebration of victory in sporting events. In this revolt only the oppressors were in peril.

On October 31, news spread that soon after the last Russian left the country, new divisions from central Asia were moving back in. We sank into disbelief, despair and fear. For days we could see them filling up the country again with tanks, cannons and gun emplacements. They encircled Budapest and large cities, taking up strategic positions. We became observers and at the same time, subjects of something beyond comprehension. Fear was palpable. We stood by stunned and in disbelief. It was a death watch.

At 5 o'clock Sunday morning on November 4th, they began a coordinated attack throughout the country. We were up against the might of a nuclear power with millions under arms, equipped with the most advanced weapons -- well, second most. The fighting went on for more than a month, before the overwhelming force won. The Russians used tank artillery to shoot at anything that moved. Budapest looked worse after that brief span of time than it looked after five years of bombing and all-out war, ten years before. Burned out tanks and blown up vehicles littered the streets. Hope vanished, despair ruled.

Hungarians used to have a naïve hope that the West will stand up to the Soviets, but actions did not extend beyond sympathetic platitudes. The revolutionary government was not given official recognition. by any western power. The United Nations was as useless than as it is now, in enforcing its vowed, lofty principles. The only thing that changed at the UN in the several decades since, is that it is even more corrupt then was then. (See the *Oil-for-Food* program, that made Saddam Hussein a man, wealthy beyond measure, while his people were left starving as before. This was possible with the complicity of high UN officials, who were paid off by Saddam and stashed their share of riches in Swiss bank accounts.)

Prime Minister Nagy withdrew Hungary from the Warsaw Pact, the Soviet led military alliance. He then sent repeated pleas to the West for support, but was ignored. A few days after the Soviet attack, Gamal Abdel Nasser, president of Egypt, occupied and closed the Suez Canal. The panic in the United States drew attention away from the plight of Hungarians. Britain, France and Israel initiated military action, that was halted by UN action. During and after that, the world was occupied almost exclusively with Suez.

Looking back, on the 50th anniversary in an editorial published on 2006 November 26, the Chicago Tribune opined:

The U.S. didn't see Hungary as a potential military ally, so [in 1956] America would fight Soviet domination with sympathy and little else... Hungary cast the mold. The U.S. first stoked the hopes of freedom, then abandoned the courageous Hungarians who rose up to demand it. By valuing stability over the spread of freedom, the Eisenhower administration ... ceded future control of Eastern Europe to the Soviets. ... Hungary's greatest impact was within the Eastern Block. The revolution of 1956 lived on in the hearts of millions of people in neighboring lands until, after three plus decades of push and pull, the Berlin Wall finally fell.

29

Leaving Hungary Forever

Late in the evening of gloomy November 13th, we had a family conference. The subject of discussion was, whether I should stay in Hungary or go to Austria, while it was possible, before the borders would be closed again. Transportation by truck, with official cover, was available to the border town of Kapuvár. (To enter the so called "Border Zone", special permission was needed, or a special document of residence for those who lived there. I was part of a crew, to do needed work.) After long discussion, we decided that I stay and make the best of my situation in that communist society, whose end at the time we did not see. We went to bed late, after the subject was considered closed. I was ambivalent, but went along with the consensus.

Mother woke me up at 3 A.M. She said, she thought it over -- I should go. I do not know whether she dreamed something or lay awake all night thinking about this -- we had no time to discuss it. In a half hour I was aboard the truck, on my way to Kapuvár with two friends, also wanting to leave.

For the most important, most consequential step in my life, I had but a half hour to think and plan. My mother, who sometimes jokingly called herself the world's biggest coward, made a decision that was beyond brave. To send me away to the world at age 20, was a cathartic act of courage. Such a thing just days before, would have been inconceivable for her, just as for all of us. The difference for me was that I saw a chance for opportunity and adventure in leaving. My future looked grim in that oppressive society. The prospect of two years in the army did not appeal to me. My academic future was bleak if I stayed.

The numbing effect of incredible time-pressure can cripple one's decision making and cognitive power. Perhaps we all were under a spell and just chose the alternative which held some promise, however laden with uncertainty. With that decision I changed my whole life without knowing what was ahead for me. I knew that there would be difficult times but hoped that long term, the choice was for the better.

In the pressured haste I left behind Magdi, the love of my youth. Without the urgency of unexpected events, I may have done otherwise. I was in love with her, and I think, she with me. We were kindred spirits with unknown future, but whatever it may have been, was destined not to happen. I left my home and family in a rush, that was forced on us by the pressure of the hour. It happened under circumstances that were as unexpected, as was their sudden command for immediate action. I, with my family were compelled to do what that day demanded of us. While hoping for the best, I still knew that I would have to live with the long term consequences of my choice. The future had promise, but also great uncertainty. I was suddenly on my own, without the long accustomed comforts and security of family.

So I left my homeland on that day with a heavy heart and in crippling confusion about the meaning of events that swirled around me and left me confused for months. When one is occupied with the immediate tasks of the day, that determine things as mundane, as where one puts his head down for the night, other things become less important. One deals with what is at hand and postpones decisions on concerns of yesterday. What was most important just days before, is relegated to occasional pondering, knowing that at present, no solution can be found to deal with them. About Magdi, my emotions were pushed back and I could only entertain vague hopes that I may see her again. I had regrets, that I chased myself into such a hasty decision that is not conducive to result in a prudent outcome. She had no input in my decision. I didn't have a chance to ask her about that. At the same time, perhaps as an effort to compensate, I had hopes, that this change will bring adventure, the thrill of going to distant places and finding happiness in pursuing my bliss, free from the restrictions of the past. The die was cast. I knew, a chapter was closing in my life and a new one was about to open, as it always does. How it would play out, was up to me now -- up *only* to me. I had my proverbial *meeting at dawn*, a fateful meeting with my future, as it was suddenly thrust upon me. Life would test me. I had to measure up. There was no other choice.

I corresponded with Magdi for about a year. During our courtship she had another hopeful suitor. She told me that he seriously pursued her, but she rebuffed him. As time past, she mentioned him in her letters. In the last one, she told me that she will marry him.

I had a few girlfriends in the following years, but nothing serious developed. I was more occupied with learning the language and finishing college.

Everything changed when I met Ildikó. Love awakened and serious emotions filled me with happy anticipation and plans for proposal of marriage. I thought that God opened a window, where a few years before, dwelt only the sense of emptiness and feelings of loss. Meeting and getting to know Ildikó, has renewed my life, optimism and hope for the future.

She has admirable qualities which, I think, are God's special blessing. For many years, in addition to my evening prayers, I prayed separately for my future wife. I also fantasized about her. Where could she be, what could she be doing? What are her interests, her life's pleasures, taste in the arts and music? What are her favorite songs? Are they the same type that I like? I knew that *she was one,* that will love family and children for whose happiness she will willingly sacrifice.

Each evening I thought of someone I did not yet know, but thought I knew something about. She had to be compatible with my values and my temperament. Not the same as me, but perhaps contrasting and in some fashion, complimentary. That, I thought would make us whole, where the shortcomings of one could be corrected by the other. Love, devotion and a romantic bond must be the basis of our union.

Ildikó came into my life several years later. She was the person who changed everything for me. The year was 1965. By then, I was completely reoriented in my emotional makeup and was looking for a woman, with whom I would spend my life and raise our family -- but much more about that, later.

* * *

My parents and the rest of us went to bed on November 13th. We considered closed, the subject of me leaving Hungary. The fateful subject was reopened before dawn the next day. Very early on November 14th 1956, I left for Kapuvár, a passenger in Mr. Benedek's truck. For the price of transportation, I was to help load the possessions, left behind by the Beringer family, relatives of Mr. Benedek, from whom we bought the two cars in past years. The Beringers, left the country a few days before.

We were busy until 3 in the afternoon, emptying the house of all its contents and loading what we could on the truck, that took it back to Jánosháza. When we finished, we looked around for some help in getting to the border. Many people were coming and going, doing the same thing. We found a man who was said to be a trusted guide. He wanted 400 forints from each of us. I thought it a little steep for a couple hours walk, but it seemed to be the going rate. I worked about two-three days for that much money.

Soon we started out for the fields. It was the preferred route of our guide, who wanted to use little known paths, rather than taking the open road. It was raining on and off. Deep mud everywhere. No matter how we tried, our shoes and soon the bottom of pants were covered. To make shortcuts, we kept walking through barren farmland, kneading mud, cursing more the Russians and the communists than the cruel weather. As time past, we began to see more people. Groups joined other groups and in time we were about 25-30, heading in the same general direction. We walked by a forest and heard the unusually loud noise of diesel engines, blocking our way. So not to be noticed, we altered course. By then darkness settled and gave us some cover. We took no chance and went around the noise. As we listened, we discerned Russian speech. The hard roar was from diesel engines. Tanks were struggling in the deep mud. We did not know how many, but even one was too many for us. We took a turn, away from the tanks which took us further from the border. We lost precious time and wasted our diminishing energy by having to go on a circling route to avoid the tanks and a sharp turn away from us, by the border itself.

A couple hours later I saw Hungarian border patrol approaching. Our guide told us not to be afraid, because they would help us. He talked to the two soldiers and said that from here on, they will take us to the Austrian border. We were not totally trusting, but fatigue set in during the last few hours that diminished our strength and stamina. The guides turned back and now we had to rely on the young border guards. It was about midnight. Tired and dirty, we continued. Our new guides said that their lieutenant's order was that they take us to the station before we can go on. After a good half hour's walk, we were approaching the guard station. We could rest, they told us, while they check in with the lieutenant inside.

I remember the utter exhaustion we all felt. We talked about the possibility of this being a trap, but were numb and could not muster the wit, or will to break out. Where would we go in the pitch dark without having any idea even about which direction to take? We hoped for the best and that we can trust our soldiers. We rested about five minutes when the young men came out and said that we can go on. He lead us to the edge of the camp to a creek about 30 ft wide. Tied to a pier was a small boat. On the other side, I could barely make out in the dark, was a flag on a post: the red-white-red flag of Austria. This was the border. In groups of three or four, we crossed the border in that little boat and left Hungary, I thought forever. The guys said good by and wished us luck. With trepidation, we continued in a direction we thought we should be going. It was solid, unbroken, deep darkness ahead.

Another seemingly endless walk began. I expected to see

some light from a house or town, but there was nothing on the flat horizon. We saw the first light about 2 A.M. It was a small town. People were up and waiting for us. Most spoke Hungarian. They led us to a school gymnasium. It was almost full with refugees. Straw was on the floor throughout. Exhausted, we sat down and soon fell asleep in our dirty clothes, as we were.

The next morning more people came and we were moved to another town. It went on like this for three days. Then we slowed down and slept two nights in the same town. We were fed and were able to clean up a little. The Austrians were very nice and provided for all our immediate needs. They especially attended to families with little ones.

We were given the opportunity to send one message through the Voice of America or Radio Free Europe carefully, just about our well being, without details. I had my secret code, as we agreed, and sent it: *The Swallow has Flown*, hoping that they were listening. The messages were repeated often and at all hours, for a few days.

One evening we boarded a train and traveled all night to the charming city of Salzburg and were housed in a large tourist hostel. It was akin to dormitory living, with food and facilities for basic hygiene. Ours was the building, that I recognized, when years later I saw the film, *The Sound of Music*. The arcaded building, where the von Trapps sing in a concert, near the end of the movie, was by our hostel. During the day we roamed, and admired the city. The weather improved, even the warming sun showed its friendly face.

I visited Salzburg twice in later years with my family as a stop on our summer vacations. We spent a day there on our way from Aachen to Hungary. This charming city has a most beautiful setting. It has Alpine vista surrounding it, small town warmth, a high hill castle, churches and more. And it has Mozart. He is all over in his lovely birthplace, even on the golden wrappers of delicious chocolate and the heavenly tasting Mozart bon-bon -- Ildikó's favorite, till this day. His statue graces the main square. We as tourists, many years later, watched other tourists in horse-drawn carriages, touring the town, and locals playing chess on Mozart

Square with figures as big as people. On our walk to the Bishop
Garden to enjoy another magnificent view, we heard Mozart being
played on a piano through an open window. It was perhaps the
music academy, or just a music lesson for a future concert pianist.
-- How much more it has to offer in summer, I thought, especially
when one has some spending money in the pocket! -- I visited it
again to re-live the nice memories which I had stored in my mind.
It was especially gratifying to take my family back to this lovely
city.

In my old and very different refugee days, I walked the streets
up and down, admiring the show windows and dreamed of times
in the future, when I can afford some of the things I saw. To the
locals, we looked distinct -- if not distinguished. As refugees,
we were easily recognizable. The way we looked, talked and
seemed out of place, must have been striking. This, despite the
position in which Austria was at the time. She was recently
liberated from her status as a defeated and conquered country,
just like Germany, occupied and divided by her old enemies. The
cold war subsided after Stalin's death in 1953, and the Russians
moved from their occupation zone, back behind the Iron Curtain,
to Hungary. Salzburg was in the US zone and was allowed much
freedom, given aid and had the opportunity for rapid economic
development. The most powerful help was the Marshall Plan,
that was also offered to countries in the Soviet block, but Stalin
canceled it, taking no chances on allowing any western influence
to cross the Iron Curtain, lest it *corrupts* his precious Dictatorship
of the Proletariat and shows other ways, that might loosen control
within his dominion. Austria benefited from the new freedom
and the Marshall Plan, that lifted her up and soon set her on the
road to prosperity. Hungary was also offered participation in the
Plan, but was forced to refuse it, claiming that it was an imperialist
plot. That was just one of the many Soviet-dictated steps that the
communist regime took in order to keep Hungary in the Russian
orbit. The Soviet satellite countries were called the "Peace Camp".
The West were the "imperialist warmongers".

Salzburg seemed so rich. The stores were stocked with luxury
goods. Just walking the streets, feasting my eyes, gave pleasure.

As I walked by a fancy shoe store, the owner must have noticed the deplorable state of my shoes. He called me in and gave me a shoeshine kit. I said "Danke schön", thanking him for his nice gesture and fitting gift.

At an earlier stop one day in a small farm town, another refugee and I were invited for lunch by a farmer family. My friend spoke German better than me. I did my best to follow the conversation. The most important thing I learned was, how the farmer managed to make a decent living, buy more land and farming machinery so soon after the war, in which the country was devastated and occupied. At the time, agriculture in Hungary was still rotting under the grip of the coercive system of the collectives, killing incentive and industry.

* * *

I came out with two other boys from Jánosháza. We stayed close and left Kapuvár together. We were friends in childhood, but grew apart later, when we went to different schools and developed different interests. Pali Hajós lived just few houses down from me on the square. He was a dreamer type, a guy with a few harebrained ideas. He often spoke of high personal accomplishments and a lot of money he would have in the future. He had ambition, but lacked discipline and organization. His father was a leather merchant, a good businessman. His mother a frail, sympathetic woman. Mr. Hajós was a stern disciplinarian. His wife was a gentle lady, a lot like my own mother.

Pali was kept under close control by his father, but entertained unrealistic dreams and occasionally acted on them. Once he had a scheme to make up for his poor school report, and score points with his parents at the same time. He was 18 years old, a senior in high school. He asked me to be ready to help, if needed. I thought his plan was too daring, risky and unrealistic, but said I will do what I can. To carry it through, it would have demanded uncharacteristically consistent effort and discipline, that I failed to see in him in the past. He thought he had it all worked out. The plan was that he leaves home one evening after a phony family fight that he would provoke. He would storm out of the house, hoping that his parents will not take him seriously and just wait for him to come back later. To make sure, that all this would work as planned, his pretext, the fake rant and the list of his grievances, had to appear obviously phony, or at least not serious. That way, adults would likely dismiss it as just one more childish eruption born of frustration and one, that should pass as others did before. Then he would get on the train, go to Budapest, where he would get a job, earn good money and finish high school. One day, he would re-appear and surprise his parents with his accomplishments. -- The plan had an element of ... *and they lived happily ever after.*

Pali's adventure had a different outcome. The parents smelled a rat. Pali may have given himself away with some inadvertent remark, indicating a major move, later confirmed by a check of his personal effects that revealed that a few important documents were missing. Mr. Hajós called his brother-in-law, uncle Sándor Ódor, our burly, but gentle mail man. He dashed over to the close-by village of Kemenespálfa -- if I remember right -- on a bicycle. This small village was downstream, so to speak, from Jánosháza, as the train was going toward Budapest. Logic, parental savvy and good intelligence paid off. Uncle Sándor boarded the train and soon found Pali. At the next stop they got off. Pali slept home that night. The great lofty plan was foiled and the family hoped that Pali learned a lesson.

I cannot testify to the latter. But I know that Pali had his dreams of business success and material riches as long as I knew him. His schemes to realize this took many and varied forms, but were as permanent as footprints in beach-front sand. We lived and worked close to one another for 1½ years, until the summer of 1958. This was the period of our life at Oakton Manor -- to which I return later.

(I recently learned that Pali died in 2001. -- At one of our family gatherings, Jim, my son-in-law, asked me how I was coming with my writings. Answering him, our conversation turned to Pali and I related the above described events to Jim. He asked me where Pali is today. I told him that the last thing

I know was, that he married and was still somewhere not far from Milwaukee, where I visited him once and met his wife Mary. Jim offered to track him down through the Internet. The next day he phoned to tell me that he found Mrs. Mary Hajós and called her. She confirmed the connection and told Jim that Pali died over a year ago. I called Mary the next day and we had a long talk about old and more recent events. She confirmed what I remembered about our childhood and later adventures, involving Pali. Mary told me about a hand written, few pages long diary that Pali wrote, describing our escape and the days we spent in Austria. He wrote it in Hungarian and she asked me to translate it. I was eager to see it. I worked on it a few hours and was gratified to see that my recollection of those days were very close to that of my onetime companion. Mary also sent about 30 photos and asked me to tell about them everything I know, and identify friends and acquaintances. Later I translated several letters for her, that came from Pali's sister, Ági in Jánosháza, and also responded to them in Mary's name, adding my own greetings and a note about my family and circumstances.)

Ervin Czinkán was the third in our trio from Jánosháza. He grew up without a father, but with a good and caring mother. I never recall meeting Mr. Czinkán and I do not know whether he died, abandoned his family or what happened to him. (Divorce was almost unknown to me those days.) Ervin was somewhat reserved and not much in our group's activities as children. He was one year my junior, and an average student. Before the time of our leaving, he began to associate with kids, such as the likes of Farkas. He was one of the younger members of the gang that wanted to beat up Imre Gaál a few years before -- the fight that was foiled by Otti. He lived next door to Imre, but I doubt that he had any dispute with him, that would have given cause for wanting to beat him up. He was with Pali and me and I saw that he depended on us for support during the uncertain days of our escape. With proper guidance he could have become a fine adult. We parted in Salzburg, when he could not complete his emigration process that

Pali and I managed to finish in the allotted time. -- Later I learned that he ended up in New Jersey and died within a year in a car crash. I visited his mother in 1963 and told her what I heard. She knew as much herself, but told me that she refused to believe that her son is dead. In her view, it was some giant lie. At the time she was still waiting to hear from him.

* * *

My departure from Salzburg was in pace with the fast moving events. One sunny morning, less than a week after we arrived, a man came to our room, soon after we got up. He announced that those who wished to go to the United States, should board a waiting bus in front of the hostel. It was an offer that I was not prepared for. I did not think very seriously about my future at that point, at least not in specific terms. Things were still too fluid and uncertain. My situation in Salzburg was stable for the moment. I was thinking of contacting my parents, to give them news about my situation. The question of where I might eventually want to end up, occurred to me a few times. My preference was Switzerland, but America, also a possibility. The distant new world held a definite allure and stimulated my imagination and curiosity. Pali and Ervin jumped at the chance. Pali's aim was from the beginning to go to America. My two guys were ready, so I joined them. I thought of that hasty decision in later years. I came across a quote that crystallized my one-time fuzzy thoughts, that I had trouble expressing clearly at the time:

Man cannot discover new oceans, unless he is willing to lose sight of the shore. (Author unknown) -- Seems, I had the yearning for adventure to take that step.

The bus took us across town to the American Consulate. It was a veritable beehive, full of personnel and about 60 of us hopefuls. They temporarily boosted the staff, by bringing in help from Linz and Graz. Only a few spoke Hungarian, and not too well. They set up about a dozen stations, all of which we had to visit and pass, to be considered for immigration. Many of them were examinations of medical or physical type. At the rest, mostly interview stations, we were screened and our data collected.

The answer by me, to a question about membership in the communist youth league was, assumed to be yes, though I do not recall anyone asking me. All students in all schools were automatically members -- they thought. Pannonhalma was a rare exception and only I knew it. We had no *KISZ* (Communist Youth Organization) there.

(This same question came up again in my interview for American citizenship in 1963. I was then better able to understand the questions and explain my answers. The interviewer showed me the paper I signed in Salzburg, stating that I was KISZ member. I stuck to my story and signed a new sheet correcting the previous error. -- The average waiting period for US citizenship was five years. My case was dragging and I made inquiries. I was told that they were trying to make up for the deficiencies of the rushed process in Salzburg. The examiner told me that in the course of investigation, my file was sent to Seattle -- he had no idea why. At that time the farthest city I visited west of Milwaukee, was perhaps Madison, and I'm not even sure about that. I knew nobody in Seattle and thought, no one there knew me. Soon things fell into place. The actual test for citizenship was easy -- too easy, I thought. I was asked only one question: name the three branches of the United States government. On November 19th 1963, I was sworn in as citizen. It was Erika's birthday -- minus six years.)

In Salzburg, we spent the entire first day at the consulate. They fed us twice between our interviews and exams. We went home to sleep. Next morning our same group boarded the bus. We were told to bring all our belongings. It was not hard to comply. I hopped on the bus with my one bag in tow.

We continued the screening process until late afternoon. By then there was a number of us who went through all the stations, and passed. Others did not make it for some reason, or could not finish on time and were left behind. One of those was Ervin. As we parted, he seemed lost and scared to continue on his own. I felt for him, but could do nothing. We ate dinner and were told to pile in a Volkswagen minibus. They told us that we were going to Munich. It was Wednesday, 1956 November 21.

We arrived at the Munich airport after 8 and were taken straight to the tarmac. A four-engine turboprop was waiting. Before boarding, we spontaneously sang the Hungarian national anthem. Soon we were aboard, ready for takeoff. Already on, were about 30 Hungarians, coming from Vienna. There they went through the same process we endured in Salzburg. The plane was about ¾ full. The charter was a gift to the refugees by the city of Milwaukee, the St. Vincent de Paul Society and other sponsors. It picked up those who were ready, but had to be back in Milwaukee, within the allotted time.

It was my first trip by air plane. Until then I saw two planes close up. One was just outside Jánosháza, in the early years of the war. It made an emergency landing in a meadow. It was a single seat civilian plane, but for me to see it, a child's experience of a lifetime. I talked to the pilot for a short while. He did not tell me anything that satisfied my wide ranging curiosity. He let me look inside the cockpit, which was a thrill. The other plane was that Liberator, smoking in the farm field a couple years later.

I enjoyed the large passenger carrier. It was amusing how the stewardesses tried to communicate with us, with little success. Despite this handicap, they did their best and served us better than I ever dreamed. We conveyed the meaning of words more by using our hands, than our lips, but it worked. There was one passenger who spoke broken English. He was our source when we got desperate. Our requests were always attended to, though I was reluctant requesting anything. I knew that things were free for the asking, but had no idea what was customary on a commercial flight. They provided food and drink. What else would one want? The view outside was nothing memorable, at least at the beginning. We flew a lot in the night, and during the day, saw nothing but gray fog or dark clouds.

After a while they informed us that our destination was

Milwaukee. The name of the city was familiar, though I knew only that it was somewhere in the central region of the States.

Our first stop was Iceland. We reached this refueling stop after about 10 hours of flying. The northern Atlantic is known for its winter storms. I do not know how common storms are there in November, but in all my many flights to Europe in the following 50 years, some on the same route and during winter, I saw nothing near as turbulent as this flight was. This was the only time I've seen people use the *bag.*

Pali sat next to me. Earlier he told me that he had flight experience in the Hungarian Air Force. As we were approaching Iceland, the bumpy ride intensified. The plane did deep dips and rolls almost nonstop, for about a half hour during descent. Many passengers used the bag. A very unpleasant stench enveloped me. Still I was holding on, despite a few close calls. I was grateful that I had a strong stomach.

As we approached landing, I found it curious, that the lights at the airport, and the streetlights in nearby Reykjavik, were of a strong yellow color. When I saw them again, on a stopover years later, I asked if it was for some special reason. I was told that this was advanced lighting technology, more economical to operate than old fashioned streetlights. I secretly hoped that they will soon find something that is more pleasant to the eyes.

Finally we landed and found out where we were. It was the American military base, Keflavik, of which I never heard before. It is on the southwest coast of the island. The time was somewhere in the middle of the night. We deplaned and were allowed to look around within a confined area of the terminal. After about 3½ hours we took off again. Conditions somewhat improved. After a long flight they told us that we would land again. This approach and landing was worse then the first one. The same people and some others got sick. I myself was on the verge twice, but managed to fight back the convulsive urge. The plane was slammed down the runway, still in one piece. I was wondering. Is this normal and expected for commercial, or any other type of flying? Without any experience, I was not able to judge. I admired the pilot, whom I instinctively trusted, and thought that he weighed the risks and was prepared for such weather. The possibility of crashing occurred to me once or twice, but I dismissed the thought. I saw it as a very untimely demise and hoped that my optimistic assumptions were correct and my guarding angel would keep me from harm. Later I learned that even one of the pilots got sick during landing.

We were in Gander, Newfoundland, another US base. Right away they sent us to a hotel and put us up for the night. I was amazed that the hotel was a wooden structure. I never before saw anything other than small shacks, made entirely of wood. The stormy weather made me even more curious about the sturdiness of wood-only buildings. But everything was so new, I did not dwell on it more than making a comment to Pali. We went to bed around midnight. About 2½ hours later they roused us. It was time to continue our journey. With trepidation and still in very high winds, we took to the air again. The pilot must have thought that it was good enough to fly. The rest of the flight was better. We flew on in more friendly skies. I was thinking again about landing, because one more was still to come. The weather improved. Light increased and we flew in sunshine the rest of the way. We saw recognizable Canadian and American terrain. The many straight roads, sometimes receding into the distance without a turn, were most unusual. This is America, I thought. This is how they do it in a modern country.

The stewardesses told us that we are were approaching Milwaukee. I braced myself, trying to get ready for another ordeal. But the weather was much better this time. As I was watching the straight streets and the distinct downtown with its tall buildings, so different from the residential neighborhoods, I noticed that we were circling the city repeatedly as we were descending. I thought the pilot wanted to make up for our suffering and anxiety of the prior, nearly two days. He made three circles as he took the plane down. Then he landed it as smoothly as a plane can be landed. So, I had experienced the ultimate extremes of the pain and pleasures of flying on the first flight of my life. It was one of the many unique experiences on my maiden journey to America, from Jánosháza to Milwaukee. -- Smooth landings are common. This was dreamy -- a most pleasant contrast to the other two.

I landed on American soil on November 23rd, a brisk, bright, sunshiny Thanksgiving Friday. My first impressions are blurred -- there were so many. Of trivial things, one I did not consider extraordinary but everyone else did, were the electric hand dryers in the washroom. The guys all admired it. This thing of curiosity to us, a wonderment of modern technology still exists, but most people I know, see it as an annoyance and a noisy time and power waster and use it only when there are no towels. If it is the only way to dry up, I shake my hand in the sink, rub it a little and let my wet hands dry nature's way. It takes barely a minute.

It seemed everybody, who was somebody in Milwaukee, was at the airport to greet us. The mayor, city fathers, state and federal officials and perhaps all Hungarians from near and far, lined up for a look.

We were *heroes*, regardless of anything else. We symbolized the valiant, bloody and violent struggle against the mighty Soviet Union. We were those who dared to raise bare hands against the tanks and fight them on their terms, with captured weapons and home-made Molotov cocktails, using only cunning and courage. We were attributed qualities that, I'm sure were generous, and romantic. We did not all deserve them, but still basked in the glory of the hour and enjoyed the attention. I did not make up stories, although I overheard a few. Simply relating the events of the past weeks were exciting enough.

Important politicians lined up to rub elbows with *us* and pose for pictures, perhaps hoping to see themselves the next day on a front page. Senator Joseph McCarthy was not at the airport, but spoke to us in an informal setting the next day at our hotel. There were speeches about our heroics, I'm sure, along with kind, encouraging words to welcome us. We were waiting patiently until it was over. We were also addressed by a few words in Hungarian. A gray-haired, elegant, dignified man, in impeccable *Bocskai* garb, decorated by a tricolor red-white-green armband, welcomed us to our new land of the free. Mr. János Barkócz, an erudite, engaging man later became a good friend. From him I learned much about America and added to my understanding of Hungary's history and knowledge about recent years in exile, for many of her children. I was a guest in his home several times. I always looked forward to his invitations. His whole family was warm and welcoming. His younger daughter, Piroska, or as they called her, Pille, caught the eye of Pali Hajós. He courted her for a while. Later I also took her out a few times and enjoyed mostly intellectual conversations with her. Mr. Barkócz died a few years later. The family then moved to a Boston suburb. I visited them there also. Ildikó and I visited Pille in Hudson, MA, soon after we were married, when I was in Norwood, for my job training course with Factory Mutual. Through the Barkócz family I met others, which was a great help for me in settling down in America. I got to know the finest of the Hungarians in Milwaukee. They partly made up for the void in my heart, after I so suddenly had to leave the warmth and support of my family.

Still at the airport, our new friends and benefactors got to work and did all the processing there in the lobby. Within two hours it was all done. I received my *Green Card* in my hand before I boarded the bus. The profound significance of such speedy and efficient action was not apparent to me at the time, because of all the new things I was continually experiencing. I did not realize the value of that card until years later. I just went with the flow and stored the impressions in my mind for later processing and a deeper appreciation of their significance.

(I am distressed, and sometimes disgusted, by the cheapening of this great symbol of freedom. My once proud and confident America seems to have lost its appreciation for this valuable document in recent years. Deserving and receiving the special gift of this land, expressed so eloquently by Lady Liberty in New York harbor, used to be high privilege. It is being prostituted and trivialized by greedy businessmen and politicians in both parties, and to no small measure, by the complacence of many citizens. Government, cowered by prevailing political correctness, has no guts to enforce the laws that it passed, to protect the country. The once precious gift of freedom and opportunity, could now be had on the cheap. It can be obtained for a mere few hundred bucks, and an added insult: contempt for our laws. Mexico's current president Vicente Fox, considers it America's *duty* to allow unlimited, uncontrolled immigration of his people, transferring his responsibility for improving their lot at home. Many a poor come here just for a job. The money they send home, sustains his corrupt regime and postpones a likely revolt by the bottom 40%, who live in extreme poverty. Fox has the gall to chastise Americans, who stand up in defense of our border. He considers America, his economic solution and, by all indications, also a dumping ground for the many felons (estimated to be 140,000) that illegally crossed our border, and stayed, in the past ten years. -- But people are beginning to see the peril of its wholesale violation and the flaunting of our laws by illegal aliens. Thanks to the Minutemen, a volunteer group of citizens, who patrol the southern borders of Texas and Arizona, the issue was highlighted, for the country to see. *They* are taking on the burden, their government is sworn to do. At this point [spring, 2006] the White House has heard the message. We are yet to see if it takes, and finally, results in effective action, not just the old, empty platitudes that serve only the illegal and those who profit by the uncontrolled, ruinous practice. The Senate seems to be oblivious, and has contempt for the nation's will.) As said before: I am disgusted.

The welcoming crowd and we, piled into our vehicles and headed for downtown. Police motorcycles were leading the procession. They had their lights flashing and intermittently sounded their siren, all the way to Milwaukee's best hotel, the Pfister on Wisconsin Avenue.

On the way we made a stop at St. Imre Hungarian church for a short, religious and patriotic thanksgiving service. Tears came to my eyes during the touching sermon by a priest and other speakers, all of it in Hungarian. I visited many times this tiny but charming church, while I lived in Milwaukee. Hungarian sponsored events were held in its dance hall. Today the church is not so distinctly Hungarian. The neighborhood has been transformed and Hungarians scattered to suburbs and other cities.

A long line of cars followed us to the hotel. With the formalities mostly over, things loosened up and the Hungarians came to talk to us one-on-one. Some inquired about specific relatives. Others offered help, lodging and other things in addition to endless, helpful advise.

I heard a heartwarming story about a special group of Hungarians who went to New York state. Among the 200,000 refugees that left Hungary, were musicians. Some perhaps, were old acquaintances, or colleagues who sought out one another in the huge refugee gathering place, Camp Kilmer. A few months after I arrived, I heard of the musicians who formed a classical orchestra. A Hungarian master, Antal Doráti assumed directorship, named his group *Philharmonia Hungarica* and soon took them on a tour nationwide. His hastily assembled and accidental orchestra was an immediate hit. They issued many recordings and even after so many years, still are active and successful. I was proud and happy for their good fortune. They found instant employment in their field, doing what they love.

Family photo (1939)

Family idyll (1938)   My Sweet Mother (1952)

The larger family. Wedding of Uncle Miklós (1942)

A peek at the camera,
while catching up with the
news (1939)

The author on horseback, brothers at the
rein -- Molnár's house in background

St. Vendel Chapel, across from our house

The castle in Jánosháza (built 1396)

Jánosháza -- Kossuth Square -- Father coming home

Snow White and her Prince in a school play (1948) --
(cannon shell 'vase' in corner)

Csikós in a school play -- by the mushrooms (1948)

On the little Csepel with Kálmán Gerencsér

Pannonhalma Abbey

My father ca. 1960

Our house, built in 1936 -- two views

Aachen, Christmas 1961 -- Father's first visit

Back entrance to our house (1960) -- Father, the Molnárs, Aunt Mala, Marika, Mother, Józsi with wife, Margit. (Behind dad, the door to the infamous cellar/prison, as was used by the Russians)

Wheat harvest

Uncle John in his Sunday   Old village street
best (age 62)

Our church in Jánosháza

Bernini - *Ecstasy of St. Teresa*

The four Magyars meet in Aachen (1964)

Festetics castle tower. The count's statue in foreground -- Keszthely

Keszthely, 1989. Otti, Miklós, Józsi, Tomi, Marika. (The old wardrobes and the Major's favorite grandfather clock from Jánosháza)

Freedomfighters waving national flag atop captured Russian tank (October 1956)

Pali Hajós -- mosquito abatement at Oakton Manor

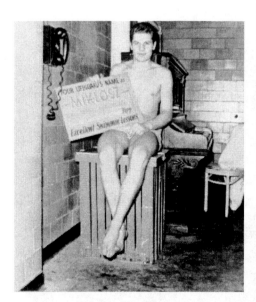

With Joe Kerényi at Oakton

"Sign at the pool: 'Your lifeguard's name
is Miklosz. Newly arrived Hungarian.
English spoken broken. Very excellent
swimmin' lessons'"

Doing the butterfly -- with
the dolphin kick

In the lab at Aldrich

"Our wedding photos -- with Father Denis

"'Aye aye, Ma'am' -- Ildi piloting a boat on our honeymoon in Florida"

Ildikó at Rockefeller Center

Erika, 5   Andrea, 3

The girls on Navy
Pier merry-go-
ground

Erika -- opening day, first grade
(dress made by Ildi)

With the Girls on Crystal Lake beach (1986)

With Mother on her 75th birthday

Ildikó

Ready for tennis

Aboard the Argentine *Amerigo Vesprucci* in New York harbor, July 4 1986

Ildikó on Washington Square

Tennis -- Snowmass Club, Colorado
Ildi won

Ildikó at Grand Hotel on Macinac Island"

Erika, Tyler, Jamie -- the
Fergusons with Maroon Bells
as background

Ildi with Edith Püski in a canyon near
Watkins Glen, in New York's Finger
Lakes region

At the Ferguson house -- Erika, Trevor, Andrea, Jim

Grandma Ella (2003)

With the Richards
and Scheiders --
desserts and coffee at
the Bellagio in
Las Vegas

Machu Picchu, high in the Peruvian Andes

Grandchildren.
Ashlyn Ella
Tyler Miklos
Elise Ildiko

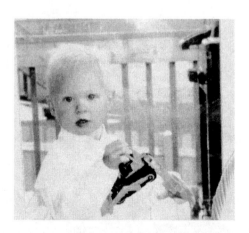

Ildi's surprise for my 70th birthday.
Otti and Tomi came to celebrate

Chicago -- With my brothers, admiring the Bean in Millennium Park

Visiting cousin Johnny in his new house in New Berlin WI

Restoring the old doll house for the grandchildren

Two Popes and an Abbot

30

The Pfister -- St. Vincent Society -- Oakton Manor -- Et Cetera

We were the guest of the Pfister, the most prestigious hotel in Milwaukee. We occupied the entire 7th floor for a week -- guests of the hotel, as if we were paying customers and treated perhaps even better. Each evening after dinner we watched a show with other guests. In one act, a woman singing, puzzled me. It looked odd but I couldn't find the reason. She sang in a fantastic voice, one that was not entirely natural. By the end I figured it out. She was a lip-synch artist. Her lips silently followed vocal music, accompanied by a recording. I heard of this before, but this was my first time to see this non-sing singing. I was close up, otherwise I couldn't have discerned the deceit. I thought it was clever, but strange entertainment. (Today several big name *artists* were caught and embarrassed doing it.)

For two days the hallway of our floor was set up to function as employment office and as a placement service. People came and went, offering and assisting us in finding jobs. Others, including several Hungarian families offered help in finding accommodations and work, that we could do without speaking English, or get by using a form of sign language. Couples offered temporary home to a few boys, aiding them in starting a new life. -- I missed out on a good opportunity. Two brothers were taken in by a nice couple. It would have been ideal for me, because I greatly missed the closeness of family.

A nice old man, a dentist walked around and gave out business cards. He said that he will donate the first dental visit. I took one of his cards just in case. The opportunity came about three years later, when I went to see him with an aching tooth. He remembered and treated me free. We had a pleasant conversation about our first meeting, my impression about America and the situation in Hungary. I enjoyed our conversation, especially that this time I could carry on fluently and be understood. I was his patient until he retired in 1961.

I moved out of The Pfister -- without ever checking out -- after an eventful stay of almost a week. A group of five of us were taken to the house of the Fenwick Club at 1409 N. Prospect Avenue. It was a neat, old, stone house, a place for meetings and parties, but not set up for lodging. (Now a modern all-glass building is in its place. I was sorry to see the old house go.) We slept there on cots and blankets for about a week, until we found our own place.

Most of us left the hotel with a job secured. My luck was again with the St. Vincent de Paul Society, just days after they provided for my trip across the Atlantic.

Pali and I started at St. Vincent on a Tuesday. Our job was, helping in the daily pickup rounds for donations. We walked to our place of work at Juneau and 7ᵗʰ Street. It was about a mile in a cold, late November morning. As I walked and watched the busy early morning traffic, I thought, how is it that we are the only ones who have to walk to work. Of course I knew why, but this rhetorical question put the answer in focus and sharpened my understanding of my situation and helped to concentrate on my objectives.

I had a place to stay, I had a job, now I was able to enroll in my *boot camp* -- my American initiation course. I had to focus my efforts to get through this difficult time of acclimation and trial period, where I had the choice to lay the foundation of a good future or screw it up, making bad choices. I was entirely on my own. I alone was responsible for choosing friends and a prudent path, concentrating on the right priorities and patiently lay a solid foundation.

I did OK, allowing for a couple detours. But God blessed my efforts, by letting me find Ildikó. The Lord gave us the gift of married bliss, children and family, that is most precious and indispensable for a happy life.

My goal was, before anything else to learn English. I had a natural curiosity about and a good feel for languages. All my waking ours were one continuous language session. I listened to everything and asked questions about things I wanted to understand. Words, grammar and phrases were all important. It was fun -- but those darn idioms drove me crazy. To remember the spelling of longer words, I pronounced them phonetically for myself. I made up my own, a *faux-Hungarian word,* out of complicated English words, in which I pronounced every letter. They made sense only to me. I was unfailingly able to commit to memory, the spelling of these newly constructed phonetic *peg-words,* with the sequence of the letters seared in my brain. I have been using this method successfully ever since. The usefulness of this method has been born out often. I *spell* words this way to my wife, when she asks about spelling. I even used it teaching my children. They too, understand the method, without a problem. My phony phonetics is *wonderphul* -- but of course only, for personal use. You should here me *spell* words, such as "Renaissance".

My learning the language, was also the highest priority for my father. In his letters he often told me that he hoped that I will soon master English. "I hope it is sticking" -- was his phrase. I told him that I'm making progress, but it was a huge project and will take a long time to speak well. Language skills stick to the brain only by constant curiosity and diligent, unrelenting practice.

Our job at St. Vincent de Paul was to load items on the truck, stuff that people donated all around the city. Work started at 7, the trucks left at 8 and returned to the warehouse mid-afternoon. Then we unloaded the trucks and could relax until quitting time. One interesting pastime Pali soon discovered, was to search through the stuffed chairs and sofas for anything that fell down in the upholstery. He found a lot of coins. I also did it and found it an interesting treasure hunt.

There, on my second day in the warehouse, I discovered Coca Cola. The famous American drink was known to me only by reputation. Behind the Iron Curtain, it was a symbol of America, in a way that is surpassed perhaps only by McDonald's today. It was a capitalist symbol that communists liked to berate and to which they attached various negative and even imperialistic attributes. I remember, tasting the *evil* drink the first time, I could not help thinking about the pervasive old, bad propaganda. My curiosity was enhanced by these memories, and I thought that the famous drink should prove them wrong. That is not exactly what happened. My taste preference was predisposed in favor of fruit flavors. It still is. The root-like taste of Coke and the dark color, was OK, but not to my best liking. Even today, when I need something bubbly to refresh me, I prefer a citrus-base drink, lemonade or just water.

(This reminds me a of couple other communist propaganda items that I refused to believe about America. Those were monster movies and wrestling. I was sure then, that it was just like all the rest: propaganda to fill the collective mind with negative images about the "imperialists", the great enemy of *precious* socialism -- maybe not sacred, but precious and one to revere, if we knew what's good for us. I also thought that such primitive pastimes cannot be favored by reasonable people. Later I was chagrined to see that this part of the propaganda was actually true. Monster movies and crude, rambunctious punk wrestling were indeed favored and, in recent years only gained in popularity. -- I see it little differently now. These popular pastimes are a certain emotional release, and primitive but innocent fun for many. -- In ancient Rome, Caesar called it "Panem et Circenses" (bread and circuses) making the point that, as long as enough food and entertainment are provided for the masses, political tranquillity is assured. The populace, with its basic needs satisfied is placated and diverted from unrest and the inclination to revolt.

There were many positive and admirable things that I found here through the years, primarily the idea of freedom. It is important to inculcate in our youth and thus repair the damage that the spoiled and shortsighted 1960s generation saw in America and does even today. Many developed a distinct anti-American attitude, while pretending otherwise. These leftists typically saw merit in communist and other socialist utopian societies, ignoring the misery, those movements brought to the people wherever they were implemented. They saw only evil in capitalism, instead of setting free its innate proclivity to provide a better life for everyone. Capitalism was attacked viciously in the 1970s, but recovered well, especially as we were witness to the widespread failure of socialism in countries around the world.)

We worked at the St. Vincent Society for some two weeks. The work was not boring. My English improved and I gained a little understanding about my new country. The Fenwick Club people provided some entertainment. A priest took us around the city one evening, to show the various neighborhoods.

Somebody even found girlfriends for us. I went out with one who was nice, though a few years older than me. She was a heavy smoker, which was a turn-off. She was good company and taught me about life in America. She explained to me that one can buy a basic used car from a couple week's earnings. I found that amazing and started dreaming about a car of my own.

My young truck driver partner, Mark, with whom I went out every day was a nice guy. One day he took me with him for a home-cooked lunch. I met his wife and enjoyed a good meal with the two of them. I would love to hear today that lunch-time conversation the three of us had. After two weeks here, I used hands, facial muscles and all my wits to convey my thoughts and they tried to do the same. It was tiring, but in a fashion, I thought, we succeeded.

Let me relate a story that happened several years later, but has to do with this subject. I lived in and around Milwaukee for a few years. Then I spent two years in New York. I came back in 1964 and lived on the east side until I graduated and got married in 1968.

After our wedding, we stayed two weeks in my tiny bachelor

apartment. Then I got a job in Chicago. When we were about to move there, we had a few things to donate. By that time, being here 12 years, I collected stuff, that I could get rid of. I called St. Vincent de Paul Society for a pickup. I knew others, the better known charity organizations, Goodwill and the Salvation Army, but I remembered old St. Vincent and wanted them to come out on my first ever donation. I wanted to see the truck and tell the people, that I started my life in America with, and helped by, St. Vincent de Paul.

We lived in a small second story apartment. The driver had to come up the stairs, to get the few things we set aside. I heard the bell and opened the door. There was Mark, standing before me. It was the most unexpected reunion after a dozen years.

This time we even understood one another. We talked about old times and how the years flew by since we were making our rounds together. He stayed a while to chat, before getting back on his truck to finish his daily round.

As we arrived to work one morning at the St. Vincent warehouse, a man was waiting, wanting to meet us. He was Joe Kerényi. He came in town from Oakton Manor, a year-round resort, for mostly Jewish clientele. The complex was located in beautiful, rural, Midwestern America. It had a bucolic setting on Pewaukee Lake, the largest in that picturesque lake-country, 30 miles west of Milwaukee.

Joe, about 40 years old, was of Hungarian Jewish descent, who came here from Austria several years before, fleeing from the Nazis. He spent time in a camp for displaced persons. He considered German his mother tongue, and spoke Hungarian with a slight accent.

He kept the books for the resort. His command of Hungarian and, as I later figured out, also of English, were not the best. He came to America about five years before. Still, it was a great help for us to have an in-house interpreter and a friendly voice. Joe had a debilitating accident in childhood, that left him with one leg shorter than the other, thus with a pronounced limp in his gate. He preferred not to talk about it, for it must have been an unpleasant subject.

The manager, Sam Sugarman and his second banana, Mike Gleiberman were running the resort. The complex offered a leisurely surrounding, golf, beach, indoor pool and a lot of other pleasurable activities. Mr. Sugarman wanted to help Hungarians and offered jobs for two.

There were about a dozen smaller lakes, rolling hills and forests within a few miles around Oakton Manor. It was God's country, in the 1950s' innocent America. In those days, out there in the country, nobody locked doors or worried about his neighbor and went to church regularly. At least that is how it appeared to me. I also attended the small Catholic church, a short walk from the hotel. I was looking forward to the sermon every Sunday. It was not for the priest's admonitions or uplifting messages. It was too early for that. Rather, I saw it as a supplement English class, where I could listen to learned, sometimes erudite and well spoken English, a kind of shop-talk for the devoted. It had its own vocabulary, but in those days I wanted to absorb everything that came my way. I was surprised how much and for how long I was able to concentrate on speech, of which I understood so little. I kept score informally, on how I improved, and directly or by inference, what new words I picked up as time went by.

Pali and I were assigned to be part of the maintenance crew, headed by a wiry, gaunt old man, Slim. He was a taciturn, but nice boss and we strove to give him the least possible trouble. Our main jobs were cutting grass, collecting refuse, trucking it out to the dump and anything else Slim wanted, to help us learn the ropes. After a few days I was asked to follow Art, another old guy, who on that day was making repairs on a damaged wall, in one of the wings, the West Hotel. We tried to communicate but did not succeed much. He was drilling me on one word, by repeatedly showing it to me and saying: "putty knife". I was familiar with the gadget and did my best to copy his pronunciation, all the while wondering, how this strange sounding word (I thought it was one word) would be spelled. No luck there. I asked Joe later and I was astonished when he showed me the spelling. I realized that the English language was even more mysterious than I was prepared for.

The resort was a large property on many open acres, adjoining the lake. I was surprised that very few people used the small beach and the other aquatic amenities. Golf and sunning were popular, but the pool was most favored. The West Hotel was one of two detached outer buildings, with about 30 rooms each. The main building, a three-story, impressive structure, featured a lot of what people come to enjoy in places like that: good food in a nice dining room, entertainment, games, pool, "Gift Shoppe", etc. (I was intrigued by the spelling over the door of this humble little shop in the lobby. I asked about it and was satisfied to learn that it is just a fancy, old fashioned version of "shop" -- a word I learned a few days before.)

On the grounds, a little distance from the main hotel, were a few guest cottages. About 400 ft. up the wooded hill was another group of cottages, used for the housing of employees. In one of those, Pali and I were given a room. They needed a couple days to furnish and set up the large room in it for double occupancy. We moved in on the third day. The first two nights I spent in a nice, spacious room in one of the six guest cottages, overlooking the main drive and the hotel.

Our first day was strange, with introductions, tours of the hotel, the grounds and getting acquainted with my first permanent home and its surroundings. I felt lost. People were kind, understanding, curious and helpful, but my feeling of loneliness hit me more strongly, than anytime prior. Gradually it became overwhelming. I was surprised, that this was the first day when feelings of a depressing, even morose loneliness, that suddenly made me feel like an orphan, have overcome me. It must have been the air of permanence, of finalized status and the sense of a final break with my accustomed, comfortable past, that seemed to be forever gone, and not yet supplanted with anything to soothe the psyche.

For the lunch-time break I ate fast and went to my room. I found it in immaculate condition, having been made up by service, as if it were done for a paying guest -- as it was done routinely every day.

After my eventful few hours, when I was always surrounded by people, I found myself in this pleasant room, just me, alone, in the company of only my own thoughts. This was the first day, when I had some time for myself and could reflect on things that happened to me in recent weeks. I was given a home, but all my possessions could fit into a shopping bag. I felt a gaping chasm and profound emotional emptiness, where just a few weeks before, there was security and the love of those I loved most dearly.

I sat down on the edge of the bed and cried. Tears came quietly, but steadily, interrupted only by my attempts of calming my sorrow, and wiping my eyes and face. I was surprised. I began to think in the past few days that my situation may begin to solidify and I should be busy with work, laying the foundation of my future. My new, wrenching bout with nostalgia and longing showed me, that I had a long journey ahead, before I feel as a stable transplant into my new and very different world.

I heard nothing from my family or Magdi since I left. It was hard to bear the lack of news. Imagination and nostalgia are no substitute in calming the soul. It was one of my most difficult time in that quaint, neat little room, furnished with everything white, from bedding, curtains, to furniture, et cetera. The room had the best view of the main hotel with its impressive Tudor style architecture and canopied entrance, with flowers all around. But it was different from what I was accustomed to for so long, and I was so alone. Rather than enjoying it, I wanted to sleep and hoped to dream something pleasant, as an escape from my misery, at least for a while. I closed my eyes, but did not sleep. Soon I went down to occupy myself with the task at hand.

I feared that my parents be subjected to questioning and intrusive inquiries about my leaving. The methods of such interrogations were always unpleasant and demeaning. I thought it best to write a letter. In it I apologized for leaving without their permission or approval. The letter was to be an admission that my action was mine alone, absolving them of responsibility and *proof* that they would have opposed it. I sent the letter and also wrote to Magdi.

It was the most difficult writing and a cathartic soul-search for me. I was in a situation of my own choosing, one that had no solution. I knew that all my letters would first be read by censors. They then would decide whether to send it on, and/or use it for their purposes to control the recipient. Letters and other information was used by them to coerce, intimidate and blackmail people. I could not risk suggesting that she escape and join me. I was cautioned by past experience. -- We corresponded for about a year. It became increasingly clear that we were parted for good, the ultimate result of the choice I made, no matter the circumstances.

I concentrated on learning the language, trying some unique ideas, such as the method of questioning. Each evening I could volunteer for busboy work in the dining room. The waitresses were kind and helpful. I tested myself and tried out the new things I learned as I was talking with Lucy, one of the waitresses. She was the most helpful. I used words and phrases that I thought I knew. I said something to her and asked if I said it correctly. This way I saw the progress I made each day. When I needed to find a word, I could go to Joe for help.

One of my proud moment was when Sam, the manager with Mike beside him, asked me to say "Oakton Manor", and when I did, praised me for my pronunciation. At another occasion, talking with Mike I used, in two consecutive sentences, the words "answer" and "reply". He commanded me for my versatility and said that it took him a year before he learned the difference. Mike's mother tongue was Russian, as I found out later. At the beginning I couldn't tell about his dialect. In time I could detect a slight accent. He probably learned English as a youngster, but retained elements of his first language in his accent, that would betray him all his life. -- People ask me occasionally about mine, noticeable in my inflections. It is not deliberate, just a tendency for a more phonetic pronunciation that makes words more Hungarian-sounding.

As an aside, this became a subject of conversation recently, in the California gubernatorial recall election of 2003. We heard many jokes and parodies, on how the top candidate, Arnold Swarzenegger pronounced *Kaliiforrnia* -- or something like that. -- English is not a phonetic language, and the famous muscle-man and actor became a popular vehicle for TV comics, such as Jay Leno. He was relentless for weeks, teasing Arnold by mimicking him nightly. -- Even Arnold's nemesis, the recalled governor,

Gray Davis joined in on the act. On another TV comedy show, he gave a list of 10 admonitions to his famous successor, after he was already recalled by popular vote. They were all funny, but I remember only one.

Said Davis: "And No. 1, Arnold -- it is pronounced: *California!*"

The company of other employees at the Manor was not the best for me. There was no friction, but we had divergent interests. In time other Hungarian young men came to work there. Each evening they went to search out bars and were cruising late into the night. I went with them at first, but soon dropped out.

Some asked me to translate or help filling out papers. I felt good that I made progress and that they trusted me with such things, after only a few months.

One, a not so pleasant event on a related subject, involved a young guy, Steve. In the fall of 1957, he bought a car. I helped him with his papers and bargained for him on the price. Next day he came to me again, saying that the dealer would not sell him the car entirely on credit. He needed a down payment or a co-signer. He asked me to sign the papers with him. I understood the concept, but was not conversant with the law and the potential consequences of this unique form of co-ownership, where one titular owner is entitled only to foot the bill, when his partner defaults. I do not remember the exact price of the car, but it was an old Nash, probably for $100. I co-signed for him in good faith.

Almost a year later, after I moved to Milwaukee, I received a letter from the dealer in Waukesha stating that Steve stopped payments after his first one and they could not locate him. (Strange, they were able to track *me* down, after *my* move.) I corresponded with the dealer and pleaded my case (ignorance, naiveté, good faith -- take your pick) but they told me that my signature binds me to the contract. At the end I paid the $80 that was the balance left by the guy whom I helped out a few months earlier. It was a lesson in caution, prudence -- and gullibility.

Joe Kerényi lived nearby, alone in a house trailer. He was a cynic about life. A lonely guy, who spent most of his time on the job, at the hotel, or watching TV at home. He ate with the brass, being part of the team and often stayed for the show after dinner, but otherwise had a limited social life out there in the country. Occasionally he took us to Milwaukee, which was a bigger thing for us than for him. He would want to marry, but did not find the right woman. His handicap affected his confidence. To boost his chances, he bought a new Dodge. It was a 1957 model with a huge blue & white body and high, two-tone fins. He was proud of it and loved the compliment on his flashy new motorcar.

(For 1957, car designers went crazy. Cars were much bigger than in previous years and almost all came with flashy fins. I loved the Chevy, as did most people. It had a daring look, but closer to classical lines. The worst example of excess was Dodge. It had fin on top of a fin, protruding high above the trunk line. I thought that of all the new models, Dodge was the ugliest. The new concept of radical design had most people talking, me one of them. I was new here and totally inexperienced in most things American, cars included. I had my opinion, but refrained from voicing it for the fear of being called a smart-aleck newcomer, making fun, at the expense of his generous host country -- so I congratulated Joe on his new, proud possession.)

His old, pea-green, two door Dodge, was for sale. He sold it to Pali for $70. The proud new owner had no license to drive, but could not wait, so he enjoyed his new found mobility by riding around Manor property. He drove in the military back home, so he knew the basics. We both drove the company truck on hotel grounds and out to the garbage dump. While this gave us experience at the wheel, it did not teach us the rules of the road in Wisconsin. Riding motorbikes for several years in Hungary was some help in that.

(I drove my father's cars occasionally without a license and without his knowledge during the last couple years before I left Hungary. I was surprised of the mild rebuke he gave me when he found out, the last time I drove the car around town. I took the car, not for any special reason but one: to show off for the girls.)

One day Mike saw Pali driving his Dodge in front of the hotel and stopped him with a friendly wave. He congratulated him, leaned in the open window, smiled and said:

"It's great, Paul! Your own car. Radio, heater, everything". -- There was a lot of truth in that, as we looked at cars then. Those were the first and most important amenities in the ever expanding list, making travel more comfortable and more of a luxury. For Pali, it was just the initial step. His dreams were always lofty, especially concerning cars and money.

Whether it was his shiny new car, or his charms, I cannot tell, but Joe's confidence was visibly enhanced and rising. He seemed happier than before. One day he saw me from a distance across the yard. He waved to me, smiled broadly and shouted:

"Miklós, I'm getting married and converting to the Catholic faith."

Then he briefly told me about a woman whom he was dating for a short time and would marry in the near future. I was happy for him, but surprised. I never saw, or even heard of the woman before. The relationship must have developed just recently.

A few days past, and one morning we heard that Joe killed himself during the night with his shotgun, in the woods near his trailer. He left a note, saying that life for him was hopeless and not worth living. He did not confide in anyone I knew, regarding personal matters. This way it was even more a sad story. Just a few days earlier all seemed well. The woman must have dashed his hopes and he saw no way out. The shock left him devastated and without a purpose that would've made his life worth living, as he saw it. My first reaction was shock, but soon sadness took over, seeing the waste of a worthwhile life. -- I could never have thoughts like this, no matter how depressed I was or how hopeless the future seemed.

As one might think, we both wanted a car, even if it was beyond our ability to afford. Pali proposed a novel solution. He and I should buy a car together. This way we could afford one that would be up to our level of desire. He traded in his Dodge for a 1952 Ford. Nice, light and darker, two-tone green, two door -- radio, heater, etc. and automatic transmission. (His old Dodge had *hydromatic*, an earlier, hybrid version, between stick and automatic, the kind that the kids sing about, in the musical, *Grease*). The shiny Ford looked and felt like beyond everything we ever dreamed of. I wonder how the dealer arranged the transaction. He trusted us to keep to this unusual bargain of co-ownership. After all, we both signed on the dotted line. It was remarkable, that the common property did not cause friction between the owners.

This was before the foregoing story about my cosigning for the Nash. Anyway, I was a full partner and volunteer in this deal. -- At first we often went to the same places. Later I went out less. Pali was always on the go. Radio and reading became more important as my entertainment. My job also changed. I worked odd hours and had to adjust. -- We'll get to all that, in a moment.

By summer, Pali wanted his own car. More important, he wanted to trade up. I agreed to buy him out and keep the Ford for myself. It was a good solution. He soon bought a new, 1958 Chevrolet. This way we avoided potential problems that co-ownership inevitably brings.

My nice car came to an ignominious end within a year. I was driving to Milwaukee from the west on single-lane Highway 16. I was in an unbroken line of heavy traffic, in a rural section of the road on a Sunday afternoon. My companion was Joe Darányi, a young Hungarian fellow refugee, who was dozing at the time. I was doing about 45 mph on the open highway, with a higher posted speed limit. A woman was traveling in the other direction, looking into an early evening sun. After waiting long time to turn left, just as we were passing by her, going through the intersection, she decided to make her turn. She could never explain why she turned when she did. The lady, wife of a doctor, driving a heavy car, was not seriously injured. I grabbed the steering wheel and bent it back a great deal, thus managing to keep myself whole. Poor Joe, totally unprepared, hit the windshield with his head. We went to hospital for checks and observation. I was out the next day. Little Joe (he was barely 5 ft.) spent two weeks there. He complained of headaches for a long time. -- My next vehicle was a 1947 Kaiser, a plush car, but affordable in its old age. It never gave me trouble. Only wishing for a modern car made me buy a 1954 Chevy in 1962 and a good looking Rambler in 1965.

I was awarded $2,500 for my trouble. Joe's case dragged out. He got about $10,000 as his settlement. During the litigation I got to know our lawyer, Charles Kersten and later also his son, Campion, who was in law school when we first met. The elder Kersten served two terms in congress just a few years before. He was an upright, conservative man, a straight shooter, very interested in Hungary and communism. He taught me a lot about life and politics in America. I looked them up later in their office from time-to-time, just for a chat. One time he asked me to interpret at a hearing, involving a Hungarian client.

I cannot say that I am proud about the disposal of my $2,500 settlement. I received in my hand less than $1,700 after lawyer's fees and other expenses. After I bought a car and a nice watch and did some long forgotten profligate spending, there was not much left. Truth be told, I was not very good handling money.

(To compensate for the lack of that talent, I was blessed with a wife, Ildikó, who is prudent with money, as with everything else and possesses temperament for restraint and discipline. Applying those with love, she often saved me from myself. Her wisdom and common sense became my guide after we were married. Thanks in large part to her, we are able to enjoy a comfortable retirement. I came to my senses about money later (she partly agrees) but she was the moving force behind a lot of good things that we did together through the years. I will always love her and be grateful. Nobody deserves more than she. She is my partner, my life's love and my universe.)

In the spring of 1957, the life guard at Oakton Manor quit. Mike asked me if I could swim -- "Yes", and if I would take over, in the pool -- "Yes sir!" It was a welcome change for me, a new, more pleasant work environment and one, where I would be with guests.

The hotel had an in-house comedian, Simmy Bow, a rough looking guy (he would've been perfect to play a gangster in a movie) who told crude jokes each evening, to rousing laughter. I did not understand any of the jokes, only was told about them by the waitresses, but I enjoyed his personal humor and kindness that he showed toward me. He had a nice new Oldsmobile. He gave me a ride to Waukesha once. We talked all the way there. It was a pleasant ride, a free language lesson and educational experience, all in one.

As a hobby, Simmy painted portraits of hotel guests during the day and made nice cash beside his night job. When I took over the life guard position, he painted a sign for me and put it on the top of the piano for everybody to see. The sign read:

Your life guard's name is Miklosz. English spoken broken. Very excellent swimmin' lessons.

I thought I understood it, but at that time the subtler aspects of his humor escaped me. I was thinking of asking him to correct the spelling of my name, but I'm glad I didn't. This way it remained original and authentically Simmy. I'm glad, a friend to took a picture of it, which I saved and still have in our album.

A few years later I saw Simmy again -- this time as a guest on television. His audience was Johnny Carson and the whole country, watching the Tonight Show. He started with a short stand-up, before the interview. He cleaned up his act for the occasion, I could tell. This time I understood and could enjoy all the jokes of his short routine. It was exhilarating to see him doing so well and eerie to see him years after his Oakton days -- which he didn't mention to Johnny. He talked mostly about Las Vegas, where he spent his more recent times. He was Johnny's guest one more time about a year later.

There was another entertainer at Oakton Manor: Chico Verlin. For months I knew him only by his stage name: Chico Holiday. A lad in his mid-20s, tall, engaging and very good looking. Girls mobbed him constantly. We became friends. He gave me a large, dedicated photo. (He signed it Chico Verlin). He sang pop and folk songs every night, accompanying himself on his guitar.

I liked to watch him and stayed around at least until he sang *Just Walkin' in the Rain*. It is a lovely, melodic song that always got great applause. The second line is: *Getting soakin' wet.* I learned the expression from the song and added it to my repertoire of colloquial English. His act was a nice break from the nightclub-style program and big band dance music that filled the rest of the evening.

In 1962 I saw him on television, a soloist in a gospel group. He was introduced again, as Verlin. Once I saw a record of his in a music store. I thought, I knew some famous people. -- I also met a few that were truly famous, ones who left me with unforgettable memories. But of those, later.

There was one more artist-type at Oakton. Next to the pool, in adjacent rooms, the hotel offered other services, including massage, to please and pamper guests. Our masseur was a handsome, personable black guy, Jerry. We soon became friends. I learned some English talking to him and he taught me a few things about America. He entertained himself singing, when he was not busy with guests -- and even sometimes during work. I got to know a few songs and enjoyed hearing his soft baritone, that was a lot like the crooning of Nat King Cole. He liked doing his own interpretation of current hits.

Once he told me, that recently on a day off, he took first place in a talent contest in Milwaukee.

"Great! What did you sing?" -- I asked.

"I Wish You Love."

It was a popular song a few years before. I did not know it, but I heard it once or twice. They still played it occasionally on radio. I asked him to sing it. It was a melodic, melancholy song about love and longing.

Jerry quit a few months later and I don't know how he made out with his talent. But the song I remembered, and it helped me to remember him. It happened later, in an unexpected way...

Simmy's sign brought me business. Soon guest asked me to give swimming lessons to their children. I found myself in a situation not very different than Father Anaklét with his Russian class, when it suddenly dropped in his lap. I had to teach -- but how? I was luckier than he -- at least I knew how to swim, but I had to invent a method teaching it. With my first pupil, I showed the little boy how it is done and expected him to copy me. It did not work. The boy was chopping the water in every direction. I realized that flailing arms do not move the body in water. Soon I began to see what was needed. Before the end of my initial lesson, I figured out that first I have to teach the function for the legs. Since I had no floating device, I had the child hold on to the edge of the pool, so I could supervise his kicking. We achieved success, when he could keep himself on top of the water. Then I told him to let go the edge. A little more about dog-paddling and things were going swimmingly. Within a half hour I had all my little charges swim well enough that could be shown off to proud parents.

I had no idea what to ask for the lessons, that usually lasted a half hour. Mike advised me to ask $5. It seemed a lot, but nobody complained, so that was the rate. After one lesson, students could practice on their own, needing no instruction, only minor corrections. The $10 per hour I charged in my first year, was a higher rate than I made for a long time -- although this was just an occasional wage. (In contrast, my salary was $150 a month plus room and board. It was equivalent to 86 cents an hour, or $1.30, including the amenities.)

I taught myself to dive and later taught it to a few kids and women. These were free lessons. I started to swim under water, for fun. After doing two of the 60 ft. lengths with one breath, I thought it was the limit. Then I went two and a half, and eventually three. I couldn't believe myself. It was 180 ft. without coming up for air. I even won a few bets from skeptics, who thought that my claim of aquatic prowess was just an empty boast, until I showed them.

In my 1½ years as life guard, I made three saves. I doubt that any of them really depended on me for life, but one never knows. I pulled them out -- two kids, and a drunk woman.

My life was easy and pleasant at the pool. The hours were unusual. Between 11:00 in the morning and 2:00 A.M., I spent eight hours on duty. My shift was divided into three segments of

2½, 3½ and 2 hours. The post-midnight segment was often empty, quiet and boring. Other times, especially on weekends, the place could be rowdy and I had to usher people out the door at 2:00 A.M. After dinner, entertainment and dancing, some people still wanted to take a dip.

In the locker rooms we had showers, tubs, a steam room and a massage room. First I thought these services were silly, but in time I learned that being pampered was the expectation of many of our guests. I had to be careful about slippery floor, broken glass, lost items and unusual requests. I went to great length to fulfill them to keep guests happy.

One day a very bad thing happened. We had a large, 5-day convention for salesmen of the Hotpoint Division of General Electric. The hotel was filled to capacity. They displayed their slogan everywhere: *Sell the Hotpoint Difference.* It was posted all over the hotel, and even on the necktie one of them gave me. Most of the participants were men and they were there to have a good time, sometime recklessly, especially in the wee hours of the morning.

On that fateful, quiet night, I went up the hill at the end of my shift and to bed. I didn't know it, but after all dancing and entertainment ended upstairs, they decided to entertain themselves. Many were drunk. They crowded around the pool, some jumped in with clothes on. Nobody from the hotel staff was there to supervise.

Mike called me about six the next morning. In the following two hours I was busy, cleaning a large portion of the locker room and the floor around the pool. Blood was all over. The rowdy night ended in tragedy.

A large group of drunken men and a few women came down to the pool to have raucous fun, starting about 3:00 A.M. A man fell through the glass door of the steam room. As he fell, the broken glass cut an artery on the inside of his upper arm. I was told that his friends wanted to help him and did what they thought best. They stuffed a pillow under his arm and were waiting for ambulance. It arrived after an hour passed. Nobody could give me a reason for the long delay. The man was bleeding during all that. He died on his way to the hospital. It was the most inept application of first aid I have ever seen. There was nobody to take blame. Hotel personnel was closed-mouthed about details. They just wanted to put it behind them. I never heard the event mentioned again.

My life as lifeguard was easy. I tried to put to good use, the free time and other opportunities it provided. Whenever I could I used it as an English lesson, depending on the people I had around me. My teachers were adults, their kids and fellow workers. In the beginning I was frustrated by my limited vocabulary and ability to express thoughts. After long conversations I was mentally spent and welcomed a rest.

One of my pool duties was to make sure that people do not fall on the wet floor. A sign, prominently posted said: "Don't Run". I adopted the phrase and tried to warn people. To my frustration, my pronunciation was poor and unintelligible to many, mainly the children. I knew I had a problem and there was a solution, but for a while I couldn't find it. One day I heard a mother yell after her child, saying the two magic words as a native would, with proper enunciation. -- At that moment I found the solution for my problem. I finally was able to discern the little difference, the distinction between understandable and unintelligible English. People are accustomed to sounds they grew up with and find other sounds strange, even when only slightly different. Hungarian is phonetic. English tends to contract sounds It is softer and muffled. I had to perk up my ears, listen closely and learn from others to bridge the gap.

Put it another way -- with her crucial scream on that day, this kind mother loosened my tongue. She gave me the *proverbial mashed potato*. I put it in my mouth, swished it about and by magic, my harsh, rolling "r" came out as a part of a nice, soft, distinct English phrase that people understood. -- My delight was surpassed only by the sense of confidence and triumph. This was a lesson not only involving one phrase, but was comprehensive instruction on an approach that transformed my way of listening and to apply myself in making English my own. This was a sea change. It ended weeks of frustration and began a new phase in my learning the language. -- Of course I kept the accent, but it's OK. It is permanent but only seldom causes problems. -- I sometimes need to repeat certain words to young people in class when I teach as a substitute in the high schools of Crystal Lake. Kids are patient, curious and enjoy hearing the difference. It often starts a conversation, that makes subbing a wonderful retirement diversion.

A few months later I got aid, that really helped me. One kind guest promised and later sent me a Hungarian-English dictionary. I could look up words at leisure, translate and understand. I thanked her in a letter, using some previously unknown words -- how well, only she could tell. She must have chuckled over it, but I'm sure, she forgave. I also exchanged a few letters with a girl, who was guest at the hotel. After I sent one of the letters, I realized that I wrote something that was a wrong phrase and really nonsense, having no meaning or at least confusing. She never mentioned it in her reply and I was too embarrassed to bring it up again, or try to explain.

The life guard position included one unpleasant duty, keeping the bottle chute clean. The bottle collection bin was in a small room, adjacent to the pool, right below the bar. According to law, liquor bottles could not be refilled and had to be broken before discarding. A large number of bottles were thrown down into a wire cage through the chute behind the bar. Some fell down whole, but many broke in the process. I had to brake those that were still in one piece and transfer them into a container. Many were sugary liquor bottles. The sticky syrup made the job unpleasant. I was astonished that good, refillable bottles were by law not reused, but had to be broken, creating extra garbage. But that was the law, probably inspired by the bottlers of the spirits. My hands got sticky and I had to repeatedly wash it before I finished. Despite being cautious, I sometimes cut myself. (Wearing gloves comes readily to mind. I am surprised they did not supply me with them. Back then, I didn't think of asking.)

Friday and Sunday afternoons guests checked in and out. Weekends were a busy time and extra help was needed everywhere. I gladly joined the bellhops during these hectic hours. We all made out well on tips for a little extra work, courtesy and cheerful

312

TWICE BLESSED

attitude.

During my life guard days I had a schedule, different from everybody else's. Being an early riser I was up at my regular time, but went down the hill to the hotel only about 10 o'clock. Until then I wrote letters, tried to read what I could and listened to a popular music station. I understood only a few words. (When I heard the songs later, it was interesting. I rediscovered old songs, as if brand new. But at the beginning I had to be satisfied with the melodies only. One of my favorite was Guy Mitchell's "Gamble". (At least this is how I remember it.) I do not know, why it affected me so much, but I found it haunting and wish I could here it again. It disappeared from the charts and I heard it only once or twice, so many years ago.)

Every morning I went to the kitchen and assembled for myself a super breakfast. It was really a *brunch*, before the word was invented, or became part of my vocabulary: eggs, pancakes, fruits, waffles, juices, the best anybody would want. I could vary my menu day to day.

I befriended our chef, Mr. Snyder. He instructed me daily on the proper use of mostly kitchen English, as he saw the need. He also tried to instruct me on baseball, always with good humor. He was a big fan. I did not understand the game at all but showed interest -- to be polite. He explained it profusely and I followed along like a good student. Baseball was very important in Milwaukee that year. The Braves, a new team in town as I remember, recently transplanted from Boston, were ascending in fame and ranking. In 1956 they did well and in '57, won the World Series. The radio was always on for the games. Excitement and tension filled the kitchen air, mixed with steam and the fragrance of Mr. Snyder's creations. His loud comments and encouragement to players added to the gay atmosphere. It may even affected the menu -- but I am just guessing on that. I prepared my own brunch and it was always superb. (I do not know if Mr. Snyder kept his loyalty to the Braves after they left town. More likely, he became the fan of the new team, the Brewers. Maybe he had mixed feelings, seeing his one-time champions to do so well in Atlanta and become the only team to win baseball's ultimate prize in three different cities, Boston being first in 1914.)

One other thing about Milwaukee baseball. The summer of 1957 was filled with excitement, predictions and high expectations. They came close before, but in '57, everybody *knew* that this was the year of the Braves. They *will* win the World Series. Sometime in that summer, George Webb made a bold offer. Mr. Webb was the owner of a large local chain of hamburger stands. This was in the very early days of McDonald's. His were the cheapest places in town -- cheapest in both meanings of the word: least expensive and meals with minimum of frills. He prided himself on the volume. The popular franchise made Mr. Webb a very rich man.

His offer was to serve free hamburgers to anyone on the day the Braves win the series. The reason was not revealed, at least not to me, but rumors had it that he was either merely taunting the team, not believing that they can pull it off, or that he was genuinely excited and was willing to make a gesture to people in the city, where he made his fortune.

He was true to his word, and on that day he gave away many thousands of hamburgers, and became even more popular and enhanced his reputation.

* * *

Word apparently got out to Hungarian families in the area, that we were at Oakton. One day a young man of my age stopped at the hotel and inquired about the new arrivals. He was Butch Virágh. He invited Pali and me to visit his family. A few days later he came again and took us to Waukesha. We went to meet the family and had dinner with them. Dr. Virágh was working in a hospital. He was an astute and ascetic man, highly disciplined. In his spare time he was working on a Hungarian - English dictionary. Pali came just once, only on that original invite.

Mrs. Virágh, a dainty, gentle, refined woman, took a liking to me. We had long conversations during subsequent visits. She invited me to spend my first Christmas with them. It touched me deeply and was a soothing balm in my lonely days. They had an older son Joe in the army. I saw him only once. He told me that he was commanding a unit of new Hungarian volunteers, who signed up with the US Army. A daughter, Gingi, was a lively girl, with a busy life in and outside of her high school activities. We had a few dates, where she told me all her dreams and plans -- and she had plenty. I wonder how many came true. She impressed me as an achiever and a girl with ideas. Butch was a good swimmer and he attended Marquette University, on a scholarship for this swimming achievements.

Mrs. Virágh tried to be a substitute mother to me. She took my interests to heart and gave me good advise. I asked her to write to my parents about me and how she saw my situation and prospects. She corresponded with my mother for a while. It was good for me and for Mother too, and I was grateful. She did it as a natural thing, willing to do a little additional mothering, beside that to her own children.

I met other Hungarian families through the St. Imre Church. It was a tiny, nondescript block building, but nicely decorated inside, with Hungarian patriotic and religious themes, statues and pictures. The church is named for St. Imre, the son of Hungary's first Christian king, St. Stephen. The prince died in his youth, early in the 11th century; became a saint, but never a king. The church had a community hall, where Hungarians got together for various celebrations, dinners, dances and plays.

I already mentioned János Barkócz. His was a distinguished family of the old regime. They invited me when they hosted dinner for other guests from the old country. After the family patriarch died, the ladies moved to Boston, where the older daughter married. I courted the younger sister, Piroska, or Pille (Butterfly) as she was known in the family and the close circle of friends. -- We almost hit it off, but I was not ready for serious commitment at the time. I never asked, so I do not know what she would say on the subject. We remained friends and at times corresponded, updating our situations. She was a school teacher and also taught ballet. She was limber with grace in her movements that people admired. An early injury cut short a possible career in dance.

There were two other houses, both in Waukesha, that I visited often: the Ivanka and the Petry families. Almost all the people with whom I came to America, were young and single. In retrospect, my attraction to members of the older generation, may have been my desire to find a surrogate family, or more likely, find attractive adult company. I was a regular and welcome visitor in their midst and found their gatherings entertaining, informative and closest to my background.

Mr. Ivanka, with a Slovak name, but a proud Hungarian, liked to talk politics. He was a railroad inspector from the northern region. He told me stories about skiing, that he loved. In the high mountains of the Tátra, now Slovakia, they skied shirtless, in the noon hours on sunny days, where a few hours later it was freezing. -- He liked to work with wood and was skilled in carving small pieces. He went blind in his old age.

One day, listening to Paul Harvey's noon radio commentary, I heard him talking about John Ivanka. He filled a whole segment in his noon report, describing Mr. Ivanka's passion and skill in carving wood. In true Paul Harvey fashion, he built up his story, telling about a nice hobby for an old man. Then at the end, he sprung his surprise on his listeners and said: "John Ivanka does all this -- while blind". It was the nicest tribute a nice man could get.

Conversations with Mr. Zoltán Petry were most interesting and intellectually challenging. He was a well read man. I went to see them as often as I could. Mrs. Zsuzsa Petry , a lady, full of heart and gentle humor, invited me for many family events. I spent two Christmases with them. She also agreed to correspond with my mother, and they wrote to each other regularly for a few years. It pleased me and also eased my mother's heart about her son, swept far away by fate.

This group of refugees that left Hungary to escape communism at the end of the War in 1946, was in large part the old elite. They were mostly members of the pre-war military or were in high positions in government. Most came here in the early-to-mid 1950s, after spending a few years in West Germany. They were ahead of me in experience, the benefit of which they freely and abundantly heaped on me. I was grateful for that, but some of it I later found to be to restrictive and potentially stifling for a

young man. Certainly, I agreed that schooling should come first.
But their general view of life and judgment about opportunities in
America was colored by their past and the age, at which they had
to start their life over again. Still, I found their company more
suitable for me, my desires and outlook, better than the activities
of others, my age.

I heard an amusing story about a member of this group, when
they first set foot on American soil. I never met him and his name
I do not recall, but he was a teacher at an elementary school in
Hungary. A studious, elderly man, he taught himself English from
a book before they set sail for the US -- and more intensively, on
ship. He crammed for his big test, that was a speech he planned, to
greet his future countrymen, after getting off the ship. As events
unfolded, after being welcomed by government people there on
the docks, he made his maiden speech in *English,* expressing his
gratitude for the opportunities, that he looked forward exploiting
in his new country.

When he concluded his remarks, there was a momentary silence,
polite applause, then a few comments. One of his friends said
that he was astonished, how fluently the old man made his speech
and gave kudos for his linguistic achievement. A member of the
welcoming committee, also with incredulity, said this:

"Interesting. I never knew Hungarian and English were so
similar. At times, as if I had heard words, that sounded almost
English."

Having to learn the language from scratch myself, I empathize
with the old teacher. This devil of a language: English with its
fiendish, no-rules pronunciation, confounds the best of us.

* * *

Life at Oakton Manor was easy, but after a whie it held me back.
I became restless. I heard of Camp Kilmer in upper New York state,
through which most Hungarian refugees were originally processed
and settled. Students there were put through two consecutive

crash English courses in preparation to entering school. Many of them received scholarship. It seemed, I was all by myself in the Midwest without the important advantages, available to those who first went to Kilmer. (Oakton Manor burned to the ground in the early 1960s. It was not re-built.)

In the summer of 1958, I looked for a job in Milwaukee. I had the Ford then for myself, so I was mobile, if need be. I was concerned about my language skills and looked for a faster way to improve it. Cardinal Stritch College offered one-on-one instructions. I signed up a for a semester. Twice a week I drove to the far south side for my lessons with a nun, who improvised a course to fit my level and needs.

The job I found in the city, was through Father Arcadius, a priest at St. Imre. The place was St. Camillus Hospital, a hospital/nursing home for elderly men, with various degrees of physycal incapacity, limited mobility and more serious ailments. There, the only time in my life, I saw gangrene being treated to no avail. It took the life of a patient. Most of them needed 24 hour care. I was an orderly, who followed a daily routine and was on duty to provide special attention when called. Patients were infirm and often cranky. With most, I developed a good relationship. We all had our little jokes and tried to use humor to ease the otherwise somber mood of the place. Mr. Walsh was a successful businessman before he began needing round-the-clock care. His mind was still sharp, his humor mostly intact. One day he reached in his dresser drawer and gave me a matchbook. I thanked him, was about to put it in my pocket, but than read what was prined on it. It said: "Stolen from John Walsh". I thought it funny. I pocketed it -- without guilt -- as a memento.

I lived in a small room. My salary was low but again, included room and board. Still, it was an ascetic life, surrounded by invalids at work, monks and nuns at meals, with little time for entertainment. It was OK for a while. I had more time for important things.

After about a year at St. Camillus, I moved. This time I found a job at a home for men. Most of the residents were vagrants, today we call them homeless. Father Arcadius was the director and he took me on as part time supervisor -- a glorified door man. The job involved minimal work. I manned a desk by the door. I had to stay close by, but otherwise could do anything I pleased. My compensation was room and board, laundry and a few amenities. For spending money, tuition and to cover my other expenses, I held a variety of other part-time jobs.

In the meantime I started school. I took an English composition course at Marquette University for no credit, to see if I can hack it. Later I entered the University of Wisconsin - Milwaukee part time, taking science courses.

One day Father Arcadius asked me to go the the railroad station to pick up a young Hungarian, who lived in Belgium for a few years and just came to America. On the train from Chicago, was Béla Bartha. Father knew his family from Eger in the old country.

I walked into the station lobby, looked around surveying the crowd. It was not hard to pick him out. I walked up to him:

"You must be Béla Bartha".

"Yes, I am" -- answered he. Thus began our friendship. Béla was my age, with a situation similar to mine. His opportunities for education were also curtailed because of his background.

He soon settled in. I played pinch hitter for him on his written driver test. He was already a good driver, but we were not sure about his skill in navigating through the special phrasing and some words on those tests. He passed the drivers part without a problem. We went to several places in search for a job. He found one, as machinist. He had some experience in shop work, and lack of language skill wasn't a limiting factor. In a few years he became foreman and later opened his own shop. He also earned a college degree.

He was a good swimmer, part of the elite group from Eger, where all the good swimmers, who did not live in Budapest, came from. Soon Béla and I, with other Hungarians started to play volleyball, and basketball with other members at a sport club every Sunday. To finish the workout, we spent time in the pool. It became the favorite weekly program for several years. The life guard in the pool was Emily, an olympic-class diver and in time, a good friend. Time and many girlfriends went by for Béla, but a few years later Béla and Emily married -- still are.

Around this time, my uncle Julius arrived to Pittsburgh from Austria. Soon he moved to Milwaukee. He needed help with a job and a place to stay. When I quit at St. Camillus, he moved in to take over my position. His beginner English was good enough. He grew to the job easily. Later, he followed me the same way and took over two other jobs, after I quit. We both were moving up in series, it seemed -- or looking it another way -- on parallel tracks.

In the next few years I moved a lot from place to place and became more independent, but still lived a bachelor life, that I now find hard to imagine. Still, there was some system to it. While wasting some valuable time that could have been put to better use, I continued my studies. I changed my major. Chemistry did not suit me. I made the best of my so far acquired chemistry knowledge and got an Associate Degree in Chemical and Metallurgical Technology at the Milwaukee Institute of Technology. At the university I continued with sophomore courses in Letters and Science.

I switched to International Relations, with a minor in economics and finance. Most semesters, I took a less than full load, but there were times when I attended full time. Part time school and part time jobs were most common. Jobs included cleaning an office at night, sheetmetal shop and night shift in a meat packing plant. I remember the last one best, for its dismal atmosphere, crude people and unpleasant work. The task was to *shave* fat from hams, as preparation to further processing or smoking. It was winter, dark days, and undesirable company of coarse, vulgar people. All were southern European immigrants from Yugoslavia and other Slav countries of the Balkans. Most of them spoke broken, primitive English, but I heard a lot of talk I did not understand. We worked in a large, dark, damp room. Only our workbench was lit up with a row of neon tubes overhead. It was the most miserable job I ever had. It was liberating to leave it after a few months when I returned to school for a semester, full time.

However, there was something during my stint there that I found interesting. Our foreman was American. I knew this from his speech. He was a nice, older man, different from his charges. Everybody respected him and followed his instructions, which he delivered part in English and often in the native tounge of the various nationalities -- or so I thought.

One day, jesting, I asked him if he spoke all the languages of the different ethnics.

"No", he said. "All these guys are Slavs, their languages are quite similar, with common words and phrases. They are able to understand one another. I picked up some from each and made up something for myself, an amalgam from all of theirs and now, never mind grammar or other refinements, I can make myself understood no matter which one I'm talking to."

(This was, before "diversity" became such fashion, and a worshiped, politically correct phrase for many, despite being a concept of little inherent meaning, parroted constantly, resulting in nothing productive, only causing friction between people. Here was a man who practiced it in his unique, constructive way and used it to help himself and his men.)

I answered a newspaper ad and got a part time job to help a handicapped person. He was Wally Dutcher a man my age. As a young sailor, he became quadriplegic, after he dived into a pool, too shallow, hit his head and broke his neck. He was wheelchair-bound, without use of his legs and hands. By the time I met him, he resigned to his condition and was working on making something of himself. He was a high school graduate, intelligent and wanted to train himself so he can get a job as radio annoncer. His family was well off on the good salary of his salesman father. They lived in a very nice home in Glendale, on the north shore. His father provided him with all he needed and catered to his whims, perhaps trying to compensate him for his misfortune. I was happy to see that Wally did not succumb to his initial woes and was working hard on his goals.

I took Wally to doctors, exercise classes and anywhere else he wanted to go. He had many friends who cheered him on, without being solicitous or condescending. I lost contact with him, after I moved to New York, but I tracked him down on the Internet to update his story. He moved to Florida, did some broadcasting, became an architect, designing handicap- accessible features for a variety of buildings. He married, adopted a girl, and now has two adorable granddaughters. I found him on his website, with pictures and a capsule autobiography. He answered my email and called me for a long chat and mutual updates on our lives for the last 45 years. -- Recently we took a drive to the Florida Keys. On the way down we stopped for a short visit in St. Pertersburg, where he now lives, retired after a successful career in business.

31

Family Matters

My brothers, Otti and Tomi also left Hungary in late November of 1956. They were students at the University in Miskolc, College of Engineering. During the revolution there was serious fighting there and they took part in it. Tomi was a courier, passing information between student groups and other fighting units. Otti commanded those on campus. He had a list of addresses and directed his men, wearing their army uniform (from prior summer bootcamps) to arrest hiding members of the secret police. After the revolution was suppressed, all were in great peril. Several were arrested and jailed but Otti and Tomi managed to escape two days later. They arrived home one afternoon, after walking for five days. By then, Father received word that the local secret police knew about them and they were to be arrested if found. The messenger was the local communist party secretary. Just days before, Father prevailed on village youth, who wanted to harm him, just because of the office he was holding. The man has returned the favor. -- Hours after they arrived home, Father took the boys to the border where they crossed over to Austria. Mother already had boxes of cookies and pastry packed, to aid a swift departure.

They were looking for me in Austria but were told that I was already in America. Germany took in many refugees. A number of students ended up in Aachen. The city boasted an engineering school of high reputation. Aachen is a beautiful city of about 230,000. It has history, unique to the European culture, as the one-time seat of the Holy Roman Empire. It also has connection to Hungary. The famous Dom, over 1300 years old, has a beautiful Hungarian chapel, built in the 1800s. Otti chose it for his wedding in 1962. He tells me that the Hungarian Club they formed in 1957, is still active and the clubhouse is used as meeting place and for various social functions.

* * *

Otti sent me a photo in 1957. It was of a car I've never seen before: *Vedette*, a French model. It was his, or rather *their*, first car. He pooled money with friends to buy it. It turned out that the car was not really viable. Soon they sold it and bought another. Since then he owned, bought, sold, transfered and reconditioned dozens of cars. The man just loves things on four wheels.

While trying to find a decent car for himself, he also started to work on, sending one to Father. By the end of the year he put one together and sent it home: a Mercedes. This was a kind of thing, the communist regimes at the time were not prepared to deal with. Their economy was totally isolated, where anything western was considered suspect, subversive and a threat. A car as gift, was unheard of. Because of the political implications of the transaction, Father had to get approval from the highest levels in the Party. Then they figured out the customs, taxes, etc. The method of delivery was a mystery for a while. For months I was asking the status of the car and where things stood, but Otti couldn't tell me. In the meantime, Father was working on having the car released, but since we knew that without bribes nothing moved, we did not ask. Father visited the car several times in a customhouse, but he couldn't touch it. My best recollection is that he finally took possession, in the summer of 1958. At our following visit I asked him about details. He had to bribe three people, costing him over 10,000 forints, plus a stiff custom charge. Overall it was an expensive car, but Father was desperate for something to replace his old one.

Since then, at least a dozen cars found a new home in Hungary, thanks to similar efforts by Otti. The gift policy of the Hungarian government went through several stages, but as freedom increased, export-import policy changed for the better. First all cars were welcome, to boost the meager car population. Later, after a lot of old cars in poor condition were sent by relatives from the West, the rules were tightened. A problem developed, where because of the lack of parts, many cars lay idle and the government wanted to improve the situation. For a few years they allowed new cars only. I like to think that we were true pioneers in those early days, sending perhaps the first one, and may even had a positive effect on government policy.

In 1961, Father was allowed the first time to visit a western country. He soon planned a trip to Aachen. Such favor was not granted before and we beleived, that it would never be possible. He was able to spend three weeks with his sons. I too, dreamed of going for a two-week visit. Until then we could only communicate through mail. This was a huge improvement. Otti and Helma, if not engaged, were already committed to each other. Tomi also courted his future wife, Ingeborg. She was a rather tiny girl and soon was given a short, catchy Hungarian name: "Kicsi" -- (something like: *Little One*). She is called Kicsi even today.

At the time of father's visit in Nonember of 1961 I also tried to find a way to go to Europe. I was not yet a US citizen, but had a Green Card, that entitled me to re-entry. Traveling without a passport had its special problems. US authorities were not averse to traveling abroad by non-citizens. But some countries in Europe demanded security deposits by *undocumented* travelers from America, lest they get stuck with undesirable persons, who might want to stay. It was laughable, and I was confident that they did not pass such a law because of me. Still I had to oblige them. Austria demanded a deposit of $350. I was told, it was for a plane ticket, in case I refused to come back on my own. I had to put it down before they gave me a visa. (Look at Europe now! They seem to have gotten stuck with a horde of undesirables.

They should've been happy to get stuck with me. I would've given them less trouble than the many thousands that ended up there in succeeding decades, people who don't assimiliate, but demonstrate and riot for special privileges and make cultural demands.)

It was difficult enough to raise the money for my trip. Now I had to come up with additional cash. Friends helped me out, trusting me with a loan. The Immigration and Naturalization Service issued a sort of substitute passport and I was ready to take to the air, first time since my memorable maiden trans-Atlantic crossing five years before.

The most important reason for my going was to see Father while he was in Aachen. We were very happy at this fortunate turn of events in Hungary. A trip to the west, so sanctioned by the state, was new. Indeed, this was a small positive gesture by the regime, one in a long line of concessions that many years later culminated in gaining total freedom. 1956 was beginning to have its effect and was leading toward 1989, when Hungary opened its border to the West, which in turn lead to the fall of the big Wall in Berlin.

Otti had a plan. The Mercedes, Father received in 1957 was in need of serious repair. He bought the parts including an engine, that he rebuilt. Father drove to Aachen, a 920 miles trip. He was happy that the car made it all the way. Otti replaced the engine and stamped the old ID number onto the new one, just in case. In fact, we did not expect trouble on that score.

Father returned to Aachen several times in successive years for various repairs and application of magic to his vehicle. He was always hard on cars and Otti had to keep up. Even with the repairs, the old "Merci" showed its age. Models changed and cars started to look different. A few years later Father came again. This time too, the trip was coordinated and included a replacement. Otti already had a car close in looks, but not the same model Father came with. This time, Father left the old car in Aachen and drove home another. Otti modified what he could, so the new car would look as close to the old one as possible. Still, important parts were different. So, Father's new car had a wider front grill, as the most glaring difference. Experience showed that nobody looked at those things anymore. This way Father got a car, nine years younger than the one he came with. The color was the same dark green, and that was really the only important thing that helped us to avoid possible trouble at customs.

Before my father 's visit to Aachen, Helma went alone in 1959 to visit my parents. It was a surprise. They knew about her only as a girlfriend of Gale. She showed up with a nice Mercedes (her own) and wanted to introduce herself as a potential daughter in law. She was an instant hit with my parents. Otti sent a lot of things, mostly mechanical stuff. She returned with a loaded car, full of mostly fruits and things my mother baked for her faraway sons. Language was not a problem. Mother spoke some, and Father was conversant in German. Aunt Mici was happy to speak her mother tounge for a while. -- In following years, Helma learned the language so well, that when she writes us, she writes in Hungarian.

During this first visit, Helma went up to Budapest, to see the city for herself. As luck would have it, she had an accident -- and with a Russian military truck, no less. The damage was not great and she drove the car home, after minor repairs to the doors and fender. The authorities (Hungarian and Russian military) were all over the case, embarrased and wanting to close the case. I was amazed to learn, that Helma returned later several times, to testify and negotiate a deal with the Russians, represented by a Hungarian attorney. At the end they compensated her for most of the damage. She also told me, that the Russian driver took a fancy to her, wanted to correspond and see her again. -- The case illustrates the guts and intrepid spirit of my sister-in- law, something I witnessed many times since.

I flew KLM on my first trip back to Europe. My father, brothers and Helma came to greet me in Amsterdam on a gloomy December day. A strange thing happened when I deplaned. Next to me on the plane sat a young women with her toddler son. She had several pieces as carry-on luggage, and as she stuggled with those while carrying the child, I offered help, as I had only a small handbag. As we deplaned, starting down on the long steps, I held the hand of the little boy and lead him to the ground, while holding mine and one of the woman's pieces. At the bottom I gave him back to his mother, and hurried to greet my folks. My family was standing just a few yards away, watching all this. During the emotional greeting they asked me about the woman and the child. It dawned on me suddenly, how cofusing it must have been for them. They thought that I surprised them with news of an existing family that they did not know about. I quickly cleared up the confusion and we were on our way to Aachen.

I met the girlfriends: Helma at the airport and Kicsi the next day. I visited Helma's widowed mother, Aunt Terese and also the Niessens, Kicsi's parents. With Father and my brothers we also paid visits to several German families, who were benefactors of my brothers in the early years. One evening we went to the Hungarian Student Club. There I met some 20 students, most prospective engineers at the university. That's where I met Imre Lendvay. He told me that he was planning to come to America.

I spent Christmas in Aachen that year. It was a simple but joyous celebration with part of my family. We were together, the four of us but missed my mother, Józsi and Marika. For me especially, this was a holiday that was meaningful beyond my dreams. It gave me hope that in the future, such meetings would be possible and maybe frequent.

I was still there when Father returned home. We were driving in two cars, taking him all the way to the Hungarian border. He drove his improved model, Otti next to him observing, to make sure that everything worked fine. He was ready to make final adjustments. Tomi and I followed. We stopped and spent the night with friends in Munich.

We said good-by at the Austro-Hungarian border station. The guard walked with us a little further, closer to the official border line. He warned us not to wave, shout or say anything to Father, after he crossed the actual border 30 ft. beyond, because the Hungarian guards frowned upon that. We thought it excessive, but remembered worse from communists. As Father crossed, checked through and disappeared in the distance, we watched and said our farewells silently.

I thought that this paranoia about anything foreign, must be a source of a lot of unhappiness. But the guards had to follow orders and did what the regime demanded of them. (Two years later, when I was at the border again, I witnessed a pleasant change. By this time, crossing was totally different. The guards were friendly, relaxed and natural in their behavior. Courtesy returned. It was a good thing and I was happy, hoping for more.)

I returned to Aachen in 1964. Then my mother and sister visited there. This time I flew Icelandic Airlines, that was known as the least expensive. The planes refueled in Reykjavik and landed in Luxembourg. Accomodations were sparse, the seats tight, but cost was my most important consideration. On this flight the weather was good over Iceland, I had a passport and even knew where I was going. It was a wonderful feeling.

Mother and my 13 year old sister Marika made their first trip to Aachen. It was another proof, that political control was easing behind the Iron Curtain. Hungary was the vanguard and the envy of her satellite neighbors.

We went to see many places, the nicest of those Paris and Versailles. We visited the top of the Eiffel Tower and on the way down, ate lunch in the restaurant on the first level. Vesailles was beautiful and not crowded. We could take our time in the palace and linger in the garden. We even walked out to the infamous Petit Trianon, though it was closed.

We again went to the border, escorting Mother and Marika. After we parted, we three brothers, took the scenic route back to Aachen. I asked Otti earlier about his favorite places in Europe. The first place he mentioned was the lovely Swiss city of Lugano. I remembered that and proposed that we go there. They agreed, but told me about possible problems with border crossings. Austrians were easy on German residents, but the Swiss were sticklers. We were planning to go from Austria to Switzerland and back to Germany. This time I had no problem with my American passport, but the boys had only German resident papers.

Within the Hungarian student group in Aachen, was one guy of German ancestry, who was recognized by the Germans, as citizen. He had a passport, that became the traveling document for any friend, who wanted to use it, to travel in western Europe. Tomi had borrowed this peripatetic pass, for our trip. Austria was no problem with anybody, traveling in a car with German plates.

There were cases when people were detained or refused crossing, but the punishment was light, if any. I heard stories told by students, indicating that the risk was bearable. Otti had misgivings, but was still willing to go.

So we prepared the best we could and took our chances. We crossed into Switzerland at the most opportune hour, 3 A.M., choosing a minor crossing point, that we were most confident using. Tomi was driving, I pretended to sleep, so that my face could still be seen clearly, and Otti was in the trunk. Tomi handed my passport to the guard along his phony one and hoped for a smooth crossing. We had no problem at all and were just waved through.

On the other side we stopped for a rest and let our prisoner out of the trunk. Driving on, the road took us through a gorge. The velley was rugged, with gullies right and left and bridges over a little creek, that we followed and crossed a number of times. (I thought back to this drive many years later, when Ildikó and I were driving to Hana on the Island of Maui. That was a similar road. We drove it with Ildi on our only vacation, while the kids were little.) Here the night was dark, but still we saw that we were traveling picturesque terrain. From time to time we stopped, looked around and wished that it were daylight. High canyon walls were on both sides, a narrow strip of sky with bright stars between them. The night was still, eerily quiet, deeply dark, yet unforgetably beautiful.

We drove through the nicest part before dawn. A few hours later we traveled north along the shore of Lake Lugano, to reach the city at the foot of a sugarloaf mountain -- one of two, that define this paradise resort city. Villas pockmark the green hills, some huge with tower, and adorned with veranda, accented by a low white, filigreened stone wall, and colorful umbrellas. A funicular's cable was shimmering as a car was inching up on the steep hillside. Along the shore of the lake, a long, gently curved walkway, following the shoreline, densely shaded by manicured trees, takes strollers from the city park, to the end of town, where the row of huge villa estates begins. At the start of the promenade, a neat bronze bust of George Washington commemorates the hero of the New World. I do not remember the inscription but I know that I liked it. I saw it a few years later and was pleased to find it exactly as I remember it. We spent the better part of a day, before going on with our trip. Lugano was unforgettable. We spent a day in Venice before returning to Aachen. A few day later I was on the plane back home.

32

Student Days

After a coule years I heard about the Hungarian Students Organization and I got in contact with them. It was a loose group of a few hundred students, scattered around the country. Among them were a few old friends. I missed the first two annual meetings before I even heard of them. In the early days, the organization was able to solicit support from a variety of sources for students. We were *heroes*, admired by many and our causes and welfare was embraced by Americans. With the leadership of a few able students we acquired modest notice and valuable contacts in high circles. Many of the Camp Kilmer students were granted scholarship and aid.

The first annual meeting I attended, as the delegate from Wisconsin, was on the campus of the University of Michigan at Ann Arbor. There I met some old friends and made new ones. (I was happy to be the representative, elected, if memeory serves, by six students in the state, none of whom I knew. My theory on my success, without additional psychoanalysis, is that I was elected because of my name. For Hungarians, without any knowledge about a candidate to elect, a *Magyar* is most natural, easier than *another* unknown guy, with a name, not so patriotic sounding.

Let's call it true -- maybe blind -- democracy.)

We had a whole week's program with a variety of academic and general interests. Several professors from the University and a couple political figures made presentations. With our past, interests and experiences being common, the meetings were entertaining and informative. Late one night, with beer in many hands, somebody started singing one of the *movement* songs. These were the ones that a few years ago, we *had* to sing in school and at meetings. They were all socialist propaganda, though many had nice, singable tunes -- the only real attraction. We sang a lot of them, but this time singing them was not mandatory. Still, all joined in. We were praising the proletariat and the *revolution* one more time, and had fun doing it. (Revolution! What a misnomer. Of course, the songs celebrated the 1917 Soviet revolution, which brought only misery for us. In Cuba they are still required to sing them, as if the Revolution were brand new, with the old tired promise by an entrenched dictatorial power, that some day it may bring a socialist nirvana to that island of many prisons.) Our crooning was shaded with nostalgic feelings for our homeland and was, in a curious way, a parody. We thought back to old times without the negative feelings that was always part of singing them in the past. Later we switched to traditional Hungarian songs that were neglected by official policy in favor of the propaganda that the movement songs promoted.

Our president was László Papp; vice president, Béla Lipták. László was studying architecture, Béla, chemistry. For the next term we elected József Takács and Csanád Tóth -- a Pannonhalma classmate -- for the top spots.

Csanád and Jóska lived in D.C. and attended Georgetown University. Csanád was a good speaker and a natural in political circles. While he was still a student, one of his speeches appeared in *Vital Speeches of the Day*. It is a select Wahington publication, honoring notable speeches. His was found to be worthy of printing and was read by the elite of government, media and academe. It was a speech, given by one who spoke the language ony a few years.

Later he held the position of Assistant Secretary of State under

Cyrus Vance, during the Carter administration. In that capacity he was a member of the secretary's delegation in 1978, that was chosen to return the Holy Crown to Hungary. The Crown was in American custody and held at Fort Knox since WW II, when officers of the Hungarian Army gave it to American Army officers for safe-keeping. After the ceremonies and before returning to the States, Csanád took his delegation to Pannonhalma for an unofficial visit.

(When our family visited Washington D.C. in our camping trip in 1982, I had lunch with Csanád and Jóska. Not much before that, Jóska, who was working at the Voice of America, was appointed director of the Hungarian Section. Csanád was still in the State Department. He died of a heart attack the following year.)

In 1962 I looked forward to our meeting on the Georgetown University campus. With the invitation I was informed that the my expenses for the trip, including a week's stay in the campus dorm would be reimbursed. I was impressed by the ability of my once penniless friends -- and a little jelous at the same time -- to be able to foot the bill for our whole group. -- I felt isolated in the Midwest, where I had to fend for myself and provide for my support all by myself. I accounted for my expenses, and told the organizers that my cost for the trip was about a third of what was allotted for it and that was all I would expect as compensation. It earned me credit and an honorable mention before the assemblage. I did not elaborate on my gesture and may have inadvertantly created the notion that I was well off, well enough not to take the money, while really, I was as poor as were they, maybe more.

Csanád befriended Senator Gale McGee of Wyoming, who was new to his office, being elected in 1960 and invited him to address our group. The senator a former professor, with a decidedly outsider's view of his new job and a humorous look at the pompous pretentions of his colleagues in his new, aloof institution, entertained and educated us in an informal gathering.

The 1-year term in office for Jóska and Csanád ended with the closing of the convention. They nominated me for the presidency of the organization, but I declined, because I felt that I could not devote enough time for the work. Underneath I did not feel confident that I could handle such responsibility. Later I regretted my decision. It would have given me needed experience.

33

Two Years In New Jersey -- And The Big Apple

Prior to my going to the Georgetown conference in the summer of 1962, an old friend invited me to visit him in East Orange, New Jersey. He was Miklós Németh, also from my Pannonhalma class. We talked about me staying permanently on the east coast and I said, yes. When the student meeting ended, I went to East Orange and stayed with Miklós, who shared, a large apartment with Kálmán, a medical student. Kálmán spent 10 months a year in Austria, at the University of Graz Medical School on a scholarship, but spent his summers in America to support himself. We got along well. I was looking for a chemical position, where I thought I was best suited. Kálmán was a few years older, and experienced. He advised me to avoid chemical operator jobs that may involve messy work in one of the large local chemical plants. He told me that instead, I should look for one in an analytical labratory.

I interviewed at Union Carbide headquarters on Park Avenue, but when my conference with the corporate personnel manager ended I realized, I did not know what I was doing. A kind interviewer advised me to go to one of their plants that had a lab where they may be able to use me. The next day I went to the Linde Division plant in Newark and in a few days I was offered a job as chemist technician.

Four of us worked in the chemlab. The work was not difficult, but demanded precision. Accuracy in results was crucial. Big decisions were made based on them. I worked with a Dutch immigrant, Tobias (Toby) DeGlopper. He had the most experience and was leader of our group. He taught me the procedures, pointing out the pitfalls and taught me good laboratory habits, that were key to precise work. We became good friends, so much more for our similar background.

Al was our resident graduate chemist. A bachelor type, he lived an active life, with girls constantly on his mind, while also working on his Masters. We often ate together and talked about our lives. He went for a week's vacation to St. Thomas in the Caribbean. He showed his pictures and told me what a nice place it was. It was the first time I heard of such places and dreamed about seeing them one day.

Once during lunch, Al made an observation which, I thought was a mere acknowledgement of facts and I didn't think much of it at the time. He said that I have a natural handicap with my limited language skills and different cultural background. Finding a girlfriend is easier for guys who grew up here. I couldn't argue with him and didn't want to. He was not gloating or had any unsavory motive, just spoke his mind. There were two particular women that we were disdussing. One he had his eye on. Nancy, a popular divorcee, was considered a catch. At the time she was already spoken for, by Al's best friend. Al told me that he was biding his time. I liked Nancy too, but competition was steep and, as he said, I was at a disadvantage. In time Nancy married the guy (Al's friend) and, as I heard they lived unhappily ever after -- or at least for a while, before I lost track. It became clear to me that pretty Nancy was a neurotic, moody, unpredictable person and I was was happy that she cast her net for someone else and not me.

There was also Joyce, the other one Al referenced in our talk, saying that he may also pursue her at the right opportunity. She too was divorced and had a sweet four year old daughter. Joyce took a liking to me, without me making an approach. It was a no-pressure friendship -- maybe a little more. She was full of life, humor, liked nature and art and was very good company. We went together for about a year, parted amicably and stayed friendly after that.

Imre Lendvay made his move to New York from Aachen in the fall of 1962. On weekends with Joyce and the little girl, the four of us went picnicking, to see the nearby country, having a lot of carefree fun. -- At work we were discrete, thus not subject to much talk, though the boys in the lab knew it. Once in company, Al talked about Joyce and obliquely congratulated me.

The lab was under the able direction of Dr. Art Prince, a Ph.D. in chemistry and a very nice man. He oversaw our operation with minimum control, because he seldom saw need for close scrutiny. -- He regularly loaned money to several men in the lab. I found out about it when I mentioned once to Toby that things were a little tight for me until payday. I made $450 a month then. It was not much, when rent was over $150, school and everything else more expensive than in Milwaukee. I really lived paycheck to paycheck. I was frugal with my daily expenses, but spent money on entertainment more freely. Sometimes things were so tight that I stayed home all weekend. I had only a radio to keep me company. It was better than TV, because I could read and study. Once I swallowed my pride and asked Dr. Prince for a small loan. He gave it to me without question. When I paid him back the next payday, he was surprised and asked if I would prefer to pay him back later. I thanked him for his kindness, but said no.

(I thought of a prior event that taught me an important lesson. Kálmán kept his summer earnings in a bank while he was in Graz. He loaned me money from that, before I got my first job. Then he went back to Graz. When he returned for the summer in July, he saw that I deposited my repayment to his account, just two months before. Although we did not set a repayment schedule, he assumed that it would be sooner. I did too, but was unable to -- or just say, didn't. He was disappointed and I ashamed. It was a seminal lesson for me about money, especially other people's money.)

Art asked me over to his house once with the expressed intention of introducing me to his niece. I spent a pleasant evening with them, talking and listening to the music of Swan Lake ballet. The young lady and I had a date later. Nothing came of it, though she was nice girl. I felt a little obliged, but it did not affect the relationship with my boss. He seemed to feel the same way, so we just went on as before.

During my stay in Jersey several intersting events took place. New York is exciting and a premier city of the world, with spectacular visual and cultural attractions. I spent many days in the city, staying until the late hours. (I remember just once, going home in daylight. After I learned every traffic light and turn of the road in the dark, it was strange to drive home in a bright day. I had to pay closer attention, for I knew the road better in the dark.)

There were many fascinating things about New York. It was a modern, lively, exciting city, at the cutting edge of societal evolution. Central Park is world class, totally integral and a fitting part of the huge metropolis. I spent much time in it, including once a carriage ride, which didn't break my budget. I now hear, it became prohibitively expensive since.

Much had been written of New York's splendor, the skyline and the list is indeed endless, so I mention only a few of them. Manhattan has a one-of-a-kind system to regulate traffic. It is not something new or contemporary. On the contrary, it is and old relic, but well designed in its day and an appropriate counterpoint for modern Manhattan, full of cars, and one-way streets. The traffic light system was designed and installed long time ago, yet it handles well the greatly increased number of cars today. The lights were perfectly timed to facilitate the easy flow of traffic on the wide, one-way avenues. One can drive from Harlem to the Battery without stopping, provided he monitors his speed and pays attention to slow-downs and occasional jams. Drivers on the numbered cross streets had to be more patient gettig across the avenues, for which the traffic lights are timed.

On several avenues, running lengthwise in Manhattan, old cast iron posts, supporting traffic lights were installed at street corners, rather than overhead. They had no amber light, only red and green. The traditional function of the yellow is supplanted by red-green glowing together. When one is driving with steady speed (about 35 mph) he could expect that the road ahead keeps opening with successive green lights. When traffic slows down he might see a red also light up, flashing above the green. It is time to stop. Then the green would go out and the red alone stay on. A few seconds before red gives way to green, allowing traffic flow to resume, green lights up with the red still on, signaling that all green will soon follow. In true New York fashion, waiting cars, a majority of them taxis, take off at this tme, showing their impatience, to urge straglers, who are still in cross traffic. -- It was confusing at first, but after learning the intricacies of this system, driving was a breeze.

I have not seen New York-type, red-green-only traffic lights anywhere else in the world. Driving in Manhattan was child's play, compared to the madhouse that is constant on the l'Etoile, the huge traffic circle around the Arc de Triomphe in Paris. (Parisians say, that there is also a system at the l'Etoile. I watched it once for about an hour, from the top of the arch with Jim, my son in law. We concluded that it was partially controlled chaos -- to be generous -- with convulsive movement of a lot of cars at once, at unpredictable times.)

Not long ago in 2005, I heard a report on radio about a proposed update of the traffic control system in Manhattan. The change would be an experiment with amber, in addition to the red and green. The idea appearently arose not from a need to control vehicle traffic, but to assist pedestrians, in getting across safely. At this time this is all I know.

Imre Lendvay came as a new immigrant to America in 1962, a year after I met him at the Hungarian student club in Aachen. His application was in the works at the time. His father was born in Bridgeport, CT but grew up in Hungary. For that, he received a permanent visa.

On the first Sunday morning we had breakfast at Rockefeller Center. It was Christmas season. We were sitting by the window in the arcade restaurant, overlooking the ice rink, facing the main tower of the complex. Music was playing, people were gliding and doing figures on the ice in front of the golden statue of Prometheus.

We renewed our acquaintance. I saw that our interests, temperament, likes and dislikes closely coincided. After a two-year stay on the east coast we seldom saw each other. I came back to Milwaukee, he stayed in New York for a while, then moved to Huntsville, AL and later to Germany. We kept in contact mostly by long talks on the telephone. Subjects often discussed, are politics, classical music, family and a lot of personal things, that could run the gamut.

Imre is a successful engineer. He worked for IBM and other prestigious firms. He has been with General Electric for the last two dacades, supervising the quality of parts, manufactured by subcontractors for large GE passenger jet engines. He travels a lot with the job from his base in Munich, Germany, but personal travel is also one of his hobbys. He visited over a hundred countries so far and wants to see more. After courting Cheryl for a long time, they married in 1993. It is a long distance marriage. Cheryl is in Pittsburgh, in a very high position with US Air. They see each other about once a month and spend a lot of money on calls over the Atlantic -- at least three calls a day, he tells me. It is an unusual marriage, but by all indications, a happy one.

Our frienship has similar aspects. It has endured for many years, despite the distance and many different busy pursuits by each of us...

While in NewYork, we saw many productions at the Metropolitan Opera. We both were avid fans of the arts, mostly music -- and its stars. After a performance of Eugene Onegin, we went to the back entrance to see if somebody famous comes out. Soon there was Leontyne Price, in the company of a few friends. She just finished singing the role of Tatiana to thunderous applause. She started speaking to us from a few steps distance, without us butting in their conversation, as they were about to part. She turned towars us, thinking perhaps that we wanted an autograph. I didn't think of that, had nothing in my hand, so just made, a red-faced excuse. After a few words she inquired about our accent. She studied in Vienna and was interested in things European, especially music related. We said that we were Hungarians. She excused herself before her friends and walked over to us. She said how she respects the music, the performers and the conductors from Hungary, known world wide. She told of her Hungarian friends and made us, intruders, welcome in her company for a little while. -- Her preformance was the last we saw in the old house. The Metropolitan closed in 1966, and moved to the spacious Lincoln Center complex.

I met other luminaries in later years, people of the artistic or political elite. I mention my encounter with some, for the indellible memory that was personal and memorable for me. The short conversations were significant for some other reasons, not for just the fact that they were famous people.

While in New York, word came to our student organization, that Otto Habsburg was in town and expressed interest for a meeting with Hungarian students. We were surprised and pleased to be invited. Otto Habsburg was once next in line to wear the Holy Crown of Hungary, then part of the Monarchy of Austria-Hungary. He would have been the next king of Hungary, but for the Nazis and the Soviet occupation of the country in 1945. According to present day law of Austria, he cannot enter his own country. He now lives in Paris, writes on matters European, and teaches at the Sorbonne.

The leadership of the Hungarian Student Organization was represented by Jóska, the president, Csanád, vice president and Ödön Mészáros, treasurer. They invited me to be fourth -- presumably to represent the grass roots.

I donned my best outfit and we showed up early for our audience. It took place in an elegant Fifth Avenue apartment of an important Hungarian, whom we did not know. The professor stayed with that family. Everything went as planned. He came in and after introductions we sat down in a circle, in a large, elegantly furnished room. He questioned us on the organization and to each of us on our personal backgrounds. Later we queried him on his life and plans for the future. At that time the possibility of him having a role in Hungary in any capacity was not in the cards. (Sometime later I heard talk of him playing some official role, even be king.) Nothing new on that subject has emerged in recent years. It is likely that the professor will stay in academe and write opinion on European diplomatic subjects. We thought that we were fortunate to meet him and talk about important issues of the day, that might effect the future of Hungary and Europe. I found him to be a pleasant, personable man, completely without pretenses and at ease with himself and others. Our initial stiffnes and caution soon desolved and the conversation flowed smoothly from one subject to another. He showed no sign, indicating his pedigree, nor had he a professorial manner or pomposity. His detailed knowledge and understanding of current and past events were evident.

I asked him a question about Hungary, as a possible factor in his future. He was noncommittal, saying that any thinking on this line was premature at that time, to say the least. It was a memorable event in my life. We spoke to a professor, but I saw in him a representative of a dynasty of royals, the grandson of Hungary's beautiful and beloved Queen Elizabeth, member of a family, that forged history for centuries, one that has been vital force in the life of millions -- and with all that, a pleasant and likable person.

In 1963 another friend came as new immigrant. The ace of the class, my friend from old Pannonhalma days, Miklós Farkasfalvy arrived in New York. I wrote about him earlier. In 1956 he went to Rome, was ordained a priest and became a Cistercian. Now he had a heavy assignment. The General Abbot sent him to America to open a school and found a monastery.

After he arrived, we met in Manhattan and spent several days together. It was good to reacquaint and talk about old times. Miklós, the student, became Father Denis and I had to get used to his new name, though most of the time I use the old one.

Through friends I got to know Roberta, a very pretty and smart girl. She was working, while attending college part time. An intelligent woman, interested in subjects that I also found interesting. She liked the arts but lacked exposure, other than in text books. I took her to the opera a few times. Seeing a large musical production on stage was a new experience for her. A Hungarian ballet company was touring in America at the time. They were top rate and she liked the program. It was her first time to see ballet.

I never really got to know her life, outside of our common pursuits, despite my best efforts.

She was insecure which made her indecisive and sometimes frustrating company. Intimacy frightened her. She apologized for it and said that she cannot help it. Once, during a long talk I tried to persuade her to open her soul, but we had only an emotional, sweet, but fruitless mutual confession session. It was beautiful in a way, but resulted in unfulfilled desires and only partially intimate moments. I liked her a lot, and hoped that I can be her knight who can save her but I was left frustrated with my inability to have her open up to me. I saw no chance for us for the long term and realized that difficulties would always lurk on the horizon. We kept our contact even when we both saw that we had no future together. It was a good way to change from serious involvement, that was not going anywhere, to a platonic friendship.

My roommate, Miklós Németh and I moved, and for a while we again shared an apartment in Bloomfield, much nicer than the old one. It had a view of a golf course, was spacious, but too expensive for me. I moved out and lived alone until I came back to Milwaukee. My next apartment was more affordable in a quiet residential neighborhood, with a lot of living space.

I took evening classes at Rutgers University, selecting courses that would fit my new major, history and economics. My studies kept me home a lot. It was just as well, because I had only a minimum to spend beyond the basics, living and school expenses being higher. In Wisconsin I was a resident and state schools were affordable. I thought of moving back.

I remember two major pop culture events, both while I attended Rutgers. The first was my discovery of the Beatles. In the window of a music shop, was a new display showing the four mopheads -- as they appeared to me on first sight. I think I heard the name *Beatles* a few days before. In the animated display, their heads were bobbing right and left in unison, in front of a fancy cardboard picture of them together. It was part of the massive publicity campaign. They looked clean, cute and innocent. Radio reports about them predicted that they would soon invade and conquer the

New World. These predictions came true in spades. Their triumph
was thorough and almost instantaneous.

The other, a true   New York event, also accompanied by
huge promotion, with interviews and excerpts on radio.   It was
a happening -- to use a contemporary phrase -- the opening
of *Hello Dolly* with the quintessential Dolly, Carol Channing. I
could't appreciate all that -- but what did I know about Broadway?
It was the first time I heard her name, though she was talked
about as a well known star of the Great White Way. Her speech
and singing sounded affectatious but the critics ate it up and the
audience loved her. (Later I concluded, that this big-haired, big-
mouthed dame was genuine. Her exaggerated manor of talk was
just the way she always was.) The show sold out for a long time
and became a standard and later a movie with Barbra Streisand in
the title role. (I saw Carol Channing recently on TV, many years
after her greatest Broadway triumph. She changed less in 40 years,
than some people change in five -- and I'm talking looks. That old,
mischievous smile and opiniated humor changed not at all.)

34

Notable Cultural
Events -- Maestro Bernstein
And Miss Dietrich

My own Broadway happening, and favorite hit, was *Camelot*. The stars were Richard Burton, Julie Andrews and Robert Goulet. Burton skillfully faked singing, Julie sparkled and Robert belted. His voice was a phenomenal baritone, but I heard it only in Camelot, where, I thinnk, he got good coaching or a director who demanded real singing. Later, in TV appearances and his albums, evidently without astute guidance, he was just walking through songs, improvising, trying to be conversational, alternating between whisper and letting his booming voice reverberate. He never really learned *how* to sing -- or likely, forgot after Camelot. It is a pity.

In New York I visited the family of Joe Zizza. Mrs. Zizza was a cousin of Zsuzsa Petry of Waukesha, who encouraged me to look them up. I saw them several times during my two-year stay and even dated their daughter, Valery, for a while. Joe was the orchestra librarian of the New York Philharmonic. He loved his job. He said, it is the most interesting work one can do for a living. We talked a lot about music, the Philharmonic and his boss, Leonard Berstein, who was the principal music director at the time. I admired Maestro Berstein. He had a collection of talents: pianist, conductor, composer and educator. His politics was on the left, with the crowd and the social phenomenon of the 1960s, that Tom Wolfe named and rediculed, as *Radical Chic.* But taking his other contributions into account, these antics were forgivable and just a sign of the time, common in his circle. His *Young People's Concerts* and *Harvard Lectures* on NBC television, were my favorite programs. The youth concerts were going for several years on Sunday afternoons.

At the beginning of one of those concerts, Maestro Lenny talked about a new discovery. He lavished praise on a young man I never heard of: Andre Watts. Young Andre was a recent acquaitance for his also. He was a prodigee, a son of a black GI and a Hungarian woman. She recognized his talent and taught her young son at home for several years.

Mr. Bernstein, introducing Watts, told a story. A while back he conducted a concert. It was one in his regular season in Philharmonic Hall at Lincoln Center. The scheduled soloist suddenly fell ill. One of his friends suggested Andre Watts as a last minute replacement. Andre, I think 19 at the time, played the scheduled 1st Piano Concerto of Franz Liszt. He dazzled his audience and apparently, also Maestro Bernstein. He found it fitting to invite back the young pianist, to play on one of his concerts for young Americans. I watched that concert and knew that I was witnessing history. These two concerts of young Andre, launched a great career. Since then, Andre Watts has been one of the most highly sought-after artist in concert halls of the world.

In the mid-1960s Harvard University invited Mr. Bernstein to present a lecture on a musical subject of his choosing. He gave four lectures that became a television mini-series, as 1½ hour lectures on four consecutive Sundays. I number those programs among my most memorable musical experiences.

Berstein made classical music interesting. His lectures reminded me of Father Kilian's Collegium Musicum presentations in Pannonhalma. I recorded the audio part of the Harvard lectures, with my primitive casette recorder, when the series was repeated later on radio. Berstein displayed a phenomenal memory, depth of knowledge and uncanny insight about his subject pieces, music theory and trends, as well personal details about the composers he discussed.

He surprised me about, and made me a fan of Brahms, analyzing his Third Symphony. But I was most impressed with his treatment and obvious love for the music of Gustav Mahler. It was on a high level, yet thoroughly clear and entertaining. The composer was new to me then, and Berstein's astute observations, erudite presentation, illustrated with examples, perked my interest in the music of Mahler. I always look forward to hear his music. His massive Fourth Symphony, was recently played at a concert in Ravinia Park -- my whole extended family attending. It was lovely.

After I moved back to Milwaukee in 1964, the Philharmonic payed us a visit on a summer tour and performed in the music shell in Washington Park. I went to see them with Ildikó and her family. Before the concert I went "back stage" -- behind the shell. There was Joe Zizza, greeting me and Mr. Berstein standing, with batan in hand, at a short distance. We chatted a few minutes, then Joe asked me if I wanted to meat the maestro. I said: "Yes, of course". So he introduced me as a friend and a lover of music. Bernstein heaped his praises on Joe, saying that he was very good, the best librarian he ever had.

After some selfconscious stutters I came up with a question that popped into my head:

"Did you ever visit Budapest?"

"Yes I did, three times. -- The most intelligent audience I ever played for."

"Wow!!" -- I did not say this out loud -- only in my mind. I restrained myself, but my chest swelled with pride. He said it sincerely, without even thinking about it. That audience must have made an impression on him. Soon he got the signal and went to conduct some short pieces and a Beethoven symphony.

Later that year I was a little more daring -- no, brazen -- at another Milwaukee cultural event. Marlene Dietrich came to town to do a one-woman show. By then she was out of the movie business for a few years. In her prime she did some singing, most notably in *The Blue Angel*, (1930) but I was surprised that she wanted to do a concert so many years later. (Since then I learned that it can be done even by a midiocre voice, with skillful control, a good agent, and well handled publicity.)

I was curious, went to see the show, and liked it. Her alluring, affected, throaty alto worked well in Hollywood and was a success here on stage. She talked to the audience in an intimate, conversational tone as part of her act, and had a repertoire, suitable for her style and image.

For her curtain calls at the end, between bows, she did her signature pose: looking seductive, while holding onto the curtain with one hand stretched high, accentuating the smooth flow of her long gown and showing her still legendary figure. -- She was no spring chicken. The lady was pushing 70, but from a distance, with aid of good make-up, she looked appealing. I thought the old gal did rather well for herself. (Now, 70 is a bit younger, as I discovered recently.)

A thought came to me during the show and after final curtains I went backstage and stood in a short line, waiting. I congratulated her and promptly advanced a proposal to see if she is receptive. We had the following brief exchange.

"Miss Dietrich, I really liked your show and it gave me an idea, if you don't mind. I remember a song that I think, would suit you and your program well."

"What song is that?"

"I Wish You Love. -- do you agree?"

"Oh, yes! How does it go? … Come on now, do it! It is *your song.*"

I tried and gave her all I knew. And it was't much. Flustered and suddenly nonplussed, I scrambled to come up with a few lines, humming and mumbling, as words came to mind.

Good-bye, … this is where our story ends...
never lovers, ever friends...

I wish you bluebird in the spring,

To give your heart a song to sing,
And then a kiss, but more than this,
I wish you love...

She chimed in crooning, helping me a bit. Together we stumbled on, humming a half-baked version with a little more of the lyrics to get to the end.

But most of all, when snowflakes fall,
I wish you love.

Embarrased, I was about to retreat, when she paused and hummed some more of the refrain, finding a few new words. It seemed, she liked my idea. She tanked me for my forward, but original proposal, in a manor a famous star would, though with respect toward her admirer, who is though, only one of millions, still one, through whom her fame is sustained. At the end I felt good for approaching her with my suggestion.

About a year later Marlene Dietrich starred in a network television special, a TV version of her earlier stage show on tour.

The titile of her special: "Miss Marlene Dietrich -- I Wish You Love". Her opening number was the title song, the contest winnig tune, I learned from my masseur friend, Jerry, back at Oakton Manor. I was astonished. It was gratifying. I hoped, Jerry was watching.

35

Life And School In Milwaukee

After I moved back to Milwaukee in 1964, I was eager to continue my studies and signed up for a few classes at the University of Wisconsin - Milwaukee.

I got a job at Allis Chalmers, the huge heavy-equipment manufacturer. In a development lab we were making electrodes for experimental fuel cells. It was a brand new thing then, and a closely guarded delevopment project. I was isolated from the actual testing process and only produced the electrodes. They were made up of fine nickel shavings, held together with some resin and pressed into a thick sheet. The job was boring and dead-end.

The pay was average, but it seemed more than what I made in Jersey. Here I could afford to live a little better. I was even looking to upgrade my car.

For a short time I stayed with my uncle, Julius, who was by then married and started his family. He met Inge, a nice German woman, who had a temporary visa, later made permanent. Before her visa expired they found reason for her to stay. In the fall of 1962, I flew back from New York and was the best man at their wedding. A daughter, Maria was born on February 5 1964, Johnnie the next year and Sabina in 1967. They are my cousins, but it took me some time to get used to it. I remember, once in Maria's presence, I referred to her as my niece. She energetically corrected me. "I'm your *cousin*, Miklós!" -- Indeed, and not surprising, I did not think of her as cousin, for they all were so much younger. Cousins of mine were grown-ups in my unconscious mind. She affirmed the exception. Since then she grew up, became Mrs. Quentin Cartier with four children of her own -- so "cousin" is natural now.

After a few months I moved out and rented a room, just off the Marquette University campus, from Mrs. McGinnis, a 75 year old widow. She rented a large apartment and sublet several rooms to students during the school year. I was her only permanent tenant.

We negotiated a special arrangement. I proposed a type of room-and-board regimen, where she would provide breakfast and dinner. She welcomed my suggestion, saying that in recent years she neglected her cooking because it became a lonely routine, not worth it for her, or at least she lacked motivation to cook for only one. This way she found a reason to get back closer to a lifestyle that she was used to all her life. She acceded to my request, but added a clause. Instead cooking on Sunday, she would treat me to dinner at a restaurant. It was unusual, but that's what she preferred, so we did that most Sundays. She picked the place and we ate out. She introduced me to chinese, and we often went there, her favorite place. Later she did other things for me, such as minor clothes alterations, but I insisted to pay for those. She took a liking to me, and found me refreshing company. We talked about many subjects during meals and it was good for both of us. She told me about her childhood in Milwaukee and illustrated with anecdotes, how the city grew. When she was little, the city ended about 20 blocks west of the Marquette campus, part of the city that is now considered just out of downtown. The area around 39th Street, where the Miller Brewery is now, was then countryside.

She recounted much of her life, her three marriages and her family. I learned a lot about middle class living at the time of the Depression and during World War II. She liked FDR and was surprised by a few things I told her about him and the unintended negative conseqences of the socialist policies of the New Deal. I too, told stories and described my background, that she found fascinating.

One Sunday, instead of going to a restaurant, she invited me to her duaghter's place in nearby Hartland, as her guest for dinner. There I met the extended family and Betty Lynn, her favorite granddaughter. It was good, because we finally got acquainted, after having heard a lot about each other from her grandma, my special landlady.

A few months later she confessed to me, what she told her family, soon after she rented the room to me. I was suprised, even though she often praised me as her favorite boarder.

"Soon after you moved in, I told them: 'I rented a room to a student and a prince moved in' ".

It was flattering, good for the ego, but excessively generous. I could tell that she appreciated the respect and deference with which I treated her. Béla came to see me often and she liked him also. I think we made a good impression in behalf of Hungarians.

In October 1966, the Marquette High Shool had a commemoration of the 10th anniversary of the Hungarian revolution. Organizers asked me to talk to the assemblage. The gym was full of students, something that surprised and frightened me a little. It seemed that they were prepared for something more than what I thought I could deliver. I had a short list of items I wanted to cover, but to make a formal presentation in front of a crowd, I was in no way ready.

The beginning was smooth, but after about five minutes I suddenly froze and could not utter a word. The heavy silence was numbing and in my panic I thought it would be better, just to get off the stage. -- Suddenly a thought flashed in my mind and I was able to resume my talk and managed to conclude it in respectable manner. I thought that the *mercy-applause* I received was partly in symphathy and in part for having the guts to go before such a large audience and make something of it with my broken English. (I would pay money now, to hear that "speech".)

A few months after this, I was back in the same gym, but in circumstances less stressful and more pleasing. A jazz concert featured *Louis Armstrong and his Band of Renown*. It was a great evening for music. At the end, the jolly master of dixyland was signing autographs for the students. I also lined up with one of his records and asked him to sign it. I told him, that it is for a friend of mine in Hungary, who is a fan of jazz and from whom I first heard the name: Louis Armstrong. I mentioned that we were listening to his music on scratchy short wave broadcasts of the Voice of America in Hungary during the early 1950s.

He looked at me with his sweet growl, smiling broadly -- then asked:

"What is his name?"

"Szimba" -- He asked me, and I said it again.

"Szimba!", he repeated me with added stress. He liked the way it sounded and asked me to spell it.

Then he wrote it letter by letter, perhaps feeling sorry that he asked in the first place. Still, he scribled it down, wrote a dedication, put his name to it and gave it to me with his toothy signature smile that seemed a mile wide.

Szimba was the nick name of my friend Gyuszi Joó in Hungary, whom I previously mentioned. He taught me about the arts of jazz and artificial insemination in Hungary, before I left.

For a few years, whenever I moved, I was able to take all my belongings in my car. Coming back from the east coast to Milwaukee, my stuff filled all the available space, including the front passenger seat. I was ambivalent about this development, because it indicated an increasingly complicated life, but also a degree of affluence -- to be bold about it. I moved out of Mrs. McGinnis' place in 1966, to an efficiency apartment at 1328 E. Albion Street. In my new place I had independence and all the comforts. For the first time, I bought a TV.

36

Space And Other Discoveries

A seminal event took place a few years earlier, that had a profound, long term effect on life in America, indeed the world: the space program and the space race. On the 25th of May, 1961, President John Kennedy addressed the joint session of Congress. In that speech, he said:

I believe that this nation should commit itself to achieving the goal, before this decade is out, of landing a man on the Moon and returning him safely to the Earth.

With this stirring call to action, he rattled the skeptics and energized the nation. His principal motivation was to respond to the unexpected success of the Soviets' launching of the Sputnik, in 1957 (Oct. 4) the tiny craft that circled the Earth three times. Sputnik came as a thunderbolt out of a blue, complacent American sky. Astronomers and space scientists were planning for the International Geophysical Year (1957-58), by sending up satellites to monitor the expected unusually strong activities of the Sun and to map the Earth. Plans were initiated by the Eisenhower White House in July of 1955. In the midst of scientific efforts to mark the

IGY, two satellite programs were under way, the Vanguard and the more successful Explorer, launched in 1958 (Jan. 31) that orbited a scientific instrument package and discovered the Van Allen radiation belt. Still, Sputnik was the wake-up call. NASA too, was formed to create a genuine American space agency.

That speech resulted in the Mercury, Gemini and Apollo programs, that put us ahead of the Russians. Looking at pictures of US and Russian space vehicles, theirs looked small (shown deceptively on a US stamp, where Soyuz looks about the size of Apollo, only because it is shown close up, with the Apollo capsule behind it). We achieved our goal, to go to the Moon and back. I followed the programs closely and enjoyed the movies *The Right Stuff* and *Apollo 13,* showing off our famous first seven (Shepherd, Grissom, Glenn, Carpenter, Schirra, Slayton and Cooper). We knew their names and even more the name of our most famous astronaut, Neil Armstrong. Bringing back Apollo 13 in one piece took technical genius and true *Guts Americana*. The Shuttle program was a success, but the unfortunate explosion of the Challenger is most memorable. I watched it on the 28th of January, 1986 while at work, inspecting a sport arena in Glenview. The tragedy stopped the whole nation for a time. President Reagan gave them a most touching farewell. Ending his tribute, he wove into his speech, words beautifully crafted by Peggy Noonan: *We will never forget them, nor the last time we saw them this morning, as they prepared for their journey and waved good-bye, and 'slipped the surly bonds of earth' and 'touched the face of God'.*

* * *

My job at Allis Chalmers was boring and I saw no future in it. I applied for a position at Aldrich Chemical Company for a position as laboratory technician, analyzing organic compounds. The founder, Dr. Alfred Bader, an Austrian native, appreciated European values and liked to hire immigrants. At one time he was one himself. After a while he befriended me.

As a hobby, he collected art. Once I wanted to sell a painting I owned, and asked him about contacts. He took me to Lenz gallery, introduced me to the owner whom he knew. The two of them appraised and helped me to sell my painting.

I rejoined our Sunday sport sessions with Béla and friends. After the workout we watched the Green Bay Packers. They were ascending in fame and stature. They were the first Superbowl champions for the initial two years (1967, '68) of this most famous American sport institution.

A few new members swelled our Sunday group, making it more interesting and challenging. One of them, Steve, was just a kid who recently immigrated with his family. He was 16 years old, a good athlete for his age. Soon he became a competitive member of the gang.

After I was hired at Aldrich, I mentioned to the guys that I was to start working there the following Monday. Hearing the name Adrich, Steve said that her sister has been working there for a few months. Her name is Ildikó and I would be sure to meet her the next day.

And, so I did. From the first moment I saw her, I knew, she was special -- but that was to be explored later. (It is a coincidence, that Ildikó was my favorite name for a girl, from early childhood. Not that I had an Ildikó as a favorite cousin or aunt, or someone in my acquaintance I especially liked. It was the melodic, to me captivating sound of the name, out of ancient Hungarian mythology that caught my fancy early on. "Ildikó" -- I was pleased with that.)

I was cautious, and Ildikó, by nature, even more. My feelings were a mixture of confidence and uncertainty about the new place. I considered the job easy, but was guarded about the new things around me.

In the lab there was a kind lady, Elfriede an immigrant from Germany. She taught Ildi the basics of the lab and the requirements of analytical work. She was a gentle, protective figure who saw the special qualities in her young protegé, paid attention to her and spent time instructing her to the language, which was a new and important skill for Ildi to learn. On the recommendation of a family friend, Mr. Glasberg, she was hired with minimal language skills. When recounting her first few months at Aldrich, Ildi says she would have run away, but for the family situation, where she was the first member to have a job and bring home money. It was uncomfortable for her to be so inadequate and rely totally on the help, good will and tolerance of others. Soon she produced good work and the pressure eased. -- I showed up after she was over the hump and was able to communicate with her colleagues. Her two years college chemistry in Rumania was a big help in producing excellent work.

Aldrich was an interesting place. Unique among chemical companies It dealt in so called *fine chemicals*. This meant a great variety of often exotic organics in small amounts, that are used in research and the development of new drugs. Our clients were universities and research labs. Aldrich bought chemicals by the hundreds. We analyzed and graded them for purity and sold them with, what I once figured, at least 400% markup. Some chemicals were very expensive. A few of them cost more than gold, in per-weight terms.

Chuck Pouchert, our manager was a student of meteorology. He received a weather map in the mail every morning. We often talked about it, for I also was interested, and learned much from him. Today I look at weather maps differently, thanks to his tutelage. A map on the Weather Channel will show short time spans. Movements in the upper atmosphere indicate major trends. Looking at weather maps tells me most of what I want to know. In a five minute weather report on TV, showing of the movements of the fronts and air masses takes less than ten seconds. Yet, that is what shows 90% of what is most telling about current or tomorrow's weather. What the weather man shows is not much more than what I can see, looking out the window. I don't even want look at the rest, thanks to Chuck.

In my second year at Aldrich, Chuck started a large project in addition to running the lab. He was assembling a catalogue of infrared spectra for all the chemicals that the company sold. The result was a huge volume full of nothing but graphs, with a name and maybe a notation, identifying unique features. -- For the initiated no more was needed. For those in the business, it became the bible or encyclpoedia to consult for information on molecular structure and purity. We worked on it for over a year. I did a large part of the graphs myself. The big book was a best seller within a very small circle of chemists, who were interested to see pictures of chemical compounds, same as doctors looking at X-rays.

The lab crew was mostly nice, and working conditions pleasant. True, some of the chemicals smelled bad, but we just had to bear it. As I got close to graduation and school work became more demanding, I switched to part-time.

Ildikó was working by herself in the "wet lab". It was where she did her analyses by the wet method, meaning, dissolving solids into solution of specified concenetration and titrate for results. That was a hand-on method, using old, established procedures for chemicals that were not suitable for analysis by instruments. I visited Ildikó often and learned about her life and the family's past. Later Steve invited me to visit his family. In time I became a frequent guest.

The family came from Transylvania in western Rumania, part of old Hungary, the region heavily populated by Hungarians. They waited 13 years for passports, after annoncing their intention to emigrate. Soon after the application, Uncle Ernest, her stepfather, an attorney, was reassigned to a minor position with reduced pay.

He was a cultured man and above all, a lover of classical music. With his pursuit of the art, he found a kindred soul in me. We had long talks about Bach, Mozart, Beethoven and Mahler. Otherwise he was not a very admirable man. Selfish and lazy, with quickly formed negative opinion of people. I argued with him at the beginning, but later let his comments go without comment. It was not productive conversation. Cultural themes were a more pleasant subject. I tried to keep our talks within that realm.

I spent increasingly more time at Ildikó's house….

37

Ildikó

Atmosphere in the lab was pleasant and easy-going. Work was steady, sometimes crammed, but we always got it done with occasional overtime. The team worked well together and we even had time for other things.

Gradually Ildikó became the center of my interests. It happened without anything unusual going on, or any outside stimulus that I can recount affecting me. Events were just rolling along as before. I tried to look at the developing changes in my feelings as an outside observer would, wanting to be objective and clear-headed, to be sure that what I was seeing were genuine sentiments and came from deep inside.

I visited her often for a chat. Our similar backgrounds provided us with neutral subjects, where we compared living in Hungary under communism with that of life in Rumania, where they struggled with deeper poverty and a truly despotic regime. It was bad for Rumanians, but even worse for the Hungarian minority that had to endure discrimination, borne of chauvinism and envy. The cultural policies of the Ceausescu regime aimed to impoverish the minority and eradicate Hungarian identity, by forbidding many activities and taking over Hungarian cultural institutions that were long established, and were for centuries, the mainstay of cultural life in many regions of the country.

Typically, the government took over a Hungarian university with its superior facilities, centuries old, picturesque campus and classical buildings, and declared it a new state, i.e. Rumanian institution. The Hungarian faculty then was relocated to teach at the previously Rumanian campus. It was a simple, but coerced swap. Most of the students also changed places in the process. The same was done with theaters, concert halls and other cultural institutions that were controlled by the government. We in Hungary were at least, in our own country. True, we had to endure the indignity of pretending, that everything Soviet was superior to things that was ours, or part of our culture. But we did not have to suffer the additional discrimination of an oppressive foreign entity overlooking everything and expropriating what was traditionally Hungarian and an integral part of our old, cherished culture.

I was interested in Ildiko's family background, her personal history, likes and dislikes. She was never the type who would talk glibly, especially on personal subjects. Most of her family history I learned later from my mother-in-law, Ella. Ildikó told me a few personal stories after some prodding, always introducing them by saying that there was really nothing interesting to tell. As time went by I learned a few important facts. A seminal event in her life was the divorce of her parents. She was three at the time. Her brother Csaba, then eight years old, went with his father and for a time the siblings saw one another only infrequently. The new circumstances, with the limited mobility, prevalent in the 1940s Rumania, was disruptive to the life of the two children. The strong bond between Ildi and her mother was reinforced in this circumstance. Her stepfather, Ernest, was a selfish man, a fact that engendered a strong sense of unrequited need for a caring father. Uncle Gábor, though not a relative, was more of a loving father figure than Ernest. He was a frequent visitor to the family and remained close to the end. I also counted him among my dearest friends.

Ildikó's father, Béla Juhász was a businessman, with excellent sense of the market, a man who instinctively recognized the need of people and was eager to provide service. He found deals where he could be a facilitator and make money in the process. Prior to the war he operated a vineyard and owned property that provided him with a good living. Even in the communists regime he played the role of contact between parties who wanted to buy or sell real estate or other property, until word got to the ear of authorities. He was ordered to cease and desist under the threat of severe punishment. He worked as an accountant until retirement.

We had long talks about his life and struggles. I got to like him a lot. I admired him for his fair treatment of people. He has come down a great deal in his societal standing and material status, but managed to retain his humor and dignity. He visited us twice, for about a month's stay each in the 1970s and was a delightful guest. We even took him camping with us once. Despite it being a new experience for him at age 72, he thoroughly enjoyed the modified outdoor life.

Ildikó's mother's side of the family, the Katonas, were prosperous and respected in the town of Radna. They were well to do merchants, had forest holdings and dealt in wood products. Both of Ildi's maternal great grandparents died unexpectedly within two days time. Their children were all under 12 years old and became the wards of relatives. The ensuing faulty and poorly supervised legal ruling resulted in some of the family wealth going to relatives and being squandered. Still, enough remained for the two boys and two girls to start a business, get a good education and marry well. Ildikó's grandfather, Izsák, apprenticed in, and later opened and operated his own general store, until it was expropriated by the state, along with the family home. In the late 1940s, from one day to the next, the family became a tenant, occupying only a part of the house, which they used to own. "Apa", as Izsák was called by the family, was left without his long-time means of livelihood, without a job or pension, and from about 1943 till his death, could rely only on the family for his daily needs. He died in 1961 at age 80.

In time I got to know Ildi's family in Milwaukee (parents, a sister, Kati, and my basketball partner, Steve) and visited them occasionally. It became clear to me, that she commanded the admiration of all who knew her, for her polite, respectful and generous ways. It took me years to discover and fully understand the unique relationship that she had with her mother. It was a study of a complex combination of deep mutual love between mother and daughter and the interaction of personalities that are contrasting in some aspects, one of which is temperament. Short-lived friction that can occur between them, soon disappears. Later in our marriage, when I felt comfortable doing, I interjected myself to smooth momentary friction. Such periods are marked with quiet, rather than shouting. Grievances by Ella, (Anyu), are expressed with caution, always with the aim to reconcile. The protective attitude and deep underlying trust is always fascinating to watch, and be a part of, as I have been for so many years. I feel, I am a part of this relationship, learned much from it and gained enormously for myself, just by being near them.

In the lab, during brakes and lunch, Ildikó and I talked about neutral subjects. But one day, suddenly I wanted to talk about nothing of that sort. Feelings that I guarded and tested in me for a time, came to the fore and I could no longer keep them concealed, and just for myself. I fell in love with her as if overnight, though I knew that my love took life through months of rising emotions and search of soul. As if by magic, my entire attitude and outlook about life was transformed. It was not love that only wanted to be with its object of dreams to be happy. It gained its force and joy from planning my whole life around her, my principal source of happiness, and the happiness we would find together in starting a family of our own. It was mature and long term -- dreaming of children and family. It was a different type of romance. Not a kind, that was merely seeking romantic bliss. It knew that happiness is living and planning together, while also being practical and down to earth, looking at life squarely. I thought a lot about self-sacrifice for a person, for children we were to have and many common endeavors to come. There was yet much to learn, more than I imagined, but I was ready and eager to embark on life's greatest adventure and most noble quest.

I was slightly surprised when instead of welcoming my proposal, Ildikó had questions for me. I had notions of sweeping her off her feet, but she was not yet ready to be so swept. With the passing of years I better understand her initial reaction. Her questions had to do with inquiries about my seriousness, state of mind, intentions and general attitude toward our possible solemn step. The first one I recall, was about Livia, a woman, she knew and thought I was still seeing at the time. I assured her that it was all in the past, in fact had been for some time.

I used my persuading best to show the seriousness of my intentions and that my love for her was sincere. I had to explain that there was an explainable reason for the way I arrived at my new state of mind and the way my feelings toward her developed in the past six months. She asked the most important question about me, as she saw me then: How did this happen so suddenly, not gradually, in a more visible manner. She said that she noticed nothing different in my behavior in the recent past. I saw these questions as serious inquiries into my deep feelings, to test my sincerity and weather I would qualify as a suitor, worthy of her affections, devotion and love. Ildikó always took serious things very seriously. This was just one of the things I had learned about her through many years. After thorough discussion, she agreed with me that there was a latent attraction between us from the start. It was gratifying to hear that. It made very happy.

An event, significant and educational, happened just a few days later. We had a rendezvous on the north side of town. I was four minutes late -- the actual number of minutes was in dispute, not that it mattered. This became our first conflict, teaching me an important lesson about Ildi. I was surprised that she considered it so serious and that my apology was not sufficient. In her view there was no acceptable excuse for such, short of something catastrophic. I agreed with that for the moment, but not necessarily to the degree of punishment meted out. That, I thought could've been applied with more mercy. The incident involved a habit of mine that, though not consistently, but occasionally caused friction between us. Ildikó has a simple view on this, as she has on most things: Being on time is the natural order of things. It is the keeping of a promise. -- Since than I thought about it more on those terms. As time passed, I realized that she was never late in her life -- never of her own fault. (She was late a few times because of me.) It is an admirable quality. Only, I have to appeal to her sense of compassion and to be more tolerant in accepting the apologies and excuses of us, fallible fellow humans. I can say that in succeeding years she has *grown*, perhaps out of necessity, tolerating my imperfections better.

After this rocky start, began a year of romance, excitement, planning and fun all around. We spent all our free time together, outside work and other duties. We were discreet, so for a time nobody at work knew. About this time, because of heavier demand on my time by school work, I switched to part time.

I went with Ildi's family on several trips. One was to Toronto where my uncle Andrew lived and also Uncle Gábor, the already mentioned old family friend. Uncle Andrew, my Mother's younger brother was one of those who had several strikes against them in the communist world. He had the undesirable family background. In addition, he was a fighter pilot in the old air force. All these added together, he was happy if he was tolerated at all. He was the favorite uncle for us boys. We admired him for his humor, his many skills and generous nature. He was excellent with his hands and picked up many skills through the various jobs he held. It could be carving, metal crafting, fine or tedious work, that needed patience and delicate fingers, doing refined art work. He also was a good mechanic. He had it all.

Andrew, as he wanted us to call him by our late teens, was a resourceful man. He dabbled in a lot of different things that provided him a living in the varying fortunes of time. In communist days, to live in Budapest, one needed special permission from authorities. He got his city permit after many tries. He was happy to find a factory job, where he stayed until 1956, when he emigrated to Canada. He had several inventions, but lacked business savvy and was unable to capitalize on them, though he peddled his ideas repeatedly.

His one successful creation was *Zebecke*, a meticulous, down to the last detail miniature of this tiny village, in Zala County. As a student, young Andrew and a classmate took on an assignment to create a scale model of this little, hidden place, left intact by time and progress. They chose it, for it was an antique folk treasure, a forgotten village, where the houses stood as they looked centuries ago. The tiny houses, all with thatched roof, and an air about them, that exuded simplicity and quaint charm, that was rare even then. Details included dirt road, a ditch, running down on each side of the few streets, with a *bridge*, connecting each house to the road in front. They made tiny copies of trees, bushes, down to the smallest shed and outhouse.

The project was finished after several months of on-site survey and meticulous work, mostly by Andrew. People admired it and after showing it off to high acclaim, the artists packed it up and put it away in an attic.

Uncle Andrew was most proud of this work and many years later, already living in Canada, started another project. It was to find a suitable home for his Zebecke. He knew where it was stored all these years and on one of his trips home he retrieved it. It took a little restoration work, then a lot of effort and persuasion, talking to people at the Göcsej Museum. As a result, his beloved Zebecke mockup is now a permanent exhibit in that museum. Göcsej is a region of Zala County, where one can still find a few villages similar to Zebecke. Looking at the meticulous work and intricate details, I appreciate the effort for building this miniature scale village. In 1975 Ildi and I spent many hours on making a doll house for the Girls as a Christmas present. I was pleased how it turned out. We had no experience but made sure that we stick to the plan and instructions. After a few years the Girls grew and we mothballed it. I took it out again in 2006. The little home received a new coat of paint, new carpeting and some re-gluing of wallpaper. The major job was the reconstruction of the picket fence around the veranda and the stair railing. It is now ready for the new generation.

* * *

Uncle Gábor was a favorite family friend of long standing. He and Ildi's stepfather formed their friendship in a labor camp during WW II. He was from a prominent family who owned a bank before the war. His family properties too, were confiscated and the family declared, class enemy. He had relatives in Toronto and eventually emigrated there.

In successive years he came to visit us many times. He was a most welcome guest. He had a dignified, quiet manner, with a touch of irony and gentle humor. We respected his opinion and advise in all matters. He delivered them with the perspective of long experience, based on good will and love for his fellow man. He had the humor of a sage, that was never biting, only slightly irreverent, unencumbered by personal impediments. It was formed with sensitivity to justice and judgment by a kind heart. We naturally treated him as a member of the family. He spent Christmas with us many a year. Despite being a Jew and a non-believer, he fit in fine.

During WW II, he spent years in a labor camp. While he was away, his wife and three children were deported and he never saw them again. This experience had a deep effect on him. It robbed him of his faith in God, but gave him a perspective that was positive. In the 1980s his eyesight deteriorated, eventually to a degree where he was not able to read.

There are many stories I could tell about our dear friend, but I chose a few, that are typically Gábor. Once he bought an item in a store, where the salesman told him that he processes sales transactions so, as to avoid for the customer to pay sales tax. Our Gábor bought the item and let the salesman process the sale as he wished. Then at home he figured out the tax, and sent it to the tax office anonymously with explanation, only stating that it was a tax due for a commercial transaction.

After college, Steve worked in a bank. Uncle Gábor asked him once about how he liked life as a banker. Steve told him, it was fine but he had a lot of hard work. Gábor smiled:

"Listen son, I am yet to see a banker with hernia. Don't worry, you'll be fine."

In Toronto, he worked for only one employer, an insurance company. He was satisfied with his lot and grateful for the bounty and the peaceful life he found in Canada. This motivated him to make that sales tax adjustment on his purchase. He found it natural to pay that tax, even in his improvised, unconventional manner. He often told us, how grateful he was to Canada, for accepting him and giving him a free and what he considered, prosperous life. He was not a man of the *what if*, but one with perspective, a man who counted his blessings.

He was a lover of the arts. Classical music, especially those composed for the violin, gave him great pleasure. An old story goes with this. His father signed up young Gábor for violin lessons. Studying music was considered essential for a well rounded education. Gábor did not then see it that way. For him, football was more important. He made meager progress with the violin, same as in school. The view of his father, regarding his prospects in life was not optimistic. His brother complained once that his own report card, full of A-s, solicited less admiration from his parents, than Gábor's, when he did not fail a subject or two. His story is reminiscent of the bible parable of the prodigal son. Not that Gábor was praised for his mediocre report. It was rather a sigh of relief for his parents, when his report contained no failing grade. His stern father resigned to the situation, as he then saw it, that his son would not amount to much. He hoped that the boy can stay out of jail and the poor house -- he was used to saying.

The violin lessons ended one day, when on his walk, the father saw the violin on the grass, at the edge of the playground, where Gábor was happily kicking the ball with other boys. He was on his way to a lesson, but decided to join a team that was short of a player. The incident was enough for the father to conclude that his efforts and money were being wasted. The event, surely for its consequences, remained memorable for young Gábor. He expressed regret several times in later years for his action that ended his violin lessons. It is possible that his love of violin music developed in compensation for a mistake of youthful excess and disobedience. In later life he certainly exceeded the promise, his father longed so much to see in him. One might say, he was a late bloomer, but when he bloomed, he produced a fragrant flower.

I was the last one from the family to see him in 1996, when on my way to Hungary I stopped in Toronto. Uncle Andrew died earlier that year and his wish was to be buried in the grave of his parents in Csehi, Hungary. While in Toronto to pick up his ashes, I took time to visit Uncle Gábor in a nursing home. His spirit was the old, I always knew, but physically he was feeble. At first glance I was guarded, not knowing his true condition, whether it was physical only, or did it also affect him mentally. Soon I saw the old spirit and the clear mind. We had a good talk, but parting was difficult. I knew I saw him for the last time. He died a few months later.

38

Ildikó, Closer

In 1967, four of us planned a trip to Europe, where we would visit relatives in Hungary and Rumania and get together in Jánosháza at the end of the tour. Ildikó, with her mother and Steve left first. A week later I went to Aachen and spent few days with Otti and his family. He gave me an Opel, that we heavily loaded with things for Hungary. Strapped to the top was a small refrigerator, intended for our cottage in Ábrahámhegy.

Soon after I entered Hungary, I saw a girl about 18, hitchhiking. I offered her a ride and we traveled some 20 miles, talking. I remember only the first subject. She asked me where I come from, with my heavily loaded car. I told her, Chicago. Hearing that, she blurted:

"Chicago, really? Are you not afraid -- with the gangsters and all?"

My first thought was: the news of the St. Valentine's Day Massacre travels far in distance and time. I tried to calm her, while silently recalling that just a few years earlier, hearing the word, *Chicago*, I could've had the same reaction.

(Actually, there was another, a most striking statistic, that I remember about our great city, despite the relentless negative communist propaganda denigrating it, along with anything Western. One was about the huge Chicago Stockyard on the south side. It spread out on more acres than the entire town of Jánosháza. Also, the record one-day kill at the yard was 190,000 hogs. It boggles the mind. -- Today, the whole thing is gone -- to the great pigsty in the sky. -- This fact was in a little book about America, that I read as a child.)

As I drove on toward home, my thoughts turned increasingly to the coming events. I had many stories to tell my parents about my intended, and our many plans for the future. After a short stay in Jánosháza my parents and I went to Ábrahámhegy. There I got ready to go on to Nagybánya, one of the old great Hungarian cities, now in Rumania, to meet Ildi's extended family.

Mother and I said a long good-bye as I was about to get behind the wheel. She had a hard time letting me go, as if she would be sending me again, as she did nine years before, to somewhere far, into the unknown. As if our bond were again to be severed, as it was then. Separation yes, but with a very important difference. While in 1956 our parting was amid extreme stress and uncertainty, this time it was pregnant with anticipation as I was to take the first step on my way to bring back the woman, with whom I would spend the whole rest of my life. This sentiment crystallized in me a week later, when I brought Ildikó with me to Jánosháza, to introduce her to the family.

I took off mid-afternoon, hoping to get to Nagybánya late that evening. Miscalculations and the atrocious Rumanian roads greatly delayed me. I decided to arrive in the morning, rather than late in the night, so I took a snooze outside of town till the dawn hours. I showed up at the house of Ildi's uncle, Lucas Katona, at 7:30. Elizabeth, his wife came out of the house, as I pulled into the yard with my loud, broken muffler, probably waking up some late sleepers in the neighborhood. -- The exhaust pipe broke and the muffler was shaken loose in the long road between Nagyvárad and Nagybánya, a distance of about 100 miles. That road was by far the worst I ever traveled. It was made of big boulders and dirt. The dirt was long since washed out and there was no escaping the huge holes in-between. Wherever I could, I drove my right wheels on grass off the road at the edge of the ditch. I was lucky that worse fate did not befall me.

Elizabeth looked out, stood by the door for a minute and came down the steps. I greeted her, as I was getting out of the car, stretching and loosening my bones after the uncomfortable night.

"So, you are the Miklós!" -- she said. This was, of course, in Hungarian. To give the true tone and spirit of her question, I would say, she said: 'So, you must be that Miklós, I heard so much about!' She said this with a faint, mischievous smile that I understood and liked. Answering her question, I confessed the obvious. We connected right there and remained good friends till this day. I was received with warmth by everyone, as if we had known each other a long time.

Soon I met Lucas and the children, Gabriella and Tibor. Some relatives came, and others we went to visit. The first were Ildi's brother Csaba, his wife Zsófi and two sons, Steve, 5 and Zsolt, 1. In the next three days I met about another dozen people, friends and relatives, and hoped that I made a good impression. One afternoon we picnicked in the surrounding hills of the Meszes.

For a long time, Nagybánya was home for a community of artists and painters. The city boasts an institute for the arts. The characteristic style of painting of the *Nagybánya School* is well known in Europe. Artists settled there for generations and produced paintings of the picturesque scenery of the region, that I could liken to the Missouri Ozarks. One of he best known was Béla Iványi Grünwald. Another noted one is Géza Bornemisza, a descendent of a historic family, and in his young days a student of Henri Matisse. (We will encounter the Bornemisza name, later.) Ildikó's stepmother, Elizabeth Erdei Juhász, was a part of this artist movement. She taught painting, exhibited and was written about. We are fortunate to have a number her watercolors.

Before we started our return trip, Lucas had one of his mechanic friends reattach the muffler to the Opel. We said good-bye to the family and the four of us were heading back to Hungary. Getting through the Rumanian border was then, and for many years to come, a torturous crossing. Communists were suspicious of anything Western. They enjoyed annoying travelers, regardless who they would be. They searched their own countrymen with the sternest scrutiny. Visitors from other, *friendly socialist countries* similarly suffered. Westerners were treated more benignly but still, often had to unload much from the car to facilitate the inspection. -- Once they found an audio tape in my briefcase. I recorded some music of Mozart for my father-in-law, to listen on his cassette player. I explained this to the guard when he asked. Still suspicious, he made me play it. No secret message found, he got tired of the music and said it was OK. -- The guards liked to go away on long lunch brakes. It made no difference for us, because no matter where they spent their time, we just had to wait. Our hope rose when we saw them return, but they often spent another hour inside, before coming out to continue with their *work*. The length of stay on the border was unpredictable, but lasted 4 to 6 hours. It improved later, but not much. Many forms of bribes were used by travelers. I never risked not offering some.

For unknown reasons, Kent cigarettes became a currency for Rumanians. It was traded by guards and in turn other people throughout the country, as money. I heard of old, beat-up packs changing hands in exchange for favors or merchandise. Even the Wall Street Journal had a long, front page article about the *Kent-trade*, detailing this curious communist practice. (Items of such iconic stature, used similarly as bribes in earlier times, were ball point pens, later felt pens, graduating to cassette tapes and players, and then to Kent. It was a sort of natural progression, reflecting fads or infatuation with new, increasingly sophisticated western products. Border guards wanted to keep up. -- Why Kent? Don't ask me to explain it.)

We arrived to Budapest on a sunny afternoon and spent time enjoying the beautiful city sights. Then we went to Jánosháza. The old house was there, awaiting its special visitors. After the formalities were over, we sat down to a festive dinner. I was pleased to see that Ildikó was received with warmth and in a manner I hoped. Marika was 17 then and took well to Ildi, as a young girl should. We toured the grounds and took pictures. Many stories and old memories surfaced in the pleasant two days we spent there. Then we went to Ábrahámhegy for a look of the vineyard and the simple little beach on the Balaton. The memories of those days are unforgettable. They contain magic moments, when my future bride was introduced and welcomed into my family. It was one of my life's happiest moments to be able to personally introduce Ildikó to my far-away family, whom just a few years before, I expected never to see again. The visit played a crucial part, establishing my sense of a new family that would be mine in the future, our own family, with Ildikó. The future parents-in-law also were happy to get to know one another and establish a warm relationship that lasted through the coming decades. All my siblings and their children were there, enhancing even more the significance of our visit.

On the day of departure of our three guests, Otti gave me his big Mercedes to take them to Ferihegy Airport in Budapest. I chose an interesting route. We drove along the north shore of Lake Balaton, then up the peninsula of Tihany, that protrudes into the lake and narrows it down to about a mile. A ferry goes across at regular intervals. We had a good view of the ancient abbey of Tihany on the hill, first from the road, then from the ferry, as we crossed.

Tihany is integral to the history of the country. King Andrew built a family burying ground and chapel on Tihany hill in 1055. He endowed the Benedictine order to establish another base here, soon after Pannonhalma. In the 18th century the monks built a beautiful baroque church, whose twin spires dominate the wide vista. We had the best view of the abbey on the hill, from our ferry.

We floated across the lake narrows to Szántód, to continue on the other side toward the capital city. I was especially careful in my driving with my precious cargo and my high value loaner. I thought it would have been appropriate to put a little yellow triangle-shaped sign in the window, fashionable in those days, with the words: *Future bride and mother-in-law aboard.* Not having that, I did the next best thing and took all precautions to ensure a safe journey. -- I put them on the plane and went home to Jánosháza to spend another week there, before returning home

-- again. ("Home". The use of this word with its special meanings and unique, double applications for people with my immigrant background, came naturally and instinctively. I noticed it only after I put the period at the end of the sentence. Indeed, I have two, and feel completely *home* in each.)

In 1967, I was busy with my school work, counting my credits earned, and those I still needed for graduation. My final courses were all in history, political science, diplomacy and finance. At the end of the school year in June of 1968, I had two credits missing. I mentioned this to a professor I had befriended, who a few years earlier immigrated from Germany. He told me that with my European high school diploma, we should be able to find several courses that would qualify for credit. He arranged that considering my major, I received credit for my geography courses, that were part of our curriculum in Pannonhalma for three years. So I graduated and received my diploma in August: Bachelor of Arts -- International Relations and Finance.

After I switched my major, I did not want to lose my roughly two years of chemical studies. I needed two courses to earn an associate degree, as I was advised by a counselor at the local technical school. Before I finished work on my BA, I also completed those two courses. In June of 1966, I graduated from the Milwaukee Institute of Technology with an Associate Degree in Chemical and Metallurgical Technology.

My busy summer of 1968 started with college graduation, continued with job search, our wedding, moving to Chicago, finding a new job and beginning training with my company.

After graduation, I was happy, relieved and looked forward to many job opportunities. But offers were scarce in the economic conditions of that year. I looked in Chicago and signed up with agencies to facilitate my search. The country was entering into a long period of economic stagnation, that affected job prospects across the board. I was naïve to think that without contacts in government I could land a job with my new diploma -- and lack of experience.

Jobs were easier to be had in industry, where a few sectors were doing well. I started looking even before graduation and spent much of that summer interviewing. I found an interesting, but not

necessarily easy job a few weeks before our wedding date. An
insurance company was looking for engineers, to be trained for a
highly specialized kind of engineering: fire protection. Since this
discipline was new and even today is taught only in one school in
the country, insurance companies developed most of the standards
and traditionally, were training their own staff. Factory Mutual
was in the business of industrial fire protection, since the late
1800-s. It was a pioneer in developing protection standards for
so called "highly protected risks" (HPR). These were plants that
were protected by automatic sprinklers and other advanced fire
safety measures and were considered to be lesser fire risks, than
plants that lacked this type protection.

In fact, the tale my Factory Mutual elders proudly told us in
the early days of training, was how the company was formed by
mill owners in the Boston area, after they were unsuccessfully
petitioned their insurance companies for lower rates. They thought
that a plant with higher level of protection, should be insured at
lower rates. After years of useless battle with their insurers, they
formed an association, a mutual company, where they pooled their
money as a reserve to pay fire damage or loss of property. The
company prospered and eventually formed an engineering division
to handle the loss potential analysis and to engineer protection,
uniquely suitable to each risk. The company today is one of only
two, engaged solely in industrial fire insurance. The Factory
Mutual standard, researched and continually developed in their
fire laboratory, is one of two sets of recognized standards, now
being used in the country and is a pioneer in fire protection for
other nations. We were training young engineers who were sent
here by European insurers.

39

A Simple Wedding

The process of planning a wedding be best left with the experts, the ladies. I wanted to take only minimal part in it -- even that, under the supervision of more experienced hands. Ildikó was no expert at the start, but with her mother's help, became one. Details fit our means, and her own common sense. I chose the place for the reception, the *Chalet on the Lake,* a beautiful, secluded garden restaurant on the north shore of Lake Michigan. I had dinner there once a few years before and considered it the nicest place around.

Ildikó and I exchanged marriage vows in Milwaukee on August 31, 1968, at St. Hedwig Church (named after a Hungarian saint, just by coincidence). The wedding and reception were simple, with 45 guests, reflecting the means of two recent immigrants, yet so much more meaningful for us. I felt we were a perfect pair. Our union was based on love, that deepened during the past two years, with common goals and mutually tuned ideas about raising a family together. A page was turned and a different life started with a new mind-set. I got used to saying "my wife" -- and it was a the thrill every time I heard myself saying it.

My thoughts and emotions about being married to the most loving person, surpassed anything I felt before. I was a little worried: will

I measure up? I chased these thoughts away with innate optimism, strengthened by my new happiness, that was deeper and more profound than at any time in my life prior to meeting Ildikó. I was full of expectations. I knew that in important ways I married *up* and saw this as a challenge. In other respects, I thought that I can be a good provider and a faithful husband and, in time, worthy of my good fortune.

* * *

I invited my Pannonhalma classmate, Father Denis, (Miklós) Farkasfalvy, to perform the wedding ceremony. His presence meant a lot to us. During his short stay, we remembered the old school days, and our reunion in New York five years ago. I was happy to introduce him to the family. He was a busy man since I last saw him. He came from Rome in 1963, entrusted with a heavy assignment. He spent his novitiate and early years in the Vatican. He became a priest and a Cistercian monk. Soon after his ordination, the General Abbot of the order sent him to America. In the Dallas suburb of Irving, he joined other Hungarian Cistercians, dispersed by the communist regime in prior years. Initiated by the Abbey of Zirc, Hungarian refugee monks established a prayer group that became an independent monastery, *Our Lady Of Dallas*, in 1961. He put his energies to expanding the abbey and opened a preparatory school in 1967. The school is patterned in the model of Pannonhalma and the Cistercian abbey at Zirc of pre-war years, taking kids through grades 5-12 just like the system, in which he and I started our education back in 1946, but finished in a revised system. Soon he was named to the office of principal, and in 1988, consecrated Abbot of Our Lady of Dallas.

His order started a grade school in 1962. From that seed, grew a prep school, which is now the pride of Dallas. The social and political elite stand in line to have their brood shaped and educated by his monks, who dedicate themselves to God, learning and teaching, just as our teachers were in Pannonhalma. Still, the school takes students from 20 surrounding schools, to maintain a broad base for the student body. It provides elite education, but not just for the children of the elite.

Some interesting facts, relating to Father Denis and his school. Long term friendship with his students comes naturally for him. It resulted in good outcomes for him, for them, and also for their old school. From the pool of the school's alumni, are his own heart surgeon who has been treating him for over a decade, the school's current principal -- now a fellow Cistercian, and the architect of the abbey church, which was one of his most proud projects. The abbot and his one-time student, by then an accomplished architect, toured Europe, visiting old churches for design ideas. He told me that his young friend brought back a thick file of sketches and notes, that helped him in planning his handsome limestone church for the abbey.

* * *

Nobody from my immediate family was able to attend our wedding. They were collectively represented by my uncle Julius. We missed them, but things could not be helped under the circumstances.

(Julius has fulfilled similar duties once many years earlier. Józsi, Otti and I were scheduled, to be confirmed on the same day -- I think in 1944. Our intended sponsors were our other uncles -- my mother's younger brothers: Miklós, Imre and Andrew, respectively. However, the war interfered. All three were in the military and with the war going on, granted no leave. So, my Uncle Julius stepped in for all three of them. I remember the clear early summer day. The bishop used the occasion to conduct the sacred ceremonies in the church yard, where we lined up in our holiday white. He walked up to each candidate, spread ointment on the child's forehead and made the sign of the cross. Julius stood behind Józsi, then stepped to Otti, than to me and put his hand on each of our shoulders in succession, in the stead of the absent other uncles. We talked about them and lamented that they, instead of celebrating with us, had to be somewhere far and in harms way.)

We went to Florida for our honeymoon, stayed at the *Beau Rivage*, a medium priced hotel, fit for our means. It was the first-time visit to the Sunshine State for both of us. We rented a car and debated for a while, weather it should be one with air-conditioning. We chose just to wing it and go without, with open windows in the still quite warm September air. Instead, we dined in better restaurants, saw shows and visited places, such as the lovely estate Vizcaya, named after the Basque province in Spain. It has architectural and artistic treasures and a beautiful, sculptured garden. We took a lot of pictures.

The wedding and honeymoon pictures became our third photo album. I already had many photos from home and my early immigrant years, filling two albums. We also put one together, to collect Ildi's family pictures. Preservation of the photographic records of our life was important for us from the beginning. I am an avid photographer and like to take pictures of everything that is important or beautiful. We developed a custom through the years, where Ildikó and I spend New Year's Day, putting all the past year's accumulated pictures in albums. We now have 25. They contain faithful records of our life, important family events and our vacations, organized chronologically, so the collection contains a faithful family history that we look at often. We believe that this is the best method to preserve family chronicles. It is always ready for viewing, easier than videos, that we also made, when Girls were little. The albums help to settle occasional arguments about chronology of events or locations we visited. I composed an index with notes to indicate times, locations and events that the pictures show, to facilitate finding the proper volume and page. We consider the photo albums our most valued family treasure.

Our wedding photographer was a good friend, László Lukács, a professional photographer and later Hollywood cameraman. He did all the photography, as his wedding gift. Photographing weddings was his first job in the US, after he came here in the mid-1960s. He also taught me the basics, the ins and outs of this specialized photo art and gave me a gig, when once he had two, scheduled on the same day. I liked it and did a few more after that.

-- We were grateful for László's generous gift and still treasure his excellent, inventive photos.

As a result of my reduced work schedule for almost a year before graduation, I had little money saved. We paid our wedding expenses and went on a strictly controlled budget. Ildi's saving account became our starters spending money.

We had the kind of time, that you see pictured in movies, where a young couple in love needs no fancy place to go, or spend much money to be happy. Ours was that kind of low key, frugal time, while we were exploring our vacation paradise, Miami Beach.

I recalled the first time I heard what kind of place Florida was. It was at Oakton Manor, during my first months in America, in the spring of 1957. Sam Sugarman, the hotel manager took off two weeks in the middle of winter. After he came back, proudly sporting a deep tan, I asked him where he vacationed. With a significant emphasis, he said:

"Miami Beacchhh".

I knew right away, this place must be something posh, desirable, and likely, expensive. Sam was a well paid and well-to-do man. I was puzzled and also amused, why he might have said Miami Beach with such emphasized stress, with his lower lip curling out. It was clear to me, it gave him great satisfaction. -- So, after 12 years of dreaming to see it, a honeymoon in Miami Beach looked attractive to me and with limitations, affordable. Ildikó concurred and we agreed that it was a right way to begin our lifetime union, dreaming of a bright future and a loving family. We dined in better places and went to see more fancy entertainment in that one week, than we did in past years, and were to enjoy for several years coming. After all, this was honeymoon. The self-imposed lean years were yet ahead. We were looking forward to a future, that we hoped would be more prosperous in the long term. We didn't yet fully grasp the opportunities this country had for us. We were still learning about life in America.

I was able to pursue my university studies, that were denied me prior to coming here. Living in a free country had many other advantages, in addition to the fact that in America, hard work was better rewarded than anywhere else on this earth. (Countries in Europe seem to prefer a different system, with a lot of long discredited socialism mixed in. They seem generously to reward little or no effort, taking it from the common largesse. I wonder how long they can afford doing that, encouraging parasitic freeloaders living off society. It is a slow, comfortable road on which to slouch toward mediocrity -- or perhaps ruin.)

I knew a little about America from prior readings. I thought I was familiar with the basics: Revolutionary War, Civil War, the Depression and two World Wars. But those were mostly facts and data. I didn't really know enough that could have given me a basis to understand the essence and attitude of the country and her people.

(I remember, once I read a small booklet about America. It was then forbidden reading in Stalinist Hungary, but I stumbled on it, rummaging through a drawer. We had it from before World War II. It was in Hungarian, perhaps from the embassy or some propaganda agency of the American government. It explained about life here. I remember best the example about small-town self government. I read it all, eagerly. It had pictures, one of a town meeting, to me a new concept, that appealed to me. It was natural and simple. People gather, discuss issues that are important to them and make decisions among themselves or at least influence decision makers. It looked like an expanded neighborhood gathering, where people knew each other and felt at ease, looking for common-sense solutions to everyday problems.)

Soon after returning from Florida, we moved to Chicago. The company paid my moving expenses. I felt important and well treated at the outset. I thought I was on my way...

I started work in September 1968, with training in the Chicago District of Factory Mutual, a division of a large insurance company. I followed an experienced field engineer, as he was doing his job, visiting plants, talking to people and spreading the idea and principles of fire safety. I started with $8,400 a year -- considered to be a good midrange salary for trainees.

We bought a new Buick Skylark just week's before. It was a beauty. Deep red, with black vinyl top. We decided that I use it for work, rather than get a company car. It expected to bring in a few extra bucks on mileage for daily travel on the job. We considered it a good deal, even with the faster depreciation of the car.

We could not afford to keep two cars. Ildikó had to manage without one during the day. A few years later I did what most of my colleagues had and requested a company car. The first was a used Chevy. The following year I could pick a new one (out of three models) that was the first of a series of company cars I drove. By then Ildikó needed some mode of transportation around town and was happy that she no longer had to depend on the favors of her friend, Edith Püski, whose husband took the train every morning. The two ladies coordinated their activities during the day and were able to shop and go places together if need be. The kids were also a common project for them, sharing activities in similar programs. It worked well for a couple years. We lived close to the Püskis and the kids grew up together. The mothers also shared many activities, to the advantage of both. The Püski family moved away long time ago, but we remained close friends through distance and time.

On the 5th of October 1968, I started my first three-week training course in Norwood, a Boston suburb. I spent time at company headquarters and in the nearby fire lab, where we watched and later analyzed full scale fire tests.

Ildi wasn't working yet and we went together on what was a second honeymoon. We certainly considered it such, for it had many of the elements of a carefree vacation -- and this one was mostly paid for by my employer. I was busy with my course during the week, but my evenings were free. We also had two weekends that were all ours. The only cost to us were a few incidental expenses. Ildi's companion during daytime was the wife of a colleague, who also accompanied her husband. The two ladies spent much time together, visiting interesting places in New England.

On our way to Boston, we made a stop in Toronto. We slept there one night and visited Uncle Andrew and his wife, Elizabeth. It so happened, that my cousin, Erzsó, the daughter of my Uncle

Miklós in Sopron, came out just then for a trans-Atlantic visit, to see the world and spend a few weeks with her uncle. After spending one night, we went on to Boston, but Erzsó's visit became a much longer stay, with one detour. She went back home only to arrange her affairs, before returning for good. On her vacation she met a young Hungarian, Alfred Chanádi. They married the next year.

We had a very good time in Boston. The training course was a lot of fun. I learned about the policies and principles of my company, a leader in the profession. It was informative and educational but I realized that my work will be complicated and difficult. I was introduced to new principles, detailed knowledge of previously unknown things and a lot of books, data sheets, containing many graphs, charts and formulas. This took place in pleasant surroundings, in the company of other novices, though they were all graduate engineers. Instructors and a few colleagues from the region, gave us ideas on what to see in nearby New England. We went to see Boston's attractions, historic places, such as Salem, Concord, Lexington and other well known places of the Revolutionary War. It was good to see and learn about the battlefields and towns where our history was forged and walk the ground that America's founders once tread.

The two weekends were especially nice. By sheer luck we caught the most picturesque period of the year. From all over the country, people travel to New England to see the turning of colors in autumn. We went up to New Hampshire on the most beautiful weekend of the year. The day was Saturday, October 12[th.]

"See the White Mountains" -- colleagues told us. We did, and enjoyed it a lot. They indeed were spectacular. It showed a thousand shades of red and golden yellow, with still a lot of green mixed in. The weather was ideal, temperatures temperate, the days full of sunshine. We crossed over to Vermont and Maine, but drove all over New Hampshire, visiting small towns in the mountains throughout the state park, named for the White Mountains. We took pictures to fill many pages in the album.

We slept in a charming bed-and-breakfast, with hand painted furniture of tulips and other flowers on furniture in our room, reminiscent of Hungarian folk art. We walked a lot in forest trails and along bubbly, babbling brooks. We said that we have to see this region again and see more of it. -- This wish came true 23 years later on another New England vacation in which, addition to Boston, we drove out to Cape Cod and up the rocky coast of Maine, to Portland. On the way we made a stop in Kennebunkport and spied from the shore (with binoculars and telephoto lens) on the Bush compound, looking ruggedly luxurious on their own peninsula, which can be seen best from the ocean beach, as it curves and runs parallel with the seashore. In New Hampshire the Old Man of the Mountain looked down on Interstate 93. We stopped for a look. Too bad that this signature landmark collapsed in a rock slide in 2003. In previous years this tourist icon of New Hampshire was commemorated on stamps, medallions and the state quarter, issued in 2000. The Flume Gorge in Franconia Notch State Park is one of the most spectacular natural wonders. We walked up the entire length, skipping on a lot of rocks and enjoying its cascades and falls. Driving by Bretton Woods, I remembered the famous post war conference by ministers and financial experts from the western world, where in 1946, they put down the foundation stones of the new monetary system to aid the reconstruction of devastated Germany and Japan. New Hampshire was a fitting state for such a conference, where the generous, victorious powers gathered to do one of history's good deeds, extending a helping hand to bombed out Europe and support the restoration of liberty and prosperity. *Live free or die* is written on every New Hampshire license plate. It is the best expression of the American spirit. Living free is the only way to live. It is naturally followed by prosperity and a happy life.

We spent an entire day in the most charming town of Woodstock VT. It is also a favorite of the Rockefellers. They used it for vacations, and own a neat hotel in the middle of town. We would have spent a night there, except for the price, and found a lovely B&B, to lengthen our stay till next morning.

We also visited Newport for a day. This city of the rich and famous is Rhode Islands best known, famous for its "summer cottages" (huge mansions) of New York's *glitterati* of old, and present, home of a tennis tournament and jazz festival. There, for the first time I saw grass tennis courts. We toured three of the mansion palaces. The Breaker is the biggest and most famous. It was the summer retreat for the family of railroad magnate, Cornelius Vanderbilt. I liked their home in Asheville NC better, for the great forest expanse surrounding it. It is also more pleasing for its architecture. The man certainly had good taste -- or hired architects who did. (I think the family considered home their penthouse, part of the block they owned on 5th Avenue in New York, with a commanding view of Central Park. -- Here I especially liked the children's house, separate from the mansion, also open for touring by visitors. They built it as a play house for the children. It is complete with kitchen and abundant living space, built to something like half scale. It's not a miniature, just a child-scale house. I'm sure the kids spent many days and nights there, free from immediate adult oversight. From the outside it looks like a charming storybook house for Hansel and Gretel, or other Brothers Grimm characters -- giants excluded. Adults needed permission perhaps, except to put the house back in order after serious playtime.

On the second weekend in Norwood, we attempted something more ambitious. We left early Saturday for New York City. I knew the city well, having spent two years in the area and much of my free time in Manhattan. I was happy to show the metropolis to my bride. -- What can one see on a weekend, which includes 500 miles of driving? We concentrated on visual highlights. That in itself was quite a task, but satisfying for her first visit. I wanted to include one thing in our programs: see a matinee at the Met.

When I first went to New York in 1962, the Metropolitan Opera was still in the old house on Broadway. Lincoln Center, with its three major buildings, was under construction during my two-year stay, and only the Philharmonic Hall and The New York State Theater were completed before I left. I watched the project take shape and now was spoiling to see the new, magnificent opera house. It was beautiful and had the most sumptuous seats and spacious leg room I ever enjoyed in any house of entertainment. I saw only one production in the State Theater. Its premier tenant was the American Ballet Theater, George Balanchine's company, that was gaining the attention of ballet aficionados around the world. The Philharmonic Hall became the new home of the New York Philharmonic Orchestra. It had poor acoustics. A lot of frustrating effort and great sums were spent on improving it. It was about 10 years before the job was considered finished with the installation of movable acoustical ceiling panels. It is still not in the class with Carnegie Hall, or other, less famous houses of music.

Ildikó and I were fortunate to catch a matinee at the Met, which was sold out much of the time. To add sweetness to luck, we saw one of our favorite operas: Gounod's *Faust*. I am sure only of the two male stars, Alfredo Kraus as Faust and Jerome Hines in the role of Mephistopheles.

(It is peculiar to grand opera, that the romantic hero roles are almost always sung by little fat men -- tenors -- while evil characters, like Mephistopheles, or Iago in Othello, by tall, handsome baritones, like Jerome Hines, Fyodor Chaliapin or Ezio Pinza. Franco Corelli and Placido Domingo are the exceptions in recent years. These two possess both of the attractive attributes: the voice *and* good looks. I could say similar things about sopranos, but there too, I would vote for the voice first. Some of those fat ladies really know how to sing.)

On Sunday morning, we drove around town, down the East Side, and up, on the West Side Highway of Manhattan. We went up north, toured the Cloisters and drove along the picturesque Hudson shores before starting back.

We spent a short, crammed, but pleasant weekend in the Big Apple, that made us both happy that we had this extra vacation, where we, just weeks after our wedding, could add another memorable experience, at the beginning of our married life. The Boston, New Hampshire and New York City trips gave us a chance to find new things that were of common interest and things that we could equally enjoy. This was gratifying and played a role in our early months.

Following this one, I had two other, 3-week training sessions in the coming years. One winter night, on my return from Boston, I witnessed something very unusual. As we were approaching Chicago late in the evening, the air appeared exceptionally clear after a heavy snowfall earlier that day. The clear, black sky was lit up by millions of stars. As we flew over Lake Michigan on our approach to O'Hare International Airport, I was looking out the window on the right side, into the pitch dark and the myriad of lights below, laid out as a brilliant carpet. I was looking north, toward Milwaukee. I knew this part of the country well. I lived here a long time and traveled its roads along the lake, up to Door County, many miles north. Looking out intently, I mapped out in my mind, the towns below. Close by were the fancy northern suburbs of Chicago to Waukegan, a larger cluster, then in Wisconsin: Kenosha, Racine, Milwaukee. I was astonished, that I was able to see all those and even beyond. We were flying at an optimum height, to make out all the towns along the sharp, black edge of Lake Michigan. I counted the cities and remember that I could account for the bigger ones, up to Sheboygan. Manitowoc I could still see, but that and Twin River were the last ones I could make out. I figured this about 150 miles. -- (Up till then, a distant clear sight I remember, was the Pilis mountains, 60 miles from Pannonhalma, or the view from the top of Sears Tower, across the south end of Lake Michigan, to Northern Indiana and part of southern Michigan. The distant shore faded in the mist at near Michigan City, a distance of about 50 miles across the bottom curve of the lake.)

* * *

(Written on September 11, 2002)

TV and radio are full of the commemoration of the events and remembering the many ordinary Americans killed a year ago today. For weeks, I dreaded this approaching anniversary, for the expected excesses by our big media. They indulge mostly themselves, telling *their* stories to *sensitive* journalist friends, as they recall their personal experiences of a year ago. For many, it was about *them* and *their pain,* commiserating, as they interview each other. This syrupy self-indulgence turns my stomach, so I listened and watched very little, while I was waiting for the official program of remembrance to begin sometime mid-morning.

I'm glad, this day did not become a holiday in any form. It was fitting that the ceremonies of commemoration were conducted in the most solemn and dignified manner. We honored our dead whose lives were taken in a monstrous attack by the world's malcontents, who instead of improving their own lot with honest work, are driven by envy and hatred toward those who are free, prosperous, and in aspects of life that really count, are leaving them in the dust. The once proud and pioneer societies of Arabs now produce these sons of the mostly well to do, who are driven by the basest instincts, nihilism, waste and ruin -- and call it religion. Terrorists would force their narrowly defined and cockeyed idea of virtue on the world, while we see higher virtue in liberty and free choice, in the framework of the law and individual responsibility.

The country remembered the victims of the barbaric event in a dignified, solemn ceremony. The National Cathedral was filled with dignitaries and citizens. Denyse Graves sang a song of remembrance, most touchingly. The major part of the event was the reading, one-by-one, of all those who perished, by individually naming each victim. The reading of the names of the 2801 dead took 2½ hours in an atmosphere of total silence by the thousands taking part in the ritual. After that, the country went back to work and continued on in an ordinary way -- continue building a happy and more prosperous America. The simplicity, dignity and solemnity of the ceremony was touching and highly emotional.

* * *

In September 1968, after I secured a position with Factory Mutual, we moved to Chicago. Our address was 6134 N. Kenmore Av., a small, four-story apartment building with parking provided. It seemed that the entire street was lined with such buildings. In the place of the demolished old multistory brick and brownstones,

the streets in the area were lined with the so called *four-plus-one*-s:
four upper stories for apartments, lobby and parking on the ground
floor.

We found our home for the next 19 months, after a whole day of
search for a small, affordable apartment in a decent neighborhood.
-- (We visited the neighborhood 10 years later and were shocked
seeing the changes, all for the worse. I hope that since then, things
reversed. -- I recall a similar decline, followed by a turn-around
in my old neighborhood in Milwaukee. While I lived there, the
east side began to deteriorate and reached a low point in the 1970s.
Businesses stagnated, closed or moved out. The neighborhood
was in the process of change, becoming a kind of beatnik beat.
By the time I moved away, it looked dirty and run-down. Change
began in the 1980s. Now we regularly drive through the same
streets on our way to visit my mother-in-law. Through a period of
another six-eight years it was pleasing to see the improvements,
as the whole area picked up itself. Merchants returned to open
new shops and restaurants and gave the old buildings a scrubbing.
Now it is a pleasure to drive through those streets again. Side-walk
cafes are all over along Prospect Avenue, and Farwell, that became
a showcase for this self-motivated urban renewal.)

Kenmore Avenue was just a block west, running parallel with
Lake Shore Drive, with its fancy high-rises, suggesting a new
affluence and providing a spectacular view of downtown. The
Drive winds gently for eight miles, from downtown to near
Evanston, where begins the long row of plush suburbs, hugging
the shore.

Joseph Gábor and his wife Maria, lived on the 26th floor in one
of these tall buildings. Joe was a childhood friend of my uncle,
Julius. They grew up in my father's hometown, Nagycenk. From
his balcony, over the top of many *middle-rise* buildings, the towers
of the Loop and sections of the magnificent lake shore, were a
splendid sight. His great view lasted only a few years, before new,
higher-riser buildings blocked it.

Our monthly rent was $185, including guaranteed parking
under the building. (Only space guaranteed -- not security. One
morning we found our Buick without its battery.) The ground floor

contained a small lobby, stairway and elevators. The rest was open and used for parking by residents. This was important, because the population density of the area was such that the streets were almost always filled with cars. A few years prior to our moving there the city mandated that at least one off-street parking spot be provided for each apartment.

The apartment we rented was the best for us. Actually, it was the most expensive of all that we looked at on our day-long Sunday search. Although the buildings looked similar on the outside, for $15-20 less, we would have had to sacrifice sizable space and convenience. The one we decided on, had it far above the others. After we agreed to take it, we found out that the storage locker for our apartment was just a few steps away from our door, down the hallway. It was a pleasant surprise. In all the other buildings, storage was in the basement.

We lived in the city for 1½ years. It was an interesting neighborhood. Many young people lived there, mostly singles and childless married couples like us. The Chicago district office of Factory Mutual was downtown, on the 22nd floor of the Kemper Building, the then home office of Kemper Insurance, a competitor in the fire insurance business. We shared the same building, while chasing the same clients. We had only our engineering division offices there. Each of the Factory Mutual family of companies had their offices in the suburbs. Kemper had everything in one place. They occupied several floors, starting with the 24th. Once I took the elevator and interviewed with them to see if I should change jobs, but found that our salaries were better and working conditions less restrictive. A few years later Kemper moved to Long Grove, into their fancy, new world headquarters and expansive green campus. Surrounding the buildings is a green campus with private golf course, no doubt to attract prospective employees and clients.

The Kemper Building is best known to me for the most famous occupant, the Civic Opera Company and the world renowned Lyric Opera of Chicago. Ildikó and I visited it every season since we moved to Chicago. It is choice, though not cheap entertainment.

For a few years my company insured the Lyric, that occupies most of the lower floors of the building. I toured their areas on the bottom nine floors, looking for fire hazards, and found plenty. One of the greatest hazards was the inadequately protected, four-story high curtains and scenery props that could feed a fire once touched off by flame or nearby electric equipment. At the end I thought that people in the arts are rarely interested in mundane things, such as fire safety or insurance. Their mind is more on providing entertainment, artistic excellence and visual beauty. The behind-the-scene tour, was a treat for me. I had the chance to do it only twice. One day, a rehearsal was going on within earshot but I had no time to spend, listening in. I was hoping to do that at a future date. Unfortunately, the insurance was canceled and the two remained my only inspection tours inside one of the world's most famous houses of music.

Ildikó found a job as chemist technician with Kester Solder Company. The job was fine, but we considered it a short-term employment. It paid a modest salary, all of which we could save for a house that seemed a distant goal. She worked there less than a year, until the birth of our daughter, Erika.

By the time Ildikó started working at Kester, I was done with my training and was on my own, doing engineering work in the field. That came with certain freedoms and flexibility regarding my time. I scheduled my own inspections. This made it convenient to take Ildi to work each morning and back home at the end of her day. In October of 1969 Ildi quit her job and prepared for the birth of our first child. She was always good with her hands, liked handicrafts, and spent her time on a few projects, beautifying our home. We bought a sewing machine and she learned to sew all kind of things, spending much time in sewing dresses for the Girls. All were well made and beautiful, eliciting comments within the family and by strangers.

* * *

This reminds me about the evolution of her cooking skills. Before our marriage, Ildi was not very interested in domestic chores. Her mother took care of everything around the house. Her brother, Csaba once said that without her mother, Ildi would be lost. Little did he know about her sister's mettle. Though on the surface it may have seemed so, he was proven a poor judge of what Ildi was made of.

Ildikó is a remarkable woman. I watched with amazement, how she approached cooking and how she, seemingly overnight, became a great cook. She took a few informal lessons from her mother prior to our wedding. Aunt Ella, as I called her then, was a great teacher of the *art* of cooking. She seldom uses written recipes. Much of the repertoire is in her head. Improvisation and the personal touch is part of the process, supplanted by monitoring and tasting on the go. Ildikó was very attuned to such instructions and made the method her own. In addition, she is inventive and excellent in following written recipes. In deciding whether to cook a dish for the first time, she reads the recipe. From that, she knows most of the important things and whether it will suit her and her intended consumers' tastes. Her rule is to follow the instructions to the letter on the first try. She makes her changes on subsequent occasions. I can say confidently, they always improve the dish. Her culinary vocabulary far exceeds mine.

She made only one meal in her life that she was ready to throw out. It was her first attempt in making *paprikás csirke* (chicken paprikash) one of my favorites. Still inexperienced, she used a little more oil in the sauce, than needed. Embarrassed, she was ready to chuck the whole thing, but I was the better judge of the otherwise good meal. We skimmed of the excess oil and ate it all with gusto. Now both of the Girls make this great dish. This was one of the first Hungarian dishes that their husbands, Jim and Trevor, also number among their favorites.

Many years later I saw that Ildi was willing to try out new dishes *on guests*. In most cases, they were old friends, who always praised her innovative creations. She feels confident even for large family gatherings, to vary the menu. This shows a certain daring, which is not her strong suit -- instead, caution and studious preparation are. She is well known by friends and family for her tasty and original dishes. A member of our long-time bridge group, Don Richards said once, that his favorite house to play bridge was ours, mostly for the delicious appetizers Ildi was serving. Don is a worldly man, one used to tasty dishes at home and the connoisseur of fine cuisine of the many countries he traveled as manager of international sales for Motorola.

* * *

Just a block south, near our Kenmore Avenue apartment, was a small beach. High-rises on Sheridan Avenue were going up at a fast clip in those days, but there was this small patch of sandy beach left there for area residents, a gift from less crowded days. Ildikó used to take Erika there, to spend some carefree time. Other young mothers also came on hot summer afternoons. -- The water of Lake Michigan is rarely warm. Chances are, that by the middle of summer, one could catch a day when swimming is a pleasure -- not depending on how hot the day is, rather on the direction of the wind. In this large, deep lake, when waves are pushing to the shore, they stir the water and cold layers from below cool the surface. But on calm days, or those with gentle westerly winds blowing into the lake, beach-side water is usually warm. I remember only one day, when the water was outright pleasant. It puzzled me and I tried to figure out this rare phenomenon. I tested my theory a few time since, and I think I'm correct.

During our time in the neighborhood, we got used to big-city living. One thing we had to endure was the noise from trains that roared by on elevated tracks, at the approximate level of our top-floor apartment. We had only our closed windows that slightly muffled the noise between the tracks and our ears. We adjusted to it by momentarily halting conversation, or resigned to losing some of the talk on radio or TV.

40

Erika, Andrea

After the Christmas holidays of 1968, we found great bargains in one of the small shops on Granville Avenue two blocks away. They were glass globe Christmas ornaments, many of which we still have. Since then Ildi embroidered others that are unique and beautiful.

Shopping was quite good on Granville. No big supermarket, but nice neighborhood stores.

There was a tiny shop of a jeweler, where I had our wedding bands engraved. In mine:

ILDIKÓ Aug. 31, 1968; in hers, corresponding markings with my name -- keepsakes forever.

We often traveled to Milwaukee. All our relatives lived there. My in-laws bought a small house on 66th Street, in the spring of 1970. It had a basement where we could sleep when we stayed overnight. It was a step up for them, a sign of modest affluence for recent immigrants.

In early November 1969, I requested office assignment, so I can stay close to the phone. One late morning, I got a call, that our child was about to be born. I hurried home and got there in time so we could get to Edgewater Hospital on Clark Street, without rushing. Ildi went into labor about 1 o'clock P.M.

I felt awkward and helpless in this new experience, shut out of the main happenings. All the real burden is on the mother. Fathers can only muster up showing sympathy and mutter about regret, how they wish, they could share the worry, the pain, etc. -- which, of course, they cannot. We try to appear part of the process but look pitiful and inadequate.

The doctor came out about 4 to inform me that the birth will be breech, but all will be well -- I need not worry. I heard of breech birth before, and I only remembered that it was rare but problematic. Now here, suddenly, it was to be a crucial factor. Poor Ildi! What introduction to motherhood! The doctor encouraged me, but he was terse, and by temperament not the most comforting person. I spent the rest of the day with waiting, pacing up and down, mindlessly watching whatever was on the tube. (Some TV movie special, with Louis Jourdan starring.) I remember only that it was a pleasant show, a nice love story. I watched with parse attention, while I was anxiously waiting for news from behind the door.

After 10:30 the nurse told me that the doctor sees no need for me to wait, because the process was on pause and he foresaw no change for several hours. I went home anxious but hopeful and returned the next morning, November 19, 1969. I had a few more hours to wait. The doctor came out once to calm me. I settled down, confused and puzzled, not understanding what was going on inside. The breech really started to worry me. I took the doctor's reassurances and his opinion as one who is an expert and involved in the process. The question: *What if...?* -- never left my consciousness.

About 1:00 P.M. the doctor came out once again, telling me that it was all over and with success. Despite his previous encouragement, it was a tremendous relief to hear the good news. Erika was born, after 24 hour labor and pain that only mothers know. Men are spared from -- and deprived of -- the pain and joy of childbirth. Fathers are condemned never to experience the elation of the pain ending, and with it, the bringing to this world a life from one's own flesh. Anthropologists and philosophers may argue the reasons. Fathers have their role which is important and noble, but the exultant state of motherhood was given by God only to women. I thought of this often since then, trying to properly understand and appreciate it, but I'm not sure that I from the outside, can fully grasp the difference. -- Needless to say, men are often reminded of this fact by our mates. It helps us to see more clearly that we got it easier in many respects. Ultimately, this is the other side, illustrating the near balance in the human experience.

We had set up Erika's crib in our bedroom. Motherhood entered into a new phase. I got used to the regular routine of nighttime nursing. Here too, I could do nothing to contribute. Ildi did it for about six months, but in time I was able to take part when we switched to formula.

While Ildikó was still in the hospital, we were recommended -- really, assigned -- a pediatrician. He was Dr. Harry Levy, a kind, calm presence, to engender confidence in parents, no matter what was happening around them. How lucky we were! We got to know him better during our repeated visits, but we liked him from the start.

Ildikó met him in the hallway of the hospital, as she took her first postpartum walk. The doctor approached and greeted her. They had the following brief conversation:

"Are you Mrs. Magyar?"

"Yes."

"I was just looking in on your baby. It is amazing how a slender woman like you can give birth to a large, healthy daughter. Congratulations. I am Dr. Levy, your pediatrician."

Ildikó still remembers this first meeting and the sense of trust and security she had about it. Just by chance, we met a man in whom we would have confidence, a doctor, a friend, to be our guide in raising our daughters for the coming crucial years.

In his office, he had two rooms and no nurse. He did everything himself. He was a doctor, totally in tune with the thinking of parents. He knew babies and children better than anyone. His other strength was his insight to understanding the psyche of parents and a sensitivity for his tiny patients. We never found fault with his knowledge, manners or advise, but the most valuable extra he could provide, was the touch, the humanity, the tenderness, that was innate -- a quality not taught in medical school.

Dr. Levy was in his mid-60s when we met him. He had a vibrant, practice in a simple medical building at the intersection of Lincoln and Peterson Avenues, a convenient distance from our house on Kenmore. We saw him monthly with Erika for another six months only, while we were living in Chicago. Then we moved to Hanover Park, a northwest suburb, almost 40 miles from our old neighborhood. Dr. Levy advised that it would be wise for us to find a local doctor, who would be more easily accessible. He said that it would be a burden for him to make house calls so far out, in case of emergency.

We were ambivalent about this advice, for we grew attached to him during the few times we saw him, but soon after we settled in Hanover Park, we found another doctor in Elgin, 10 miles away and asked Dr. Levy to send our records to him. We soon learned a lesson that lead us to reconsider and reverse our decision. The manner and treatment of babies and parents by the new doctor and his nurse were so strikingly different that we never wanted to see them again. We were among the first four patients in the morning, on our first and only visit. Apparently, all four had the same appointment time. We saw the nurse go to the four rooms in succession, to spend a few minutes with the babies to start her day. She did one thing in each room: take temperature. She left the doors open for the doctor, after she finished with the preliminaries. We were in the last room of her round. As she progressed, the babies in each room began crying. When she was done with Erika, it became clear to us why. The way she inserted the thermometer, made Erika cry also. Then she left the room and returned to the others to take readings. It was a painful experience for us, just to watch the rough treatment of her tiny subjects. We looked at each other, shocked. Each of us, without saying a word, have decided that this will not go on, whatever sacrifice we have to make. -- This experience gave us our secretly-wished-for excuse. We contacted Dr. Levy and asked him to take us back. He obliged and we were relieved and happy again.

Andrea was born on June 15, 1971 at Sherman Hospital in Elgin. We started her with Dr. Levy right away. He continued to see the Girls until Andrea was 6, when we moved to Crystal Lake in 1977. By that time they were ready to be under the care of a family physician.

There are many memorable moments to recall about Dr. Levy and here I mention a few. One time early, when Andrea was due for a routine immunization shot, the doctor prepared his syringe. He told me to hold her in a way, that she was looking to my back, over my shoulder. Then, with a smooth, swift motion he administered the shot. The entire move took about a second. Andrea cried out, protesting the sudden, unexpected pinch. She quickly turned around to see who caused her pain. By that time the good doctor was two steps away, looking innocent and benign, the syringe nowhere in sight.

Then, discretely, he winked at me:

"Now she is angry at you, but she will forgive. I do not want her to associate me with the pain, because it would spoil the relationship between us for a long time."

His clever trick happened in a flash. He did not prepare me either for what was to come. We agreed wholeheartedly with his philosophy and method about what just took place. Our respect for his judgment and experience, tempered with the gentle humor of a sage, endeared him to us even more.

There was a different but unavoidable event. Andrea had a chronic ear infection that he had to see through, involving several visits in quick succession. During those visits he had to be a little invasive, checking out the ears and causing pain to his little patient. As a result after the second ear-visit, Andrea started crying as soon we entered the office. This lasted a few months but faded, along with her pain and subsequent tender treatments.

Dr. Levy held an open-line period from 7 to 8 each morning, 7 days, when he invited, free of charge, phone calls from new mothers. He did this from his home, before he started his day. We used it occasionally to report progress of the kids' condition or ask advise on little things. Ildi often said what comfort it gave her to have the doctor at her beck and call. He did not consider it a bother, no matter how trivial the problem, simple the question or obvious the answer.

At the end of each visit Dr. Levy sat down at a tiny desk he had in the corner, and on a 4x8 in. sheet he recorded progress, noted treatments, wrote reminders and gave detailed instructions. Printed on top, was his logo, with name, address and telephone numbers, at the office and his home. Below, he wrote with neat, pearl-like letters a summary of all that happened during that visit. We could follow the progress in weight and height of each child. He told us what we had to do at each stage for each child, with reminders, cautionary notes et cetera, more than we could ever think of. His notes often spilled over to the back page. The rest of the sheet was filled with dietary suggestions and other reminders, to call him about possible problems and progress in the kids' condition. He used red ink to note vaccinations, planned for the next visit.

Each time, his special *prescription* was for us to take, as a record. We still have the sheets and we count them among our family heirlooms and as a remembrance of this gentle human being. --

He said a few times that Andrea will be tall. Once I asked him how he knows, and what makes him so sure. He said that he can tell by looking at her feet. He became more sure as she was growing. It was an accurate prediction.

On one visit in the waiting room, before going in, I overheard part of a conversation, between two women next to me. The subject was interesting. It was about a *Dr. Harry Levy Chair*, scholarship or endowment, that was established or was in process of being so, at a medical school. It was a project, planned by grateful patients of Dr. Levy, who wanted to honor him.

41

Moving To The Suburbs

In the spring of 1970, we started going to the suburbs on weekends, looking at houses. We saved about $3,500 by then and hoped that it would be enough as down payment on a house, suitable for our needs at the time. Most of the homes we looked at, were 2 or 3-bedroom, on a small lot, with a carport or single garage. Despite that, existing houses in Schaumburg or Hoffman Estates were beyond our budget. Houses closer to Chicago were even more out of reach. Several weekends we spent time with agents. Our search seemed fruitless, except for the experience we gained, until we we spotted a large sign, advertising an existing development: *Hanover Highlands*. As our last stop before going home we checked it out on our own. We found what we wanted: bigger house for less money, though another five miles out. Immediately, we started to talk price and other important details. I was eager to push for commitment -- not an easy task with Ildikó. She likes to sleep on even smaller decisions, and this was certainly one she wanted to think over carefully. Before we left, we put down $200 to hold our option for a few days. The young salesman, little too eager, encouraged us, saying that 10% down can buy the house. We felt comfortable; we had 15% in the bank, so we committed with a small sum down, just to hold our option to buy. On the advise of the salesman, we applied for mortgage at Talman Saving and Loan. After more than week of anxious waiting, we contacted Talman, inquiring about our loan. They said it was in limbo and demanded 20% of the $28,500 price.

It is often said that in purchasing a house, people buy beyond their means. We were about to become one of those. Ildikó especially, worried that we may take on a burden beyond our ability to carry. I always looked at things with more optimism than she, assuming a modest gradual increase in my salary. Also, housing prices were going up at a fast rate and I heard of stories from friends of making a killing on homes, owned for a few years, or even just one. Of course, new home prices were also on the rise, for inflation was inching up.

Our house was one of the last two on the tract before they opened the next phase, with smaller homes at higher prices. Ironically, we became one of the *lucky victims* of the inflation years of the 1970s. My salary increases kept up with increases throughout the economy, thank God. So it was very important to buy a house as soon as we were able. With the mortgage rate fixed, although historically high, still was a boon, because we were able to pay our installments with increasingly cheaper dollars. Hanover Park was a rapidly growing area and the price of homes were increasing at an even higher rate. So I was more right than Ildi, just by the luck of the draw and without a complete understanding, or ability, to predict future economic trends. We simply joined the herd of buyers when, for several years, buying a house was the smartest move one could make.

Our house was already built, but we were pleased with its location, design and other details. It was the Stratford model, a *tri-level*, three-bedroom with attractive design. We felt lucky to have found it and thought the price much better than what we were accustomed seeing on our tours with real estate reps. We felt ready for our first big purchase -- but not just yet. We were short on the down payment.

We took on an additional burden, by borrowing from family. Ildikó's parents and my uncle Julius loaned us $1500, to make

up our $5,700 down payment. This expedited things at Talman.
The loan was approved within days. We had the house at 8010
Berkshire Drive.

It was a happy switch from the 1-bedroom apartment to a 3-
bedroom house with all its amenities, back yard and open, suburban
spaces. Yet, our monthly housing expense did not increase too
much. Our $185 rent was replaced by a $275 monthly mortgage
payment, with property tax and insurance included. (I was making
$10,000 by that time.) The added good feeling of building equity,
was icing on the cake. But before we could enjoy all that, we had
to make sure that we were able to repay the two secondary loans,
and keep up with the Talman payments. We did not mention the
extra loans to the mortgage company. This way we were more
exposed, in case we faltered on the bank's monthly installments.
As it turned out, we simply continued with our frugal ways and in
a year repaid the family obligations.

Erika was 6 months old when we moved to Hanover Park in
May of 1970. It was a slow, cold, unpleasant spring, a kind when
one is spending many days waiting in vain for a sunny day. The
wind was blowing non-stop and for weeks we saw only gray skies.
It also rained a lot. This helped us with the grass. I seeded the
lot and waited impatiently for some green to show. It was a slow
process, with frequent rain, but cold ground. It would've been
tedious and a real chore to constantly move the sprinkler. For
over a fortnight it was not necessary. Then the rain stopped and
I had to run the sprinklers continuously. The ground was still
muddy and it contained clay. I stomped on the tender grass shoots,
partly defeating my purpose, as I picked up heavy chunks of soft
mud on my shoes. Then the green became thicker and we had the
beginning of a nice, if not completely even lawn.

Hanover Park was a new town, a bedroom community, in large
part the creation of developers, bordered by Barrington Road on
the west and State Highway 20 at the south end of town. Highway
19, the extension of Chicago's Irving Park Road, cut through not
far from our house. The area was farmland just a few years before.
At the south edge of town was the railroad station, still named
Ontarioville, which was an old, tiny town along Route 20. It was

in Hanover Township, hence the name for the new suburb.

My mother visited us in 1972. One day she said: "This town is called Hanover Park. Where is the park?" (Hers was an early version of the noted question: *Where is the beef,* as asked on television by the old lady, advertising Wendy's -- and later shamelessly borrowed by Walter Mondale in a political debate.)

Indeed, the park had to wait a few years, but they have more than one now. Other things were more urgent and had priority. Ontarioville had a railroad station, just a small hut really. It was along the track on a curve, so when the train stopped, it was leaning slightly. It used to serve the few farm families nearby. Now it had to accommodate at least three growing towns. Bartlett and Streamwood also sent commuters to this station. Around it were a few old houses and farm buildings. A nearby large barn was renovated and became the retail store of a lumber yard. The old farms became burgeoning suburbs with winding streets and new shopping strips.

I took the train for a time, when it was my turn for periodic office duty that we did in rotation with field work. Parking at the station was very limited. It was a good thing that I took the early train. But as the town grew, so did the number of riders to Chicago. It happened a few times, especially on rainy days, that people had hard time getting their car out of the mud at the edge of the unpaved lot or the grass. One evening my car was blocked by other cars, so that there was no way for me to get it out. Someone offered me a ride home and I had to come back later to pick it up. (After we moved to Crystal Lake in 1977, they built a new handsome station some distance away from the old shack, with ample -- but this time paid -- parking.)

Dominick's, the once Chicago neighborhood grocer and K-mart were beginning to expand about that time. We were happy to see that each chain opened a store in town that year. There was an ACE Hardware, and a True Value, to help new home owners. Without these stores, the closest ones were some distance away, in Schaumburg. The entire area kept growing, and in time there was ample opportunity for shopping nearby.

Gradually we were able to spend some money on entertainment.

We went to see the vast collection of the Art Institute of Chicago, on occasional visits. Our favorite was and still is the European collection. It is comprehensive and has good examples of all the major schools and movements. The most famous is the impressionist collection. Special exhibitions come often.

A few years ago the Institute added a major piece to its collection. It may be a city project, but is on institute grounds. It is not inside the building but outside, along Columbus Drive. It is the great arched, beautifully carved entrance to the old Chicago Stock Exchange. The building was demolished, but the stone entry saved for posterity. Nestled among the trees, it is an eye-catcher, a symbolic entry to the past of Chicago.

Our social activities and entertainment were mostly *self-service* and could be had on the cheap. Minor extravagances we allowed ourselves after a while, were occasional movies and a few opera or ballet events. Prices for such entertainment were cheaper in Milwaukee, so we tried to coordinate them with our family visits. As children, neither of us were exposed to quality productions, available here at the Lyric Opera or world class touring international ballet companies that we can see in Chicago.

I never had a chance to visit the opera house in Budapest while in Hungary. In Milwaukee, there was the Florentine Opera Company in a small house, founded in the early sixties. I saw a few productions there. The Lyric was founded a few years earlier, after a period of decline of opera in Chicago. The first manager of the new Lyric was Carol Fox. She was instrumental in the long-term success of this world-renowned house. Today the Lyric is among the few greatest opera companies in the world. Miss Fox brought the biggest names to the Lyric stage. She was held in very high regard by artists, critics and the public. One of her most remembered decision was to fire Luciano Pavarotti -- and at the zenith of his illustrious carrier, no less. The golden tenor was summarily dismissed, after canceling one too-many performances. He never again sang at the Lyric. Miss Fox was true to her word, serving her public and the integrity of her house, above all else. It must have been an agonizing decision, but she showed gutsy courage. Star power has clout and Pavarotti had more than most.

For his many admirers, who regretted no longer being able to hear him -- we among them -- her decision evoked mixed emotions. Still, people admired her for it. -- After her death in 1986, the great operatic tradition continued under the direction of her protégé, Ardis Krainik, who started with the Lyric as a clerk/typist/ mezzo-soprano and sang several roles from 1955-59. I caught a glimpse of her at a Chicago Opera Theater production, a small company on the north side, where she came to observe and learn. I asked her, with a leading question, if she was spying on the competition. She smiled and said that she wants to learn as much as possible, using every opportunity. The production was Hector Berlioz' *Beatrice et Benedict*, an opera, based on Shakespeare's comedy, *Much Ado About Nothing.* The Lyric never produced that opera. Only Miss Krainik knew why. She died since then, so we may never know.

In the world of ballet, our favorite is *Giselle* by Adolf Adam. It is an amazing fact, that he composed the entire ballet in three weeks. The story goes, that he was in a very low emotional state -- and as often is the case, a very productive one -- following an episode of unrequited love. It is true, the music is full of beautiful, melancholic passages, colored with sumptuous orchestration. To me, it is one of the best music written for ballet, along with *Don Quixote* by Léon Minkus, Sergei Prokofiev's *Romeo and Juliet* and some of Tchaikovsky. They all have a combination of beautiful music, a great story with stirring dancing. I am partial to the choreography of the French master Marius Petipa (1822-1910). Ballet productions are much better seen, than read about. I only wrote this, to let the reader know, how much artistic pleasure ballet gave us through the years. In time, I looked at ballet as perhaps the highest form of art. It expresses feelings, drama and beauty, tells stories and evokes emotions without a word spoken -- all done to gorgeous music. How physically demanding and athletic it is, should not be noticeable to the audience. Its movements, with characteristic exaggerations are most graceful, unless viewed at close range, where the physicality is discernible. I learned this from Pille Barkócz. She was the only person I know, who from personal experience, could talk about ballet, its mechanics, little secrets and demand on the body, especially the ever pointed toes of the tough, yet gentle ladies.

I knew nothing about ballet, until about age 26. I lacked understanding because general ignorance about the art and the fact that I never saw a ballet. I formed a vague idea, that it was a feminine art and had my doubts about the role of men in it. I had no idea what the male dancers did, since the ladies did all the pirouetting and pretty dancing in pretty dresses. Later I learned that I was not entirely right. Yes, the ladies look good, but it is often because they are showcased by the men in lifts and in graceful poses. Man do the lifting, while making their own steps. They also do the spectacular and most showy leaps.

One Saturday afternoon in 1962, while I was visiting, Zsuzsa Petry mentioned that there will be a ballet program that evening in the auditorium at Carroll College in Waukesha. She told me that the director and star of the show will be a student, Tibor Zana, a fellow Hungarian refugee from 1956. I went gladly and curios, expecting an amateur production. I thought, this was an opportunity to expand my cultural horizon. The program was instructional, with narration, demonstrating various classical and modern styles. It touched me in a way I did not expect and taught me a lot. Tibor was the director and did most of the dancing, very well, I thought. I came away with a different view and a respect for ballet. I wanted to see more. Two years later I had my chance to see first class ballet in New York and a lot more later, in Chicago.

In New York, the American Ballet Theater was the new resident company, now in its own house, the New York State Theater. Under the direction of George Balanchine it soon made a name for itself. It was able to attract the best as guest artists, while also producing the future domestic stars of ballet. I saw my first Giselle, a production by the famous Danish Ballet, with their renowned Dancer Noble, Erik Bruhn, in the role of Prince Albrecht. That production was in the old Met building on Broadway. At a later time, the role of the Prince was danced by Rudolf Nureyev, just after he escaped from the Soviet Union. He was touring the world with the British dance icon, Dame Margot Fonteyn. Balanchine produced major stars, such as Gelsey Kirkland, Suzanne Farrell and Patricia McBride, but the really big names were still those of the Russian principals, most notably, Maya Plisetzkaya and Natalia Makarova, another escapee from the Soviets. Security, or fawning groupies were not a problem back then. Stars were sought out by admirers after productions, but it was still a different world. During the day they could be just themselves, walking freely, recognized by only a few, who respected their privacy, perhaps asking for an autograph. The mindless idolatry of mostly rock stars affects all show business today.

One evening, after the program ended at the old Met, I was walking to my car, parked on the street nearby. Suddenly I saw Nureyev, stopped by a fan, asking him to sign his program booklet. They were talking and I joined in. He told us in his broken English, that he was just down the block famished, and wanted to quench his hunger with a hamburger. He said that he can never eat before he dances and gets very hungry by the end. He spoke with a unique accent, softer than I was used to hearing from a Russian. I do not want to speculate on the fact that his ancestry was Tatar, and whether it, or perhaps Dame Margot, had this benign influence on his elocution. After a brief chat the famous dancer excused himself with an awkward smile and strolled away, back to the theater building. We all thanked each other and parted.

The one, my most striking memory of Nureyev occurred during this production. It was his *grand jeté* the arching forward leap, that is a staple of all dancers and some figure skaters. That is what he did, but the way he executed it made a mark forever in my memory. He lunged his body up high, spread like an eagle, then seemed to stop momentarily in mid-air before completing his leap. Confirming that I was not the only one noticing, or that I just imagined the whole thing, I also recall the gasp heard through the packed house, followed by thunderous applause.

Time magazine wrote this: *His trajectory is beyond the proper limits of the body. At the apex of his elevation he hangs in mid-air for one long, impossible, crucial moment, as if suspended by piano wire, before making his feathery descent.*

A few years later another huge name in ballet, the Latvian

Mikhail Baryshnikov bolted from the communist world to escape restriction on freedom and its tyranny of cultural confinement. He was also able to do those halting leaps. Others followed, and did it almost as well (Alexander Godunov, Fernando Bujones). Baryshnikov's career was similar to that of Nureyev, but he was also great in the contemporary repertoire. He stayed at the top of his profession for many years and contributed enormously to his art. He found time to teach, coach and act in several movies. His best film was *The Turning Point*, a good story with a lot of dancing with Leslie Browne, a budding star in those days. Other stars in the movie were Shirley McLain and Ann Banckroft. They played two dance moms, rival dancers in their youth, but now best friends -- until the reflexive urge to compete surfaces again in an argument over one's young daughter, the rising ballet star of the new generation. Their old, suppressed rivalry gets the better of them. A street quarrel of the dignified matrons degenerates into an all-out, hair-pulling cat-fight, until they suddenly realize the sheer silliness of it, break out in hysterical laughter and embrace, in one of the great scenes of moviedom. I discovered Don Quixote in this picture, where it is the main dance repertoire of the movie. I wish that this beautiful ballet were performed more often.

42

Travels

In 1972 we made plans a to visit our families in Hungary and Rumania. This trip was our first, as a family. Andrea was 1 year old, Erika 2½. I was looking forward to take my loved-ones here, to those over there. On this trip we again took KLM, rather than the narrow, tight-seated planes of Icelandic Airlines, though they were less expensive. The flight was smooth, pleasant and included a special treat, a surprise to Ildi and me. After supper, as we were getting ready to put the girls down (at 36,000 ft.) for the night, a stewardess came with a *Moses-basket*, a special amenity of the airline, to be used as a bed for tiny passengers, such as was our one year old Andrea. Erika had her own ticket and seat, but Andrea was to share ours for the whole trip. This ingenious and original contraption was designed for babies' overnight travels. It was a long wicker basket, measured for a baby, equipped with hooks, to be hung overhead, secured to the storage compartments. It worked like a charm. Andrea was always a good sleeper and within minutes she was out, not to bother anyone until morning.

We also tried to sleep through the short night over the Atlantic -- no in-flight movies, back then. Soon we were in a slumber, induced by the low murmur of jet engines. After a few toss-and-turns, we were in sleep with reasonable comfort -- and for longer than we expected.

As I woke, I heard cooing noises, as if adults were talking to a baby. As I looked up, there was Andrea, entertaining half the cabin. She was sitting in her basket, smiling and *talking* in her sweet way, with those who were awake, joining the interactive show. I woke up Ildi and we watched together for a while, then we fetched the little princess from her special perch and let a hostess return the basket to storage.

We landed in Frankfurt, where Helma greeted us and took us to Aachen, to spend a few days. Otti gave us a car, that he selected just for this trip. It was a big Mercedes Benz, with ample room for the long trip.

Early morning on Pentecost Sunday, we took to the road and were on our way to Hungary. The first leg, about an 8-hour drive, took us to my younger brother's house. By then Tomi lived in Gilching, a Munich suburb. We were looking forward to see his new home. With some difficulty we found his nice, spacious, three-level townhouse. I was impressed how well it was constructed and how much comfort it offered.

Gilching grew out of farmland, just as many suburbs did in the States. Houses in Germany were smaller, yet more expensive, at least in part because of the quality of construction. The entire house was made of concrete. The interior had many attractive features and nice, solid wood finish. Higher land prices in Europe also drove up home prices. Backyards were small and always fenced.

We spent two days in Gilching and early on Pentecost Sunday, we continued our drive to Hungary. We drove less then an hour and not yet reached Austria, when the nice big Mercedes broke down with some strange defect in the engine. The motor suddenly started shaking violently. I knew that something was seriously wrong. I pulled off the road, looked under the hood, but could not detect any reason for the trouble. We limped on and exited as soon as we could, stopping on the main square of a small village. It looked like a ghost town, not a soul to be seen.

It was Pentecost weekend, a two-day holiday in Germany, as

it is in most of Europe. It is one of the three, two-day holidays (Christmas and Easter, the others). The day was bright and sunny, but very grim to us. Everything was closed for both days. Many people left town. We knew that Otti and Helma went away for the weekend. I called Tomi, but could not reach him. The line was always busy with a tone that had an unusual sound -- a line problem, to add to our woes. I got through later in the afternoon.

Tomi came right away and was there within an hour. We packed everything into his smaller car and went on, this time without a problem. He hitchhiked home, telling us not to be concerned about him. He said, hitchhiking is never a problem. He was home before evening.

Otti, when heard of our misfortune, was distraught and emotional. Helma said that tears filled his eyes. He told me later, that after working hard to make that car a reliable one, he felt cheated by fate, having this hidden flaw inside the engine, undetectable in advance of the breakdown. By the time he learned of our problem, it was solved, at least temporarily. He was unable to do anything to help. He put himself in our position after the fact, frustrated and felt that he failed, despite his best efforts. -- A week later he brought the Mercedes to Hungary. The old war horse was problem-free for the rest of our trip. I drove it to Zilah and back to Aachen, some 3000 miles without a hitch.

We spent a few days in Jánosháza, enjoyed showing off our children to grandparents and relatives and rested up for another long trip to Transylvania.

The playpen for the Girls we built in Aachen, using a plywood board over the back seat, was still in the car. It was cut to size, extending to the front seat back rests, on top of the back seat and leg room space, that we used for storage. It was a perfect way to travel. The spacious back seat was a playroom and sleep-room, always within sight. In the space under the board, we put seldom used items and things we wanted to take to relatives in Rumania. Only at the Rumanian border did we have to show what was under the board in front of the back seats.

After a few days we took off for Zilah in Rumania, where Ildi's father and stepmother lived. We chose to travel at night, to make it easier on the kids. We arrived at the border at daybreak, rousing the young border guard from his slumber at the quiet, small border station at Ártánd. He was not pleased and either couldn't speak Hungarian, which was unusual in that border area, where Hungarians are the majority or, more likely he wouldn't, out of spite. (It could also be, that he was from a faraway part of the country, put here on purpose, where he knew no one.)

Ildi fumbled through some Rumanian, that she have not spoken for a decade. The kids were sleeping peacefully. After some terse questioning about our purpose and destination, the young man said:

"Don't you feel sorry for these kids, dragging them through the night, like this?"

We looked at him in disbelief, thinking that perhaps he was trying to crack a joke. But no, he was stern and outright scolding. We told him, that we were sure, this was the best way to travel with toddlers. They sleep all night, wake up rested and are happier in the morning, making the day easier on us all. He seemed un-persuaded and muttered something unintelligible, but pursued the subject no further.

He then asked me to open the trunk. It contained our usual traveling cargo and a few inexpensive gifts. A few calendars, thrown on top of a suitcase caught his eyes. I could tell right away that they captured his fancy. The calendars were all nice on shiny paper, with beautiful pictures of scenery, nature's splendor in faraway places, with a small advertising logo on each page. I know that at least two were from chemical companies, who put out the ones with most spectacular pictures. -- Half of the year was already over, but I still brought them, because they were a favorite of my father-in-law who, in prior years gave them as gifts to friends. Here was proof, how popular they were with Rumanians.

The young soldier also wanted at least one -- I could tell. He was alone at this minor border station and perhaps did not feel as powerful as his colleagues at the more important crossing points. I resented his being so cross with us earlier. The following conversation took place between us as we were staring into the trunk, without eye contact and with Ildi behind us looking on, haltingly translating:

"What are those?" -- he asked.
"Calendars."
"Really? Do they sell those, in America?"
"No. They use them for promotion and give them away as gifts."
"Oh."

Then there was a moment of tense silence. I did not know what to expect, but soon the stalemate was over. He chickened out. I did not offer the bribe he had in mind. In fact he felt it better just to let us go. I closed the trunk and off we were. (This was the only fast crossing we ever made in or out of Rumania.)

Talking about border crossings, an experience, quite different, though even more swift, awaited us weeks later on our way back to Aachen, as we were leaving Hungary for Austria. We were waived to a stop by a Hungarian guard at the border. For a better understanding of what happened, I should stipulate that this was after a five-week period, that we spent in the circle of relatives, all of them seeing the Kids the first time. Our usual instruction to them, when we entered a house of some uncle or cousin, was:

"Give a kiss, Sweetheart. This is uncle-, aunt- or cousin- so and so".

It was too early for Andrea, who at age one was oblivious to these courtesies, but Erika caught on fast and was eager to oblige, expressing her natural warmth and cuddly personality. This went on for weeks in many places, with a lot of people, all new to her, yet very kind and solicitous.

So, we stop at the Hungarian side of the border, looking forward to a stretch of limbs. There stands a young guard in his usual garb, large boots, service hat and a rifle on his shoulder. We all get out of the car. Before I say a word, Erika is in his arms, kissing him on the cheek, as it feels natural for her, a lesson well learned, reinforced and repeatedly practiced during the past few weeks.

The young man was defenseless and totally taken with his tiny admirer. We had to give an explanation in a hurry, lest somebody misunderstands. That done, we did not even have to open the trunk. The young, blushing soldier just motioned us to go on.

In the 1970s the cold war eased somewhat. *Détente,* the highly touted, but mostly meaningless easing of tension with the Russians, was the constant subject of political talk. The plus side of this phony arms stalemate was that traveling to the satellite countries in the Soviet sphere became less cumbersome. Getting a visa also became a little easier. Harassment on the borders was less, and less frequent. For the first time, travel to the West for ordinary citizens of the eastern block became possible.

Between these contrasting experiences at the two borders, we had the most wonderful time, showing off our two little girls, who captured the heart of everyone they encountered. They were always the source of our pride. The greatest compliment should go to Ildikó, who was more of a disciplinarian than I. She was stronger and more willing to endure their resentment, never forgetting the ultimate aim and knowing that she is doing the right thing by instilling in them a sense of duty, restraint and honesty, along with patience, common sense and the value of virtuous living. It was satisfying to hear my mother often refer to our marriage as the best one among those of her children.

In Zilah I renewed my acquaintance with Ildi's folks and met some others. We picnicked again in the romantic Meszes. We drove up on its curvy, poor quality roads. The scenery reminded me of national parks in America: rugged wilderness with great natural beauty. We picked mushrooms and searched out small patches of wild strawberries. Erika had a grand time, loudly announcing each find.

One day we traveled to Kolozsvár, (Cluj) an ancient historic city of Matthias (Mátyás Hunyadi) Corvinus, one of Hungary's greatest kings, also king of Bavaria. (In Italy, between his two assignments in Buda Castle, Galeotto Marzio wrote his *De egregie, sapienter, iocosedictis ac factis regis Mathiae* -- "The excellent, wise, humorous sayings and deeds of Matthias".) His was the golden age of Hungary. In the words of the Encyclopaedia Britannica:

He was, indeed, a remarkable figure. A true Renaissance prince, he was a fine natural soldier, a first class administrator, an outstanding linguist, a learned astrologer, an enlightened patron of the arts and learning. His collections of illuminated manuscripts, pictures, statues and jewels were famous throughout Europe. Artist and scholars of European repute were welcome at his court, which could vie in magnificence with any on the continent. Sumptuous buildings sprang up in his capital and other centres.

When we were in the Vatican Museum several years later, I saw two of Matthias' codices prominently displayed, as shining examples of the high art of calligraphy and codex illustration, mostly by monks in the middle ages. -- Matthias was born in Kolozsvár, imprisoned in Prague with his brother, László, who was murdered by jealous nobles, vying for the throne.

In the center of the main square, surrounded by ornate buildings -- some from the 15th century -- is the gothic coronation cathedral and the huge, composite equestrian statue of Matthias. Though born in Kolozsvár, his family name derived from Hunyad, where his family's castle stands. His father, János Hunyadi, was governor of Transylvania and the defender of Europe, against the initial onslaught from the Ottoman empire. He recaptured Belgrade from the Turks in 1456, that we still continue to celebrate. To commemorate his victory, Pope Callixtus III ordered the ringing of church bells throughout Christendom at noon every day -- a tradition, that continues today. After the Hunyadis passed from the scene, the Turks ravaged half of Europe, plundered its wealth and people, and occupied the continent -- parts of it for 500 years.

The Matthias statue is an elaborate composition with many minor figures and animals, around the magnificent king on horseback. It escaped abuse from the communist state of Rumania, I think, because Matthias was a truly great figure of European history. (They didn't dare touching it.)

The statue is the work of János Fadrusz, who also made the smaller, but equally famous monument in Zilah, to Count Miklós Wesselényi, one of the wisest and most sympathetic characters in Hungarian history. In an attempt to deny the Hungarian past in this large region of Rumania, the government moved the Wesselényi

TWICE BLESSED

statue, later moved it back, then covered it with a plywood *box*, like the communists did in Hungary, for the statue of Count Festetics in Keszthely. The Wesselényi monument stayed hidden behind the ugly eyesore for almost 20 years, ruining the look of a lovely square.

In Hungary, we attended Father's 50th high school reunion in Sopron. The old Benedictine institution was still there, run by the state, but a couple of his teachers attended, coming over from the cloister. This included his class master, from the mid 1920s, who also taught my brother Józsi for a year, in 1943-44. It was a rare occasion, where Father had all his children and grandchildren in attendance, making his grand occasion even more special.

The vacation in Aachen, Hungary and Transylvania was refreshing and filled me with joyful pride. Connecting my two families, separated by ocean, was the reward for years of planning and dreaming.

While home, we invited Mother for a stay with us in Hanover Park. She never before traveled west of Vienna and was not the traveling kind, as was Father. The trip was a huge event for her. She wanted to see how we live and to spend a little time with her grandchildren. During her stay she wanted to stay around the house. We only managed to take her once each to Chicago, Milwaukee and Toronto. She had the opportunity to see the local highlights and spend time with Ildi's family and Uncle Andrew. The trip to Toronto included a stop at Niagara Falls.

Mother and Ildi were spending a lot of time together. They talked all day and did a lot of craft work. They almost completed embroidering valances for two windows. Ildikó finished them after Mother went home. We picnicked in the park, took leisurely walks and just enjoyed ourselves, blessing our good fortune that her visit became possible. A trip such as this was unimaginable just a few years before.

By the end, though she was pleased with her trip, she was ready to go back to her usual surrounding, sleep in her own bed along her husband, where she belonged. Father died, the following spring at age 69. At the time he was still doing occasional work to help out old colleagues. He suffered his third heart attack during work in

Kemenespálfa, the closest and one of the smallest village in his old district. I was not able to attend his funeral. The suddenness of his passing and our circumstances at the time, forced me to make the difficult decision.

Mother remained alone in a huge house with diminished income, overwhelmed with the daily upkeep. After a few years she sold the house to the eternal regret of Otti who, should it happen a few years later, would have bought it himself. As things stood, we all were not yet in a situation where we could have kept the house. - - Market for homes in the 1970s was weak, especially for a large house in a small town. At the end, the local agricultural cooperative purchased it, and with a small addition and remodeling, divided it into dwelling units for four families.

43

Unpleasant Events

About that time, Józsi had his second painful incident -- this one relating to his work. Here I will recount the two juxtaposed, for the common elements in them and in part as a tribute to my oldest brother.

Józsi never shied away from expressing opinions, that did not sit well with the official line of the all- powerful Party. This streak of a gadfly brought him grief twice in his life.

The first was more than 20 years before, during his senior year in 1951, while in high school at Sümeg. It happened, that on a Communist Student Club bulletin board, somebody scribbled a derogatory comment under a picture of Stalin. This was a serious offense. In school matters, the club was empowered with the official investigation and limited judicial power, under the aegis of the Party. It was ready to punish the perpetrator -- or at least a scapegoat. His peer investigators and accusers were his classmates, office holders in the club. They professed to possess proof of guilt and were ready to mete out punishment: expulsion from school (all high schools of the country) and as a consequence, permanent banishment from further academic pursuits, allowing him to hold only menial jobs in the indefinite future.

It was a daunting task and a very difficult fight, but Józsi acquitted himself with distinction by his clever, aggressive, lawyer-like defense and at the end with panache, when he accused his dilettante accusers with dishonesty and vindictiveness. He demanded to see proof (habeas corpus). He knew that there were none, and *his* claim to the truth was much more credible than that of his classmate thugs. The *proof* in contention was his handwriting. The evidence presented against him by the amateur graphologists contended that a certain letter, "g", was recognizably his. Józsi demonstrated, with samples, that two of the interrogators on the panel wrote "g" in a way, that would make them indistinguishable from his. "Was it one of *you*, who wrote the line on the board?" -- he asked.

That collapsed the case. They admitted defeat and dropped the charge. It was a mini show-trial, typical of the era. Those, in the political big-time, usually involved prominent members of society, of whom the Party wanted to make an example in widely publicized trials, thus maintain control over the population.

As an ironic twist, toward the end of this month-long ordeal, Otti confided in him, that he was the guilty one and he was sorry to see his brother twisting in the wind, while at the same time being proud seeing him, so ably extricating himself from this difficult situation. Józsi seriously reproached him, for telling him this *now*, while the trial was still under way. He told Otti, that by his admission before the matter was over, he made it more difficult to defend himself. Józsi told him, that throughout the trial, he never lied, including when he said that he has no information or clue about the identity of the culprit. This new knowledge made his defense more difficult and thus might jeopardize his case. Fortunately things were far advanced by then and no new information was presented, that could have aroused suspicion and lead to reopening the case.

Things came to full circle more than 50 years later. While we were in Hungary in 2001, Józsi had his 50th class reunion. He told me, that during that gathering, his onetime chief accuser apologized to him. He said that what they were doing was wrong but they were ordered to conduct the trial, directly by the County Communist

Party and they dared not to defy that ultimate authority. This
brought enormous satisfaction to Józsi and he gracefully accepted
the apology. It came just in time. By then he was seriously ill with
cancer, which took his life four months later.

Józsi told me this story in the summer of 2001. He also told me
about his writings, chronicling about two years of his life at age
17-18. It is a diary, hand written in a notebook and kept in a folder.
Marika had a copy which I brought out with me. I was astonished at
the ease of his pen and his simple, conversational style. The pages
are filled with school events and reflections on happy moments of
a summer past (1951), nature outings, friendly girls and potential
girlfriends --and one that he distantly dreamed about. Reading the
dialog, one feels present and right in the middle of the action, or
inclined to share the author's sentiments . He wrote about his long
summer vacation in Csehi and how hard it was to leave and start
school again. Several girlfriends and a nostalgic *could have been*
is mentioned. I was pleased to read that he was discriminating
and judged girls primarily on character and qualities he found
admirable, rather than on physical beauty. For him, honesty and
constancy were before charm and good looks. I think it is time
to read it again. It is 72 pages, long hand. A significant part of it
details his account of the foregoing story about defending his good
name against great odds and unfair accusations.

His more recent case had similar elements, typical for the time,
but brought with it severe consequences. As everything else, the
veterinary profession too, was subjected to the purposes of the
state, as represented by the communist party. He was a practicing
veterinarian for almost two decades, when in 1975, his superiors
brought charges, accusing him of dereliction of duty and causing
spread of a disease.

He was sure of his innocence and also, that he can prove it. He
got his papers and documents together and sent it to the professional
supervisory body. A few weeks later the papers were requested
again. He had no copies -- no copiers back then. He never saw
his original papers again, some of which were indispensable for an
adequate defense. While his case was pending, he was suspended,
his district taken from him, leaving him without income for more

than a year. He again defended himself, this time against greater odds and handicapped by the deliberate destruction of evidence by his superiors in his case. He was sure of this, but determined to vindicate himself. After a few dead ends he befriended a lawyer, who previously worked for the regime but was sympathetic to his plight, had experience and connections. With a newly created file for his defense, while lacking key documents he still succeeded at the end. The cost was great, but the triumph, sweet. He was restored to his district and position. -- Years later, after the communist regime collapsed, his chief tormentor confessed to him, that it was a witch hunt, in which he was forced to take part. Józsi said he understood, for he remembered the times and the oppressive forces that prevailed on everybody back then. He reconciled with his one-time accuser and they were on old terms again.

These cases illustrate the destructive power, dictatorial regimes often bring on society. The victims are good, innocent people whose real crime is that they are not inclined to towing the line. The even greater casualty is the good will and trust that is the foundation of a civil society. Such events leave in their wake, basic institutions that are deeply marred and may need more than a generation to recover, so that they can again fulfill their intended role and be the cornerstone of long established order.

44

Work And Associated Pleasures

By the early 1970s I was promoted and achieved a status in the company that made me eligible for work assignments that everybody desired. The work was the same, but the locations to be visited made these trips plum assignments. The biggest *plum* was a trip to Colorado. There was a lot of work in Denver, where I spent my first two-week assignment out west.

In March of 1972 I was assigned a tour that, with some effort and a little extra expense, we made into a family vacation, just as we did it a few years before in Boston. My experience with the Ramada hotel chain was pleasant, based on prior long distance field trips. Looking through my Ramada catalog, I saw one in Golden, called *Ramada Foothills.* It was appealing. Indeed, we found a lovely place, with perhaps the best combination of location, view and isolation from the bustle of the big city. Golden was known by lovers of beer, as the home of Coors Brewery, though I was not aware of this fact, until several of my colleagues asked me to bring them six packs. (Coors is now available in Illinois and I think, nationwide. One of the reasons for the good beer could have been the water, whose great taste I still remember. It is mountain water, from reservoirs high up the Colorado Rockies.)

Denver often suffers from atmospheric inversion, when in calm days, polluted air is trapped over the city. On such days, they often measure high pollution levels. Golden was always free of that, situated conveniently higher, on the foothills. We looked down on the city and, especially in the morning hours, saw it enveloped in a cloud that often stuck around all day. In Golden, the days were always sunny.

Ildikó and the Girls spent much of their time at the pool. Some evenings we went up the mountains and drove around, sightseeing. It was a vacation for me too, because the day went by with fieldwork and time on the road. I had to make copious notes, especially on this trip, because the days were crammed with inspections and travel. By habit, I usually wrote my reports in the hotel room following inspections. This time I did not much feel like sitting down with papers, rulers, pencil and slide-rule. So I had to write some of them several days after the inspection. By then, memory about details tended to fade.

One afternoon, I scheduled a visit to a radio transmission tower, fairly high on the mountainside. I took Erika with me. It was a simple, short inspection and I was sure she would be no burden. Everything went as expected. On the way home we spotted gliders in the air and searched around for the launching site. It was at a steep drop of a hill, where updrafts lifted gliders, and carried them on and on, to seemingly unending, effortless flight. It was the first time I saw gliders up close. Erika also watched them with wonder. Some of the crafts seemed never to come down. A good run to the edge of the cliff was enough to take up the winged contraption and keep it in the air indefinitely, with a skilled pilot guiding it. We watched them until dusk crept in. It was a nice side-trip to complete the day's work.

On my next western trip, in the spring of 1972, we had the best of all treats. It was the *western slopes* tour. During this fortnight we covered much of the western half of Colorado, including small towns in isolated valleys, surrounded by snowy peeks and green mountainside miles around.

We drove all day on a Sunday and slept in North Platte, NE, starting again early next morning. This drive was shorter, but I had my first stop, scheduled at 10 o'clock at a Union Carbide plant in Rifle. In the brightening Colorado dawn we drove through Denver, across the mountains, past Vail and Avon, -- wishing to stop -- but postponed it for another time. We were in Rifle at 9:30. I finished work by noon and went on to look at a cement factory in Ouray, late afternoon. The nicest part of the tour lay ahead. Next job was the inspection of a mine in Telluride.

In recent years this sleepy, quaint town was made famous by an annual film festival, founded by Robert Redford. When we visited, it was beautifully quiet, no movie folks about. I was astonished to see a beat-up sign in *downtown* on a large, redstone building: "Opera House". I wondered whether this was just a fancy name for a local theater or was it truly a home for serious music. Somebody told me that it was real, and in its hay day, when the mines brought in a lot of money, it was the center of culture in town and its surrounds.

The weather was ideal and dandelions were in their first bloom. It was the time when millions blossom at once and their yellow paints the meadow bright. In many spots they dominate the lawn's green matrix. The Girls collected big bouquets for Ildi, than rested in a meadow in the middle of town square, as if been dropped there, sitting on a huge, deep yellow carpet. Looking at the pictures in our album, we sometimes re-live the lovely day and think back to simpler times.

Telluride is an old mining town at the end of a wide, 7 mile long valley, a mountain *cul de sac*, where the road ends. My mine was at the end of a dirt road, just out, east of town at the foot of a steep, high mountain range. It was dug deep into the belly of the mountain. I had a simple inspection, only the outer buildings and the staging and processing area, where the shafts began. We insured property, not safety.

Driving back to the hotel, I met my family, taking a walk on the only road in town. They looked tired. It was a long walk for them (Andrea was not yet 1 and barely walking) so they welcomed a lift to the hotel.

On the map, Silverton lies just a dozen miles from Telluride on the other side, but to get there, one needs a mountaineer's truck. The short dirt road up and over the mountain is open only a few months each summer. I surveyed the steep hillside and with my binoculars, spotted a Jeep, tracking up slowly. Next day we followed the regular highway and have covered 75 miles to get to Silverton.

Two other towns where I had work, were Durango and Cortez. To reach them we tracked back and took the most spectacular road, the Million Dollar Highway through Silverton, the Red Mountain Pass, Molas Divide and Coalbank Pass, all above 10,000 ft, in the San Juan National Forest.

On Friday of the first week we were in Cortez. Here I began a week's vacation and we kept on going west, to California. Our intended stop was San Diego, to visit Imre Lendvay, then Los Angeles, to see relatives. On the way, we stopped for a day at the Grand Canyon. It was awesome, more spectacular then I imagined it. Seeing the depth, the details, the proportions, was impressive beyond any picture or video I saw before. In the afternoon we drove around and saw what we could in one day. I was reluctant leaving and next morning, walked with Erika up to the rim of the canyon one more time, to take it in just once more and see if I could discover something new with binoculars, searching the vista below. I spotted a few people in the distance and thought that some day I want to go down myself.

Then I turned to Erika, standing next to me:

"Look down there Sweetheart. Is this not the most beautiful sight you have ever seen?"

"Igen Apuka" -- said she in Hungarian, using her endearing, customary version of *Daddy*.

Than, after a pause and a sigh, she added: "Now, let's get some ice cream."

I understood her perspective. I took my last look and tracked down to the car, where Ildi was waiting with Andrea. Before heading out on another long leg of our journey, we obliged Erika and also treated our own sweet tooth.

We arrived in San Diego in the middle of the day and used the time to explore the city. We liked it, and I understood Imre's feeling about his city. He told me once, after he lived there for about a year, that he never again wanted to move. (He considers his present assignment in Munich, temporary.) We walked through the famous Hotel del Coronado. It was the setting for a great film, one of the best comedies ever, Billy Wilder's *Some Like it Hot*. In my mind I visualized the great trio: Marilyn Monroe, Tony Curtis and Jack Lemon, parade down the sandy beach, with the magnificent red wooden spires (in black and white) behind them.

We spent a night with Imre, then went on to Los Angeles, to visit Aunt Pepi and Gerti. Looking back now through distant decades, seeing California was quite a feat, original and rewarding. I was able to take advantage of favorable circumstances and the company's flexibility, by taking off a week in the middle of a faraway field trip and see a beautiful part of the country.

With Pepike and Gerti we spent the time recalling memories we shared, while sunning poolside, and catching up on years of missed conversations. -- I ate the last orange from her tree. The taste was remarkable, juicier and more aromatic than any I ever tasted in an orange before, or since.

Gerti had a beautiful house on a hillside in Burbank. Her address, 700 View Drive, was an apt description. She had a commanding view of the city below. The backyard, terraced higher on three levels, was a sculptured jungle, with a variety of plants and flowers. Between the main house and the guest quarters -- she called it the Cabana -- was the pool, making a splendid picture of a luxury home. She collected paintings, bronzes and other treasures of fine art. (Those fabulous days are gone. Pepike died in 1998 at age 98, and Gerti after a short but severe illness of cancer, in 2004.)

On the way back, I picked Phoenix for an overnight stay. We arrived early in the afternoon. When we got out of the car, we felt as if we were in an oven. It was totally unexpected, stepping out from the comfort of a pleasantly cool car. We hurried inside for relief. After a short nap to freshen up, we ventured out again. The sun was not yet set, but quite low. It was a totally different world. A nicely warm evening was approaching. We stayed outside and enjoyed the cooling temperatures. In time it became outright chilly. By dusk the temperature dropped more than 50 degrees below the day's high. I thought of what I learned about travels in the Sahara.

Within an average day you were baked during the day and froze in the night. Phoenix came pretty close to that.

On the way back we stopped at Four Corners, climbed the spectacular Indian cliff dwellings in Mesa Verde National Park and were amazed, walking the high bridge above Royal Gorge. A toy train, as it seemed, puffed through the narrow gorge a quarter mile down, trekking the wild Arkansas River.

By Sunday evening we were back in Colorado Springs, ready for my second week of work. We spent two days and had a chance to tour the campus of the Air Force Academy and marvel at the futurist looking chapel and the fighter planes that decorate the grounds. Before leaving town, we stopped in the Garden of the Gods and drove up the hill to picturesque sites, that overlook the city in the light of the setting sun.

Our last stop, for two nights, was Pueblo. The Girls, all three, spent much time by the pool sunning -- forgetting that they were at high elevation, where the power of the sun is more potent. Their fair, winter skin was exposed too long. Ildi protected the kids better than she did herself. The last night in Colorado she hardly slept, nursing her sensitive skin, that was in the process of acquiring a vibrant, pink tone. By morning it was in full bloom. Poor soul, she had a difficult time on the way home, which was a 24 hour drive, nonstop. We kept making jokes about it, but my Love suffered all the way. Sitting in the car for such a long time was hard, but it could not have been much easier in a hotel room either. After a while she found a few tenable positions and managed the trip with courage.

We were pleased with our trip. We had a good time, without serious problems. It widened our horizons and gave us an appreciation for the vastness and the beauty of our country.

45

From Hanover Park
To Crystal Lake

As Erika and Andrea were growing up, my nightly bedtime goodnight kiss evolved into a custom of longer visit with each girl in her room, after they both were already in bed. In time, these *tuck-in* sessions acquired a life of their own. The girls were past the age when parents read them a story. Instead, with each I had a longer, one-on-one session of freewheeling talk, where we discussed life, dreams, wishes and other items of interest. The girls did most of the talking, usually about their day in school, problems, events and sad or happy stories. These delightful nightly sessions went on for a good number of years. Subjects evolved and gradually became more mature. I fondly think of how they came to me for advice, telling me about their day and things planned for tomorrow.

I have fond memories of those talks. A few times in the early years I tried to record our talk on audio tape. This was not easy, because the presence of a recorder affected the carefree atmosphere. I know, that the best moments of these evenings were lost for posterity and only live vaguely in my memory. I listened to the few passages I have, and muse over the problems that were so important back then.

There was one for Erika, perhaps her saddest day, when she told me about her broken heart, caused by their short-lived break-up with Jim. This was near the end of one of our heart-to-heart talks. She was a junior in high school. I tried to console her and suggested that she should look at other boys.

She would not hear of it and said that though she is miserable now, the good times outweigh the bad ones many times over. Indeed, the lamentable episode lasted only a few days. (Now, nearly 20 years later, they are in their 10th year of blissful marriage, awaiting the birth of their first child.)

Andrea was also imaginative and enthusiastic story teller. Her best moments were not the recounting of events, but the dreams and planning of new ones in the future. She told me one evening of an upcoming trip to Great America. This was to be her second or third. She would be with all her close friends. Her face lit up with wonder and anticipation, as she described the absolutely most beautiful, fun-filled time they would have the following Friday. She was flying on her wings of fantasy, inspired by the memory of previous experiences. Great America, instead of school -- can anything be better?

It made me think back to my two days in Keszthely in 1948 just before Easter vacation, as I was in my emotional high, with the first Tarzan movie still in mind, and my thoughts increasingly occupied and full of plans about going home the next day. Our nightly little gab sessions started while we were living in Hanover Park and continued for years after we moved to our second house.

While in Hanover Park, we befriended a nice young couple across the street. Olaf Hanson was a son of Swedish immigrants. His wife Annalise, was born in Austria. Both grew up in the States, but acquired continental values from parents. They also had small children. We kept up our friendship and spent time together, until they moved to California a few years later.

Olaf was an architect at the prestigious firm, Skidmore, Owens & Merrill. We talked about his interests and his stint in the Navy, that was a defining experience for him.

One day in 1976, he told us that they saw a beautiful house in

Crystal Lake, that sure would appeal to us. Olaf had plans to build one just like it on a big lot but somewhere else, away from the development where he saw the model. It was a *California design* he said, distinguished by an open interior, a loft with a view of the lower level, made bright by many large windows. After he told us about the dream house a few more times, we also traveled to Crystal Lake to see for ourselves.

Usually I do not expect too much, based on someone else's enthusiasm for anything, but this time we were surprised how right Olaf was. The house was too good to believe. After touring the model, we stopped in the sales office. The price was $70,000. My salary was $18,000 at the time. Our house, though we bought it for 28 thousand, handsomely appreciated in the inflationary times of the previous years. After holding it for six years, we saw similar homes sell in the low 50s. The math about a possible upgrade was sobering, but appeared not to present insurmountable problems. Once again, Ildikó needed some persuading. It was much in my favor, that she also liked the house. We acknowledged that we were comfortable in our three bedroom house in a nice neighborhood. Still, what we saw, excited us beyond our expectations. The Girls also saw it as a new adventure. When we first entered the model, Ildi and I admired with gaping mouth, the splendid view of the loft from below. By the time we had a chance to say a word, the two girls were up in the loft, hanging on the railing, smiling down on us.

We said that we will sleep on it and count our money, to decide if this upgrade is doable within our means. Ildi did not have a job yet, except for a stint at Marshall Field's at Woodfield Mall in Schaumburg for the previous Christmas season, working evenings. At the time, she was selling ladies accessories about 20 hours a week while the kids were in school. We had to think of the considerable jump in our mortgage, higher taxes and other ancillary expenses, such as furnishing a larger house. After a few weeks of thinking we signed the papers. It was November, 1976.

Before going home, we drove around town and stopped at the elementary school, where the Girls would be enrolling. Erika was in first grade, Andrea would start her schooling here. We went to the handsome beach, that was familiar. We came to swim in the actual Crystal Lake the previous summer and picnicked in the attractive beach park. The entire town made a good impression on us.

* * *

We had a pleasant surprise in that autumn. Berci -- Dr. Bertalan Varga -- looked us up. His call out of the blue came from Kansas City, saying that he will be in Chicago for a few days. He came to attend a medical convention and wanted to know if we can get together. I happily assured him: yes, of course. He stayed at the Hilton on Michigan Avenue.

Berci was one of my classmates in Pannonhalma. He was in Kansas City for a six months research fellowship. It was fortunate that he could arrange to attend this Chicago convention. Andrea and I went in to pick him up on a Friday evening. At the time I knew little about him, only that he was a doctor and lived in Budapest. -- We did not even graduate together. Berci had a serious illness in the middle of our sophomore year and missed months of school. He was in the top quintile of the class, but missing so much, he dropped a year and came back again as a sophomore. He was fond of saying that this entitled him to attend the reunions of both of his classes -- and he did go to most.

I saw him again at our 25th class reunion in 1979, the only one I attended. Berci was a simple guy from a smallholder farmer family but had done very well for himself. Having a family background that the regime favored, he was accepted to medical school, despite being the graduate of Pannonhalma. Married another doctor, and while becoming a member of the professional elite, he remained a down-to-earth fellow and the nice guy I knew back in school. He loved intellectual conversations and politics, so we had a lot to talk about. He and I saw things quite the same way. I liked that we could exchange personal experiences that affected and shaped us in different worlds, since high school.

We got together twice more in later years, when we visited them in Budapest. The last time, at the end of our visit in the summer of 2001, I stayed behind to spend another day, after the rest of my family came home. Berci was not well, but his wife Ági said that with medications, his condition was manageable. A stroke in 2001 partially incapacitated him, and he died as a result of the second one a year later.

* * *

In the middle of buying a new house, I changed jobs. We lived in Hanover Park, but were committed on the new house. I went to work for Wausau Insurance Companies, where the Highly Protected Risk program was being initiated, using the model from other companies, that were in that sector of the business for many years. I was well versed in the field and took part in training employees, who did not previously deal with the discipline of this type of fire protection. The change added its own measure of uncertainty, but I soon proved my worth to the company and advanced at a greater rate than I would have otherwise. I also found the work environment more to my liking, with the less structured inspection and review procedures. (This condition lasted for about ten years, when I began to see signs of increased centrally controlled bureaucracy that reminded me of Factory Mutual, the kind that stifle creativity and bring on more burdensome working conditions, but do not really produce a better product.)

The winter of 1976-77 was the coldest I ever remember. A freezing air mass settled over us that winter. It arrived suddenly in mid-November and let up only in early March. In the middle of it we had a 32 day period, when the temperature did not rise above 0 degree F. The ground froze 5 ft deep. I know this from personal, or rather professional experience. I was still with Factory Mutual. The famous amusement park, Great America (now Six Flags) in Gurnee, IL was under construction and we insured the entire project. I spent many hours there, looking at blueprints, water systems and construction drawings of some 60 buildings and rides. The campus was criss-crossed with underground piping for the fire protection system. The pipes were laid the previous autumn and were already charged with water. There were three underground pipe breaks that winter. They were detected by maintenance employees, after water came up and froze into large patches of ice along the sidewalk. I was present at the dig-up of one of them. There I saw that the pipe was buried five ft. deep, instead of the recommended six, designed for Midwest winters. It was a rare lesson. Here we had an example of a contractor fudging a little on standards. The pipe could have lain there for many decades, nobody knowing. -- Six ft. is good, why not five? It surely was not -- not in this case. During this cruel winter I witnessed many frozen sprinkler systems, all over around Chicago.

It was a pleasure to see this huge project come to life in the following months. I received a gift from the park: free pass for the family. We were among the first visitors when the park opened. It was one of the most treasured gifts to Erika and Andrea, who visited the park many more times in succeeding years.

Great America was the largest construction job I worked on. There were two other big, famous projects, early in the 1970s: Sears Tower and Woodfield Mall. We at Factory Mutual insured the general contractor for the building phase. My responsibilities involved a lot of plan review and many visits to the sites. At the time, the Tower was the tallest building and the Mall, the largest in-door shopping center in the world. It became only bigger since. -- Other long term, big insured projects, were the many plants of Caterpillar in the Peoria area and Joliet, the farm equipment manufacturer, John Deere, both with many huge buildings and the Brookfield Zoo on large, varied acreage. Inspections of unusual businesses brought surprises and were an opportunity to get an insight into interesting processes and operations. -- I found one of the most inventive solutions to promote employee efficiency in the office at the Caterpillar corporate office, downtown Peoria. On the top of their six-story, glass block office building, they built a small penthouse to contain only one thing, a giant coffee brewer. From there, the favorite beverage was piped to coffee stations throughout the building. When I saw it, it has been in operation over a decade without a problem. The "V.P." of coffee operations (a building custodian) worked there full time. His work was likely subject to more scrutiny by fastidious fellow employees, than any other job in the office.

46

Family Life — Growing Up In Crystal Lake

In Crystal Lake, we were told by the builder, that our new house should be done by June. During that cold spring, we visited the area a few times, trying to find our *street* (for months, just tracks of frozen mud) to check on progress, but saw none for many weeks. The ground was unworkable until a thaw in late spring. A lot of snow also fell in that cold winter. First we had to wait for that to melt. The area was farmland prior to development. Later the ground let up and we had mud, knee deep. All this delayed the start until middle of March. We had to time the sale of our old house, to coincide with the completion of the new one. In April we put it on the market. To save money, we wanted to sell it ourselves. One Sunday we put an ad in the paper and four days later, sold it.

In late March, we were able the first time, to approach the construction site. The outlines of the street were not well defined, but we saw hydrants. After the ground sufficiently dried, we were able to get close enough to take pictures of the foundation and later of the frame, partially up.

The Hanover Park house sold in April 1977, for $55,000, thanks in part to our attractive interior decoration. The price reflected the inflation of intervening years. We were happy with our gain. When we signed the contract on the new house, we added basement, a fireplace and some other extras, that increased the purchase price to $80,000. The house was the Augusta model, the nicest and largest of those offered by the builder. This move-up gave us a feeling of accomplishment with and a sense of luxury, that appealed to us but took a while to get used to. It was a new adventure, full of promise. The town was clearly more desirable than our old address. It was an older, established town, with existing comforts and services. The lake, with its attractive park and beach house has always been a draw for Sunday bathers from around the area.

Crystal Lake schools had a good reputation, that they retain till today. We saw this during our parent's night visits and years later, when we went college hunting for the Girls. When we signed up Erika at Illinois State University, we told the registrar that she graduated in District 155 in Crystal Lake. She said, that was the only information she needed. She said, it was not important to see Erika's ACT scores. The district's reputation alone was satisfactory for admission.

Crystal Lake got its name from the lake, that was known for its pure water. Ice cut from it a hundred years ago, was the cleanest, and most desired by hotels in Chicago and industries around. Then it was the only means of cooling things in hot summer days. The ice business was the largest employer for years.

Our interest rate on the new mortgage was 7.45, ½% higher than the old one. We were happy, because in the Carter years, inflation and interest rates were on the way up, peaking above 12%.

With the old house selling so well, we were able to put down more, while also leave some money in the bank. Our new mortgage was $46,000. The revised date for the completion of the house was early August. We closed on the 5th and moved in the next day.

An interesting thing happened two weeks before we took possession of the house. During a visit we noticed a 12 ft long crack in the tall chimney for the fire place. Talking to the builder, we learned that they already knew about it. Lightning did the damage in a storm the night before. They assured us that it will be fixed in time. When the house was turned over to us, the chimney was repaired. They had to tear down and rebuild, brick-by-brick, the upper 2/3rd of it. The day we moved in, the house was immaculate, cleaned and vacuumed throughout. It was good to see. We felt that we bought a house that we thought we can never afford. Its comfortable size, the four bedrooms and the general plush looks were pleasing. The woodwork especially, was appealing with its nice dark color and matte finish. We valued the luxury we could provide for ourselves, after coming to a new country with nothing, and speaking no English, only 20 years before. We've been counting our blessings and gave much of the credit to America.

It was exciting to start new things, as we did in Hanover Park seven years earlier. This time we sodded, that gave us a nicer lawn with less work. I installed shelves and started the garden, where we grew beans and tomatoes, for the nostalgic pleasure of seeing things grow.

Our neighbors were friendly. Occasionally we got together with a few, but in time they all moved. I recall only one unpleasant neighbor, living next door in the late 1980s. Thank God, he stayed less then a year. He had two dogs, that he kept outside. They barked several hours, any time of the day or night, without reason that I could see.

Our assigned address was 835, the first house built on Huntington Drive. By the fall, half the street was done. In the next spring the city planted trees. We also planted some in the yard, along with flowers. On the second summer I brought home a maple sapling I dug out on the beach at Moose Lake. It was just a stick, about 2 ft. high and barely ¼ in. diameter. A friend told me later that it is a giant maple. Indeed, it is now the tallest tree on the block, despite being at least four years behind the others.

I was surprised how soon the first change in ownership occurred. People were just as mobile here as were in our old neighborhood. We count as special blessing, one neighbor, Jim and Helen Moore, who live behind us. We face each other through our joining back yards. Today we are the only original owner on our street. All the other houses changed owners at least three times. The original children grew up and moved out one way or another. A *second generation* of kids moved in the street a few years later. Today, we have yet another group of little ones. They are the third such generation in the neighborhood.

We got to know the three daughters of the Moores and saw the grandchildren grow up. They played in the backyard at various family gatherings, to some of which we also were invited. Marilyn had Heather, Kara and Victoria, all successful adults now. We attended the wedding of the youngest Moore daughter, Nancy, in 1980; and the wake of Shirley in 1996, who died of cancer at 44, leaving behind Jimmy and an infant daughter, Hana. Through all this we remained good friends, often sharing stories and took part in each other's family events. We are grateful for our good fortune, that of all the people who moved in around us in 1977, the Moores are the ones that stayed here the longest. Nancy's husband Oscar has beautiful operatic voice. He is singing small parts at the Lyric Opera in Chicago. Recently he gave a solo concert, to which he invited us. He was very humble about his fame, but Nancy and her boys, Michael and Matthew were gleaming. Recently he sang Alfredo, in Verdi's *Traviata* at Court Theater at on the campus of Northwestern University.

* * *

After Erika was born and while the Girls were growing up (1969-84) Ildikó had no full time job. She worked part time, starting in 1976. The first in the series was as Christmas help at Marshall Field's, later at Paddors, a women's dress shop, also in Woodfield Mall. After we moved to Crystal Lake, she had a similar position locally (Lynn Stevens). She was home to greet the children after school. Later she spent two years in the china department at Bergner's -- now Carson Pirie Scott & Co. This was perhaps the most satisfying of these temporary positions. The atmosphere at Begner's was not hurried and less demanding. Toward the end of her stay, she bought a most beautiful Mikasa china set, at a very attractive saving, combining the manufacturer's, seasonal and employee discounts. It is our favorite dining set, along with a uniquely delicate sterling silverware set that her mother scouted out in a Milwaukee antique shop few years earlier. Whatever Ildi earned, we put toward the Girls' college fund.

For years, Ildi sewed the Girls' dresses and got many compliments. Indeed, those were the nicest garments they wore in childhood.

The Girls were always good sisters. I recall only a handful of short-lived quarrels between them, none lasting longer than overnight. Erika was a leader, always full of ideas about play and games, some of which she invented. This talent and her profession as a teacher are aiding her mothering instincts, that makes her a wonderful mother to the apple of her eye, Tyler.

Andrea was her admiring follower, in the early years. She grew up to be a self-assured woman, with well considered, strong opinions. As a mother, she is effective instilling in her children courtesy, good manners and the principle of fair play. She is raising two wonderful girls.

* * *

One day in 1974, when I was working at home, I heard noise from the yard below. I looked out and saw Erika, directing her sister and neighbor friend Christie, as she put on a show for mothers in the neighborhood. She lined up folding chairs for her audience and was directing her friends, prompting them when they faltered and taking the starring role herself -- of course. The audience was Mrs. Moore, Mrs. Dollahan, Mrs. Bucklar, mother of Christie and two small neighbor kids. I had the presence of mind to take a picture of the *cultural event*, so we have a permanent record.

For Erika, beginning in her pre-teen years, the important things were not material but the principle that some privileges were due the older sister, before they are granted to the younger one. In her view, to achieve this has taken too long. I was not fully aware of her frustration, for we raised them with even hands, applying control and granting privileges equally. Around the time she was in junior high, she challenged us about curfews, free time away from home and about the places she wanted to frequent. She accused us of favoring Andrea, by granting her the same privileges, for which she alone fought hard and long. She argued, that it was not fair, that as soon as she achieved them for herself, we also granted them to Andrea.

We certainly wanted to be even handed. Since they had only 1½ year between them, it was easy to treat them, dress them and love them the same, as one would do twins. I thought, sometimes we overdid it. There were occasions when they received not identical gifts, but comparable ones. The one who perceived to have been shortchanged, complained. Also, when one had a birthday, the other also received some gift -- thanks in large part to doting relatives. At one point I explained to them that life is not always fair and things don't always have to be the same for both.

The attainment of some extra freedom was one issue that caused friction. An interesting aspect of the problem was that Andrea was far less active in advocating them. But when we granted Erika a later curfew, soon Andrea too received it though she did not ask for it. It was not favoritism, we just didn't consider it important. Eventually we worked out the differences and the issue faded.

Erika had separate friends, a few girls and many potential boys in waiting. She could pick as she wanted. For Andrea, solid friendships were more important. At times, each was jealous of what the other had. Erika was looking for a kind of fun in school, that we did not consider strictly part of the high school experience. She liked special activities and others that she pursued by friends. Among electives, she liked photo class in which she excelled and astronomy, that she liked. We talked about stars and galaxies and compared knowledge. She knew more than her father.

They played tennis, starting as juniors and were quite successful as No. 2 doubles. Erika quit the program for her senior year. Andrea continued, but her favorite was basketball, that she played all four years. She continued in both sports in college. They were not just sport, but also important part of her social life.

Erika taught me the phrase, *senior ditch day.* She explained, that it was an *honored* tradition, at least for some students, who it seems, were considering it a warm-up for parties in the coming college life. Still, our prior efforts of instilling in her good values, kept her on the straight and narrow. This experimental period ended in her last year.

Something crystallized in her, as she approached the end of high school. She wanted to be a teacher. Her senior-year foolishness passed and in its place I saw purpose, that suddenly occupied her thoughts and concentrated her efforts. We found it the most natural development and thought that the profession she chose suited her well. Our, and her expectations were fulfilled and today it is a pleasure to see what meaning and enjoyment she finds daily, in handling, teaching and attending to kids.

The defining change in Erika's life was Jim. Jim, is James Ferguson -- Jamie, as Erika affectionately calls him. He was Erika's first and only love. They were married on the 11th of June 1994.

Erika was pursued by a number of boys in school, but took none of them seriously. It was love at first sight with Jim, or something close to it. After their memorable meeting at K-mart, I remember only two short brakes in their relationship. Proms and other events followed. After 7 years of courting, that included the four years at ISU, they thought themselves mature and ready for matrimony.

Even early on, it seemed that they were meant for each other. Now, with the perspective of the past dozen years, it is even more evident. At the outset we could not be so sure about either of them, for they were too young. We were not sure that they could take commitment seriously. The relationship endured a few minor bumps, but overall I see it as a success, we rarely see today. They love each other and cherish a special friendship with intense fervor. For each of them the company of the other fills the day with pleasure and joy. Their marriage made them better, happier and more loving people.

I recall the few ups-and-downs, early in the courtship. They met at K-mart in their junior year, as fellow employees. Erika's favorite story is, that when she first met him, they exchanged just a few words. Minutes later another girl told Erika about the high shelves, from which she had trouble taking down boxes. Erika told her that she cold not be much help, but knows someone who surely could.

"I just met this tall, strong guy, Jim. I'm sure he can do it." (Jim is 6'6").

Jim was there soon and the problem with the high shelf was solved. -- Something else also started -- and never ended for them. Dating, courtship, prom and other good times followed. The relationship endured, getting stronger with time. We saw, how much they loved each other's company. -- There were a few glitches, that were painful for her. She never looked at another boy, after she met Jim, though he may have looked around at times during the first year of courtship. I recall two occasions, when our usual evening talk was spent discussing Jim and the pain he caused by avoiding her. One was especially painful. Toward the end I said that she should forget him at least for a while by liberating herself from him.

"Look around you Sweetheart. You are young, pretty and popular. It is not the end of the world, in fact it may open new doors for you. Look at yourself, how miserable you are. With all my consoling, I still can't make a dent in your grief."

"Dad, it is hard and painful now", she answered. "But the good times greatly outnumber the bad ones and they are more meaningful. I'm sure that he is the right one and he will come back to me because he will want to". -- And she was right. That was their last serious quarrel. Since then, they are inseparable.

Andrea was consistent in picking friends, all classmates, going back to elementary school. They are still close. Erika considers them her friends too, which they freely reciprocate. Sleep-overs at our house were frequent and enjoyable for kids and parents alike. I, an early riser, remember carefully stepping over them in the family room, where six-seven girls were sleeping in their bags in front of the fireplace. Their nonstop gab-sessions lasted late into those Friday nights and it made it harder for them to wake up next morning. They provided us with entertainment that originally was meant for them alone. They put on a *show* for themselves, but soon Ildi and I were invited to watch.

This gave me a window to their world, that was imaginative and sweetly innocent. It was a pleasure to see the abandon, with which they pursued their pure, unique and seemingly limitless *happiness*, that is the exclusive province of adolescent girls. (I wonder if our founders ever thought of such, when they pondered the special and daring phrase in the Constitution about that *right*, that God bestowed on all "men". I have rarely seen a more eager *pursuit* of it by our girls.) Once the mouth got going, telling some important story, the words came out faster than I could listen.

I know that sleep-over at our house was a coveted event. Our little guests were behaving impeccably, seemed to enjoy and felt free in the ambiance we and the house provided, while always conscious of the rules and the care we placed on order in the house and the respect we had for our furniture and decorative objects. Years later I found out that they were impressed with this and had a name for our house, based on how it seemed to them. They affectionately dubbed it the *museum*. I considered it as a compliment and was happy that they recognized the value of nice things and art objects that can enhance the beauty of a home and how one feels in it.

Now those old friends of Andrea and Erika are married and most are mothers. We see them as friends too and keep in touch with them through the Girls and sometimes directly. The favorites were two Sharons, that were perhaps closest to Andrea. Both are still living nearby. We see them in church, at family gatherings and while walking or biking.

Sharon Flaherty -- now Oeffling -- was a psychology major. Their friendship began in elementary school. She now is working in the local school district as a social worker. Her first job, right after graduation, was working for Ildi at Sheltered Village.

I consulted Sharon on the four personality types I wrote about, on the first pages of this book. I asked her to confirm that those arcane terms are still understandable today. She put my mind at ease, saying that she remembers them, and the categories still make sense. -- Sharon had twins last year. Seeing her attending to them, I saw the change that motherhood makes in a woman. I saw an interesting blend of a responsible adult, mixed in with her old perky self, full of jokes, vigor and good times.

Sharon Nicholson -- now Blake -- affectionately called, Rose (a word-play within the family, derived from the *rose of sharon*) was jogging once, pushing her son Wyatt in a three wheeled jog-stroller. I was on my way to the bank when I spotted them. I doubled back, interrupting her exercise for a little update on their life. In 2002 she had Madelyn, a sweet addition to her family.

Today, Sharon is teaching English, to be specific: creative writing, in Cary-Grove high, Jim's old school. I asked her for some pointers about writing and if she would be interested in reading parts of this text. I wanted an outside opinion on the feel of it and whether she would find it worth reading. She read a good part of it, approved and encouraged me to go on.

Another friend, a true artistic soul, Ericka Plate -- now Lavin -- is doing well as a glass artist. We admired the gift she made for Andrea's wedding. It is an elaborate stained glass picture frame with lilies interwoven in a white background. The flowers and leaves, with their number, *spell* out the date of the wedding: September 4. -- She also made a decorative Hungarian coat of arms, dedicated to "Magyar". It was Andrea's Christmas gift to us in 2001.

Another close friend of Andrea is Tricia Morrison -- now Galagher. Tricia was the point guard on the team in high school, where Andrea played post. Basketball was the most favorite sport for them. Much of their friendship was around that, and they kept close in recent years, after being separated during college years. Tricia lived far away for a few years, but settled nearby after graduation. Now they play as much as their busy schedule allows. Tricia has two children, that forced her to limit her favorite activity, but the friendship and the dominant new interest -- motherhood -- brings the girls together often.

47

Pleasures Of Camping

For about 20 years, our favorite mode of vacationing was camping. I was surprised how much I liked it, after at first being skeptical about *roughing it*. Ildikó encouraged me to change my attitude toward this simple and nature-friendly way to see beautiful places in the country.

I soon realized how simple and commom-sensical her idea was. Also, that this could be an economic and practical way of vacationing as the children were growing up. For a few years it enabled us to go on family vacations, stay within our means and see the country on the cheap. Ildi thought that taking most of our vacations this way, would helps us saving for college and for our own future. Soon I took to camping, as a fish to water. The experience alone, separate from seeing sights, was enjoyable. The kids liked it from the get-go and are still doing it with their families. Both men had to be taught, just as I was, that there is a lot of fun in camping, having good teachers. They enjoy going several times each summer.

(Recently Erika and Jim took us along on a long weekend in their new camper. We were glad to go and had a good time.

We spent the time like in the old days, except this time we were the guests. It was great, nostalgic fun.)

People who go camping are a special lot. With very few exceptions those who pitch tents or pop up their campers, and even those who travel in luxurious motor-homes are down-to-earth people. Roughing it, came to mean something different than what the words imply. Most people joke about it, implying only minor discomfort, perhaps referring to the lack of TV, that we have to walk to the toilet and to take a shower and a few other things. Camping today could provide all that and does too, at many camp sites. To me, this aspect of intimating forest living was the proverbial spice that made camping interesting and more fun. Going to take a shower early in the morning, I usually was the first up so early. I am a kind, that likes to greet the cock before it crows. Campfires are every kid's favorite. It allows them stay up late, because bedtimes and wake-up times are a flexible rule when camping.

I like to think that we got more out of the experience than most, just because the way we set our priorities. The important thing was to have a relaxing vacation. But we planned the bigger trips carefully and with purpose. Ildikó deserves most of the credit. She is a thorough and excellent planner with diligence and good judgment on where to go, what to see or avoid. Erika inherited her talent. The Püskis were frequent companions and very good company, adults and kids alike. They were camping, years before we did. Their experience was helpful for us in starting and selecting places to go. They started with a small tent, then a bigger one, but bought a camper similar to ours, after they saw the advantages of living off the ground and having a real door and roof, that can better shut out the elements.

For us, the experiment started in 1975, when on a summer Friday afternoon we all went about 180 miles west to the Mississippi for a trial run. The Püskis brought their new large tent and loaned their old one to us. We went to a campsite near Savanna and set up for a week's stay. Ildi and I had the old Püski tent for two nights. Gabi, Edith and the four kids slept in the new big one. It was not the most comfortable two nights I spent, but hoped that later things would improve. Gabi and I stayed two days, then left our wives there with the four kids for the week.

Gabi and I came home on Sunday and returned again the following Friday. The five girls and Richard, had a wonderful time living in the big tent. Next weekend Ildikó and I again slept in the tiny canvas contraption. I knew that camping for us will not be in a tent. Otherwise it was fun and just needed a little getting used to.

Another practice run helped us further. It was an upgraded form of camping. We found Crazy Horse, a campsite in the Great Smoky Mountains where they rented out campers that were permanently parked on site. Ildi's mother came along. It was a new experience for all of us.

After that pleasant experience we visited all the camper dealers in the area and in Elgin we found a one year old Coachmen, a 16 ft. pop-up camper, for $1,500. It had comfortable sleeping room for six, great for the four of us. We considered it a luxury after our short stint in tents. The Püskis also saw it as a better way to spend vacations and in about a year, bought their own. Ours had ample room for storage, as campers go. It had gas stove and ice box. Soon we made simple changes to fit our purposes better. The ice box became a storage compartment and we put a small refrigerator on top of it. This way we had a proper way to keep perishables. The cooler and the refrigerator allowed us to take frozen things on long trips and keep them from spoiling. Hookup, directly to camp site piping supplied our ready fresh water. In many campgrounds a site with electricity and water hookup cost $4-5 those days. (Ironically, one of our worst camping experience was near Virginia Beach, where on a holiday weekend we paid $24 for one night. The place was the only one in this popular vacationing area. That was why the owner could ask such exorbitant fee, despite operating an unattractive, dirty place, with garbage left out from the day before. The campground was huge and crowded. Even the clientele was different than what we've been used to. A rowdy bunch of motorcyclists kept us up half the night. Edith had enough after a while and confronted them and their rude noise-making. They quieted down after that -- perhaps because it was already past 2 A.M.)

I had a permanent hitch installed on the car and we brought our camper home. The first night we parked it in the garage at the kids' request, before we permanently parked it by the side of the house. They wanted to *christen* their new "little house on the prairie", by having a sleep-over. It was enormous fun for them so they did it a few more times after that.

Driving with a camper in tow, was a new experience for me. Everything was clumsier and a little slower. It affected acceleration and made me very cautious passing. The most difficult things, however, were parking and backing up. I admire the skill of drivers of big rigs. The double jointed moves the car and camper made while moving backward, were not easy to master. I had to do it with only the mirror and people yelling instructions to me, but I learned. We loved the pull-through sites that made parking easy.

We went to nearby campgrounds for a while. This we could do for a weekend on the spur of the moment and with minimum of planning. Later we went to places far away that became great vacations. We told friends about a few memorable trips. They were surprised how versatile this type of vacationing could be.

Before going on, and to complete the list, I should mention two more family vacation. Ildi and I took off time, while grandparents moved in to watch the kids. We went on a Caribbean cruise in 1975 and spent a fortnight in Hawaii in 1980. The trips were memorable for being such new experiences for us.

After a couple weekend trips nearby, we went to Florida on our first, long camping vacation. On the way there, we stopped in Cumberland Gap Park at the border region of Kentucky, Tennessee and Virginia, along the Wilderness Road. Trailblazer and explorer Daniel Boone cleared those valleys in 1775. We did our own pioneering, camping overnight and in more comfort than did old Daniel. There was a difference between this and a motel: the setting. It was closer to forest- rather than urban living. The experience of our first night under the stars was exciting.

The first long distance tour was wonderful. We settled down for more than a week near Fort Myers. The city was Thomas Edison's winter residence. He had a large estate with elaborate laboratory facilities (now exhibit halls) where many of his inventions are displayed and his creative life documented. He had a pier at the end of his property, where he's said to have spent time fishing -- though according to our guide, rarely caught anything. Maybe needing a rest, he only pretended to pursue this passive sport. His mind was probably working on things other than catching fish.

The Girls were busy in the sand and water all day. I learned a thing about hair on this trip. Ildi used to curl Erika's very straight hair on special occasions. If it was on a humid summer day, the curls soon went back to straight strands. Andrea had her natural curls and never needed such artificial training. The difference between the hair of the girls became glaringly obvious as soon as we arrived in Florida. Erika had her strait hair hanging as it always had, but Andrea acquired a new do in the natural way: her waves became tighter and gave her a new and distinctive look with the dense, exaggerated curls. It was obvious that humidity enhanced the natural characteristic of hair in either tendency.

To explore the area on a Sunday afternoon, we drove around beautiful Sanibel Island. It is almost white, because its *sand* is all crumbled sea shells, broken to tiny pieces and polished through millennia. We drove and drove, enjoying the sights and nearly ran out of gas, because almost everything was closed on this peaceful place.

Our next vacation was again in the Smokys. In 1976 we went back to the Crazy Horse campground in Tennessee. The Püskis also came, still in a tent. On a rainy night it collected water on the roof that was not pulled taut enough, collapsing the tent. I think this was their incentive to switch to a camper.

The biggest attraction for the kids this time was the newly installed water slide, something we saw the first time. We did all our favorite activities: swimming, tennis, hiking and sitting for long hours by a campfire. The park was just a few miles outside Gatlinburg, the charming center of the region, full of shops, hotels and restaurants. To our surprise we found an antique shop that had beautiful and expensive things, we did not expect to see in a small town. Of course, we bought nothing. Prices were far above our pay-grade, but just perusing the art pieces was a pleasure. It had European antiques, the likes of which I saw only in the best galleries.

We were always on the lookout for good places for camping. Once at work I overheard conversation by colleagues, talking about a camping place, a state park in Indiana: Turkey Run. I never heard of it before, and was curious. One guy was extolling its picturesque beauty and fine facilities.

I told Ildikó about it and soon we went there. It became our favorite place for years. It had gorgeous gorges, a creek with waterfalls, big pool, tennis courts, trails for every taste, level of hiking skill and endurance. It was surrounded by forests and lush central Indiana farmland. We found it clean, well run and equipped for camping comfort. I think we attended every nature outing or presentation they offered. Naturalists lead daily walks and put on nature programs, interesting and informative to all ages. The kids signed up to clean up part of a trail and earned their *Junior Park Ranger* badge.

The park had an attractive lodge, with dining and entertainment. We inquired about a possible stay there for the future. The rates were quite high and reservations were taken for a year in advance.

Years later, after we sold the camper, we came back, this time to stay in the lodge. In 2001 we reserved a room just for Ildi and me, to spend a few days there. It was a nostalgic and emotional return where we saw reminders behind every turn. The place was a little different. We visited the campground only in passing. We were just as busy on that weekend as during past visits. We tracked through most of the trails and refreshed our fading memories about details and noticed a few changes. It was comforting to know that the loveliness of the park was retained by leaving it to nature and allow her to make the changes as she saw fit. Trees grow and some fall, but the air and feel of the place is constant -- and that's good.

The Püskis, just the two of them, joined us there again, as they did times before. They also stayed in the lodge. We again took advantage of the programs the park offered. In the front courtyard, the inn sponsored free concerts of country and folk music on two consecutive evenings.

During the first concert, I noticed a huge flock of swallows circling above the lodge as dusk approached. Their circle was getting smaller and suddenly they disappeared on the far side. I got up to see if I can spot where they went. My guess was that they went into a tall chimney at the back of the building. It was too late to find out for sure. The next evening they were back, doing as they did the night before. This time I walked around the building and watched their progress. Indeed, the gradually shrinking, swirling circle was around the big chimney. When it was reduced to a size of about 20 ft. in diameter, the birds suddenly, en masse, dove into the opening at the top. At the end, the swirling circle of about 150 swallows, disappeared into the opening within a minute.

Next morning I described the event to hotel employees. They received it as news, and were not as excited about it as I was. (They knew and cared *less* about their swallows, then I did.) A lady in the office told me that the tall chimney of the dining room fireplace was decommissioned several years ago. For me this interesting event was a rediscovery of one of nature's wonders. It was a lucky, accidental find and it involved my favorite birds, evoking childhood memories. I recounted the event to Józsi, when I called him after we returned home. He was not surprised. He said, a chimney can be good nesting place for swallows. It is a quiet and undisturbed home in the summer months.

We visited many camping sites and can count most of them as pleasant stays. Some of the most picturesque places nearby, were Devil's Lake in Wisconsin and Starved Rock State Park along the Illinois River near Ottawa.

Later we ventured far, to see parts of the country, that were famous for their spectacular beauty, wildlife, and known as camping vacation spots. Ildiko's father, Béla, (Apu) was visiting us in 1979. This was his second trip to the States. He was eager to come camping with us to Kentucky and North Carolina, despite lacking relevant experience. He liked to picnic and walk in the hills and forest around Zilah, but camping was an American thing. We assured him, that we can provide the basic comforts. (No indoor plumbing at home. That was one of the things that was taken from him, when the communists took away his house and land. So in that respect camping was more comfortable for him, than his circumstances at home.)

On the whole, the new experience agreed with him. He took things in stride. He was not a whining type. During the day we went on hikes, on some of which he joined us. Evenings were spent with long talks around the campfire, usually after some nature movie or slide show in the amphitheater.

We made a whole-day outing to Asheville NC, to the magnificent Biltmore Estate of the Vanderbilt family. We visited the place once before, but were glad to see it again. The building is a beautiful example of the French chateau style architecture. It is on a huge estate of forests, rolling hills, meadow and farmland. It seemed to me that after we passed through the gate which is within the town of Asheville, we would never see the building, at the end of the longest driveway I've ever traveled. It was a true forest drive, winding through pleasant woods, by farms through picturesque scenery. (On the way out I measured it: 3 miles long.)

I cannot remember the number of rooms. Most of them we did not see anyway. The main part of the ground floor, the aviary, dining room and the double stairway were unforgettable. No expense was spared on its construction. The double-decker spiral stairway (two independent stairways sandwiching each other, as two corkscrews placed tandem) is a copy of the one at Chambord and a few other chateaux in France.

My father-in-law had a good and comfortable time for most of the trip, but at the end we all suffered from stifling, humid heat. On the way home we had to find a motel to cool off for the night. In Benton IL, after much search, we found one motel room, big enough for five -- one with air-conditioning. The girls were happy to take to the floor, as long as the cool air was flowing.

* * *

For my 50th birthday the family treated me to a hot air balloon flight. I was wishing for and talking about it for a while, so it was a welcome gift. Windy City BalloonPort is in Fox River Grove, where the other big attraction is the Norge Ski Jump that is open year round. It has been operating since 1905.

Ballooning is a pastime that requires specific conditions: calm air and mild temperatures, if possible. Thus, balloonists fly only during summer. The most important factor is wind. It must be less than 5 mph, otherwise the mission could be in jeopardy. Even this way, the direction of the craft is totally subject to wind. A skilled pilot can move higher or lower by firing up his LP tanks and if he is lucky, find air movement slightly different in speed or direction from where he is at any moment. Flying is only practical early morning or late afternoon until sunset. I was on standby for a few weeks, but early one morning I received a call that they are ready for a go soon after 6 A.M.

Andrea came with me for the take-off. The big, colorful, flat-on-the-ground bag was slowly tilting upward as hot air was directed into it. Soon we had to jump in the gondola and were rising ever so smoothly in silence, interrupted from time-to-time by the hissing noise of burning gas.

It was eerily quiet. Noise from the ground was minimal. A few people yelled up to us, shouting morning greetings. We flew over rural and suburban landscape. People were getting into their cars, ready for the morning drive. I saw deer several times, running in and out of wooded groves looking for water.   I was watching our chaser following us the best he could, taking turns trying to find roads, so he can be close when we touch ground.

We crash-landed at the edge of a large home development project in Bannockburn, where at the early stages, they were still grading and pouring foundation. The slight breeze still dragged us a distance, while we held on for dear life, leaning 30-40 degrees to the ground. It was a little rougher than I expected, having been spoiled by such a smooth flight. As the chase car approached, we popped open a bottle of champagne to celebrate the event. This, and a bumpy truck ride back, are the customary finish for this unique flying experience.

48

Camping In America
And Visits To Europe

In 1979, after seven years we again flew to Europe. The Girls were 8 and 9. It was the highlight of the year. This time, beside family visits, we also saw other nice places, others than Hungary.

At Tomi's suggestion, we traveled north from Munich, on the *Romantic Road.* This name was given to the region in Bavaria, from Munich north to Heidelberg and Würzburg . The name is apt. The Road takes the traveler from one nice town to another, through charming countryside. The crown jewel of the region is Rothenburg on the Tauber river, a beautifully preserved medieval city, protected by high, 15 ft. wide stone wall with many gates. On the top it is a spacious walkway that tourist use on their walk to circle the city. We spent a day, discovering as much as we could and took part in a few activities. At the end we wished we could stay in Rothenburg, but there were other places to see.

In 1981 we took a trip with our camper around Lake Michigan. It was an easy ride, with stops wherever we wanted. Holland, MI was the first. The city prides itself as the tulip capital of the US, but is quiet when tulips are not in bloom. For us then, it was not much more than a curiosity and a place for lunch. Sault Sainte

Marie, was interesting. It is a Canadian border town on the St. Joseph Channel, connecting Lakes Superior and Huron. We stayed the night and in the morning, watched the heavy ship and barge traffic through the locks.

The real treat on this trip was Mackinac Island at the north end of Lake Huron. We took the ferry, and explored the island on foot with everyone else. Cars are not allowed there, only horse-drawn carriages and bicycles. We biked around the island -- about an eight mile trip. The weather was exceptionally good, clear, warm with a slight breeze. The girls rented a tandem, but were not happy at the end. Each found it restrictive, but it was OK for once, as a novelty. In the yard of Fort Mackinac, which is now a museum, we saw a demonstration of military gear, including a cannon shoot and shots by rifle. I was amazed what loud bang a simple rifle could make. After that, soldiers in full, period military gear, conducted a mock court martial, patterned from history. It concluded with conviction and execution -- also mock, of course, but convincing.

We had the idea to use the camper in other ways. I proposed seeing Washington D.C. while camping nearby. We found a site near Fairfax, VA. There we slept and spent our evenings, but we were in the city every day. It was Ronald Reagan's second year as president, a good time to visit our capital city. We again were with the Püskis. My mother-in-law Ella also came and enjoyed the history trip.

The week in D.C. flew by as in a flash. I liked the plan and setting of the city. The most memorable places we saw were the White House, Arlington Cemetery, the National Museum and all the main memorials, including those to Washington, Jefferson, Lincoln and Teddy Roosevelt -- this one on his own island.

I was surprised by the intense security of the area near Capitol Hill. It was infested with cops at every turn, even in early morning hours. I shudder to think how oppressive people-control must be today. For a tour through the White House, we just lined up with the others and were inside a short time later.

On Memorial Day, President Reagan was scheduled to make a major speech on the mall behind the Capitol. We lined up as early as we could to be close to the podium. It was very hot, but we sought shade only after the conclusion of ceremonies. It was interesting to see how the press operates and behaves. They all crammed on one platform, higher than the president's, with their mikes and cameras working constantly. I saw Sam Donaldson throw a fit over some minor cosmetic issue, abusing his cameraman, before he settled in for his broadcast with pretended dignity. Ronaldus Magnus, (my favorite name for Reagan, given him by Rush Limbaugh) made his usual great speech. It was at the time, when his policies were still called by his enemies, gleefully and disparagingly, *Reaganomics.* They chided him for trying to govern by "simplistic", supply-side principles. The good effects of his policies were not yet evident. Inflation was still high (though on the way down from the 14% high of the Jimmy Carter years). The big employment boom and the doubling of the gross domestic products were still in the future. In 1986, when the economy was in good shape, the president talked about earlier times, humoring his detractors, who were mostly silent by then -- at least on this issue. He quipped: "They don't call it 'Reaganomics' anymore!" (Two of my other favorite quotes by him, are his comment on Lyndon Johnson's domestic policy, *We fought the war on poverty, and poverty won*; and how to deal with the Soviets, *We win, they lose* -- and they did.)

We inquired about other places to visit in the area. Hillwood was highly recommended. It was the estate of the Post family. Emily, the famous author on etiquette and manors, and collector of fine art lived there. Her daughter, Dina Merrill of Hollywood fame, narrated an introductory film shown before our touring the estate. Mr. Post was the American ambassador in Moscow during the turbulent times after the Soviet proletarian revolution. For them, it was a fortunate time. The Bolsheviks were getting rid of hated vestiges of the czarist era. One can imagine the climate, when uneducated proletarians suddenly get into power. They have little appreciation for anything that was favored by the nobility and the members of the old regime. Some clever comrades took advantage of the situation, when in one swell swoop, such a trove of treasures fell into their lap, to do with them as they pleased. Most, however, had no respect for works of art and sold them for a pittance. Mr. Post and especially his wife, were collectors of fine

things and the most eager of buyers. They also had the means
that very few others had. So, the Posts made out like a bandit and
accumulated a large, sophisticated grouping of exceptional objects
of art. This added to their highly valued existing collection. In
Hillwood, I saw one that was most attractive. Many of the famous
eggs of Fabergé were on display. They are examples of the best in
art of that era.

Ildikó was also impressed by the meticulously appointed
Japanese garden behind the main house.

Our tour of the estate was one of the highlights of an eventful
and rewarding visit to Washington D.C.

The next morning we broke camp and moved on. There were
other places to see. One important stop was Mount Vernon
VA, the museum and estate of George Washington on the bank
of the Potomac. We took a guided tour to learn about this most
important father of our founding. After we toured the house, we
were delighted by the lovely garden, the outer buildings and the
burial crypts of George and Martha.

We headed south to Williamsburg. This is a fascinating, unique
town, as one of the principal cities of early American history. We
saw television programs, detailing its brilliant past, its decline
and later resurrection. Reconstruction of the town, left in ruin,
was based on a French Lieutenant's drawings, that meticulously
detailed topographic and architectural elements of the community.
I read about this huge project and wanted to know more. We
were looking forward to see a slice of life at the time of George
Washington and Benjamin Franklin. John D. Rockefeller Jr. was
similarly interested, and in 1926 agreed to finance the monumental
project. Since then, more than 150 government buildings and
homes of historic persons had been restored.

We were not disappointed. The flavor of the place was
illustrated by hostesses, craftsmen and militiamen who, in the
many houses open to the public, acted out, demonstrated and
documented life, as our ancestors lived it. The guides, dressed
in authentic period costumes, described daily duties and activities
of the servants in each house and that of occupants, whose names
are known, for they were prominent people in town and often,

historic figures. The town illustrated history with a sense of being back in time. Williamsburg was the capital of Virginia named in honor of William III, Prince of Orange, who governed the Dutch American provinces, fought the French and English, but became king of Great Britain after marrying the king's daughter Mary, with whom he jointly and successfully reigned. The College of William and Mary is one of the prominent institutions of higher learning, named in their honor.

We took tours through several houses and watched demonstrations that illustrated life at the end of the 18th century. The most interesting was a music shop. The intricate art of building a violin was explained in detail. Violins produced in that shop are sought by musicians. We also toured the Armory and later saw a demonstration by Minutemen, that brought the town square to life.

The next day we rewarded the kids with entertainment they favored.   Nearby was a wonderful amusement park, Busch Gardens, with fun and frolic for all. We got fashionably scared when prompted by creepy ghosts, drenched in the open boat at the bottom of the water slide, and by the end we were dead tired.

The next president to explore was Thomas Jefferson. Monticello is also a lovely place, a companion piece to Mount Vernon. The intellect and endless curiosity of Jefferson is well illustrated in his home, if the visitor is to listen to the guide and look at the books and scientific objects, displayed in the house.

Founding the University of Virginia was Jefferson's most proud achievement. The campus was quiet on a Sunday in early summer. We walked the attractive courtyard, circled by an arcaded walkway. This was our last stop before heading home.

In 1985 we planned an ambitious European trip, that became our seminal romantic vacation. Brother Tomi wrote me, detailing his plans to celebrate Mother's 75th birthday, on July 6. We last visited home in 1979. The Girls grew up and we were ready to take them to see the world, not only their grandparents. Ildikó made a change at her work. I was happy about that, regardless of everything else. She was working with chemicals, in an environment, that was unhealthy. She quit, which solved her vacation problem. I extended my three weeks vacation and we set out to see half of Europe.

Helma picked us up in Luxembourg and before leaving for Aachen, treated us to some fabulous creation of raspberries and ice cream. A fancied fruit for all of us, raspberries are the favorite of Ildi and Andrea. Made into a most delicious dessert, it was a memorable treat, served elegantly on the lovely veranda of a sweet shop, overlooking the gorgeous green gulch in the middle of the city.

We spent two days in Aachen. The night before we left, Helma and Otti gave us a lavish party, with over 20 friends invited. For the trip, Otti gave us a Volvo, a nice, big, reliable car. Early on the third day we left for Paris and spent five beautiful and exhausting days in the City of Lights. This was before the Internet became such a great source of information and travel aid, but a friend offered to arrange our hotel reservations in Paris, Lugano and Venice.

Don and Cindy Richards, neighbors, bridge partners and good friends, offered the services of Don's colleague, Walter Bortolaso, who lived in Lugano, Switzerland. Walter worked for Don, as one his field men, selling electronic equipment in Switzerland, Italy and other countries. Don was the international sales manager for Motorola and talked with Walter almost daily. This was nothing for Walter, he assured me. In fact he did a lot more than calling a few places, making reservations and arrangements for us.

Our first stop was Paris. He found rooms in a cozy old hotel in the middle of the city, at the height of tourist season. Walter even apologized, that he was not able to secure room at the hotel he thought were best for us. We were more than happy with our accommodations, but I still want to describe a few features of our little hotel. The elevator was designed for at most two people. We used it only to send up our suitcases and bring them down at the end. The rooms also, were able to accommodate no more than two. This worked out well, for the Girls had their own room and felt special. Theirs had only a sink, ours boasted a shower (designed for the skinny). We all were slim then, so it was OK. The room reminded me of the cabin on our first cruise, 10 years earlier. There too, we could hardly turn around without bumping into something. (Today's cruise ships are luxurious, with rooms as spacious as those in many hotels.)

I was happy that we had such a good location. We liked to walk, and see the city at street level -- so to speak. We made a judicious use of the Metro, but covered more kilometers on foot than under ground. We covered more of the famous places in those five days, than most tourists ever could. (At the end, Erika wanted to stay another week, but we had to keep to a tight schedule.)

We started with the best known place, the symbol of Paris, the Eiffel Tower. I enjoyed looking in, to Mr. Eiffel's tiny office on the top platform, his figure sitting at his desk, as he supervised the construction of his famous tower, 96 years before. We viewed the city in all angles, as we walked around at the top more than once, and looked down to this spectacular city, as would a bird on wings. Other tourist stops were the Invalides, Montmartre, Rodin Museum, Arc de Triomphe, and others I forgot.

We were disappointed at two highly anticipated sights. The crowd at the Louvre was such, that we thought better not to waste time standing in line, and said -- maybe next time. (The *next time* came 16 years later, when the Girls brought along their husbands -- and the crowd wisely stayed away.) My other big wish was to see Versailles. I walked through it in 1963, with Mother, Marika, Helma, Otti, Tomi and Kicsi. My memory of the palace and grounds was most pleasant and I could hardly wait to see it again.

We were there at opening time, but had trouble finding a place to park, because of the many that came before us. But the most disturbing was the more than 20 tourist buses, already disembarked. The crowd was so big, that it made the walk trough the palace unpleasant. In most rooms it was difficult to see anything but the ceiling. Our tour became a hurried walk through the long row of magnificent rooms, full of people, blocking our view. The gardens were also a let-down. They were neglected for several years and at the time of our visit, dug up in many places, as they were being put back to presentable condition, it seemed. It was ironic, that when this once beautiful and historic place was in the worst shape, so many people came to see it. Many, I'm sure, were as disappointed as we.

Beside visiting famous places, we tried to absorb the spirit of this great city. Each evening, when we got back to the hotel, we rested our aching feet and often went out to visit the neighborhood markets, to see how the locals live and have fun. The dollar was at its peak value that year. Still, the trip was quite expensive and we economized where we could. We ate at a few restaurants and tried some of the local delicacies. Brie was not widely known in the US back then. We bought some and I heard Ildi and the Girls gush over it, as they enjoyed it with a fresh baguette. I took a bite, but saved my palate for the sweets. One evening we ate an entire tart in one sitting, filled with wonderful fruits, and agreed that we were living the good life.

We looked around in the famous department store, the Gallerie Lafayette and admired its huge Tiffany style glass dome skylight on the top floor. -- As we were walking down the avenues, I would not miss the flower shops. There is no comparison. The Parisian florist have the nicest flowers and the best arrangements. The bouquets and elaborate creations they sell, can not possibly look better at their fancy destinations, than the multitude of flowers, tastefully crammed to fill all available space in their little boutiques. The inside of each shop looked like one enormous *arrangement*, a lovely picture of a flower jungle. Artful presentation of the merchandise is the best sales tool -- in no place more than a flower shop. I always looked in and was delighted with the mix of exotic and ordinary flowers, creatively arranged, hardly leaving enough room to move around. And the fragrance? Magnifique!!

Ildi scouted out a small church that I have not heard of before: San Chapelle. She wanted to see this old chapel, after reading about it. We had to search before we found it. It has beautiful gothic architecture and the most spectacular stained glass windows, the tallest in Paris, maybe in the whole country.

The last evening the Girls went to pursue their own bliss, walking the neighborhood. Ildikó and I walked to Luxembourg Garden, that was just a few blocks from our hotel. We found a little gazebo on a hill, near the middle of the park. We sat up there on a bench for almost two hours, as if Parisians, listening to the city at dusk, with its muffled noise, filtering in from the distant streets, through the old trees around us. We reminded each other of the splendid time we had sitting there quietly in the middle of the big city, just the two of us, enjoying a quiet evening at the end our last hectic, eventful day.

Leaving Paris, we went to Chartres. It boasts one of the most famous gothic churches in the world. We walked and looked, and for a while, listened in on narration of a guided tour. The guide explained in great detail the many little pictures and stories in the large, rotund, florid, stained glass window above the altar. That alone was a lesson in theology and French history. Soon we had to leave. A long road lay ahead.

We headed south toward the Loire valley, to see a few of the famous chateaux. The drive proved to be longer and more time consuming, than I expected. We wanted to sleep in a chateau-hotel for the night, but we had to find it ourselves. Around mid-afternoon we stopped at a tourist information office and learned that most of them were fully booked. At the end, the mademoiselle found one, a good driving distance away. We got lost and had to ask for directions a few times before we found it. It was a small chateau, but they gave us the best they had, the ultra luxurious suite. A beautiful, carved wood baldachin bed, with a gorgeous canopy was in the middle of the room. The Girls had their bed in a cozy alcove. The wall was decorated in impeccable taste with delicate wall-covering, giving the entire room a soft hue of pale blue. The bathroom alone, with modern, sumptuous appointments, was about the size of our room in Paris. We stayed only one night, but wished we could spend a week. A great breakfast, (no, brunch) with choices galore, was included. With all the amenities, the cost of a luxurious night seemed reasonable.

We had to postpone visiting the other famous country houses for a few years. We only saw Chateau de Chambord in a distance, but had to go on, for we did not want to fall behind our well planned schedule. We spent a pleasant night in Tours and started out fresh, early next morning. The long road lead us by Lyon, through beautiful Provence, Avignon, near Marseilles, toward St. Tropez. We were at the threshold of the famous French Riviera.

In Toulon we rented a room for the night. Our hosts, an elderly couple, advised us to put the Volvo somewhere safe. The man asked his neighbor to keep the car overnight. He obliged us, gratis. We spoke with the hosts the next morning, using the little French we knew and picked up in the past week. They spoke no English at all. We mentioned that we were going to Cannes, the famous resort and home of the world famous film festival. Upon hearing that, they became animated and most adamantly wanted to warn us of the perils in Cannes and all the thieves and pickpockets who collect there. They were gesturing forcefully, saying that we should never venture far from the car and keep our eyes on it constantly. We wanted religiously to adhere to their admonition and discussed our strategy, as we drove by St. Tropez and St. Rafael. In Cannes we were attentive, taking shifts to watch the Volvo. -- Cannes is a lovely place, with palmed paths and palaces along the seashore, wide, flowered walks and happy people -- as we could tell. With our studied vigilance we must have scared away those pesky thieves and could go on, with our pleasant memories intact.

Next stop Nice, perhaps the most famous of all the French cities, after Paris. It was a little less crowded, and as nice as we dreamed. We arrived at lunch time and settled down on the terrace of a restaurant. Ildikó said that she was wishing for a long time, to once have bouillabaisse for dinner -- but she was hungry enough and lunch would be just as good. Andrea volunteered to be partner for the large meal, made usually for two or more people. Soon our waiter brought out the huge bowl, of this sumptuous meal, containing a veritable ocean aquarium, with tentacles of lobsters and crabs hanging out on the side. Erika and I had a more mundane, but satisfying meal. We took special delight watching and listening the praise, mother and daughter lavished on the complex fish soup they were consuming with rare pleasure. Andrea was not sure about her choice at the outset, but became a true believer in French seafood concoctions, as they ate all that was in front of them. After many years, Ildi still remembers that meal as the best she ever had. She has two others to remember, that are runners-up in our family's culinary archives -- a paella in Madrid and another fantastic fish concoction in Normandy, 16 years later.

After Nice, came Monte Carlo. To me it was the ultimate of the

Mediterranean cities. This principality has a panoramic setting, that bests all others. We walked up long steps, toward the palace and discovered ever more spectacular vistas, improving on prior ones. The opulence in architecture, the yachts, the shops, captured our imagination, as to the wealth and luxury, that surrounded us as far as our eyes could see.

We peeked in at the door of the casino, but had little interest to go in. If I remember correctly, we were told that the casino had strict rules of entry (even before they would ask one about money). Irony of ironies, the principal rule for this house of vice (gambling) was the same, as the Vatican had for its churches: enter in proper attire. Wearing our shorts was more important for us than seeing the inside of this most famous house of games.

We were more keen on seeing the palace. We took the one-hour guided tour and I could not avoid thinking of Grace Kelly, the American princess, who occupied those rooms for a few fleeting years, before her untimely death, not long before our visit. As we were walking through the row of rooms of this pink palace, we came upon a large painting, depicting the Grimaldis in a casual family pose. The children were still quite young, smiling innocently in an idyllic, bucolic setting. I lingered a long time by the painting, remembering to buy a post card of it before we leave. To my disappointment, it was not among the many cards for sale in the gift shop. As we left the building, we saw that a guard took note of an approaching car and opened a small gate nearby. I noticed too, and took a better look. It was Princess Caroline driving in, letting us catch a glimpse of her.

Soon we were on our way east. Leaving Monaco, we entered Italy. The drive, hugging the seashore, seemingly, often by fingernails, became more and more spectacular in the rugged rocky terrain, through many short and a few longer tunnels. Driving demanded full attention. The view was full of beauty all around us. We *ood* and *aad* nonstop. Despite the many curves, we often saw several tunnels ahead, receding in the distance as seen through tunnels, closer up. I saw three several times and once I saw four in line ahead of us stacked up, so to speak, as so many tubes that are fit into one another. It was an unforgettable ride for 150 km, most of it breathtaking. As we approached Genoa, things settled down a little, as the huge seaport came into view.

Genoa was important in the life of Ildikó and her family. This was their second city, a semi-permanent stop after leaving Rumania. (The first was Vienna, where they applied for visa to the U.S.) -- It is another story, with interesting anecdotes, how the family managed communal living with other displaced people, biding their time, hoping that a day soon comes, when they can be on their way to the land of their dreams. Aunt Ella shared the kitchen with other women, trying to avoid being in each other's way, while each was cooking her own meal. The children, Ildikó, Kati and Steve went to catch all the movies they heard about in Rumania, but had never had a chance to see. Each received money for bus tickets, but instead of taking the bus to the theater, they walked great distances and saved the money for other films. After all, there was no school, not much work around the house, but a lot of delicious time to kill. -- Ildi lead us to the neighborhood where they once lived. For her, it was a strange feeling, remembering old times and seeing familiar places.

Later that day we drove down the coast, to Portofino. This drive was the most spectacular, even surpassing sights we saw in recent days. The view behind every curve was indescribably beautiful, with one added feature. The coast is fully built up, as the rugged terrain allows it, at times even defying imagination. The result is a spectacular combination of God's nature and the ingenuity and creativity of man. We made a number of stops to take in a part of this enchanted world laid out before us, often viewed from cliffs, high above the Mediterranean.

Portofino is in a pleasant, peaceful, picturesque bay, reminiscent of the fishing villages of the Amalfi coast, that we visited in later years. We strolled the bay, that was lined along the shore with a row of colorful buildings. We rested a little on a terrace, spooning sweet ice cream. Then we headed back, to be at the hotel before dusk.

As we approached our place in the city, we witnessed one of the finest examples of an old European tradition: promenading on the wide esplanade on the shore, along the bay. Sauntering there was the best of Genoa, leisurely talking -- surely gossiping, -- animated, about the latest goings on. We joined the throng and had hard time leaving this joyful, carefree crowd, that stayed on late into the night.

Before we went to the hotel, we remembered the most important rule of traveling in Italy. We emptied the car totally, not leaving a spec in it, as other people also advised us since Cannes. In the morning we loaded everything back in and were ready to see new sights.

Ildi told us about the world-famous cemetery in Genoa, full of great art. Wealthy Genovese honored their ancestors with beautiful statuary and elaborately decorated family mausoleums, that fill the city's main graveyard. This place is something to be seen, for it is difficult to describe. It is a veritable city, self contained within its high stone walls, massive, yet elegant gate, rows of large, beautifully decorated sarcophagi, on wide, straight rows, as so many houses on an elegant street of a city. The monuments are true works of art. We saw marble statues of patriarchs, grand ladies, children, valued pets and precious objects. They depicted family scenes, expressing sorrow for, and reverence toward the dead. There were many that would do credit to fine museums. The most touching were the ones, honoring the memory of those who died too early, especially young brides, shown in their splendid wedding regalia. On beautiful faces, artists tried to show the presage of a happy life unfulfilled, the joys and promise of motherhood, that never was. I remember, I was full of anticipation to see these historic, sacred grounds. Ildikó's prior description was vivid in my mind and proved accurate, as soon as we entered the gate. However, it took time for me to fully appreciate the true solemn beauty of this place, consecrated by the church and the memory of all those it reveres and honors within. We saw many family coats of arms and allegorical figures to help family ancestors live on in the memory of succeeding generations.

Coming out, I was muttering something about how right Ildi was and what an unforgettable experience this was for us. -- Little did I know about something else that happened while we were inside. We went to our car, thinking of new places we wanted to see, down the coast further east.

Our idyllic planning was suddenly interrupted. Trying to open the trunk, I noticed that it *was* open. We looked in and saw that a small and a large hand bag and two suitcases were gone. Left was only two, containing Ildi's and my clothing. Several major items, and the most precious ones in small suitcases were taken. All the Girl's clothing, including the two special dresses they bought for their grandmother's party, were gone as well. They were left with only the clothes on their back. I had a gold ring with black onyx and a few other things that I was sorry to part with, especially in this manner. The most precious items though, were the 21 rolls of film I shot of our trip up to that day. They contained our memories of Aachen, Paris, churches, museums, palaces, Chartres, Loire, our chateau, Toulon, Cannes, Nice, Monaco, Portofino and part of Genoa. Mementos of cities, buildings, tunnels, seascapes were lost forever.

It was difficult to pick up and just go on with the day, but there was no choice. We had to keep to our itinerary. We went strait to Milano, to do some serious shopping. Items needed ranged, from things such as tooth brushes, to party dresses and shoes. As we were heading north, the weather more and more reflected our mood. We arrived in Milano amid gloomy sky and cool rain. We were trekking through the big city with wet clothing, ducking under awnings when possible. Of the many stores we visited, only Benetton was familiar to us. It was one of the stores back in the States, for everyday fashions for girls. It was a favorite for the Kids at home. (The chain almost disappeared since then, at least around Chicago.) This familiarity was comforting and we bought several pieces for each of them. Finding affordable dresses was more difficult, but by late afternoon we found two nice white ones, and we were happy. We took only a peek into the famous gothic cathedral, then continued on our way. It was raining buckets when we arrived in Como. There were signs for bed-and-breakfast places along the road. At the end of our tumultuous day we were relieved to find a nice one. The host, a cheerful, tall, patriarchal figure spoke broken, but understandable English. We tried, but couldn't keep it inside, and told our sad story, in part to explain our state of exhaustion and long faces. He did his best to cheer us up and to a measure, succeeded. He came out with me and helped to park the car for the night, assuring me that no harm will come to it -- not under his care.

We woke up to a day, gorgeous in every respect, giving an instant boost to our collective spirit. Part of breakfast was hot cocoa. Till today, we talk about that drink. Whatever the lady did with it should be patented. We did not ask for the recipe but should have. Maybe she used magic ingredients. This breakfast, the pleasant people and the beautiful morning helped to perk up our mood.

We went to town, looking for a boat ride. The lake is long, narrow, with shape of an upside-down Y. Stretching north from Como, the largest town located at the south end, the opposing sides run parallel with each other, close enough to see both shores. The view was spectacular wherever we looked. High cliffs, adorned with villas and church steeples, made for unforgettable pictures. I tried to compensate for those we lost and shot many new ones. The boat took us up to the town of Nesso, where we got out for a half hour. We climbed steep steps to the road above the cliff and took in the view and walked down slowly, licking ice cream. The boat took us to the fork, with the view of beautiful Bellagio, that gave its name to the fabulous hotel in Las Vegas many years later. It is the point, where the right leg of the lake goes south to Lecco and the main body continues north to Domaso. Here we turned and cruised back to the city, completing another one of our unforgettable visual experiences.

Our next destination, Lugano, was not far. Entering this lovely city, we drove up the shore to our hotel, just off city center. It was a quite luxurious, modern, facility with a large pool and garden restaurant. After we settled in, we went for a swim. A handsome life guard caught the eye of Erika, saying that it would be nice to meet him. It was imaginary romance at first sight, but Andrea prevailed on her, pointing out our transitory status and busy schedule. We went to lunch.

Just as we ordered, the waiter came saying that I have a phone call. I went inside. It was Walter, wishing us "bon apetito" and wanted to know whether we found everything as we expected. I assured him, that accommodations here too, exceeded our fondest hopes. The other purpose of his call was to invite us out with his family for dinner that evening.

He came to fetch us mid-afternoon and took us to meet the rest of the Bortolasos. We toured his house, that included an atom-bomb-proof shelter. He told us that every house in Switzerland, by law, had to have one. (Ironic, I thought. The country that managed to stay out of all the big world conflicts, saw no war, perhaps since the days of William Tell, and cannot today name an enemy country, is paranoid about an atomic attack.) After that, we went to his favorite restaurant and sitting at a long table under large trees, we exchanged stories and got to know each other during a wonderful dinner.

They had two children, Katja and a younger brother, Peter. Katja's age was between that of our two girls. She spoke little English, but the three had no problem understanding one another. Soon they compared knowledge on, and challenged each other's enthusiasm, for their rock stars and discovered that their tastes were similar (no surprise there). We went back to the house and stayed late. Walter gave us good travel advise and ideas for the rest of our tour.

He also proposed that we do a girl-exchange. He thought that it would be good for Katja to see America and learn English. We welcomed his suggestion and invited Katja, setting a tentative date for the summer of 1987. Katja wanted to give herself time to polish her English . The girls were excited and immediately started planning their future vacations. We were also happy and agreed that it will be a wonderful experience for all three of them.

The next two days we kept open, just for us alone, to enjoy this beautiful city of Lugano. Walking along the shore we noticed a sign, advertising a unique cultural opportunity. Villa Favorita, on the other side of the lake, owned by the family of Thyssen-Bornemisza, advertised tours to show off the family's renowned art collection. The sign said: "Capolavori da Musei Ungheresi" -- *Masterpieces of the Hungarian Museum*. I could hardly believe my eyes. It was a most serendipitous discovery. I never heard of this collection before, though I thought I should have.

* * *

May I please digress for a moment and delve into a little Hungarian history. The Bornemiszas have an old and interesting family tree. Theirs is a fabled historic name, that produced Géza, the previously mentioned student of the painter, Henri Matisse. Earlier key figures were Péter, a 16th century poet, known for his verses of melancholy lament, popular in his day. Also Gergely, a "King's Lieutenant", who played a crucial role in defense of the Fort of Eger against the Turks. I remember learning about them in my history and Hungarian literature classes in Pannonhalma.

Gergely Bornemisza was one of the two heroes in the historical novel by Géza Gárdonyi: *Egri Csillagok* (The Stars over Eger). That was the first serious book I read as a youth and perhaps the one I enjoyed most. Till today, I remember phrases verbatim, from its pages. (A few others that come close, are *Les Miserables* of Dumas and books by Stendahl.) -- It was the story of the siege of Eger, a city northwest of Budapest. It was attacked in 1553, by the then invincible armies of the Ottoman Empire. Eger was a key fortress, whose loss would have exposed a large part of the country to conquering by the Turks. -- The story of the long battle was made into a movie at least twice, but did not live up to the level of literary beauty and excitement of the book, that they tried to bring to the big screen.

A group of residents of Eger and the surrounding region were holed up in the fort, behind high, thick walls. Soon they were transformed into a hastily trained, poorly equipped, but spirited soldiers, along with some riffraff, sufficiently scared of, and motivated by an impending plunder of their country by the Ottoman Turks. Men, women with families, locked themselves up in the city-fortress upon the hill, awaiting the onslaught. They did not perceive themselves to be protagonists of a great victorious battle, with episodes of unbound heroism and romance.

The Turks joined two armies at the gate of Eger. Pasha Ahmed, emboldened by great prior conquests and basking in the glow of his recent victory at Temesvár, joined his fellow Pasha Ali, who was victorious at Drégely. His soldiers massacred every defender in taking that fortress. The combined force was 150,000 men, with the most advanced armor of the day and bolstered confidence borne of past triumphs.

Among the Turkish soldiers were many Janissaries, the most fierce of fighters. Janissaries were those soldiers, who were taken from Hungary in infancy, raised as Turks and instilled with vicious hatred for the Christian Hungarians, preparing them for military conquests of their old homeland. Many died, never learning the truth about the sinister plan that victimized, and so cruelly used them. (Young Islamic suicide bombers are a parallel, for our day. History repeats!)

Eger's defense was lead by István Dobó and his able lieutenant, Gergely Bornemisza. They were an extraordinary pair. Dobó was a soldier's soldier, a Patton type, great leader of men -- and women, as history would have it. He commanded 2000 men, women, and later children, who had to become replacement soldiers by the end of the 38 day siege, after their sons, husbands, and brothers fell. The young Bornemisza was an intelligent and inventive engineer. He designed and built *fire wheels*, that rolled from the high walls, down the attack-ladders, sweeping off the Turks climbing up. -- The "decrepit pen", as Ali Pasha called it the day he set eyes on the fortress, still stood, after he decided to withdraw his army under cover of darkness, after more than five weeks of frustrating losses. It took him that long to realize that he failed, after his totally demoralized soldiers refused to fight. He heard one of his lieutenants say:

"Only Allah can help here. God is with the Magyars. And who can fight against God?"

His initial clue should have come on the first night, when Dobó, in a surprise nighttime raid, killed a number of his troops and destroyed many of his canons, before retreating back into the fortress. The pashas never had a successful day at Eger.

* * *

About four centuries later, one of Lieutenant Bornemisza's descendants married a Thyssen, member of a very rich and prominent German industrialist family, collectors and patrons of fine art.

Ildikó and I were eager to see the renowned Bornemisza-Thyssen collection. Its unique claim to fame is, that beside holding a high quality collection, it has important works, representing all major periods and schools of painting. Only few of the world's leading museums are able to claim that.

The collection is smaller than others, but compact and most complete of its kind. It is designed to present a well rounded collection, that represents the best of the fine arts.

A small, nicely appointed boat was moored at the shore, under a prominent sign, advertising the permanent exhibit. It provided the only mode of transportation to the villa. The price of the ticket included a 20 minute ride to the villa and entry to the exhibit. The ride alone in the small motor boat to this exquisite estate was a treat. We passed by sumptuous palaces on shore and tried to guess, which was the one, where we would dock. (Our captain chose well. He stopped at the one I had picked.) It was one of the nicest properties we've ever visited. The exhibit included a few paintings that we recognized from catalogs and art programs on television. After viewing, we walked the grounds and admired the architecture, the setting, the view of the lake and the picturesque mountains in the distance.

The Girls showed less interest. They stayed behind and spent their money on beach front entertainment. As we were sailing back from the villa, we spotted them pedaling a tandem foot-powered boat, waving happily as we passed by.

(The Thyssen-Bornemisza Museum was moved to Spain about 15 years later. When we were in Madrid, we walked through it again in its new, larger home, just a short walk from the other more famous museum, the Prado.)

We left Lugano next morning. The road took us into the Veneto region, by the cities of Bergamo and Brescia. The latter was a town, known to me from my history classes. For Hungarians, the town was made infamous by an Austrian general, during the great revolutions that swept Europe in 1848-49. Haynau, the "Hyena of Brescia" is remembered as an unduly harsh soldier. He demanded and was instrumental in the execution of 13 Hungarian generals and statesmen in the city of Arad on October 6, 1849. Before that, he earned a reputation in Brescia, where he cruelly repressed the rising of Italian patriots against the oppressive Habsburg regime. Old history classes came vividly to mind. I have not thought of Haynau for decades, until I saw the sign on the roadside, directing travelers to this otherwise ordinary city in the luscious Po valley.

I related the story of Haynau to my children, but soon we turned to Shakespeare. They were more familiar with the story of Romeo and Juliet. We were approaching Verona, where we rested, ate lunch and looked for the famous balcony, where one of literature's greatest love scene took place in sentimental innocence and gentle beauty. It seemed that the town wanted to profit from its literary fame and *designated* a balcony to lure tourists. No guarantee of authenticity, in fact, the place and the story was Shakespeare's lovely fiction. It lives on because it is a classic, expressing fundamental human emotions, treating power, love, hatred and murder -- done seductively well. As we walked around the yard, I photographed it and thought of my favorite versions of Romeo and Juliet. They are the Franco Zeffirelli movie and the Prokofiev ballet. The balcony scene, as choreographed, and danced by the artists of the Joffrey Ballet is our favorite. We also saw it danced by other companies, but would again choose the Joffrey.

We stopped in Padua, the city of Mother's favorite saint. Father took bus tours through Italy in the late 1960s. I remembered him telling me in 1972 during our visit home, that to him the cathedral, dedicated to the local saint, Anthony, was the nicest he has ever seen. Since then I am comparing churches I visit, with the one in Padua. There is one other church, that Father mentioned at the time: St. Mark in Venice. I do not know what other churches he saw on his two trips to Italy, but I have seen many more than he, and I also have my favorites -- in fact too many. The best ones are St. Peters -- I could name several others in Rome -- Westminster

Abbey in London, the cathedrals in Toledo and Seville, beside the many glorious baroque churches of Europe. These are all massive edifices that overwhelm with their size, yet are impressive with their beauty, their proportions and richness of decorative detail.

Next came Venice, where again, a reserved hotel was waiting for us in the outskirts of the city, thanks to Walter. We arrived in the afternoon and the clerk informed us at check-in, that we were invited that evening to desserts and a tour of a castle. It was not very clear what it may be, because the offer was unusual and an unexpected treat to guests.

Our hotel was owned by a wealthy family, which also had, as one of its family properties, a palace with large tracks of farmland nearby. As an amenity with our stay in the hotel, we were invited to the palace for coffee and dessert. After dinner we traveled a few miles in a bus to the estate: Villa Widmann Foscari. The road took us through lush farmland. Near the palace were huge fields of corn -- *elephant high* -- shimmering in the descending sun. Along the road, as markers to identify the farm property, I saw handsome cement columns, spaced about 100 ft apart, topped with carved stone statuettes. It was the only time I ever saw a farm field so decorated. "Only in Italy!" -- I said to myself.

Our visit to the late-Renaissance palace included a guided tour and walk through the beautiful garden, before we sat down under the arcades where our dessert was served. It was a pleasant and tasty treat.

There was one other reason why we remember that coffee and sweets so much. We were served by a young man, who had movie star qualities. Good looking, yes, but he had more. He had style, that is not subject to description by words. Very courteous and correct, and at the same time captivating with his gestures, smile and impeccable manners. I commented to Ildi, who confirmed my impression. The more detectable impression, however, was on our two girls. They tried to be discrete, but responded with polite, but meaningful smiles. It was fleeting infatuation, lasting only until bedtime, but remained subject of family talk for a while. -- On the way home Ildi and I agreed that while he was certainly impressive, a lot of his appeal was well learned and rehearsed, necessary for his job. He did it better than either of us had seen before.

The next morning we took a bus to Venice. It was the best choice, giving us time, free of worries about parking and the huge crowd. Along the way to town, the bus followed a creek, not wider than 20 feet: the Brenta. We saw at least a hundred men fishing along its banks, seemingly trying to catch each other's fish. I wondered if they expected to catch anything or it was just time to take it easy for awhile.

Talk about a crowd! No wonder Venice is sinking. People were everywhere, filling streets, squares and the many bridges. The variety of people included a large group of Buddhist monks whom we encountered several times, as we -- and they -- were criss-crossing town. They were shaved bald and wore bright orange. Not a surprise that I remember them so well. One alone would have been noticeable, but twenty-one?

We were on our feet until late afternoon, with the exception of a nice lunch in one of the busy, back street cafes. We sat down very tired on St. Mark square, at the base of the fountain, where others, for the same reason sought refuge, nursing aching feet. While Ildi and the Girls took a rest, I climbed up the tall tower on the main square, to take my visual and photographic bird's eye view of this magnificent city. The panoramic view of the red tile roofed city, the Duke's Palace and St. Mark Cathedral was impressive. After that we went across the bay to the Lido and into Venice's other church of note, the baroque, Santa Maria della Salute and its chapel, the Campanile San Giorgio.

Venice is truly unique. I am especially grateful that we were able to see it together. The Girls were quite young but already had an appreciation for the beauty and the cultural significance of the place. This great mercantile city is one of those that they may want to see with their husbands and children.

The next day we said good-by to Italy and entered Yugoslavia. (A historical footnote: As I write this on 4th February, 2003, I want to cite a news item, I heard earlier this morning: Yugoslavia ceased to exist today. The reason for its demise is that it ran out of constituent states. Slovenes, Croats, Macedonians left it earlier. The Serbs and Montenegrins saw it better no longer to call it *South*

Slavia. Rather, they decided to stay in a new, smaller union, just for the two of them. I do not yet know what the state is to be called, but it would not surprise me, if after a few years, this new creation would also dissolve.)

We took our long drive through the old Yugoslavia. It was markedly different, with its poverty and distinct Balkan flavor. We drove all day with minimum of rest. Late afternoon we entered Hungary near the city of Barcs, that I visited with my railroadcar-full of cows 32 years before. This time we were just passing through Hungary. Our next destination was Transylvania in Rumania, where Ildikó's father, stepmother and relatives lived. We wanted to go there first then return to Hungary to see my family.

Our first stop was Pécs where we were looking for a hotel, but found a bed-and-breakfast we liked. Soon we hit the sack, to be ready for an early rise.

We drove through Szeged. The city lies on the banks of the Tisza. It is one of the big cities, and a nice one. We decided to eat lunch and look around. It was my first time in Szeged. The main square was set up for the famous outdoor summer theater season that I knew about and saw pictures in magazines. On Cathedral Square huge productions of opera and plays are done every year. The most famous is the grand production of Giuseppe Verdi's *Aida*, where they bring animals, including elephants from the zoo as part of the production. As a boy, I heard it on radio and dreamed to see this larger then life production and wondered, what would happen if the elephants decided to sing....

Crossing the border to Rumania was just as dragged-out and nerve-racking as before, but we made it to Zilah by dusk. Other than Apu, the relatives saw Erika and Andrea the first time. They wanted to give us the best they were able to, in their meager circumstance. Shortages of all kinds were the order of the day. Inventive cooking made up a lot for the material shortages.

We took a day to go to Beszterce to visit Gábor and Baba Imreh and their family. They visited us in Crystal Lake a few years before. The Girls found a distant cousin, Ildikó, with whom the connection was instant and warm. They corresponded for years afterwards.

With Gábor, I walked the streets of this lovely city, that showed the signs of its prior greatness amid its current dilapidated state. On a large square I pointed to a very well kept mansion, strikingly different from anything else around it, surrounded by manicured lawn, trees and a brightly painted wrought iron fence. Gábor told me, it was one of the palaces of Nicolai Ceausescu, the dictator and communist party chief. He was not there, but the building was always ready to receive him, in case he came for a visit. In all the years, Ceausescu stayed in it only twice. He had many other such palaces, more than thirty throughout the country, similarly kept just for him. This shiny, all white mansion was in stark contrast to the rest of the city, that reflected the neglect and poverty of the country. (Saddam Hussein copied Ceausescu in this fetish, taunting the people in poverty around him. He too had about 30 palaces, for his exclusive use. The two men shared similar fates. Ceausescu was overthrown and executed in 1989.)

Later Gábor took me to the building that was once his, where he had his business, before it was taken by the state. He was processing vinegar and had a comfortable life doing it. The business he built and operated gave him security, a sense of achievement and comfortable living. The building I saw was in ruin. Gábor was declared an "exploiter", a class enemy, and ostracized from society. The state operated the factory for a while, then closed and abandoned it. They also took his home. After much effort and with the help from friends, he found an apartment to rent in one of the many, multi-story, ugly block buildings, the state assigned to people. He was unemployed for a while, then assigned a job as a clerk.

It was a somber walk. He reminisced about happier times, but was optimistic about the future. -- It was difficult for me to listen to his depressing story, though he has reconciled to the past and put it behind him. For me the story was new and affected me deeply. Gábor was one of the most decent and generous man I've ever met. He was among those who suffered a great reversal of fortune, as was Mr. Lippai. They were determined to go on with their lives and do the best with the hand they were dealt by fate.

Early next morning we went back to Zilah, then on to Hungary.

Preparations were under way for the big party, Mother's 75th birthday celebration. At the time my sister, Marika was working in Termal, a resort spa hotel in Héviz, where we planned to hold the party. Marika helped Tomi with the arrangements. More than 50 close and distant relatives attended. Most of us gathered in Keszthely and went down to Héviz in a caravan of cars, loaded with people. The Termal made the event special. Excellent dinner was served by waiters wearing white gloves in elegant setting. The atmosphere was joyous, with many children running about. Among the gifts was an arrangement of wild flowers, sent through Teleflora from my cousin Gerti and her mother Pepi Néni, from Los Angeles. The thought of sending a bouquet of wild flowers from so far away was touching. Mother loved the simplicity of nature that was best represented to her by the flowers of the meadow and hills, she grew up with in Csehi.

I took pictures in many combinations of the members of our family tree. I remember how much trouble I had in taking the big group photo. First, I asked all to squeeze together and I had to move back, so everybody would fit in. Then the harder part, getting them all stop talking and look ahead, without blocking others. I took two shots and if I could combine them, taking the best part from each, I would have a good picture. So, we pasted them both, alongside in the album and ask the viewer go back and forth between the two, if she wanted to catch a good likeness of all who were there.

A few days later we left for Aachen and soon for Chicago. Thinking back to the days we spent in Paris, the Rivieras, Como, and all the beautiful ones following, we forgot our misfortune and frustrations in Genoa and considered this vacation one of our best. Our expectations were high at the beginning and they were more than fulfilled and canceled the two glum and gloomy half days in Genoa and Milano.

The Girls started their correspondence with Katja soon after we returned. She was eager to write, so she can improve and practice her English. Plans for her visit the following summer were soon formed. It was a new experience for us, but we felt comfortable to have her as guest. She was to stay with us for more than a month, planned for 1987.

* * *

The gathering of tall ships in New York was in 1986. It was perhaps the largest number ever in one place, appropriate to celebrate the 100th birthday of our Lady Liberty. The Girls were still in high school. We drove there and met up with the Püskis who provided our lodging for the week. Gabi's parents have emigrated to New York a few years before, both past age 70. They established a thriving book selling and publishing business in the middle of Manhattan. (It was their business in pre-communist-day Hungary.) Gabi's brother Steve also came out, followed the parents in the business and with his family, settled in New Jersey. They put us up in their house for the whole week. Through Gabi, we were also invited at his parents' place for meals, anytime we were close enough to drop by. It was a very generous arrangement and we often made stops for meals, refreshments, a good rest and a good time. We roamed Manhattan all day on foot, looking at and boarding those beautiful ships, that were moored all around Manhattan and in Brooklyn. On July 4th, we were at the shore of the Hudson, watching the spectacular Thunderbirds, the Air Force flying team. In the evening, we crowded in with more than a million people, to watch the biggest fire works ever. Six battery stations were floating on the water around lower Manhattan, and together, impeccably timed, produced the show that kept the sky around us lit up with fiery wonder for an hour. It was incredibly exciting. We were a little bit like sardines, throughout Battery Park and the surrounding streets. Many came early with blankets, but soon had to fold them up. During that evening, I literally rubbed elbows with more people, than in all my prior years, or since.

We had an uninvited, but exciting episode on our way home. Driving through Pennsylvania, in heavy rain and traffic, we barely escaped a crash. On the Pennsylvania Turnpike, a black bear ran in front of us, trying to cross the busy road. I swerved, but sill hit its rump. We had no chance to stop or even look what happened to the poor beast. It was a close call that could have ended tragically for all of us on that very busy, wet highway, with semis all around us.

Katja arrived in June, 1987. The short acquaintance/friendship, forged in two days in Lugano proved to be solid. For some six weeks the three were like sisters. Katja, brought up well, was respectful, courteous and no problem for us. There was one thing however, that her mother hinted about but we understood fully only after a while. She had an eating disorder and saw herself as -- let's say, not thin enough. She was indeed a slender girl, with a finicky appetite, that we accommodated the best we could. I had two exhaustive talk with her about the subject, but felt that I gave her no real help. I was ignorant about the subject and tried only appeal to her common sense. Psychologists would say, that these problems are deep seated and it is naïve to think that merely talking about them helps. Still, after she returned home, we were happy to hear from her parents that Katja's stay with us was a happy one and that they were gratified seeing that she put a few pounds on her slim bones.

One of the girls' favorite pastime was scrabble. They spent hours playing it and filled almost all their travel time with it. We had some long drives with Katja. We took her on an eventful western camping trip. Our main destinations were Yellowstone and the Tetons. First we went to the Black Hills of South Dakota to see Mount Rushmore. For years we wanted to do this, but it is out of the way of and too far from Illinois. Mount Rushmore was on the way, just a good day's drive. For us it was customary to start very early and rest at the end of the day. By evening we were in the neighborhood, so to speak, and the next day we could explore the Hills and the magnificent granite carvings up high. We drove around the back of the monument and saw George Washington's profile close up, as the road circled behind him.

We also went to see the other monumental work carved out of a mountain, the memorial to the Sioux chief, Crazy Horse. The work had been going on for years, but the Chief and his horse were just barely discernible. The outlines of the figures were chalked on the rough rock. In the visitors yard, we gathered around the white model replica, as it was conceived by the artist and his family, when finished. (Not long ago I saw a photo, showing the progress they made in intervening years. It was impressive.) The project was a noble obsession of one man, the late Korczak Ziolowski and his large family who are still working on their dream project. Ziolowski, son of immigrants from Poland, served in the U.S. Army with distinction. Later members of the Sioux invited him to make a monument to Crazy Horse. He answered the call with a lifetime of dedication to this project. The rough work is done by blasting. We saw big Caterpillars moving around in the distance, as we watched from about a mile away. There is a museum, showing the project from its inception, illustrating the difficulty and monumental size of the work. It was inspiring to see the dedication of the family as documented by exhibits. It will be a triumph and a gigantic permanent monument to the human spirit. Its size is enormous, dwarfing anything that man has made before, surpassing even the giant statues of Zeus or Colossus, two of the famous, ancient seven wonders. When done, it will be in the class of the Pyramids. Looking at the mockup, I was impressed by the design. Astride on his horse, the Chief, leader of his nation, points forward with outstretched arm, commanding attention from the viewer, as he commanded allegiance and obedience from his braves in battle.

We went on to Yellowstone National Park, where we spent a day, driving around the long northern loop, encountering dear, crossing our path. We stopped by the main lodge, where Ildi and I once slept on one of my Colorado trips. We waited for Old Faithful to shoot up its geyser steam a few times and we were on our way to Grand Teton National Park. By evening we reached our campsite. The view was magnificent as we came out to the clearing from the wooded camp. The whitecap mountains are famous and their setting is such that they are the background for the panorama of the wide, flat valley, Jackson Hole. The unique, combined view of the two, is the signature image of the park. We drove up and down the valley several times, between our campground and the town of Jackson, just outside the park. As one travels south, one can see a flat green meadow several miles wide, cars inching on distant roads. I always looked forward to a certain slow curve in the road, that follows the Snake River. The view of the river bend, the green pasture, with the white peaks behind, were unforgettable. The best picture was, as we approached the bend, especially near sunset. The river and nearby marsh glittered in the reflection of the golden setting sun. I took several pictures and still bought a postcard in the shop. I knew, my photos could not vie with the professionals' pictures and I wanted the best image of this remarkable sight. It is the most essentially western panorama, that shows so much of nature. And it is so very American. I also bought a framed, 360 degree, super wide-angle photo of the valley that shows everything and does justice to this special place.

We drove all the roads in the valley and walked many of its trails and nature walks. Park naturalists warned us not to get too close to moose, because they were known to run down and trample curious tourists. We hung around Jackson, the only town, checked out the shops, watched birds and grizzlies on trails and early bird walks. On a nice, warm afternoon we walked around Jenny Lake and rested on the beach, just soaking up sun. Andrea and I went in for a swim. The water was quite cold but the vigorous exercise, refreshing.

The western trip was a great success. For Katja, it was a once-in-a-lifetime experience, one that showed America and left her with singular memories. The following summer a great fire in Yellowstone Park burned for weeks and devastated about a third of the forest in the park. For many days, pictures and news reports filled the pages and television screens about the ugly scene the fire left in its wake. Some overly eager but shortsighted forestry officials let the fire burn freely in the mistaken belief that it will burn itself out without much damage. They forgot that earlier regulations encouraged clearing brush, as part of forest management. After the fire was raging for weeks, frenzied fire fighting proved to be of little use. Several of the hundreds of volunteer fire fighters from all over the country lost their lives before the fire was controlled. It was painful to see such damage to one of our most precious national treasures. The Forest Department, deeply embarrassed, returned to the old policy of conservative forest management -- I hoped.

I wrote Katja, that she was lucky to see the magnificent park in its full glory. We will have to wait years before it recovers and will be able to show its beauty again for the millions of its visitors.

Shortsighted *benign neglect* policies resulted in a similar, more devastating series of fires in 2003, when a huge area of southern California was devastated and nearly a thousand homes were consumed by a fast spreading fire. Cause of the rapid spread-rate was again the abandonment of long-time forestry practices -- the old mistake. Politicians, at the urging and heavy lobbying by the tree-huggers, increased the number of areas affected and with it, the cost to home owners and society. Will they, or we, ever learn?

* * *

Next summer Erika and Andrea prepared for their trip to Lugano. They spent three weeks there. For the first two, they were home with the Bortolasos. On the third week Walter took them to Italy on an extended trip, where they met boys, through friends of the Bortolaso family. They came back with a tan, deeper than they ever had. They treated us to many stories of fun and exciting adventures.

While the girls were in Europe, we went to California. Ildikó said once that for her, the nicest place in the whole country was Yosemite National Park. She remembered little of the details, but the impression of the park on her was profound. For many years I also wanted to see it and was happy to go. We planned a trip, an ambitious driving tour, beginning in San Diego. We rented a Pontiac 6000 sedan and drove up the West Coast Highway to San Francisco, with many stops on the way.

We flew to San Diego, where we stayed one day with my friend, Imre Lendvay. Then we drove to Los Angeles and visited with my cousin, Gerti and her Mom, Pepi Néni. Gerti was still in the travel business and quite busy. Pepike entertained us and showed us around in her neighborhood. She made for us her famous *beigli strudel*, one log with poppy seed and another with walnuts. It was exceptional, one of the few things that anybody could make better than Ildikó or my mother. Ildi wrote down the recipe and has made it a few times since, even passed it on to her mother.

On the way to Los Angeles, we drove through the Wild Animal Park and toured the abbey of San Juan Capistrano. This cloister is one of the best examples of rugged, mission-style Spanish architecture. I could hardly stop myself taking pictures. The large courtyard, nicely spaced with old trees, flowers and lawn patches reminded me of parts of Pannonhalma, where a placid surroundings are conducive to contemplative life. Arcaded walks around the court also made for excellent pictures. We saw a Civil War era medical exhibit, with instruments, documents and pictures, collected by a prominent doctor, showing today's generation the hardships that was part of everyday life in those days. A case of amputation of a limb was described in detail. It made me appreciate the fantastic advances medical science made since then. I admired the courage and the capacity to endure pain by those who preceded us.

I remembered the 1960s song about Santa Catalina Island by the Four Preps, and wanted to see it ever since. We took an early morning ferry. It was *26 miles across the sea,* just as the song said. The island is a popular vacation spot. We spent the entire day there, along with many day-tourists. There wasn't much else. On a bus tour, we saw the airport at the desolate top of the island. The shore is nice, but it is the only real attraction. Most of the island is nothing but a semi-arid forest on a hill.

The next day we went to see two famous local curiosities. Some 20 years ago the city of Long Beach purchased the decommissioned ocean liner, *Queen Mary,* to use it as a tourist attraction. In her day she was indeed the queen of the seas, the most luxurious ocean liner and the crown jewel of the Cunard Lines. (As I write this in 2003, a worthy successor, *Queen Mary 2* has just been launched.) We walked through the old lady. It was indeed, top of the line. Today's cruise ships are opulent in a different way, with 21st century comforts and frivolity -- huge atrium, casino and spacious rooms. Eighty years ago, the Queen Mary was the standard that was not matched. Before air travel she, and for a while, huge airships, were the mode of travel for the well to do -- and oh yes, the *Titanic.*

Nearby is the *Spruce Goose,* the wooden *albatross* of Howard

Hughes. It is a strange curiosity, despite being a true engineering marvel. By albatross, in this case, I refer to the size of the craft, rather than the meaning, in which this word is more often, pejoratively used. There was a need for large transport aircraft during WW II, to ease the vulnerability of surface transport ships, that were decimated over the Atlantic, by German U-boats. Hughes dedicated his engineering and business talents and took a risk to his fame and reputation, by designing and producing a plane that could effectively take over a large part of this burden. To save on vital metals, needed in the manufacture of all other aircraft in the war, he built it out of wood. He was ridiculed, hauled before Congress several times, but remained steadfast and committed to his dream. The design was daring and ambitious. The plane was to carry two Sherman tanks or 750 soldiers, fully equipped.

Officially called HK1 (in honor of his friend and associate Henry Kaiser) but soon affectionately known only by its nickname: "Spruce Goose", this flying boat proved its air worthiness when Hughes himself at the controls, took off and flew the 170,000 pound craft, on a 1-mile test flight, with its 80 ft. high tail, 320 ft. wingspan and its 8 Pratt & Whitney 4360 engines roaring. It was the 2nd of November, 1947.

We toured the cockpit and some of the interior of the plane, but did not have the chance to see the number of its interior inclines and the spiral staircase to the upper level. The interior finish was exposed to show the extraordinary craftsmanship and the fine and ingenious use of wood for the purpose that the world first saw applied by the Wright Brothers, but not much since, except by modeling enthusiasts.

We watched a short film on the history and the maiden flight of the Goose. I thought of Hughes, who died a recluse in 1976 in his Las Vegas hotel suite. He lived there in total isolation, in filth, watching old movies during the last years of his life, a victim of obsessive compulsive disorder. It was a sad ending to an extraordinary life.

A 2005 motion picture, *The Aviator*, chronicles his career, successes and the tragedy of his illness. He is ably played by Leonardo di Caprio. Hughes, a multi-talented genius is effectively portrayed on the big screen, except for his dashing looks (sorry Caprio). It was a good movie. I was pleased to see that it included much of his testimony before Congress, where he made mincemeat out of blowhard senators and taught them a basic economic and business lesson. They tried to ridicule him but Hughes turned the table on his audience of fools, heard nationally on radio. -- His case is reminiscent of the World War I General Billy Mitchell, who advocated the modernization and build-up of his Army Air Corps. In 1925 he got court-martialed for it, only to be proven a man of foresight and an original thinker, after his death.

We left Los Angles late in the afternoon and drove into Oxnard, looking for a place to spend the night. The town did not look very attractive. At the edge was a row of motels, that we did not find inviting. We picked the one that looked best and registered at the curbside check-in window. Soon it became obvious, why we had the feeling about all the motels we passed by. The first thing we noticed in the dingy room was the mirror on the ceiling. (Ildi joked that we should've asked if we could get a better price on the room if we paid by the hour. After all, it was late and we were planning to leave early the next day.)

To me, Santa Barbara was the epitome of California, a city that best represents the life style in the Golden State. The hedonistic life of the rich was the title subject of a soap opera, full of neurotic people. I watched little of it, but this is the impression I came away with, other than the beautiful setting and the striking red tile roofs of a lovely city. We spent a few hours, looking over this storied town. It is indeed a nice place. I loved best a hilltop view, enjoying the sea of red tiles. We looked in the court house on the advice of a local resident and were impressed with the painted wood panel walls. Other famous and very Californian places were the Biltmore Hotel and exclusive Pebble Beach golf course. I was surprised that nobody was bothered or curious as we walked the grounds.

Early next morning we set out north and looked for the Pacific Coast Highway. After a short drive on Interstate 5, we took the narrow, two-lane road with its many curves, simple construction and spectacular vistas behind its many bends. We were on this road for two days, stopping often to rest, or just linger and absorb the view before our eyes and ingrain in memory the unique experience.

We took a detour from the main road to see San Simeon, the fabulous, 165 room, estate on 124 hillside and hilltop acres, of William Randolph Hearst, the ultimate media magnate between the world wars. He named it *La Cuesta Encantada* (Enchanted Hill). The tour of the estate is organized, like I have not seen before or since. It begins in the distant visitor's center. Buses took us up on a winding path, to show off and explain the nature preserve and open zoo that takes up much of the hillside along the road.

It is not easy to describe this hilltop palace complex and I will rather not attempt it. I found the style, especially of the main castle, (*Casa Grande*) a tad strange, as I looked at the facade. With its twin steeples, it intimated to me a church, which it is certainly not. I liked the interior, that contains priceless and well selected art treasures, housed in opulent rooms, more pleasing to my taste. The setting of the estate is what may be remembered by people who come to visit. The three bungalows, Casas: *del Mar, del Monte* and *del Sol*, betray Spanish quality and the preferences of Mr. Hearst and his faithful architect, Julia Morgan. After the tour we walked the grounds and enjoyed the captivating view of the valley and the distant hills.

That night we slept in a small, simple hotel, isolated from everything else, with only the murmuring sound of the ocean, lapping the shore. After sunset we spent time to watch hummingbirds, zipping around on the hedge, feeding on nectar from funnel shaped flowers. For us from the Midwest, these tiny birds were a rare sight. Here they were common and more daring, ignoring the presence of humans. We went to bed only after our tiny birds flew off for the last time, to tuck in for the night.

Next morning I was up early and went out to the shore. I sat on a rock, watched the waves and waited in vain for sun rays to warm my back. It could not, for the dense fog, that is constant along the shore. This narrow coastal strip has its own unique weather pattern. Many photographers tried to capture the misty air and ghostly shapes that lay in the distance. I also tried my best and brought home beautiful images. One needs patience -- and luck -- to be able to snap the picture quickly, when the ever changing sight yields the best image. A few seconds hesitation and the result is mediocre, or gone altogether.

As we approached the north end of the long drive, we saw a viaduct that we instantly recognized. Many car commercials were filmed there, using it as a backdrop, one of the most spectacular spots on Big Sur. As the terrain changed we saw small towns with strange names, and two near San Francisco, that were familiar. They were those that people talk about, and are known as nice places to visit. The first was Carmel, known also, as a town that had Clint Eastwood as mayor for a few years. We cruised up and down on the main drag to absorb the atmosphere of this charming place. We parked at the beach and walked some more. The town has a rocky shore, populated with sea life, mostly seals and walruses. These animals spend much of their time warming the rocks and letting the sun warm them. They probably are sleeping, but one cannot be sure because from a distance, it is not easy to tell. The difference may not be great in any event.

Next was Monterey. We spent more time there. The aquarium is one of a kind. From the ocean, animals can enter the large inner pool, stay a few hours or days and are free to return to sea. Inside the complex, huge glass tanks are filled with a great variety of aquatic *fauna and flora.*

The former is a vast array of fish and other creatures that we saw in Jacques Custeau's *Silent World,* the first underwater film and many other successive ones, shot in the ocean depths. They show the ocean to millions who could never go down on their own and see what lies beneath. We lingered, looking through the glass about 40 ft. tall, watching the graceful spasms of jelly fish, floating by. It was a very peaceful world. Best example of ocean flora was the giant kelp, reaching to the surface and gently waving in the simulated movement of ocean water, probably induced by a pump hidden somewhere. We waited for a feeding before we ventured out to the seashore, where the open basin was constructed for the itinerant members in this collection, coming into this friendly compound for voluntary captivity. One would think that the smarter ones appear regularly to find an easy meal, that might require work to find in the wild.

Nearby Cannery Row is different now. Decades ago John Steinbeck made it famous in his novel of the same name. All factories are closed and the buildings used for other purposes.

We heard of the *17 Mile Drive* before, and saw pictures of the most photographed small tree (I think it's a cypress) on a high rock at the shore. I joined the lot of innumerable professionals and amateurs, who tried their best to record an image of this famous tree, that I saw many times before on postcards. I felt that, because of private property around, I could not approach the spot, which may have yielded the best angle and was satisfied with what I was able to get under the circumstances, using my zoom lens to bring it in.

The Drive is within an exclusive, gated community. It winds along the rocky seashore, that boasts the most spectacular views of the Pacific shore, seen between huge homes of unique architecture and grounds magnificently landscaped. This terrain makes the area prohibitively expensive for even some of those who consider themselves well to do. We did our obligatory slow drive, stopping often to take pictures. The fact that there is an entry fee to drive this road was odd, but one has to appreciate the need for a semblance of privacy for our moneyed oligarchy. We paid the fee, not wanting to have regrets later for missing this most spectacular drive.

That night we slept in Sausalito and went on the next morning to San Francisco. The city had one of its rare heat waves. People were talking about it as temperatures rose to the high 80s. It was unusual there, but not too hard to bear for a couple of Midwesterners. We walked a lot and covered most of the famous sights. Lunch was at a very attractive Hungarian restaurant, the *Paprikás Fonó*, while we were listening through the open windows, to music on Ghirardelli Square.

Next we went to see Muir Woods, the home of the nicest, tallest and best proportioned pine trees in the world. The park is clean, and simply landscaped to show off its main assets, those towering redwoods.

Our final treat was a week in Yosemite. One of the world's

great treasures, Yosemite National Park is on the top of my list of God's gifts to mankind. The setting for its many parts compete with each other for top honor. One has to see El Captain with his own eyes, to fully comprehend its enormous rock face. Nowhere in the world is another place, where one can look up on a rock wall, over a mile high. We spent an active, enjoyable week. We saw all the main points at least once, but never enough of them. Yosemite is a place, one has to revisit at least once a decade. (We have to correct our dereliction soon. I feel a void in me.)

49

Life With Wausau, And Beyond (1988-2001)

Changes at work began to accelerate . Wausau Insurance Companies, that was such a fresh air for me after the over-regulated atmosphere at Factory Mutual, was taking up ways, similar to those at my prior work place. Policy decisions were made at the highest level, then filter down to the troops in form of more complicated work rules and meticulously prescribed bureaucratic procedures. Our report format gradually resembled the ones I knew years before at F.M. It was progress in a certain direction, that management thought wise or felt compelled to introduce to stay competitive. For us in the trenches it meant more work, much of it pushing paper. Computers were introduced that at first was an exciting change, but in time report review demanded a lot more new things from us. The reasons had to with competition and probably followed ways where the industry was evolving. At any rate, I did not welcome the changes and none of my colleagues did. They complained more than I did. I was able to compare and put it in perspective, but it was all new to them.

There were a couple good years, when the company rationalized that long-term, maybe permanent good times have arrived.

Ironically, the property division was consistently making money during times good and bad, yet we, a stepchild in the large, mostly casualty company, were the ones most affected by internal changes and reorganizations that were made to suit the larger part of the business. The workers compensation and casualty business has suffered as a result of shortsighted pricing policies and the prevailing business cycle, that favored buyers, rather than sellers of insurance. Business cycles in insurance are not like waves, rather like huge, slow moving swells of sea. Using another nautical analogy, to change course for an industry that moves like an ocean liner is difficult, takes long time and causes disruptions. Cycles effecting business are inscrutable, even when in the vast ocean of worldwide business, they are lurking just around the proverbial corner. Cycles are always part of business and usually come unannounced and leave no time to restructure the underwriter's book of business, that would aid him to compensate for new conditions. -- For us, bad results began to show, signaling long term problems. In the meantime it meant losing a lot of money and the freedom of taking risks on upcoming business opportunities, without a larger risk of jeopardizing further the company's financial standing before the rating bureaus. We arrived to a difficult crossroads with the accustomed cushion of reserve cash seriously depleted. Making defensive moves absorbed most of the time of company directors.

This process began during the good times in the late 1980s. In the boom years of President Reagan's second term, the company built an ambitious project, a new corporate headquarters. The Wausau Company logo, the small-town depot -- modeled after the railroad station in Wausau -- was on every letterhead since the founding of the company in 1911. I began to see it increasingly in fancy magazines. It was promoted as a sponsor of the most popular weekly news program, *60 Minutes.*

With the decline of railroading in the 1970-s, the old depot in downtown Wausau was neglected and the area surrounding it, deteriorated. Talk was of buying it and moving it up the hill, pretty far away and placing it next to the corporate offices. The idea proved too difficult, so the top brass decided to build a replica, with a few hundred feet of tracks, and make it a reception center for VIP guests. The new depot was built on a hillside, with a commanding view of the city. It was a small part of a huge project: new corporate offices and the Training Center. The complex was big, plush and imposing, a large and extravagant undertaking, with luxurious training facilities for employees and clients. I have never seen more spacious and plush seats, than in our main auditorium, bettering even the ones I remember at the new Metropolitan Opera. The design, setting and architecture of the Training Center rivaled any I have seen in similar structures. They also built the first rate fire research lab for training employees and to show off for clients. It was as good as that at Factory Mutual. The even larger home office complex was built adjacent to the training center and all the offices from downtown Wausau were moved to this site. As one approached it, coming from the airport in the company limo, one could not help being impressed. In front of the large office building the little depot looked like a quaint accent piece.

For my first training session I drove to Wausau. Later I flew on company planes from Chicago's O'Hare International Airport. In the hay day of seemingly unlimited profits, the company bought two small turbo jets. They were hangared, and were the showcase at the tiny Wausau airport (I once quipped: "Wausau International"). It seemed the planes spent more time at O'Hare then in Wausau. Top brass used it for their schedule-free travels and to entertain clients. It was convenient for us too, when we traveled between home and home office. I could park my car at a remote corner of the airport, board the plane at the nearby hangar and fly, as if door-to-door.

I spent a lot of time in Wausau during my employment, in two- or three-week training sessions. The training complex included a private Wausau Companies hotel, operated by Marriott, the worldwide hotel chain. Accommodations were the finest. It was an upscale hotel. Meals in an attractive cafeteria were of high quality. As an extra service, by each piece of dessert, a label was provided, stating the calorie count. Thus I learned, that the highest calorie content was in a slice of pecan pie (over 400). It was a life lesson for me. Ever since, when I see pecan pie or see it listed on a menu, the first thing that comes to mind are those record setting calories. I am sure, there are other slices of cakes or desserts -- but the humble pecan pie? It was a blow, and an education. It was an interesting way to inform us about eating well, something that since became a fetish of our health police. They at Wausau were clearly ahead of their time. (How ironic: the size of meals at Burger King and other fast food places keep increasing. Current calorie count is above 1500 for one of those super-duper whoppers.)

By the late 1980s, dark clouds were gathering and the company was losing money at an increasing rate. Once I was talking to a colleague, Ron Marx, who moved to home office from Chicago a year before. In his position Ron was familiar with the financial status of the company. While discussing Wasau's problems, I asked him if he also thought, that all this prior reckless spending got the company into financial trouble in recent months. I specifically mentioned the Training Center, for I knew that best and I thought it was a very expensive project. He smiled and made a quick calculation.

"You know, what? With the money we lost in the past year, we could have built 81 training centers, like this one."

With that he put in perspective, what deep hole we were in at the time. Officially top management was upbeat and promised better times. But one day real bad news hit. Nationwide Insurance *helped us out* with a large pledge and promise of more money if needed in the future. In return, one of the Nationwide vice presidents took over the helm at Wausau. They said it was a perfect fit, claiming that the book of business of the two companies were compatible and complimentary, equally helping each. We were to continue operating freely, just as before. In a few years the changes that were underway accelerated, increasing discontent. A few years later Nationwide sold Wausau to Liberty Mutual. I had my 401K account with Wausau, then with Nationwide for several years. They gave me good service and a nice portfolio increase. The markets were doing well during those years.

In the summer of 1992, Wausau offered me early retirement and strongly advised me to take it, which I did. People all around me were let go and it was typical of the goings on at the time. The employee roster was reduced and new trainees at lower salaries were replacing some. A few of my friends stayed on for a while, but were painting a dismal picture and described an increasingly draconian atmosphere. They were eager to retire when the opportunity came.

I saw my early retirement as forced and too early. I was at my peak earning period. It was also clear, that the situation the company placed itself in the past two years, some form of drastic cost reduction could not be avoided. Apparently, they wanted to do it this way. They contrived a reason to force a number of us into retirement.

The following year was difficult. Things looked bleak, for the job market was in decline for many months and nobody was looking to hire. Time was marching on. I sent out many resumes, got a few nibbles from insurance companies, but they were looking only for safety engineers.

One day Ildikó showed me an ad in our local paper, the *Northwest Herald*. Our school district was looking for custodial help. It was low pay, but better than sitting at home with dwindling hope of finding anything in my field. The school was our neighborhood high school, where our girls went and graduated 4-5 years earlier. I went for an interview and met friends. I knew them casually, from prior brief encounters, having to do with parental and sport events. Larry O'Meara was the principal. He had only one question. After he told me the salary ($14,000) he just wanted to know if I'm still interested. I said yes, though I wasn't really sure. An hour later he called me and offered the position. He mentioned, just as an aside, that there were over 60 applicants. I tried to feel important and appreciated. The job turned out better than I expected. The position was in the laundry. I was put in charge of all uniforms and *clean issue* of the athletic department, taking care of things the teams wore on games and in practice. It was a very full time job in season, especially in late fall, with football going. Later basketball started, while football was in post season. Usually it took me till Thursday, to catch up with the heavy load from the weekend. The spring was more fun. Things were less busy and more pleasant overall.

There were other aspects to the job, that I slowly got used to and really enjoyed after a while. I remember Uncle Gábor asking me once, after a few months:

"Well my Miklós, how is it going? Do you like it by now?"

"No".

"You will, and it will be better for you."

I reflected on the few months I spent on the job and thought that with lower expectations I can still find happiness in my simpler circumstance. The job was easy, without serious responsibilities and with free time, though not one that I thought fulfilling. I pondered his answer and admonition and thought, "I hope so", though didn't yet see how he could be right. -- I thought of his personal story and experience. He came to Canada and soon was hired with low salary in a position that was much below his education and training, though he had the language handicap. He was keeping books at an insurance company. He grew to like his job, his circumstances and fellow workers. He retired after more than 20 years. The company and colleagues gave him a nice retirement party.

I started work in South High School on March 1, 1993. It was the easiest time of the year, that helped to acclimate myself to the job and the environment. I spent most of my day working alone. At the beginning I asked if I could have a radio. The answer was, even a TV if I wished. The radio and reading occupied and entertained me. I listened to a lot of music and Rush Limbaugh, an informative and entertaining conservative talk show program. -- Another aspect of the job was that I worked with the teachers of the Physical Education department. In time I met other teachers, who came to coach or work out in the faculty exercise room, during their off-hours. -- I enjoyed this company, but enjoyed even more the company of students, the kids that came to see me every day. In a small way, I assumed the role of a surrogate teacher. I commanded respect and watched them observe it, while trying to smooth their rough edges. I asked them a few times, 'What would your mother say hearing you talk like this; or seeing your rough behavior?' I made and posted a sign: *In Loco Parentis* -- (In Place of Parent). A few asked me about it. When I translated it, they understood the meaning and understood me better. We joked and had a lot of fun. I got a touching sendoff message on my last day, from members of the football and basketball teams and the teachers I worked with. -- Summers were different. The crew did the large cleaning in labs and classrooms and installed new equipment. This work was more physically demanding, but not too difficult. Since I left, I return often as a substitute teacher. I like visiting staff, working with the kids and teachers, a few of whom were students back in my custodial days. I told one: now you call me Miklos, but he insists on " Mr. Magyar".

50

The Girls Growing Up

To backtrack a few years, Erika graduated from high school in 1988. To our chagrin, she took her senior year a little lightly, but had grades good enough, so she had no trouble being accepted in any of the colleges where she applied. She chose one of the best teacher's colleges, Illinois State University. Jim, her boyfriend also went there, apparently by coincidence. At the time we thought it unwise for their sake. There was, as we saw it, a little cooling in their relationship, and a pause, with opportunity for reflection, and meeting other people would have been good. We thought their being at the same school was a distraction. As it turned out, they liked the closeness. Their relationship deepened in those four years.

Erika (and Jim) graduated from Illinois State University in 1992. She substitute-taught in the spring and was working hard on finding a permanent position, though jobs were scarce. We heard that for each position there were 600 applicants. (It completely turned in 10 years. Supply-and-demand corrected the imbalance and filled the gap. Today teachers are in demand.)

One Thursday afternoon I was with my cleaning crew, preparing the floor of the cafeteria for the new school year, when the principal,

Larry O'Meara stopped by.

"Did Erika find a job, yet?" - he asked.

"Not so far".

"No? Let me see, I may be able to do something. I'll let you know. A position could be opening up."

He asked me a few questions and walked off. I was full of hope, despite knowing how low the chances were -- although help from Larry was encouraging. He had connections in the right places.

I told the story at home. Erika was still living with us.

On Friday, when I came home from work, she greeted me with good news: she had the job. She was called in for an interview Friday morning and offered a position later in the day. A new fifth grade class opened at Husmann Elementary in Crystal Lake. It was the week before instructions began. Erika went through a crash-orientation and started her class the following Tuesday.

We felt lucky, and I grateful, to Larry, who came to see if we needed help. I already forgot that a few weeks before, we talked about old times at South High and what the Girls were doing since graduation.

More than ten years passed since then. Erika is still teaching fifth grade -- a good age group, she says. I visited her in class several times and saw how well suited she is to her job and the profession -- one in which she was born to bloom. Just recently she asked me to spend an hour before her class, talking about history as I saw it growing up. I covered the two World Wars and the time, until I arrived to America, as I lived through it. The kids were attentive and asked many questions. It was a good session.

At that time Jim also tried to find his place in the world. He changed jobs several times but, to steal a line from the Rolling Stones, none gave him satisfaction. His major was public relations. We saw his struggle in trying to find fulfilling employment. A few years later Jim made a decision. He went back to school, enrolled to study nursing and received his sheepskin from Lake County College. It seemed, he has found something, in which he has personal fulfillment. He went through several departments in his hospital (Northern Illinois Medical Center) and liked emergency care best, where he still is today.

The young people spent time getting to know each other and find permanence in the grown-up world. After more than 10 years of courtship they were sure about each other. Their relationship deepened, and it became clear that we were looking forward to a wedding.

On June 11, 1994, in bright sunshine and great weather all around, our young couple got married at St. Thomas the Apostle church in Crystal Lake. Otti and Helma were among the 160 guests. Their presence meant a lot to us. Reception was at the Barn of Barrington, our favorite place for such events. Since then they have been living happily together. It is still a very good marriage. With their honeymoon, a cruise in the Caribbean, they were on their way to ever after...

Jim was brought up by his loving mother, Barbara and later by stepfather, Peter. His father died before he was born, so he was deprived of the love and tenderness of a dad. Yet he grew up to be a fine young man with many talents, good humor, cheerful personality and always willing to help others. Erika often talks about him as a *my great guy* – and she is right. He has common sense, a huge capacity to work and talent to plan, build and repair things, which is a great asset in saving money on projects around the house.

Since they married, they rented for a while, then lived in two different homes that they bought in poor condition and sold with a sizable profit, after Jim made major improvements so they were attractive to sell. Erika helped mostly in the painting. Today they live in their third house, walking distance from ours. This is a closeness we all wished for, one that makes things pleasant and convenient for us all.

About the time Jim became a nurse, Erika received her Master's Degree from Concordia University. Later she earned a requisite additional 50 credits, that took her to the pinnacle of her profession and the top of the salary scale.

Andrea graduated from high school in 1989 and spent her undergraduate years at Augustana College in Rock Island, IL, enrolling in the biology program, as preparation for a career in physical therapy. Augustana is a lovely little place, a choice

college, academically and otherwise. Its campus is on a gently
sloping hillside, up from the banks of the Mississippi. It has a
mixture of old, stately buildings and newer ones scattered among
the trees and along winding walkways. Central to the campus is
a Lutheran chapel, marking its founding by Swedish immigrants.
While Andrea attended there, a beautiful, spacious library was
built, giving the campus a striking new look. Her first dorm was
Andreen Hall. It was on top of a steep run. The walkway up to it
in large part was stairs, a good exercise track for freshmen.

The impressive modern sport complex was the other center of her
activities. She continued her basketball career and soon joined the
rank of top players. We attended all her games, as circumstances
allowed. We were lucky in that the majority of the schools in her
conference were located within easy driving distance for us. We
got to know other parents, several of whom we saw regularly at
games. Some we also visited at after-game parties. A drive to
Augustana took about 3½ hours, so we saw only a handful of home
games, but during basketball season we saw Andrea frequently
in nearby towns. The girls did quite well, winning conference
three times. Taking part in this intensive program meant usually
a truncated Thanksgiving weekend, because it was the time for a
very important annual tournament. We tried to work around it with
our Thanksgiving family programs. Erika also joined us for a few
games. One of the colleges in the conference was Illinois Weslian
in Bloomington, just a hop and a skip from ISU. We even made
a larger family gathering once in Waukesha, at a Carroll College-
Augustana game, with a lot of Milwaukee relatives attending. --
For a season, Andrea also played on the tennis team. It was nice
to see her play again in our favored sport.

In 1992 she had a chance to take a semester abroad. Augustana
rotates trips between Europe, South America and Asia, for an
entire trimester. Her year was Asia. She was away 12 weeks,
with members of her senior class and faculty, while school went
on, more or less as normal. They visited Japan, Taiwan, Hong
Kong, and China. On the way home, they stopped for five days in
Hawaii, completing a trip around the world.

She loved her school and formed close relationships with many classmates, members of the faculty and some of the coaches.

Andrea graduated *Summa cum Laude* in 1993. She was in very select company at the top of her class of a lot of smart students. It was a source of pride for us, and a fitting recognition, certainly better than her father received for his less than brilliant school days. She always applied herself totally to task, a gift she inherited from Ildikó, who was also very diligent -- and successful -- throughout her schooling.

With a major in biology/pre-physical therapy, she was well prepared for the next big challenge: Master's Program in Physical Therapy at the School of Medicine at Washington University, St. Louis. It took me a while to comprehend the amount of knowledge they had to make their own. Once, just for comparison, she told me, in answering my question about her study workload:

"Dad, the physical therapy curriculum and pace is different from Augustana. Here we cover material in a week, that we covered in a semester at Augie".

For this reason, admission standards were strict and selective at Washington University. In that year, *Wash. U.* was listed No. 1 in the country, for its program in physical therapy. Andrea was very happy to get in. She researched other major universities and also applied at the other two top schools (Iowa and Northwestern) just in case. All three accepted her.

We saw her a few times in St. Louis. I also took business trips that way and stopped by for a couple hours. Time flew and at the end of two years of academic studies she went on a three-city internship to gain experience in the various sub-disciplines of the profession. While in Houston, with her classmate and good friend Jean, they visited Father Denis for a day. In Chattanooga, TN, she stayed with a landlady, Vera, who became her good friend. She went to see her a few times since.

The last city on her internship tour was Charleston, SC. Ildi went to see her there, to spend a few days together. They had a good time visiting this historic city and the region that has much to offer.

Charleston turned out to be significant in another way. Something happened there, that happens in life often by chance.

She met the young man, to whom she is now married. Trevor Gadson is an electrical engineer, a bright and engaging man. She told us about him, soon after she came home. I sensed trepidation in her presentation, and we soon found out why. Trevor is black and Andrea knew that this may produce reason for deep thought on our part. We could see that she was quite fond of him and that the relationship may lead to serious steps down the line. She knew that we will respect her choice and intentions. She also knew that, not for the question of race but potential societal issues, we had our reservations.

We talked a lot about it, raised questions and weighed probabilities. But I will remember forever, how Andrea summed up her case and explained her mind clearly to us, during a dinner at a restaurant.

"We also talked a lot about this" -- she said. "We know the challenges. It may not be an easy road. But for me, the positives outweigh the negatives. We are ready and strong to face our challenges in today's society." -- It sounded a well considered, thought-out and determined choice. Right there, in Riverfront Restaurant in Algonquin, we closed the subject and talked no more about it.

She also had encouraging words, explaining that things today are different than they were decades ago and the trend was positive. We agreed with that, for times are indeed changing and attitudes noticeably relaxed and more tolerant, than were a few decades ago. Things that were a problem, are now treated more as natural phenomena and accepted as normal. This has been confirmed in the past few years. To be a racist in today's America is anachronism and out of place. For most people it is anathema. *Content of character* is what increasingly determines a person. (Thank you Dr. King.)

There was one more thing left for us: to persuade her grandmother, who understandably held more conservative views. As time passed, we all warmed up to the idea. Trevor came to visit us twice for a weekend and later moved to the Chicago area. They assigned themselves a year as test period.

After the passage of about that length of time, one evening

the doorbell rang. It was Trevor, coming unannounced, without Andrea, but of course, welcome. It seemed, something important was to unfold. After a little idle chat he told us, that Andrea did not know of his coming. A few minutes passed, a good pause for the three of us to relax a little.

Then he simply, forthrightly told us: he came alone, to ask us for Andrea's hand in marriage.

I cannot say that it was unexpected. Still it was a big thing and I just sat there speechless, stumbling over my thoughts, as they were in process of becoming words. Ildikó came to the rescue, giving her approval. I chimed in, seconding the motion. So, after a few awkward moments for all three, we managed to relax. We gave them our blessing. Trevor thanked us and departed.

Wedding was on September 4th 1999. Otti and Helma came again. The reception was in the Barn of Barrington. Many of Trevor's relatives attended, that made it a grand event. We have met Trevor's parents before, on a trip to Myrtle Beach in the spring of 1998. Ildikó attended a seminar there. I went along for a free vacation. During that week, we spent a pleasant time with the older Gadsons.

* * *

Grandchildren update: The following few paragraphs were written and added to, as changes occurred. During the writing of this story, two girls and a boy were born as additions to our family.

The Gadsons

Ashlyn Ella, a sweet and adored granddaughter was born on the 28th of October, 2002. We were all in the hospital on the day -- and two days earlier too, when it seemed that she was ready to be born, but decided on a delay. She is a bright and happy child, who was the center of our love and attention alone, for a year and a half.

At Andrea's request I watched Ashlyn two days a week. Andrea went back to work on January 21st 2003. Ashlyn fills my days more than I ever imagined. Each day I spend with her, I bring back stories that delight her grandmother. This way she feels a little closer, in constant touch and up-to-date on the little one's progress, her antics, ever changing idiosyncrasies, and just how cute she really is. She is a very good baby, even better than her mother was -- and that is saying a lot.

On December 1st 2004 *Elise Ildiko* was born, to add great joy to our life, with her sweet innocence, a teasing sense of humor and impish smile, that grandparents find impossible to resist.

Ferguson Update

After years of anxious waiting, Erika conceived through in-vitro procedure. Little *Tyler Miklos* was born on May 9, 2004. This miracle child was a highly expected and delightful addition to the roster of grandchildren. He is the absolute center of the Ferguson house and adds immeasurably to our daily joy. When we have him here or at home with his mountain of toys, he has the run of the house. He has energy that never wanes. -- Since the Fergusons move into their close-by new, third house, we see them more often and can help on the spur of the moment, in case something urgent comes up.

Latest entry: 2006 August 15.

Erika, Jim and Tyler came by this morning. They brought great news. It was the confirmation by ultrasound, that Erika is expecting twins. Projected birthtime is March of 2007. Everything looks fine. We are elated. Nothing else needs to be said.

Last Entry: 2007 March 23.

The twins were born. Soon after 8 AM, within a 20 minutes period, *Heather Erika* and *Adam James* came to greet us with their sweet cry of lung exercise. It was easy, and a wonderful event. Mother and babies are fine and in good health. This is really the last entry. Thank be to God.

51

Joys Of Travel

In the past few years we took vacations, visiting places that we long dreamed about. For us, going to Europe was always a valued and special trip. Mostly we went to see relatives. Our customary route was flying first to Germany, where we would get one of Otti's cars to use. Often we drove straight to Hungary and back in one stretch to Aachen, stopping maybe to see a few sights. The 1985 trip, to Mother's 75th birthday, was different. We thought, that could be the last time we travel together as a family and was happy that we did it. (As things happened, we went together three more times. On the last two Jim and Trevor completed the family. The one in 2001, was an extended trip to Europe.)

College came with the natural loosening of family ties, as the Girls were looking increasingly to forge their future in a family of their own. Ildikó and I looked for interesting and beautiful places to see. The most memorable trips were England, Southern Italy, Spain, Florence, Tahiti, Scandinavia and wonderful Peru. This last one included five days on the Amazon. The highlight in the jungle was a canopy walk on rope bridges at the top of giant trees, 120 ft. above the floor of the cloud forest. In Machu Picchu and central Peru we were treated to great natural and human-created beauty and stories about the Incas before and during the cruel Spanish rule. Now (2006) we are looking forward to an *Ultimate Africa Safari* (South Africa, Botswana, Namibia, Zimbabwe).

Our first trip for just Ildikó and me, was to London in June, 1993. This great city has more to offer than I ever hoped. We were lucky to pick a fortnight, that had only sunny days. Again, walking was our favorite mode of transportation. The city is clean and pleasant, the people friendly. (Most of them spoke English.) We saw many of the city's museums and art galleries and a few important castles. A day trip to Avon included everything Shakespeare, and a tour through Warwick Castle. We also went to Windsor. I could write a lot about each, but they may show up better on some travel video. On a late afternoon we took the train out to Wimbledon, where the championship tennis matches were in progress. We had no tickets or time to spend, with all our other plans. We walked the grounds and even saw a few notables coming and going. Everybody was commenting on the good weather and how rare it is that none of the events were rained out. Each evening on our hotel room *telly*, we caught up with the day's major events.

As we emerged from the subway coming back from Wimbledon, we had a one in many-a-million chance meeting. As we emerged from the Earls Court subway station, waiting to cross on the other side of the street, stood Pisti (Steve) Juhász, Ildiko's nephew. He was amazed, also wondering if he saw ghosts, just as we were. The odds to run into each other was prohibitive, but such things still happen. Steve was living in Budapest. He had tickets to see Wimbledon and saw some tennis the day before. When we met, he was on his way to his hotel, that was not too far from ours. Neither of us knew of the other's plans about coming to London. We spent the rest of the evening talking and dining together.

Ildi and I spent time in the parks, experienced *Speaker's Corner* and stood outside the Queen's palace, which then was not open for public tours. Don Richards told us about Speaker's Corner, in Hyde Park, where a figurative soap box can be had by anybody. It was an interesting lesson about free speech. Not that one may speak on any subject. That is basic. The more interesting aspect of this freedom is an important corollary. While one can speak to his heart's content, no one is obliged to listen. Some speakers commanded a sizable audience, while others struggled to hold just a few.

One morning we came back to see the changing of the guards at Buckingham Palace. We heard that the Queen was scheduled to take part in some state event, which included a procession from a barracks to her palace. We spent an hour watching the guards practice in the yard, then proceed to the palace about ½ mile away. Queen Elisabeth and other royals came later in their fancy carriages. We walked through Harrod's, the Portrait Gallery and saw the hugely diverse exhibits of the Victoria and Albert Museum.

* * *

Southern Italy in 1995 and Spain in '96 were guided motor coach tours. It would be hard to enumerate all the beauty -- natural, architectural and artistic -- that we were able to cram into the two weeks in each of the countries. I just want to mention a few highlights.

We began in Rome. Touring the Vatican, the gardens and Sistine Chapel were a must, as is probably for most tourists. The treasures in the *Museo Vaticani* are impossible to list, describe or remember. (We did the tour again a few years later.) Our first big stop was the magnificent gardens of Villa d'Este - Tivoli. The bus took us to Pompeii, Sorrento, the Amalfi Coast, Capri, Naples and around Sicily. From the island we ferried overnight to Naples, than back to Rome, where we stayed four days after the tour ended. We liked the guided tours, but the free time at the end was a wonderful finish. It gave us a chance to see more of the best churches and all that we could catch on the way, as we walked tirelessly on aching feet.

We attended one of the Wednesday Papal audiences, where we had a chance to see John Paul II close up. We had to reserve tickets for this very popular event before we left home. The most touching part of it was when the already ailing Pope received about 50 newly married couples, dressed in their festive best. He attended to each couple, touched them and talked to them one-on-one, that made it a spiritual event even for us, just watching. All who attended and the many who participated were in the best mood in the stifling heat. I saw how dedicated the Holy Father was to his flock, braving the heat, receiving a long line of delegations, sitting through the program and speaking to the crowd in about 20 languages. It is the second time I heard him in Hungarian -- this time live.

The most memorable places for us were the side tours to the *Isle de Capri* and the drive along the *Amalfi* coast. The extended day-trip to the small off-shore island from our base in Sorrento, is one of the many treasures of Italy. We heard that it is a nice vacation place, but nothing could prepare us to its charm and beauty. We took an afternoon ferry and spent a night there. The island is one of those rear places -- the other notable ones are Mont San Michele and Machu Picchu -- which are very popular for day-tourists. The visitors thin out after dark, when the boats take most of them back to the mainland. The little *downtown* square was full of music and happy people, none happier than Ildikó and I. Our hotel room was a spacious suite, with a view of the famous *I Faraglioni*, the two famous rocks just off shore, that I see on cards and in many travel brochures. The next day a bus took us up a good climb to Anacapri, the old town on top of the island, that we explored on foot. There on a square, I spotted an blue-and-yellow hand painted enamel street sign. I read it, as I read most of the things that cross my path. This square was not named after any famous Italian, but after a special group of Hungarians. It read:

Piazza Martiri d'Ungheria - 1956.

(So full of pathos. How Italian! -- naming a square for the Hungarian martyrs of 1956.) It felt like home, for a moment. Not that I am in that select group, for they have all fallen in defense of their country. But it was an extraordinary feeling to see that residents of a town, so far from Hungary, value liberty so much and want to keep alive the memory of martyrs, who fought tyranny and were ready to give their life in the cause of freedom. I lingered a while, before Ildi called me to catch up with the others.

The road lead to the top, to the summer home of Emperor Tiberius almost 2000 years ago. The view was to kill for -- which we know he did often, by tossing people off the cliffs. His reasons had nothing to do with the view. It was to seek some sick pleasure, that made him do it. His reign was not a success and this demented habit was perhaps a grotesque release for a frustrated ruler. Emperor Augustus also favored Capri. A botanic garden carries his name. Looking down from a cliff in the garden, we saw a serpentine road below, that looked very out of place, going nowhere. Our guide told us, that the German Wermacht built them during WW II. The purpose or reason? He couldn't tell and said, nobody knew for sure.

The drive along the coast to Amalfi is also something that cannot be described. It is a place for the senses. In it, nature and human creativity join to produce beauty that must be experienced to fully appreciate.

After a few days in Sorrento we continued south. Our bus was loaded on a ferry in Reggio di Calabria, at the tip of the Italian boot and we crossed the Strait of Messina to Sicily. On the island, beautiful Taormina is most memorable. It is also a hilltop town, though larger than Anacapri, high above the shore, that it has a tram to take tourists uptown. Beautiful and historic, it boasts a Greek amphitheater, a charming, yet very lively main walk, full of shops, restaurants and of course, people. Locals, all older men, were sitting in shade, playing chess. Not a tournament, it was all for pleasure and just passing time with friends and kibitzers. In the evening we went to the park, where Mascagni's *Cavalleria Rusticana* was performed by a local group of opera lovers. It was a production, different from regular opera. Much of it was dialogue. They sang just the highlights and the best known arias.

We loved Palermo. It was most interesting, with its vitality, attitudes and culture. It has the craziest rules for driving. We tried to find some system in the chaos, but nothing made sense -- until our guide explained, that the lights do not determine who can go and who must stop.

"In Palermo, the traffic light is not the rule, it is a suggestion." -- OK, I got it!

Monreale, a monastery outside Palermo, and the nearby catacombs were informative about ancient lives and customs. We drove around Sicily, just touching, or stopping in cities with historic names, like Syracuse and Agrigento. I heard of, or knew something about a few others and was eager to expand my knowledge. The most surprising revelation to me was the important role this island played throughout ancient and medieval history. During its long, fascinating past, everybody and his brother owned, or ruled over this strategically important island in the Mediterranean. Records go back to 6th century BC. Since then, with hardly a breath for independence, it was ruled by Greeks, Arabs, Spaniards, Normans, the kingdoms of Naples and Austria -- to name the more important periods. I was blown over by the volume of history, relics and artifacts of its varied past. It was a fascinating journey to places I've been to in classrooms or books only, prior to this trip. I enjoyed all the new things and surprises behind every turn.

* * *

In Spain we traveled from Madrid south to Toledo, from there northwest, with stops in Avila and Salamanca, crossing into Portugal, to Coimbra, Fatima and Lisbon, then across the Strait at Gibraltar to Morocco. After taking the ferry back to Spain, we saw the beautiful cities of Granada and Seville. Tracking east and north, we drove the Costa del Sol and circled back to Madrid. On this trip we had the best guide one can ever want. Vicente worked very hard, told wonderful stories, answered all questions and was a delightful, good humored company.

Coming into Seville, we saw the Harp Bridge, one of the most beautiful and interesting bridges I have seen. It was built for the world's fair, the city hosted in 1992. That was the year, commemorating the 500th anniversary of the first journey to America by Christopher Columbus. -- For several years in the 1980s, Chicago agonized over and planned for a worlds fair, 100 years after its very successful World's Colombian exhibition. At the end, Mayor Daley, scared of cost-overruns, chickened out. Seville stepped in and made a success of it. It is a beautiful city at the foot of the mountains, with the snowy peaks of the Sierra Nevada in the distance.

The lovely *Harp Bridge* at the outskirts of Seville is supported entirely on one shore. It is a flashy, yet graceful structure. From a massive base, a giant arm is jutting in the air, pointing away from the river at a 45 degree angle. It supports cables, that are attached to the span for the entire width over the river, Rio Guadalquivir. The brash, provocative, show-off design gives it a striking look. From a distance, the cables resemble strings of a giant harp.

The weather was very hot, but dry. We went on an afternoon walk through Seville, to take a look at its historic marvel: Plaza Espana, dedicated to the country and championing the art of public architecture. Ildi and I wanted to see the details, walk the length of its exhibit circle and the number of bridges over its labyrinth of canals. The monument honors the 53 provinces of Spain with impressive mosaics, depicting historic events. It celebrates each region individually, with its unique picture gallery. We walked its entire length, the bridges over the lagoon, climbed the many steps, stopped by a wedding party and took pictures, as I once did in Palermo and later in Prague. This way, I have a couple unknown brides, in picturesque settings in our photo albums.

When we started our walk from the hotel, we were not sure that we could go all the way, constantly looking for shelter from the scorching sun. It was a good distance to go, but rewarding. It took us by the cathedral, where we spent a lot of time the previous day . It is similar in style to the one in Toledo, but even bigger (third in the world, after St. Peter's and London's St. Paul Cathedral). Books have been written about it, telling of its treasures, architecture and historical significance. Columbus is buried there in a magnificent tomb. Four soldiers are holding his coffin on shoulders, representing the four major provinces that united to make modern Spain: Aragon, Castile, Leon and Navarre. Each man is elegantly dressed in the garb of his region. The design and its patina makes for a most impressive monument.

In Granada we walked through the Alhambra. I left with a better understanding of the Moors, their reasons for coveting the paradise, that in their mind was Spain. I gained a greater appreciation of the work of novelist Washington Irving who, for a few years lived in and wrote about this magnificent palace.

We were glad that we set aside an extra five days in Madrid at the end. Our leisurely tour extension allowed us time to see the Royal Palace, the Prado, the new home of the Bornemisza-Thyssen Museum and take a train ride out to El Escorial.

Since we saw the Bornemisza collection in Lugano in 1985, the family heiress married a Spaniard, who persuaded her to move it to Madrid. It was the same exceptional selection of the world's finest, more spaciously exhibited, but not the same without the old house, the splendid palace on the shore of Lake Lugano, where we saw it ten years before. I was nostalgic for the old, enchanting palace on the lake.

Monasterio de San Lorenzo del Escorial is an impressive royal retreat, about 30 miles from Madrid. It was built during a 21-year span by Philip II, and completed in 1584. The complex includes the palace, monastery, library, college, art collection a splendid garden and a fine Renaissance church. The most impressive part of the palace is the mausoleum for many Spanish sovereigns, beginning with Charles V. The rotund, golden domed, marble walled room is home for more than a dozen beautifully decorated, matching marble caskets, placed on four levels, around the room. I have never seen a more magnificent display for the remains of royal ancestors. The chapel is the Pantheon de los Reyes.

One of the highlights of our few extra Madrid days was to see a bullfight. The same ritual is repeated with each bull. We had some ten opportunities to study the process. The matador follows an exacting routine, teasing the poor beast in various ways with his red flowing cloth, before he administers the *coup de gras*. It was a somewhat bizarre process, but enthusiastically applauded in every step by the crowd, interspersed with occasional boos, for most of which we could not discern the reason. As a final act, a team of horses dragged the bull's carcass out of the ring. This ceremonial carnage has a positive side. Poor people are said to receive the gift of free meat.

Domestic vacations included Colorado, once with the Püskis and in the following year, with the family. Both were great, to this special part of our United States. -- Then, we were looking for some other nice area, not so well known to us. I remembered long time ago traveling through the Finger Lakes region one night in 1964, when I drove from New York to visit Uncle Andrew in Toronto. I took a shortcut on secondary roads, to avoid the expensive New York Throughway. This way I could go on minor country roads that I usually prefer. The drive was different, I drove all of it at night. For a long time I followed a car on the twisting roads in pitch black, with very few cars on the road. It was a big help, because he was leading, showing the road ahead in the darkness. After more than an hour, I sensed that he wanted me to pass. After that he followed me for many miles. As much as I saw of the terrain, it seemed a very nice region. Later I heard friends praise this area as an interesting place to visit. So, we decided to go there. We rented a cabin with the Püskis and spent a week exploring the area. This is New York state's wine producing region. The geological formations produced many canyons, that are now state parks. We visited the Cornell U. campus in Ithaca and the Corning glass factory, which is one of the best of its kind.

Coming home we took a detour to Akron OH, to see Hywet Hall. I saw it once in 1985, on my way back from a business trip. It was the home of the Goodyear family -- of tire fame. The estate has beautiful setting, garden etc., but its most appealing feature is, that it is the best example in America, of Tudor style architecture. I enjoyed taking Ildi through, after talking to her about it for over a decade.

1998 was a busy, peripatetic year for us. We took four vacations -- or at least I did. We spent a week on Margarita Island, off the coast of Venezuela. We left after Christmas ('97). It was a nice, low key vacation. Ildikó took time off to soak up some sun by the pool in the middle of our Midwestern winter. Mid-week we flew into the jungle and hiked up in a canyon. I happened to mention it to Otti. He told me that they did the same trip. The flight also included a fly-by, over Angels Falls, reputed to be the highest in the world. Back at the hotel, we enjoyed watching the locals putting on a show, celebrating and ringing in the New Year.

Ildikó had the seminar in the spring, in Myrtle Beach. She spent several hours a day inside, while I had the almost empty beach for myself. She still considered it a vacation, away from the daily grind of running Sheltered Village. That part of the country was mostly new for us and we saw a lot of it. We visited plantations, spent a few days in Charleston and also a day with Trevor's parents.

Later that year we went to Colorado with the Girls, Jim and Trevor. We also spent a week on St. Lucia, that we substituted for a more ambitious trip, that had to be postponed. In the spring we went to Toronto for the confirmation of nephew Danny, son of my cousin Erzsó and a visit with uncle Andrew's widow, Elizabeth.

St. Lucia was an all-inclusive stay in a hotel, where we found things that were surprisingly nice. I spoke with several workers and found them happy, dignified and interesting to talk to. During our stay, the hotel hosted a picnic for the families of employees. We saw a big party begin. I found it difficult to tear myself away from watching the happy children around me, looking impeccable, with ribbons in hair for little girls, dressed in lace, carrying their gifts and consulting parents about where to go next to receive additional presents. It warmed my hart to see care and gentleness that surrounded the little ones, reflecting security and good family life.

We signed up for an excursion, a cruise around the lush island. I had a chance to dive into the sea from a platform, extended from the side of the ship over the water. It was built just for that purpose.

Talking with a lady, a member of the crew, I learned about the history of this volcanic Windward Island of the Lesser Antilles, one in the Caribbean West Indies. The island changed ownership 14 times, always between England and France. It ended up British, ceded by France in 1814, in exchange for the French part of modern Canada. St. Lucians are proudly recounting this fact. It shows, they say, how highly the great powers valued this little island, equating it in value with Quebec.

For a long time, Ildikó and I have been talking, that we should see Florence. This Tuscan city is a vital part of Italy and her culture. We saw Rome, the north and the south, but I felt a void, not ever having seen the middle: *Toscana*, with its lush landscape, wine, art and magnificent cities.

In 2000 we spent two weeks in Italy again, this time on our own. We began and ended the trip in Rome, but spent most of the time in Florence. The great Renaissance city was our base, from where we also toured Tuscany, on day-trips. Our first evening we had dinner on a restaurant veranda, built above the bank of the Arno. We basked in the setting sun, looking at the high Renaissance building of the famous Uffizi Museum across the river. It was a beautiful picture from our lovely spot, one that would be fit for a postcard -- I thought. (Looking through cards in a shop the next day, I found two: one showing our view from the terrace and another, depicting a reverse view. This picture was taken from the Uffizi side, showing the river and, on the on the opposite bank, the restaurant veranda overhang, perched above the water, with flowers on the railing, looking just as I remembered from the night before.)

As we tasted our first authentic Florentine meal, we were looking at the Arno, smoothly flowing by. With my eyes, I followed a lone kayaker. With his narrow vessel, he was splitting into a widening V, the smooth surface of the river, to leave fleeting pockmarks on both sides of his vessel, as he paddled his way downstream, with powerful, rhythmic strokes.

(Looking at this river, so calm and innocent, I remembered November 1966, when the Arno swelled and flooded a large part of the city. Thousands from all over the world volunteered to help. They labored at the tedious task of drying and pressing books, and papers, hoping to limit the damage, thus saving more art and literary treasures, than many a city can count in its museums or archives.)

I have trouble remembering the museums, galleries and churches we visited. I know, we did not see them all. The last day we added one to our list, the Bargello. It was in some ways the most satisfying. It has two of my very favorite bronze Davids, those of Donatello and Verrocchio. It was uncanny to find day after day, pieces that I have seen in books and on television all my life. Verrocchio's slender David was surrounded by visiting high school students from Provo, Utah. They all sat on the floor, with pencil in hand, looking up and down between strokes, trying to sketch their own master copy. Their teacher guided them with suggestions and answered questions, occasionally posing his own, to provoke thoughts and perk up the youngsters' imagination.

The most famous David is also in Florence. It is the prominent display in the Galleria dell'Accademia. Michelangelo's white marble is massive, also weighing heavily on the senses. The colossal statue is on a pedestal too high, I think. True, this way we could see him from a distance, away from the adoring mass below, but from close up, the height distorts the perspective of the figure as a whole. Still, he had the biggest crowd, even bigger than those that came to see Moses, the other world-renowned Michelangelo work, in the charming, sedate little church, the S. Pietro in Vincoli, in Rome.

We learned a lot about the art and history of Florence. The city is easily covered on foot and we cris-crossed her river and many squares almost every day. The two main art galleries have an endless inventory of the best in the world. Some of my favorite historic figures are entombed in her churches. We stood at awe by the tombs of all those Medicis in their own large chapel, the Capelle San Lorenzo. They are decorated, with marble figures, carved by Michelangelo, some of them originally intended for Pope Julius II. Marble statues, historical documents and Medici memorabilia filled the chapel and many exhibits. The floor, richly colored with a variety of marbles, itself would qualify as a masterpiece.

We visited the house of Dante Alighieri. His bust is on the wall of his ordinary house, facing the ordinary street. Many less important people have more elaborate monuments. But this is Florence. There is so much here that dazzle the senses, one has to put it in perspective. He is buried in the church of Santa Croce. There he is one in a very select company, which includes Michelangelo Buonarotti (known to most, by his first name only), my namesake: Niccolo Machiavelli, Leonardo da Vinci and Galileo Galilei, who in America is known by his first name only, and in Europe, or at least Hungary, by his last: Galilei --

don't ask me why.

A day-tour took us to Pisa, then to Siena, our favorite. Another, to a wine tasting in a lovely, old, hilltop estate. Sitting in the garden, we were treated to a number of appetizers, alternated with a series of the house wines. We all felt elated at the end -- to different degrees, depending on the body's tolerance for spirits. We made brief stops in picturesque hill towns, such as Lucca and San Gimignano, a city of many towers. Seeing the lush, varied Tuscan landscape was also part of our afternoon wine tasting tour.

In 2000, we were able to put together our year-ago postponed trip to Tahiti. Starting a week early, we flew to Los Angeles, visited my cousin, Gerti and went up to Kings Canyon for a week. The stately Sequoias, the rugged, unspoiled beauty of the California high country was fitting prelude for Tahiti.

It was the Polynesian *winter,* around 80 degrees every day. (They told us, summers are barely bearable.) We visited four islands, beginning with the best: Bora Bora. It is indeed paradise. Our garden hotel, the Moana Beach ParkRoyal had a low key, high elegance air. In our beach-front thatched cabin, understated luxury included a large creeping vanilla plant, with its faint fragrance and fresh flowers brought in twice a day, on the table, the kitchen, the bed and the bathroom -- yes, even on the toilet tank. We had our fill with Tahitian music, at least for the duration. We bought two CDs, that we played a lot since. They are classic. No matter how many times you play them, you give them only temporary rest, before you want to hear the lovely songs again.

One of the seminal musical experience of our life was in the most simple and dignified setting. On a Sunday morning we inquired about a Catholic mass. The desk clerk said that a car will take us down the coast to the church, for the 12 o'clock service. It was the gathering place for the locals. Their life had the air of informal joy, with smile and kind words among friend.

As the mass began, people went up into the sanctuary, gathered around the organ and gave God a concert, that was divine. Even today, it seems like a long, glorious morning, stretching into endless hours of music that would have made Saint Cecilia proud. She, the patron saint of music, may have blessed this church and its people with the ability to present God with a special kind of devotion which was musical ecstasy for the ears. We thought ourselves blessed with extraordinary luck, that by chance, we could be present at this joyous ceremony, which was probably just an ordinary Sunday for happy Tahitians. The music was all new to us, a blend of the gentle, undulating melodies of the south seas, yet somehow different from the familiar Tahitian songs -- mainly in harmonic structure. They had no formal choir, only those in the church for that mass. A few minutes into the celebration, about thirty, mostly women, gathered to become the informal choir. They may have been regulars, at least for this mass, but the joyful music making seemed spontaneous, unrehearsed and free spirited. On the way out I tried to hum a few melodies, but soon they faded, leaving me only, with my special Tahitian memory.

We took the long walk back to the hotel, savoring the view of the seaside and observed the scattered communities along the shore. We stopped in one of the open air restaurants for refreshments and a chat with the proprietor.

An enjoyable pastime for us was watching the great variety of tropical fish. The colors are fabulous and can be seen in books, TV documentaries and aquaria. What was different here, was the number, as they gathered around corral formations. We walked around in the shallow lagoon among the thatched cabins over the water. The color of the water was a very pale blue and so clear that one could see in it to a long distance. The bottom is crumbled shells, that make it so. We watched the fish on all the four islands and found that the variety was inexhaustible.

The next island was Huahine. The luxury continued. We had the nicest house on the water with two differently furnished decks on opposite sides of the cabin, and outdoor shower to wash off the salt of the sea. We toured the twin islands and learned about life -- and death. A grave for ancestors, for most of the houses, was in the front yard. They choose to honor their dead by having them close, we were told.

Moorea's highlands are accessible by car. We took a bus tour around the island, that included a lot of local flavor and a spectacular view of Cook's bay. By the time we arrived on the main island of Tahiti, we were acclimated to this most enchanting way of looking at life and in our own way, adopted it. I could write long on the beauty of this archipelago, the smiling faces, the flighty spirit of its people and all the beauty it offers for the senses. The only way to fully appreciate it, is to go there. Our two weeks were unforgettable with memories for life and a desire to return. (It was worth it, but I rather not mention the price.)

In the summer of 1998, Erika and Andrea helped to celebrate our 30th wedding anniversary. They threw a big party for us in Erika's house, with our close friends invited, some coming from distant places.

In October I had a sudden turn, that affected me for the rest of my life. My routine exam showed elevated PSA level. A biopsy followed, to confirm, that I had prostate cancer. Within a week I had a second opinion and a radical operation to remove my prostate. I recovered, but within a year my PSA was on the rise again. Since then I am on hormone therapy that is working so far. The cancer is under control, but residual problems persist. They make everyday life cumbersome, but are limiting normal activities only in minor ways.

I retired on the 5th of May 2001 and the same afternoon we left for Texas to visit relatives and friends. We took the new Cadillac DTS that Ildi bought for me as my retirement present. We were looking forward to ride in luxury, but the comfort of the ride still surprised us. The real measure was, that we were not tired after driving many continuous hours during this trip.

First stop was Irving at the Monastery of Father Denis. We stayed overnight and were guided through the expanding campus. We saw many new buildings shown us proudly by the Abbot. The best was the church and its ancillary buildings, that I wrote about earlier.

Next stop was Ildi's uncle Lulu, then the Richards in Cypress, a Houston suburb. We saw the first time, the new house the Richards built. (We visited their cottage on the lake the year earlier, when we spent a few days with them, going down with Clare and Merv Scheider. The four of us drove together and met the Richards in Branson MO, to see this show business town and some of the many shows it has to offer. Most astonishing were the Chinese Acrobats, whose unbelievable stunts I previously seen depicted only in Disney cartoons. Skills and flexibility of the human body they exhibited, I could not imagine before. The six of us had another common vacation a few years earlier in Las Vegas, where we had a wonderful time. We walked and talked a lot, but gambled little.) On the way home, Ildi and I took a detour to New Orleans. From there we drove home without stop, the longest nonstop stretch of the whole trip.

Last year Father Denis sent me a photo, a copy of his original, that was taken by a Vatican photographer and sent to him by an aid of Cardinal Ratzinger -- now Pope Benedict XVI. The chronology of events, surrounding the picture is interesting. For a number of years Father Denis was a member of the *Pontifical Biblical Comission, or Sacred Congregation for the Doctrine of the Faith*, working on church doctrine. The Prefect of the Committee was Cardinal Ratzinger, the then long-time right-hand man of John Paul II. -- On the picture are the Pope with the Cardinal, as he is introducing our Father Denis to the pontiff. The picture took its time to arrive, and when it did, we already had our new pope. As instructed by the new pope, his aid titled the picture: *Two Popes and an Abbot*. It is a unique and wonderful gift. I'm glad I have a copy.

52

Retirement

S uddenly, I had no job, a lot of time, but less worry then before. After a few months, germs of this book sprouted in my head. A lot of writing, editing, then endless reviews that took longer than the original write, occupied me for long hours since then. At first I had misgivings about the project, but now I see that nothing prepares one better for this, than the doing it.

This is what flowed out of my pen -- one keystroke at a time.

(Things continued to happen since 2001. In fact, they seemed to accelerate. So I decided to write an appendix of sorts, which I call: CONTEMPORARY NOTES. I will add to it as events dictate.)

THE END

ISBN 142511198-X